LAW & AMATEUR SPORTS

LAW&
AMATEUR
SPORTS

EDITED BY

Ronald J. Waicukauski

INDIANA UNIVERSITY PRESS
BLOOMINGTON

Library of Congress Cataloging in Publication Data

Main entry under title:

Law and amateur sports.

Papers from the national conference, Law and Amateur Sports—Issues of
the 80s, held in Indianapolis, August 1981, and sponsored by the Indiana
University School of Law Center for Law and Sports.

Includes index.

Contents: The emergence of law in amateur sports / Ronald J.
Waicukauski—Due process in the enforcement of amateur sports rules /
William G. Buss—Liability for injuries in sports activities / Cym H. Lowell
Legal approaches to sex discrimination in amateur athletics / Mark A.
Kadzielski—[etc.]

1. Sports—Law and legislation—United States—Congresses. I. Waicukauski,
Ronald J. II. Indiana University, Bloomington. Center for Law and Sports.

KF3989.A75L38   1982   344.73'099   82-47773

ISBN 0-253-13730-6   347.30499

1 2 3 4 5 86 85 84 83 82

Contents

Preface: The Emergence of Law in Amateur Sports

By definition and tradition, amateur sports and money are not supposed to mix. To some extent, they probably always have, but the thickening of the mixture that has occurred in the last decade is unprecedented. With the masses of participants and spectators who have been attracted to amateur sports in recent years, particularly through the medium of television, transactions in the hundreds of millions of dollars are now occurring. Although most of this money does not filter down to individual athletes, they know that if they successfully traverse the training grounds of amateur sports, prosperity lies ahead in the lucrative professional sports market. Thus, they have an increasingly significant financial stake in the decisions that are made and the events that occur at the amateur level. Similarly, the rewards now available to the successful coach, athletic administrator, school or amateur sport organization provide increased incentives to be concerned about those decisions and events. Accordingly, when misfortune occurs in amateur sports, those aggrieved have become likely to seek relief wherever it might be found, including by resort to the law.

Simultaneously with these developments in sports, there have been significant changes in the law. Since the early 1960s, legislators, administrators, and courts have all expanded the scope of the law they make, execute, and enforce. Litigation has reached epidemic proportions. The convergence of these developments in law with the developments in sports has led to an explosive growth in the relationship of law and amateur sports.

That relationship has developed in every way the law acts: litigation, legislation, and regulation. This book explores the myriad dimensions of this relationship by focusing on the critical issues of the 1980s. Professor William Buss begins the exploration by examining the constitutional problem of what process is due when an athlete, coach, or team is excluded from competition. The issue has been a major source of litigation in recent years as, it seems, virtually every person affected by an adverse eligibility decision has sought relief in the courts. Chapter 1 provides a comprehensive treatment of the issue and develops new insights into how the problem should be analyzed and resolved.

The most active area of sports litigation is liability for sports injuries. Injuries are common in sports, and courts have in recent years been more receptive to efforts seeking redress for such injuries. In chapter 2, Cym Lowell canvasses the primary issues arising in sports injury litigation and describes the applicable legal principles, thereby providing a useful primer in this important area of sports law.

Another area of much sports litigation in recent years, as well as legislative and regulatory activity, is sex discrimination. The law in this area has had a tremendous impact in expanding sports opportunities available to girls and women over the past ten years. Chapter 3, by Mark Kadzielski, explores the two primary approaches to sex discrimination in athletics, the Equal Protection Clause and Title IX of the Education Amendments of 1972, notes the areas of continuing uncertainty, and analyzes prospects for the future.

In 1978, the United States Congress overhauled the organization of Olympic sports in this country by passing the Amateur Sports Act. In the first published assessment of this important legislation, Professor James Nafziger describes in chapter 4 the background of the act, reviews its structure, and examines its substantive provisions in terms of its objects and purposes.

In intercollegiate sports, regulations administered by the National Collegiate Athletic Association serve to control conduct for a variety of objectives, including the protection of academic standards. Chapter 5, by Ronald Waicukauski, examines the NCAA regulatory scheme by focusing on rules and litigation relating to the academic integrity of intercollegiate sports. In light of recent scandals, deficiencies in the regulatory scheme are perceived and remedial regulations proposed.

Another area of NCAA regulation focuses on the relationship between the student athlete and agents—a relationship much abused by agents in the past. In chapter 6, Robert Ruxin examines this relationship in light of the NCAA rules and suggests several approaches to reduce abuses by agents, protect and enhance student athletes' rights and interests, and preserve the educational and financial interests of our colleges and universities.

The regulation of high school athletics is analyzed in chapter 7 by Professor John Weistart. After reviewing the revolutionary litigation of the 1970s, in which the courts struck down high school rules in areas such as personal grooming and marriage, he examines the legality of high school transfer rules. The result is an illuminating exposition of where the courts are and seem to be going in reviewing regulations and decisions in interscholastic sports.

We conclude with a comprehensive bibliography of articles, books, and government publications about law and sports. Librarian Keith Buckley has organized these materials in a format that should be useful for any lawyer or scholar seeking additional information in this area.

Twenty years ago, there would have been little to say about most of the legal issues in sports. There was no Title IX or Amateur Sports Act. The courts had not extended notions of due process and equal protection to sports. Sports agents were unheard of. There was comparably little litigation concerning sports injuries. Only in recent years has law emerged to play a major role in controlling the affairs of amateur sports.

For many people involved in amateur sports, that role is unsettling. Government regulation is perceived at best as a nuisance, and the prospect of litigation is frightening. For many spectators, the emergence of law in sports has been greeted with indifference and occasionally hostility. They value sports in part because it offers an escape from reality. To them, it is a special world of fun and games, where people want to play or be entertained. Law represents an intrusion of the real world that detracts from the enjoyment sports can give.

It is, however, a detraction that cannot and probably should not be completely avoided. Properly applied, law can serve to improve sports. Tort law, for example, by encouraging more concern for safety, can reduce sports injuries. Title IX has undoubtedly contributed to a reduction of discrimination against women in sports, and the Amateur Sports Act of 1978 has served to eliminate much of the friction among amateur sports groups in America.

In time, there will no doubt be diminished legal activity in some areas of sports where, for example, the law becomes settled and people adjust their behavior to comply. But the restraints of civilization as represented by law do not and should not stop at the edge of the playing field. It is now clear that law will continue to play an important role in sports in the years ahead, and indeed, as long as sports continues to experience the dynamic growth it has enjoyed over the last decade or so, the level of legal activity is likely to expand further.

As subsequent chapters of this book attest, the impact of law on sports has been considerable and promises to become even greater during the next decade. Whether that impact will be favorable or not depends ultimately on the quality of our understanding of the issues. The Center for Law & Sports was established at the Indiana University School of Law at Bloomington in 1981 with the mission of enhancing that understanding. In August 1981, the center sponsored a national conference in Indianapolis entitled, "Law and Amateur Sports: Issues of the 80s." This book is an outgrowth of that conference and represents the initial efforts of the center in pursuit of its mission. It also represents the collective contribution of several distinguished legal scholars to expand our knowledge about these complex and increasingly prevalent issues. The information and analysis provided should be helpful to any professional in law or sports who is confronted by these issues and provide an essential foundation for further scholarly work in the area.

Ronald J. Waicukauski

LAW & AMATEUR SPORTS

[1]

Due Process in the Enforcement of Amateur Sports Rules

William G. Buss

I. INTRODUCTION

No doubt, there is a kind of luxury embodied in the very idea of associating law and sports; there is something very nearly hubristic in applying a majestic concept like due process of law to athletics. Due process, we intuitively think, is what may stand between a person and death or imprisonment. We have extended the idea, because we are civilized, to protection from loss of job and loss of subsistence welfare payments. But sports?! It seems at first incongruous.

Yet, in one sense, the connection between the two is as American as apple pie. After all, our courts and our legal system have been heavily used by business interests for business purposes. And, of course, sports —even "amateur" sports as we use that term loosely outside the Ivy League and the Mid-West Conference—are big business. It is altogether fitting, then, that we should think about giving the little cogs legal protection from the large and powerful wheels that are spinning their ways toward postseason bowl games and national television contracts.

The cogs, in my picture, are the players and the assistant coaches— or, in the antiquated terminology of another day, the students and their teachers. As is often the case, what is cog and what is wheel may sometimes be unclear, and the head coaches and even athletic directors will occasionally find themselves on the cog side of the circle. Nor do I mean to invest the cogs with a character or value that places the glowing halo over their heads. We may assume that they are striving, in the good old American way, to escape their cogness—to receive lucrative professional player contracts or head coaching positions under the generous professional (or the sometimes even more generous collegiate) arrangements that do not stop with attractive salaries. Nor should we assume that, on the merits of any given controversy, the cogs have right and justice entirely on their side. On the contrary, the protection of

1

procedural due process is designed to avoid a prejudgment about where justice lies in any particular case.

A. Activity covered by this chapter

That brings me closer to the subject at hand. It will be helpful, I think, to identify the kinds of cases in which a claim for procedural due process concerning amateur sports might be expected. First, and perhaps most important, there is a range of cases involving student ineligibility to participate in sports. This category of cases can be subdivided in a number of respects. (a) Over a wide spectrum, the extent of ineligibility may vary substantially—a student may be suspended from practice for a short period; "benched" during a game; or declared ineligible for a single game, a season, a year (in all sports), or the remainder of school or college career. (b) The ineligibility may apply to a student at either the high school or college level. (c) The ineligibility may be based on varying grounds that differ in kind. For example, ineligibility may be based on a rule dealing with a transfer from another institution, the age of the student, or the total number of years of playing time; it may be based on grade-point requirements—the grades or test scores required for admission or a scholarship to an educational institution or the grades that must be maintained throughout the student's educational playing career; ineligibility may be based on a misconduct rule, such as a special "training" rule concerning "hours," alcohol use, or cigarette smoking or a general student rule that prohibits fighting, property destruction, or use of drugs.

Second, parallel to the various levels of suspensions of students from sports activities, there is a group of cases involving sanctions against coaches, including dismissal and suspension.

Third, a student who voluntarily or involuntarily discontinues participation in sports may lose a scholarship, and, in some cases, this loss would have the effect of terminating the student's education.

Fourth, an entire team (or all teams from a school) may be disqualified from participation in competition of a specified sort—for example, postseason bowl games.

In all these cases, I am assuming that the athlete or the coach or the team (school/college) is claiming that the action was taken in a manner that denied the claimant due process of law and is claiming a right to "procedural due process." I am assuming, specifically, that the claim is based on the United States Constitution—ordinarily on the due process clause of the Fourteenth Amendment.[1] It is important to note in passing, however, that such a claim for procedural protection could be based on other legal sources, alternatively or additionally—for example, state constitutions, federal statutes, state statutes, or regulations of a school, college, or governing "conference," such as the Big Ten, or a supervising organization, such as a state high school athletic association or the National Collegiate Athletic Association (NCAA). For example, a high school student excluded from participation in football by reason of being deaf might rely upon the procedural rights created to govern education for the handicapped by federal statute.[2] A high school coach, who is also a teacher, might claim the procedural rights governing teacher dismissal cases under the applicable state tenure law.[3] Many of the cases that would involve students, coaches, or teams at the collegiate level are governed by the rules of both the NCAA and some league or conference. These NCAA and conference rules are replete with provisions that spell out procedures and procedural rights.[4]

B. A paradigm due process sports case

To bring this chapter more clearly into focus, a paradigm due process sports case will facilitate a succinct overview of recurrent issues. Suppose that an unmarried student athlete who is the star of a girls high school basketball team (in a state that cares about that sport) becomes pregnant and is disqualified under two distinct rules promulgated by the state high school athletic association. One rule prohibits participation by "unmarried pregnant girls in contact sports"; the other rule prohibits participation of any student in competitive sports if such competition presents a "serious risk of injury by reason of the student's physical disability." The girl has consulted a physician who has informed her that there is no risk whatsoever in her playing the particular brand of basketball that never involves running more than half court or taking more than three dribbles in succession. The girl wants to play. She has her parents' support.

(1) Preliminary to reaching any procedural due process issue, there is an issue whether the rule is invalid on its face—as sex discrimination violating constitutional or statutory law,[5] or as an invasion of the student's constitutional right to privacy concerning marriage and pregnancy,[6] or as an *ultra vires* rule involving the personal life of a student beyond the power of the school or the state athletic association to regulate educational matters.[7]

(2) An additional preliminary (non–due process) issue is whether either rule has been properly applied to this case. Girls basketball may not be a "contact" sport; certainly, there is a question whether the student athlete is "disabled" or whether her playing entails a "serious risk of injury."

(3) A threshold due process issue is whether there is any action by the "state," without which Fourteenth Amendment due process never

comes into play. The answer is that both the public high school and the high school athletic association will be treated as exercising state power.[8] (4) A different threshold issue is whether the student has a constitutional right to procedural due process under any circumstances. The answer is clearly yes; a student is a "person" under the Fourteenth Amendment.[9] Note, however, that if, in our illustration, the student's public high school initiated the action to challenge the rule, the *school* might not be regarded as a "person" with constitutional rights. Whether or not a public school is a person under the Fourteenth Amendment, the school might have standing to assert the rights of the student.[10]

(5) The next question, a major one, is whether the student has a protectible "liberty" or "property" interest, without which there is no right to procedural due process. My answer is "probably yes," but meaningful discussion must be deferred on this point.[11] It may be noted in passing, though, that the answer might vary as the period of ineligibility is reduced or expanded; also, my "probably" would get more certain if we were talking about a college athlete in a sport for which there was a professional counterpart; and the answer would be influenced toward a definite "yes" if the high school athletic association rules, taken as a whole, may be construed to say, "You may be excluded from participation for these reasons and for no others."

(6) Assuming that the basketball player gets by the preceding issues, the ultimate issue is, what procedures must be given to her? As it is frequently framed, the issue is, what "process" is "due"? The only dependable answer is "It depends," and this issue, too, requires more complete discussion.[12] In a general anticipatory way, one can say, her right to procedural protection will increase as the period of ineligibility expands. Furthermore, she may be entitled to more procedures of a particular kind (like presenting evidence, cross-examining witnesses) if there are fact issues (as there appear to be under the disability rule but not the pregnancy rule). Finally, if we change the grounds of her ineligibility to academic failure, and if we assume that her challenge concerns only the validity of one or more low grades, she would be entitled to only very minimal procedural protection.

II. PRELIMINARY QUESTIONS ABOUT DUE PROCESS RIGHTS: "STATE" ACTORS WHO VIOLATE THEM AND "PERSONS" WHO HAVE THEM

The Fourteenth Amendment language focuses attention on what it takes to allege the bare bones of a due process claim under the United States Constitution. According to that language, "No State shall . . .

deprive any person of life, liberty, or property without due process of law." The central questions raised by the end of this sentence (from "life, liberty" to "of law") will be taken up in Parts IV.A and IV.B. In this part, I will consider the questions centered in "state" and "person."[13]

A. State action

It is well established that "state" action includes action by all state agencies, including state colleges and universities[14] and local school districts,[15] and all officials acting on behalf of the state or any state agency.[16] It is also well established that the restrictions of the Fourteenth Amendment apply to state, not private, entities.[17] So, for purposes of examining the law of sports and due process, it is clear that action by a state college or university or a public school or by an official of such a college or school is "state action"—and, therefore, any such action must be taken in a manner that is consistent with the strictures of the Fourteenth Amendment.

By the same token, the actions of private educational institutions at every level ordinarily are not subject to Fourteenth Amendment restraints. Yet, what is private in form may be public in substance.[18] With few exceptions, the courts have rejected the argument that government financial assistance to private education or government regulation of private education will convert private education into state action.[19] Similarly, the public function performed by private education has not been treated as a basis for finding that private schools and colleges exercise state power within the meaning of the Fourteenth Amendment.[20] It has sometimes been held, however, that the relationship between a private educational institution and its students is contractual and that, by an implied term of the contract, Fourteenth Amendment due process *standards* govern as a matter of contract interpretation despite the absence of state action.[21]

In two related lines of cases, the courts have held almost unanimously that high school athletic associations[22] and the NCAA[23] exercise state power although both are private organizations in form. These decisions have been based on the combined circumstances of extensive state involvement in these organizations and extensive "delegation" to these organizations of significant power to control the athletic activities of state institutions. As the court said in *Parish v. NCAA*, "[I]t would be strange doctrine indeed to hold that the states could avoid the restrictions placed upon them by the Constitution by banding together to form or to support a 'private' organization to which they have relinquished some portion of their governmental power."[24] For comparable reasons, athletic leagues or conferences of colleges have been treated as state entities for purposes of the Fourteenth Amendment.[25] This treatment of state action seems consistent with current Supreme Court doctrine, under which private entities are imbued with state power when there is significant governmental involvement in the particular "private" action challenged or when there is a "symbiotic" relationship between public and private entities.[26]

The significance of attributing state action to high school athletic associations, collegiate athletic conferences, and the NCAA can hardly be exaggerated. Most obviously, it means that all of the many actions taken by these organizations to regulate high school and collegiate athletics are subject to constitutional limitations. Even beyond that, it is arguable that action taken by private colleges in compliance with NCAA regulations is tantamount to state action.[27] Two courts have expressly reserved that question in dictum.[28] In each case, the court expressed its reservation about an action taken by private universities that "voluntarily" concur in the NCAA's decision. It is understandable that these courts choose not to answer a question not unavoidably before them. But the conception of a "voluntary" compliance with an NCAA decision does not reflect the reality of the potentially severe sanctions against a university and its athletic program that would result from a failure to take the action dictated by an NCAA decision.[29]

B. "Persons" who have constitutional rights or who have standing to assert them

The Fourteenth Amendment protects "persons" from violations by the state and those who are treated as exercising state power. It is clear that individual students are "persons" entitled to this protection and that neither their youth nor their status as students disqualifies them from asserting constitutional rights.[30] Although constitutional rights are frequently said to be "personal" rights,[31] corporations have been regarded as "persons" having constitutional rights under the Fourteenth Amendment.[32] Thus, it would seem that *private* schools and colleges have constitutional rights under the Fourteenth Amendment. It may be questioned, however, whether *state* colleges and universities and *public* schools have constitutional rights.

On several occasions, the Supreme Court has held that a local government may not assert constitutional rights against the state in which it is located.[33] The rationale of these cases emphasizes the fact that a municipality is the creation of the state and should not be able to assert constitutional rights in opposition to the will of its creator.[34] These cases have not been treated as controlling by lower federal courts when the government entity was not suing its own superior sovereign.[35] Once corporations as well as individuals are afforded constitutional protections, there is no clear and obvious reason why all corporate entities that sometimes exercise state power should be disqualified from having constitutional rights. Indeed, it seems clear that private entities, such as the NCAA, which are sometimes imbued with state authority, continue to have constitutional rights in many circumstances. Despite the relatively weak authority on this question, it would be reasonable to argue that a public school or a state college or university is a "person" with due process rights against an entity such as the NCAA or an athletic conference that is exercising state power but is not the sovereign that created the school or college.[36]

The validity of such a constitutional claim could be important when, for example, the NCAA, exercising state power, disqualifies a college from postseason competition in a particular sport. Even if state educational institutions are not "persons" having constitutional rights of their own, however, the NCAA's action might be challenged under one of three alternative approaches. Under the first approach, an individual student (or group of students) would bring an action alleging that the NCAA's ban on postseason competition violates the constitutional rights of individual students. Under the second approach, the college would bring the action alleging the individual student rights and claiming standing to assert the rights of a "third party," the individual student who is not in court. Under the third approach, a college *official* would bring the action claiming a derivative personal right to avoid participation in the denial of the student's right.

Each of these approaches would, of course, necessitate the existence of an individual constitutional right—a subject that will be discussed in the following two sections.[37] Under the approach involving an assertion by the college of the student's right, the college also must satisfy "third party standing" criteria. The general rule is that a litigant does not have standing to assert rights of the "third party."[38] But the courts have recognized various exceptions to the general rule.[39] For example, the college might argue that it has standing to assert the rights of a student athlete third party because, otherwise, the student rights would be diluted or destroyed[40] or because, practically speaking, it would be impossible for students to bring actions to assert their own rights.[41]

The third approach that was suggested entails a derivative claim by an educational official based on that official's duty not to violate the student's constitutional right. For example, if the effect of an NCAA decision were to cause the college to take an action adverse to an individual student, the official called upon to carry out that action might believe that the action violated a constitutional right of the affected student. In such a case, the official would have a duty not to violate that right and, arguably, would have a right to judicial relief from the pressure tending to cause such a violation.[42] Of course, there would be

no basis for relying upon a duty-derived right if the alleged violation
related to an injury to the college itself.

III. THE ESSENCE OF PROCEDURAL DUE
   PROCESS AND WHAT IT ISN'T; HEREIN
   OF "SUBSTANTIVE DUE PROCESS"
   AND OTHER SUBSTANTIVE CLAIMS

The subject of sports and procedural due process will be brought
into sharper focus by identifying the distinction between *substantive*
and *procedural* due process and noting briefly the wide range of substantive claims that may exist in addition to the claim for procedural
due process. Suppose a student is informed that she is ineligible to
participate in intercollegiate tennis competition because of a college
rule prohibiting competition within a year of a transfer from another
college. The tennis transfer student may challenge the *validity of the
rule* on its face or as applied to her. In either case, she is making a substantive claim. The tennis transferrer may, additionally or alternatively,
challenge a denial of an *opportunity to show* that the transfer rule
should not be or may not be applied to deny her eligibility. In this
latter case, she is making a procedural claim.

A. "Substantive due process" and other substantive
constitutional claims

Despite the seeming contradiction in terms, a "substantive due
process" doctrine is well recognized. According to this doctrine, a legislative (or regulatory) provision violates constitutional norms if the
provision is not rationally related to a legitimate government interest
or if, it is sometimes said, the provision is arbitrary, capricious, or unreasonable.[43] Except in specialized situations,[44] the doctrine exists more
in theory than in fact—which is to say, litigants who rely on this theory
(without the something special) do not win. A substantive due process
challenge to the transfer rule, for example, would have to argue either
that the "state" (for which, read: college, university, conference, or
NCAA) had no legitimate interest at all in making such a rule or that
the year of ineligibility did not tend to accomplish any legitimate interest that does exist. This is not an argument with any appreciable
chance of success.[45]

A substantive challenge to the validity of a governing rule can also
be placed on more specific constitutional grounds. For example, the
tennis transferrer might argue that her freedom of speech and/or association was curtailed by the transfer rule.[46] Although that may seem
a plausible argument, the decided cases would not encourage the ten-

nis player to expect the argument to succeed.[47] Based on analogies readily suggested by decided cases, it is easy to imagine situations in which an athlete would have a much stronger substantive claim based on freedom of expression: ineligibility to participate in sports might be based on a general student conduct rule concerning student expression.[48] Or, ineligibility might be based on a rule directing athletes to stay out of political demonstrations[49] or on a rule prohibiting homosexuals from participating in athletics.[50]

In addition to general substantive due process grounds and specific substantive constitutional grounds such as freedom of speech, the validity of the transfer rule might be challenged on equal protection grounds.[51] Of course, the tennis transferrer would have an easy equal protection case if, for example, only women were ineligible during the year after transferring. That would provide the basis of a classic sex discrimination claim.[52] But even without such a patent discrimination, the tennis transferrer might make a plausible equal protection argument. She could argue that the transfer rule imposes a burden on the right to travel and thus discriminates against those who have recently traveled. Some support could be found for this view in decided cases.[53] But the argument would probably not succeed in the present state of the law,[54] because the "travel" involved does not entail migration, and the reason for the rule (presumably to deter "raiding" between colleges) would be regarded as an adequate justification for any restriction on nonmigratory travel.[55]

B. Nonconstitutional substantive claims

Just as the tennis transferrer may challenge the validity of the transfer rule on the basis of various federal constitutional arguments,[56] she may be able to challenge the rule's validity on the basis of a federal or state statute.[57] It will often be the case that the strongest legal argument available in a sports case will not be an attempt to argue that a particular rule is invalid but that, properly understood, the rule favors the position of the student (or coach) resisting adverse action taken in the name of the rule.[58] For example, the tennis player may argue that the rule does not apply because she is not a transfer student at all or because she had transferred from junior college or because she has taken a year off before enrollment in her present college or because she did not participate in intercollegiate tennis at the college from which she transferred.[59]

In a parallel fashion, the tennis transferrer may want to rely upon a contract between her and the college to which she transferred. Suppose, for example, her scholarship is terminated by reason of her ineligibility due to the transfer. She may want to argue that her contract

with College B guarantees her scholarship even when she is not playing. Such a contract claim would often be founded upon an "implied"
contract—not one spelled out in writing but one inferred from the various words and actions that appear to summarize the parties' understanding.[60]

C. The qualified protection of procedural due process

The role of a procedural due process claim falls somewhere between
a challenge to the validity of a rule or contract and simple reliance on
the application of the rule or contract. On the one hand, for purposes
of the procedural due process claim, the *validity* of the rule is *irrele-
vant;* on the other hand, the procedural due process claim is a *means*
by which the *applicability* of the rule is challenged. In the illustrative
transfer rule case, the tennis player might be told simply that she is ineligible under the rule. In lieu of, or as an alternative to, a challenge
to the rule's validity,[61] the tennis player, asserting a right of procedural
due process, may insist that she be given an opportunity to show that
the transfer rule is inapplicable. If the right is recognized, she is given
a hearing of some sort, at which, aided by appropriate procedural safeguards, she hopes to be able to convince the persons with decision
power that the rule does not, after all, make her ineligible. Under her
procedural due process claim, she would seek the opportunity to present facts and make arguments and to rebut facts and arguments adverse to her. Her procedural due process claim would encompass a
demand for an impartial decision, but it would otherwise assume that
the decision would be made by the college that had declared her ineligible. The decision-making, to satisfy procedural due process, would
be conducted in a manner designed to give the claimant assurance that
the decision rule would be applied fairly and accurately and with an
awareness of the claimant's position.

IV. PROCEDURAL DUE PROCESS
IN AMATEUR ATHLETICS

A. Constitutionally protectible liberty and property interests

In any constitutional due process case, there is a threshold question
whether the person claiming procedural protection has a constitutionally protectible interest. In the words of the Fourteenth Amendment,
the question is whether the state is depriving the claimant of "life,
liberty, or property."[62] These terms mean both more and less than at
first appears. For present purposes, we may assume that capital punishment is not one of the hazards of amateur athletics, and thus we

may put the interest in "life" to one side.[63] The Supreme Court has said, "'liberty' and 'property' are broad and majestic terms," but they "must be given some meaning,"[64] and the Court has attempted to fill in some of the content in a variety of situations, none of which have involved sports. Below the Supreme Court level, a number of judicial opinions have addressed the question whether a protectible liberty or property interest was presented in connection with college and high school athletics. On the whole, the courts have been reluctant to find the existence of the required liberty or property interest.

1. *Liberty.* a. *A general analysis of protected liberty interests in sports cases.* The most obvious meaning of liberty is freedom from bodily restraint. When someone is threatened with imprisonment, the deprivation of a liberty interest is clearly threatened. But liberty also includes such interests as the freedom to make contracts, to be educated, and to engage in an occupation.[65] The Supreme Court has held that liberty includes a person's interest in avoiding damage to his or her reputation in the community[66] and in avoiding substantial restrictions on the opportunity for future employment[67] and further education.[68.] In the context of amateur sports, this line of authority suggests that a student athlete's liberty may be involved when athletic ineligibility results *from* conduct attributed to the student that would be regarded as "stigmatizing" or "defamatory," such as breaking a training rule, or when the ineligibility results *in* a substantial foreclosure of future opportunity, such as a high school student's loss of possible athletic scholarships that could ensure a college education or a college student's loss of playing experience, competition, and exposure that could lead to a professional sports career. In a parallel fashion, a coach may claim that a liberty interest is affected by a discharge that alleged stigmatizing grounds or foreclosed other coaching opportunities.

The general proposition that damage to reputation implicates a constitutional liberty interest is subject to important qualifications. First, disparaging actions or statements or record entries will not make out a liberty interest unless the defamatory content has been communicated in a manner that would be likely to result in a curtailment of the claimant's social or professional mobility.[69] This limitation obviously raises questions of fact. For example, in the context of a student athlete dismissed from a team for misconduct, there would be a question whether the reason for the dismissal was "published" in a manner likely to affect adversely the excluded athlete's future by damaging his reputation in the community or by reducing his opportunity for education or employment.

The availability of reputation damage as the basis of establishing a protectible liberty interest is also limited in a second way. In *Paul v. Davis,* the Supreme Court held that, to be able to claim a liberty deprivation by reason of injury to reputation, a person must suffer not only damage to reputation but also a separate loss at the hands of the government.[70] This additional requirement would seem to be satisfied in the typical case arising in an amateur athletics setting. For example, a discharge of a coach for wrongdoing or the suspension of a player from a team for misconduct would implicate a constitutional liberty interest because the reason (wrongdoing, misconduct) would be damaging to reputation and the action (discharge, suspension) would entail an independent loss (of a job, of playing eligibility).

In a case dealing with the discharge of a football coach,[71] it was argued that the coach had already been terminated and, therefore, the only interest at stake was the coach's interest in his reputation; thus the required independent loss was missing.[72] The court avoided the problem by finding that the coach would, in effect, be "blackballed" from other coaching jobs in the same conference and, perhaps, at any college within the NCAA.[73] The court also indicated, correctly in my view, that it should not be possible to circumvent a constitutional duty to provide due process by the simple expedient of a precipitous discharge.[74] That is, practically speaking, the coach lost a job *and* suffered reputation damage.

Although damage to reputation will often be the vehicle to the diminution of future prospects, that will not inevitably be the case. The curtailment of future opportunities is a distinct basis for showing the deprivation of a liberty interest. As the Supreme Court articulated the question in the *Roth* case, the inquiry should be whether there was any "stigma *or other disability*" that foreclosed the freedom to take advantage of other employment opportunities.[75]

b. *Liberty and the "speculative" interest in a professional sports career.* A recurrent question in the amateur sports cases is whether the effect of a loss of college eligibility on a professional sports career gives rise to a constitutional right of procedural due process. Because of the economic value involved, the interest arguably implicated in such a case is sometimes—understandably but incorrectly—characterized by the courts as a "property" interest.[76] The correct question in these cases is whether the student has a "liberty" interest in attempting to obtain a career in a professional sport. Very often, the courts have rejected the liberty claim on the ground that the interest in a professional sports career was too "speculative."[77]

Especially after *Paul v. Davis*, one must be cautious about any prediction of what the Supreme Court will do with future "liberty" claims. Nevertheless, it appears that the rejection of a liberty claim because of the inability to predict the athlete's eventual success in the professional sport misunderstands the nature of the liberty interest claimed. The interest involved is not the interest in having the future career but in having the "opportunity" for a future career in a professional sport. Time and again, the Supreme Court has emphasized the significance of action that forecloses a person's freedom to enter an *entire line of employment activity*.[78] The question should not turn on the odds of a player's making it in "pro ball," but on whether exclusion from college competition results in the sort of disability that, practically speaking, closes the door to the possibility of a professional career. That amateur college athletics plays such a doorkeeping role is hard to refute. As the court acknowledged in *Colorado Seminary v. NCAA*, the characterization of "the college athletic forum as a training ground for professional careers . . . may be a sadly accurate reflection of the true significance of today's amateur athletic competition."[79]

Despite the recognition that college athletics acts as a forum for certifying qualification for professional sports in this fashion, the *Colorado Seminary* and other courts evidently find the relatively small proportion of college athletes who have successful professional careers a basis for rejecting the liberty interest as speculative. That reasoning might be examined by comparing the connection between obtaining a law school education and having a career as a lawyer.[80] If a student were expelled from law school, the student would have a strong basis for claiming that the liberty interest in pursuing a legal career had been adversely affected, even if legal jobs were scarce and difficult to obtain.[81]

It does not follow from this line of argument that a declaration of ineligibility automatically triggers a liberty interest. For example, courts have sometimes rejected a claimed liberty interest by pointing out that there is no future professional opportunity whatsoever for an athlete to compete in a sport such as track.[82] It is conceivable, furthermore, that courts could draw factual distinctions based on the level of competition involved on the ground that certain colleges were not regarded as training grounds for professional careers by the colleges themselves, professional scouts, or college athletes. Clearly, factual distinctions would have to be drawn on the basis of the length of ineligibility; it may well be that only ineligibility for an entire college career, or perhaps the last year[83] or two of college competition, would amount to the de facto withholding of certification for a professional career necessary to bring the liberty interest and the right to procedural due process into play.

Still, despite its relatively narrow scope, a liberty interest does appear to be implicated in those cases in which college athletic ineligibility acts as a practical bar to opportunity for a professional career.[84] The very fact that college and professional athletics have been deliberately structured to make the college athletic competition a sort of minor league preparation for professional sports careers argues against deval-

uing individual claims as too speculative. Of course, the odds against
any individual athlete are long indeed, but athletes, generally, have
been channeled along the college route with the implicit, and often
quite explicit, counseling by their college mentors that this is *the* path
to a professional career in sports.

2. *Property.* a. *A general analysis of protected property interests in
sports cases.* Based on a common understanding of what "property" is,
there would very rarely be an amateur sports case involving the loss
or a threatened loss of property. Perhaps one can imagine a property
claim in a case involving forfeiture of a team jacket or the use of athletic equipment taken away by reason of a student's ineligibility.[85] But
such a far-fetched example is not required to invoke the much broader
concept of "property" as that term has been construed in the Constitution. As used in the due process clause, property is often explained as
an "entitlement," and it is used in contradistinction to a "subjective
expectation."[86]

Property interests are created by state (or federal) statute, by regulations of an agency authorized to act for the state, or by contract with
a state institution.[87] Of potential significance for sports cases is *Goss v.
Lopez,*[88] holding that state compulsory attendance and universal education statutes created a property interest in not being excluded from
public school for even a very short period of time.[89] It would seem that
the property interest in school attendance would encompass any interest in receiving the educational programs that schools are established
to provide. Unless written off as "extracurricular" or in some other way
treated as superfluous, sports activities would be included in such educational programs in which students were "entitled" to participate.[90]
At the college level, statutes and regulations similarly establish educational programs and the terms of eligibility for participating in them;[91]
thus, such statutes and regulations would appear to be a potential
source of a property interest in participating in college sports.

It is important to stress that the existence of a property interest does
not depend on an *a priori* claim of a *right* to participate in sports in
either the public school or college setting. *Goldberg v. Kelley*[92] illus-
trates this point clearly. Under the federal statute involved in *Goldberg,* welfare payments were made under statutorily specified conditions. Apart from the statute, there was no "right" to receive welfare
payments. Yet the *Goldberg* case recognized a constitutionally protected property interest in continuing to receive such payments by
those eligible in accordance with the statutory terms. Apart from any
governing statutes or regulations, property interests might be created
by express contract or by implied "contract," custom, or usage.[93]

If the NCAA exercises state power (as the courts say it does), it
would seem that the rules and regulations of the NCAA are also sources

of constitutional property claims. So too are the rules and regulations of a collegiate athletic conference, such as the "Big Ten," or a high school athletic association, as such conferences and associations have also been regarded as exercising state power. Take as an illustration the NCAA rules concerning student athletic scholarships.[94] These rules specify the forms and amounts of financial assistance that *may and may not* be provided to student athletes. NCAA member colleges, in effect, are bound to apply and enforce these rules. When a student demands procedural due process in connection with alleged financial assistance violations,[95] the student would often be able to assert a property interest based on these NCAA regulations.

A helpful insight can be obtained by asking whether the state agency whose action is being challenged was intended by the pertinent grant of authority to have "discretion" to take the action for any reason chosen by the agency.[96] For example, if one concludes, in a particular case, that a head football coach at a state university was given unqualified discretion to decide whether and when and why to dismiss assistant coaches, an assistant coach would have no property interest on which to found a right of procedural due process. The assistant coach might have had an expectation of continued work with the head coach, and that expectation might have been very reasonable, but, according to the illustration, the expectation would have been only subjective— not founded on anything sufficiently objective to amount to an entitlement.

If, to vary the previous example, an assistant coach may be dismissed only in accordance with the terms of a contract between the assistant coach and an employing state university, the assistant coach would have a protectible property interest. Similarly, the assistant coach would have a property interest to the extent that the terms of his employment were fixed by a regulation of the NCAA (or a conference or a high school athletic association). In these illustrations, the contract or the regulation would provide an "entitlement" such that the assistant coach was "entitled" to insist upon dismissal only within the terms of a contract or regulation.

To say that the assistant coach has an "entitlement" is not to say that he or she has a *right* to continue working as assistant coach under all circumstances, independent of the contract or regulation relied upon. It is to say, rather, that there is a constitutionally recognized *interest* in continuing in the assistant coaching position and that that interest may be terminated only pursuant to the terms of the contract or regulation that created it. As another example, let us revert to the earlier illustration concerning the recruitment of student athletes subject to NCAA rules regulating financial assistance. To say, as we might, that the student athlete has an "entitlement" based on the NCAA rule is not to say that the student is entitled to keep the athletic scholarship under all circumstances, but that the student has a constitutionally recognized *interest* in keeping the scholarship and that that interest may be terminated only in accordance with the terms of the NCAA rules that created it.[97]

b. *The judicial treatment of property claims in sports cases.* Based on the foregoing analysis, it should follow that students and coaches would often be able to argue successfully that they have property interests affected by adverse actions of schools, colleges, or controlling agencies such as the NCAA.[98] There is some authority for this proposition,[99] and some courts have reserved decision on the question of whether a property interest exists.[100] But, in a very sizable number of sports due process cases, the assertion of a property interest by a student athlete has fallen on deaf judicial ears.[101] Perhaps it is fair, also, to say that the courts' opinions in these cases do not reveal very much of the reasoning behind the decisions. That leaves a good deal of uncertainty about the correct explanation of the results. Despite the uncertainty, several partial explanations are suggested by what the courts do and do not say in their opinions.

First, the courts may be reading some of the broad language of *Paul v. Davis,* discussed earlier in connection with liberty interests, as signaling a general hostility toward federal protection of interests that are commonly governed by state law.[102] All one can say for certain about this possibility is that most of the courts are not explaining their results in these terms,[103] and the Supreme Court has not yet provided an analytical framework to go with this new mood.

Second, a disproportionate number of the cases rejecting property claims involve high school athletes complaining about their ineligibility under rules that proscribe participation in the first year of a transfer to a new school,[104] and most of the students in these cases had no serious factual or legal claim that the transfer rule did not apply. This lack of a colorable claim might suggest that these cases are similar to *Dixon v. Love,*[105] in which the Supreme Court held that there was no right to a pre–revocation-of-driver's-license hearing when there was no allegation of factual error in the revocation. That is, when there is no issue other than a request for a discretionary exception, the process due is very limited.[106] This explanation is less than satisfactory, however, both because it was not articulated by the courts deciding these cases and because, even if it had been, it would have been incorrect. It would have been incorrect because it is a very different thing to say that little or no hearing is due despite the existence of a protectible property interest (relying on *Dixon v. Love*) and to say that there is no affected property interest whatsoever.

A third explanation for the cases rejecting property interest claims, also suggested by the high school transfer cases, is the idea that the courts regard many student athlete property claims as *de minimis.* Once again one can say that this explanation has not been sharply articulated, although there is language in some of the opinions indicating that the *de minimis* ground is what the court had in mind.[107] The *de minimis* exception requires an honest judicial judgment based on a consideration of other decisions and of real world consequences. Since the Supreme Court indicated in *Goss v. Lopez* that a suspension of ten days or less was not *de minimis,*[108] that becomes a bench mark against which to test *de minimis* claims in cases of athletic ineligibility. For example, for an exclusion from an entire football season to be *de minimis,* a court would have to conclude that the impact on the affected student was so clearly different in scope from a ten-day suspension as to make *Goss* distinguishable. Furthermore, apart from precedent, a court would have to conclude that, in light of the significance attached to playing competitive football by students, school officials, and community members, the consequences to the average athlete of disqualification for a football season are so trivial as to be beneath the dignity of the judiciary duty-bound to protect constitutional rights. Notwithstanding the value-laden nature of the required judgment, I find it hard to believe that a conscientious judge could reach such a conclusion. When a student is given a "dirty look" by a teacher for what the teacher believes is misconduct, *that* is government action affecting a *de minimis* interest. Possibly, suspension from practice for a day may be *de minimis.* As the Supreme Court has said, "lines more nice than obvious" often must be drawn.[109] But I think a reasonably placed line will leave most of the due process sports cases to be decided on grounds other than *de minimis.*

A fourth possible explanation for the general tendency of courts to reject property claims in student sports cases is the concern about the burden that requiring procedural safeguards would entail for the educational institution. One court seemed to say this expressly.[110] Other courts, acknowledging that athletics is a part of the interest in education recognized in *Goss,* nevertheless have stated that the components of education do not separately constitute property interests.[111] Although the burden resulting from due process of law is clearly a relevant consideration, it is relevant to a different issue. The burden of providing procedural safeguards is an important determinant in deciding what process is due;[112] this burden is not relevant, however, to the issue of whether there is any protectible interest requiring some due process.[113]

The practical consequences of this distinction are potentially far-reaching. If a court says, *"This property* interest is *so slight* compared to the great burden it imposes on the school that only the most limited due process is required,"* then the court has left it open, for another day, to provide greater constitutional protection to a property interest that is like in kind but different in scope. If, however, the court says, "A student interest in participating in athletics is *not property*," as the courts seem to say, exclusions from athletics of a very different magnitude have been prejudged not to be the source of a property claim.[114]

Fifth, it is possible that many of the courts that deny the existence of a property interest may be doing so on the ground that students do not have a "right" to participate in athletics.[115] If so—if the courts are denying property claims on the basis of a "right"-"privilege" distinction, it is easy to say, unqualifiedly, that the reasoning is flawed. The Supreme Court has repeatedly indicated that the constitutional right to due process does not depend on an independent right that due process is claimed to protect. On the contrary, the Court has stated emphatically that the right-privilege distinction has been abolished.[116] No one claims (or should claim) that a student has a right to participate in sports, in the sense that the student has the right to exercise freedom of speech. If a school or college has no sports program, the student has no grounds on which to complain. But, in the cases about which we are talking, there is a sports program. If a program exists, a student's interest in participating in the program may not be taken away, except in accordance *with* due process, simply because the interest may be characterized as a "privilege."

A final possible explanation for the unsympathetic treatment of property interest claims may be traced to the labyrinthian relationships between student (or coach) and college and "conference" and national (for colleges) or statewide (for high schools) athletic associations. Conceivably, these relationships are so confusing that courts sometimes overlook the obvious. What seems obvious is the fact that the athletic association or conference that, the courts have recognized, exercises state power is also a source of property entitlements. For these purposes, the extensive array of NCAA regulations is the equivalent of a state statute setting forth the conditions under which students must be excluded and also, necessarily, the conditions under which they may not be excluded. Yet the courts seem to overlook even the possibility of this source of property interests.[117]

In the end, a conclusion that a student does not have a property interest on which to ground a claim of procedural due process can be supported only if the school authorities were given uncontrolled discretion to determine who participates and who does not. But it seems clear that such discretion has not been conferred. No one would argue that students could be excluded from a sport by reason of race or religion or the politics of their parents. The argument for procedural due process is like in kind though different in detail. According to the excluded student, the discretion of the authorities is limited by a rule, whether explicit or implicit. Procedural due process, the student argues, will increase the likelihood that the student's eligibility will be determined, like the eligibility of all other students, in accordance with the rule that specifies the conditions of participation.

B. The "process" that is constitutionally "due"

If the coach or athlete is unsuccessful in convincing the court that a protectible liberty or property interest has been "deprived" through state action, that is the end of the case: NO procedural due process is available as a matter of constitutional right. If, on the other hand, a conclusion is reached that a liberty or property interest is implicated, that is only the beginning. It is quite possible that a claimant's victory on the liberty/property issue will turn out to be Pyrrhic, as the "process" actually found to be "due" will often be very minimal.

The content required of procedural due process is phrased in many different ways. It is sometimes said that the right to procedural due process is a right to "*some* kind of hearing."[118] It is sometimes said to entail a trade-off between fairness and efficiency.[119] Sometimes, procedural due process is said to mean, simply, "fundamental fairness."[120] In *Mathews v. Eldridge*,[121] the Supreme Court articulated a three-factor "test," which is often accepted as the starting point in deciding what procedural due process requires in a particular context. According to the *Eldridge* test, the critical variables are (1) the importance of the interest affected, (2) the benefit to the claimant of any procedural safeguards requested, and (3) the burden on the administrative agency of providing that procedural safeguard.[122]

1. *Outlining the* Mathews v. Eldridge *test*. By way of illustration, suppose a student is declared ineligible to participate in intercollegiate football competition because (a) the student's academic record is below a specified minimum, and (b) the student has already had four years of competition. Let us suppose further that, despite the student's athletic prowess, it is his own (state) college that, regretfully, determines the ineligibility and notifies the student of its decision. Now, assume that the student wants to challenge the grounds of this decision and requests a "hearing," including the right to "discover" the evidentiary basis in advance of the hearing and, at the hearing, the right to be represented by counsel, to present evidence, to cross-examine opposing witnesses, and to present arguments. Finally, let us assume, for the present, that the student has a liberty or property interest.

We turn to the *Mathews v. Eldridge* test to determine which, if any, of the requested procedural rights the disappointed football player will be entitled to receive according to the Constitution. For reasons that

will soon be obvious, let us defer any consideration of variable one—
the importance of the interest in playing a season of college football.
Variable two asks about the benefit of a procedure to the football
player in challenging the grounds of exclusion—poor academic record
or prior use of four years of eligibility. If, for example, the football
player would be able to improve the presentation of his position materially by having representation of counsel, variable two should produce
an affirmative weighting toward a conclusion that the student is entitled to that procedural safeguard. Variable three—the burden on the
college—should produce a negative weighting if permitting the football
player to be represented by counsel would be burdensome to the college—e.g., by making resolution of the question more expensive or,
perhaps, by causing bad feelings between player and college athletic
officials.

Let us assume, now, that under the *Eldridge* formula the indicator
for each requested procedure is positive when variable two is considered and negative when variable three is considered. Still keeping variable one in the wings, we would next have to balance the negative and
positive weights. If we concluded, for example, that the benefit to the
student of having a procedural safeguard would be very great and the
burden of providing it very small, that would move us closer to a resolution in favor of saying that the student has a constitutional right to
that procedure. Conversely, if the benefit of a particular procedure
would be slight and the burden great, the formula points in the direction of denying the constitutional claim for the procedure.

But let us assume, for a particular claimed procedure, that the balance of benefits and burdens is relatively even—at least not clearly
weighted in one direction or the other. We must now call in variable
one, concerning the significance of the football player's interest. According to variable one, if we decide that losing the opportunity to
compete for a football season is a very substantial loss, the balance
shifts toward requiring the procedural right claimed. That is, the more
important we say the loss is, the more careful we must be to provide
procedural safeguards that will minimize the likelihood of an erroneous
deprivation. Thus, the more important the loss, the less benefit is required to demonstrate that, on balance, the procedure is constitutionally required, and the greater the burden on the college it will take to
demonstrate that, on balance, the procedure is not constitutionally
required.

It should be noted that the *Eldridge* formula focuses on one procedure at a time—such as right to counsel, presentation of testimonial
evidence, or cross-examination. But in each instance, the formula as-
sesses the benefit of that procedure in the light of the other available
procedures. It is commonly assumed that the strength of the claim for

any particular procedure may be weakened by the availability of some other procedure.[123] For example, the "need" for legal representation is diminished when there is an impartial tribunal that can be expected to protect the claimant's interest. The potential interplay between procedural safeguards gives the process of applying the formula a kaleidoscopic dimension, since, in actual practice, a due process case deals with all procedural demands at once.

To eliminate a possible source of confusion, attention should be called to a point of contrast between the *Mathews v. Eldridge* balancing test and the antecedent question whether a liberty or property interest is involved. We saw earlier that the *nature* of the individual interest that is adversely affected by the government's action determines whether a protectible liberty or property interest is at stake and, thus, whether the individual is entitled to any procedural due process at all. Now we have also seen that the *significance* of that interest is a variable influencing the scope of the constitutionally required procedural due process protection. The former question, concerning the nature of the interest, is an either-or question; the governing legal test is technical and mechanical. The latter question, concerning the significance of the interest, is a question of degree; the legal context calling it into play asks for a value judgment about the worth, in our society, of such an interest. So, to decide our illustrative case, the exclusion of the ineligible football player, we would have had to ask, initially, whether the foreclosure of future opportunities to play professional football implicates a liberty interest or whether the existence of an applicable statute, conference rule, or the like implicates a property interest. Only if we decide that there is a liberty or a property interest do we go on to ask, as a part of determining the extent of the process "due," just how much value our society attaches to the interest in playing intercollegiate football.

2. *Translating theory into practice: procedures required in sports cases.* It should be apparent from the preceding discussion that the *Mathews v. Eldridge* test requires extraordinarily difficult judicial judgments.[124] To anticipate such judgments and to avoid denial of constitutional rights, these same difficult judgments must be made by parties governed by this body of law. The educational institutions and state-acting organizations such as the NCAA must make these judgments in order to determine which procedures they are constitutionally obligated to provide. The affected individuals—student athletes or coaches and their lawyers—must make these judgments in order to decide which procedures may reasonably be requested and which denials of requested procedures may reasonably be appealed in court.

Although the *Mathews v. Eldridge* formula is nearly mathematical in form, it is anything but mathematical in application. In fact, in attempting to juxtapose the formula with the results and opinions in actual cases, a cynical person might conclude that the formula is not taken seriously by the courts. The courts seem sometimes to ignore and sometimes merely to give lip service to the three-part *Eldridge* test.[125] But the apparent gap between theory and practice may be deceiving. What courts do in procedural due process cases entails highly elusive, highly intuitive judgments that Justice Frankfurter once explained in the following way: "Due process is not a mechanical instrument. It is not a yardstick. It is a process. It is a delicate process of adjustment inescapably involving the exercise of judgment by those whom the Constitution entrusted with the unfolding of the process."[126] *Mathews v. Eldridge* should be read not as an attempt to convert the process into a yardstick, but as an attempt to articulate the variables that the courts intuitively draw upon in carrying out the "delicate process of adjustment" pursuant to their constitutional mandate.

There is a gestalt dimension, then, to due process decision-making. There is also a short chapter of history that will tend to make the results of that decision-making more intelligible. In 1970, the Supreme Court decided *Goldberg v. Kelly*.[127] In that case the Court held that a welfare claimant whose AFDC[128] payments had been terminated was entitled to a pretermination hearing, which included representation by counsel, presentation of evidence, cross-examination, transcript, and argument.[129] At the time, *Goldberg v. Kelly* was thought to usher in an era of due process protection so extensive and so pervasive that it was called by many the "due process revolution."[130] As it turned out, *Goldberg v. Kelly* was probably the high-water mark of that era. Protections of comparable magnitude were held by the Supreme Court to govern administrative actions other than AFDC termination.[131] But the thrust of the due process revolution was much criticized, and it soon came to be realized that the Supreme Court was not in such a revolutionary mood after all. The criticism leveled at the expansion of due process protections argued that benefits of due process were overstated and, especially, that the cost of due process was often great and had seemingly been underestimated.[132] It seems reasonable to conclude that, for the present at least, this point of view has carried the day on the Supreme Court, and many recent decisions bear its stamp.[133]

With this historical perspective, we can move toward a more specific statement of what due process might require in the kind of sports cases under consideration here. The history tells us that we should anticipate that the courts are becoming more grudging in their recognition of a right to various procedural safeguards. The history also reminds us that the law governing the scope of constitutionally required procedural due process is often in flux. This, in turn, means that a great deal of caution must be exercised in reading any particular opinion, as there is a high risk that isolated cases will reflect where the law has been rather than where it is going.

One case that provides an important bench mark for sports due process cases is *Goss v. Lopez*.[134] *Goss* held that a student suspended for ten or fewer days for violating school conduct rules was entitled to a "hearing" that consisted of informing the student of the charged misconduct and, if the student denied the charge, informing the student of the evidence on which the charge was based and giving the student an opportunity to present the student's side of the story.[135] The Court in *Goss* clearly anticipated that this entire "hearing" might take place in a very short time,[136] and the Court evidently contemplated that due process would have been done even if the disciplinarian, in effect, heard the student out and then adopted the teacher's view of what happened simply because it was the teacher's view.[137] Although *Goss v. Lopez* was decided the year before *Mathews v. Eldridge*, the *Goss* opinion reveals that the three *Eldridge* factors were considered. The procedures required were thought to provide a beneficial check against erroneous decisions, and more extensive procedures were denied because of their burden on the school; in dictum, however, the Court indicated that more extensive procedural safeguards would be required if the student's interest were significantly greater—as it would be if the threatened sanction were an expulsion or a long suspension.[138]

In a sports due process case, the court must decide how the interest adversely affected compares with the ten-day suspension of *Goss*. If, for example, the loss of a football season is equated to the loss of ten days of school, such a loss would presumptively call for minimal procedures comparable to those in *Goss*, unless there is a basis for concluding that either the benefits or burdens of those, or alternative, procedures would be different—a possible but unlikely result. If exclusion from a football season is thought to entail more serious consequences than the ten-day suspension—perhaps because of a judgment that the loss of future employment or educational opportunities would be greater—more extensive procedures would be required. If, to change the hypothetical, a college student athlete loses a scholarship for nonparticipation in athletics and is thereby forced to drop out of college, the case may be tantamount to an expulsion and thus require quite extensive procedural safeguards.

Goss is frequently mentioned in the sports due process cases, although the most common reference occurs in connection with a conclusion that (unlike *Goss*) there is no liberty or property interest and, thus, no due process right in the case at bar.[139] *Goss* has also been invoked for the proposition that, whether or not the litigant has a liberty or property interest, whatever procedural protection may have been constitutionally required was received.[140] In such cases, there is sometimes an indication that the court has actually attempted to compare the significance of the short-term suspension from school in *Goss* with the interest deprived in the case before the court.[141] But the main point usually appears to be that *Goss* is very easy to satisfy, and the courts simply do not address the question whether something more than the minimum might be required. Of course, when the court specifies the procedures that were available and says that they satisfied due process[142]—with or without citing *Goss*—that indicates that more is not required; but it does not indicate how much less might have been enough.

In a very few of the cases, the courts have found that the claimant had a right to procedural due process and that the procedures were inadequate. In *Wright v. Arkansas Activities Assoc.*,[143] the court found a denial of due process in the failure of an athletic association's regulations to give notice that a coach could be terminated for violating a prohibition of off-season football practice.[144] Cases such as *Goss* require "notice" of the *misconduct charged* so that the affected individual may defend against the charge at the "hearing"; cases such as *Wright* require that the rule allegedly violated be sufficiently clear so that an individual is given "notice" of *what is expected* and thus given an opportunity to avoid the misconduct. As the *Wright* case reveals, a rule is not sufficiently clear unless it not only identifies what is prohibited but also identifies the level of seriousness of the prohibited conduct. Other cases have made it clear, however, that the affected individual need not have actual knowledge of the conduct prohibited; it is sufficient if the individual has an appropriately accessible *source* of information.[145]

Just as notice without actual knowledge may satisfy due process, it seems clear that a right-holder may "waive" procedural rights. Accordingly, a student who knowingly acquiesces in being represented by a university may have waived the student's right to direct participation. Nevertheless, it seems incorrect to assume, as some courts evidently have, that there is such a "unity of interest" between student and university that the student has no independent procedural right.[146] Under the NCAA rules, the college is the "party" directly subject to NCAA sanctions;[147] students' hearing rights are very uncertain;[148] and the college has an obvious incentive to comply with an NCAA decision adversely affecting student interests both to avoid other sanctions and to terminate the disruptive tensions generated by an NCAA investigation.[149]

Behagen v. Intercollegiate Conference of Faculty Representatives[150] involved the suspension of college basketball players for participating in a violent brawl in an intercollegiate basketball game. The court held that the players were entitled to a hearing to challenge their suspension from participation in intercollegiate basketball and to be informed in writing of the charges against them, the grounds for penalty, and a list of witnesses at least two days before the hearing;[151] at the hearing, they were entitled to present their position and to hear all testimony but not to cross-examine witnesses; following the hearing, they were entitled to have access to a tape recording of the hearing proceeding.[152]

In *Stanley v. The Big Eight Conference*,[153] the court specifically refused to follow the part of the *Behagen* decision that denied the right of cross-examination.[154] The *Stanley* court contemplated that, in some circumstances, written statements of witnesses and written responses might be used in lieu of live testimony and cross-examination.[155] But the *Stanley* court held that, if there were factual disputes, "a fact finding hearing would be required,"[156] and that merely providing an opportunity to respond to summaries and paraphrases of statements based on an informal investigation "does not satisfy the requisite level of due process."[157]

In the *Tarkanian* case, the court held that a coach who was given a two-year suspension for recruiting violations was entitled to an extensive hearing that included notice of specific charges and the facts on which the charges were based, effective representation by counsel, presentation of evidence, and cross-examination of witnesses.[158]

As a general proposition, the courts have taken the position that little or no hearing is required when the factual accuracy of the charged misconduct is conceded.[159] It is arguable in such cases, however, that a hearing is appropriate for the purpose of making policy arguments, showing exonerating circumstances, or appealing to the discretion of the decision-maker.[160] In a case raising a question of the harshness of declaring athletes ineligible for all intercollegiate competition on the basis of minor infractions, the United States Court of Appeals for the Eighth Circuit said there was no constitutional due process right to appeal to the decision-maker's discretion.[161] But the Eighth Circuit was dealing only with the question of a hearing *prior* to the eligibility determination,[162] and the court expressly observed that a subsequent mitigation hearing might be held by the NCAA.[163] Furthermore, the Eighth Circuit relied upon *Dixon v. Love*,[164] which held that the absence of factual issues supported the denial of a *pre*-revocation hearing when a more complete hearing would be available before the revocation of a driver's license became final.[165]

3. *"Academic" due process.* The absence of factual issues partly explains the special treatment that has been given to "academic" actions that adversely affect students. I have found no sports case involving such an action, but a simple illustration will demonstrate how such a case might arise. Let us revert to the disqualified football player, but let us assume, now, that the grounds of ineligibility are (1) a grade-point average below a specified minimum; and (2) violation of a train-

ing rule prohibiting the use of alcohol of specified "proof," in specified amounts, at specified times and places. The first ground might be characterized as "academic"; the second ground as "misconduct."

In *Board of Curators v. Horowitz*,[166] the Supreme Court held that dismissal for "academic" reasons leads to much more modest procedural safeguards than a misconduct dismissal.[167] According to *Horowitz*, misconduct dismissals raise fact questions, whereas academic dismissals raise questions of judgment. So, if the excluded football player is claiming that he really didn't violate the alcohol rule—e.g., that it was a case of mistaken identity or that the amount consumed was below the forbidden level—a fact issue would have been raised, and legal representation or presentation of evidence or cross-examination of witnesses would be beneficial to the student in presenting a case. If, however, the excluded football player is claiming that his academic performance was not below the established norms, the claim could be characterized as merely questioning the professional judgment of the professors who had done the grading. For that purpose, *Horowitz* indicates that conventional trial-type procedures such as legal representation, presentation of evidence, or cross-examination of witnesses would be of no value. This conclusion fits into a general due process principle according to which the remedy for claimed defects in testing is retesting.[168]

But suppose the challenge to academic ineligibility were not based on a direct challenge to the grades. Suppose the football player claimed that his average had been miscalculated or that some of his grades reflected not an honest professional judgment but personal bias by his professors against football players. Under *Horowitz*, one has only murky answers to the questions raised by such a claim. It is possible to read *Horowitz* to say that an academic action is an academic action—period. But it seems more reasonable to read *Horowitz* for the proposition that the issues in question rather than the characterization of the college's action should control. Under this second view, the football player's right to procedural safeguards such as representation by counsel or cross-examination of witnesses should be evaluated on the basis of the utility of those procedures in proving that the grade had been miscalculated or that personal bias, rather than professional judgment, caused a particular grade to be entered. It can be expected that the courts will take a cautious position in dealing with a claim of personal bias. In such a case, the claimant has been required to establish a prima facie case of bias before being entitled to any right to a hearing on the bias issue; the mere allegation of bias would not secure the hearing.[169]

Horowitz clearly would not govern a case in which a grade reduction was a result of misconduct, and the student was challenging the misconduct determination. For example, if a student athlete is accused of stealing a book from another student and, as a punishment, is given a failing grade in a course, the student athlete's request for a hearing to contest the *stealing charge* would not come within *Horowitz*. The character of the stealing case as a student misconduct case would not be altered by the imposition of an academic sanction.[170]

In addition to its conclusion that conventional procedural safeguards would offer very limited benefit to a student expelled on academic grounds, the Supreme Court concluded in *Horowitz* that providing such procedures in an academic dismissal case entailed added costs. Although the Court's reasoning was not altogether clear,[171] it seemed to be saying that to permit a challenge to professional judgments in an adversary proceeding would tend to destroy the academic atmosphere that is characteristic of an educational institution and indispensable to the performance of its educational function. If *Horowitz* is to be followed true to its spirit, it will require courts to apply the *Mathews v. Eldridge* formula in a way that places added weight on the cost (or burden) scale whenever the nature of the student athlete's claim entails a challenge to academic judgments.[172]

V. CONCLUSION

Although the action of a "private" (nongovernmental) entity is not subject to constitutional limitations, action that is private in form may be treated as "state action" in substance. In this fashion, the courts have treated high school and national athletic associations and "conferences" or leagues as if they were government agencies for purposes of constitutional law. Because these interscholastic and intercollegiate organizations exercise such pervasive influence in the field of amateur athletics, most of the field is governed by the constitutional limits applicable to the state and its political subdivisions and officials.

Among other governing principles, the Constitution prohibits the "state"—and thus athletic associations, such as the NCAA, exercising state power—from violating the "due process" rights of students and coaches. In a suit to vindicate the right to procedural due process, a student or coach—or a school or college on behalf of the constitutional right-holder—must establish the existence of a "liberty" or "property" interest within the meaning of the Fourteenth Amendment. Even though the applicable constitutional doctrine is riddled with unsettled issues, there often would seem to be a strong liberty or property claim in a sports due process case. It is arguable that the "liberty" of students is implicated by termination of athletic eligibility because of the effect of such action on opportunities for higher education (in the case of high school students) or on opportunities for a professional career in a sport (in the case of college students engaged in certain sports). For coaches, the argument is that coaching career opportunities may be significantly curtailed. Both students and coaches would often have "property" claims based on express or implied contracts or on the "state law" that often takes the form of regulations of the NCAA or other regulating agency. For students, the liberty or property claim might apply either to participation in sports or to retention of scholarships.

This suggested analysis has been only infrequently adopted by the courts, which have tended to find no liberty or property interest in these cases. Based on actual decisions and on statements contained in reported judicial opinions, it appears that the courts are most sympathetic to liberty or property claims in a case involving termination of a coaching position—especially if stigmatizing grounds are involved; next, in a case involving loss of a scholarship that might terminate a student's education; and, next, in a case involving a loss of athletic eligibility for an extended period of time—perhaps especially when the student appears to be an "innocent" victim of a college-rule violation.

The distinctions between affected interests represented by this hierarchy of judicial protection is clearly relevant to procedural due process cases, but these distinctions should influence the extent of procedural protection available rather than whether any protection at all will be required by the Constitution.

If and only if a protectible liberty or property interest is found, the courts must decide what procedural protections are constitutionally mandated. Relatively few of the sports cases have had to decide this question. But a number of courts have said, in dictum, that the student litigants have received all the process that was "due," *even if* they were entitled to any.

At a very general level, one can say that the courts indicate that due process requires notice of the existence of the rule prohibiting particular conduct and the penalty a violation might entail and also notice of the violation charged and an opportunity for the accused person to defend against the charge. Generally, the opinions dealing with the sports cases have reflected a view consistent with the usual constitutional pattern, which requires a greater opportunity to defend as the potential loss is greater. Similarly, these opinions have recognized that the opportunity to defend will be significantly affected by the presence or absence of factual issues.

The more thoughtful judicial responses have reflected an awareness of the complexity—and possible constitutional repercussions—of the layers of relationships between the individual students and coaches, the educational institutions that offer students education in exchange for athletics, and the collectives like the NCAA that regulate educational institutions directly and students indirectly. One can often detect in a court's opinion a nervousness about being drawn into this world of amateur athletics in which so much money is involved. One can detect in these opinions, too, an element of condescension about "sports." Yet, whatever one may think about the influence of gargantuan amateur athletics or the integrity of the educational process at the institutions involved, it is hard not to take seriously the fate of the individuals who often have such a big stake in this enterprise.

NOTES

The valuable assistance of Cynthia L. Winkler, J.D. 1980, University of Iowa, and Brian P. Leitch, J.D. 1981, University of Iowa, is gratefully acknowledged by the author.

1. U.S. Const., Amend. XIV, Sec. 1: "No state shall . . . deprive any person of life, liberty, or property without due process of law."

2. Education For All Handicapped Children Act, 20 U.S.C. §§ 1401–20 (1976), Pub. L. 94-142 (1975). *See also* § 504, Rehabilitation Act of 1973, 29 U.S.C. § 794.

3. *E.g.*, Iowa Code, §§ 279.12–.18.

4. *See, e.g.*, 1980–81 NCAA Manual, "Official Procedure Governing The NCAA Enforcement Progam," pages 149–63; Handbook of the Intercollegiate (Big Ten) Conference (July 1, 1981), pages 12–18.

5. *Compare* General Electric Co. v. Gilbert, 429 U.S. 125 (1976), *and* Geduldig v. Aiello, 417 U.S. 484 (1974), *with* Nashville Gas Co. v. Satty, 434 U.S. 136 (1977).

6. *See* Bellotti v. Baird, 443 U.S. 622 (1979); Zablocki v. Redhail, 434 U.S. 374 (1978); Ordway v. Hargraves, 323 F.Supp. 455 (D. Mass. 1971).

7. *See* Goldstein, *The Scope and Sources of School Board Authority to Regulate Student Conduct and Status: A Nonconstitutional Analysis,* 117 U. PA. L. REV. 373, 391–94, 395–98, 407–11, 425–26 (1969).

8. *See* section II.A, *infra.*

9. *See* section II.B, *infra.*

10. *Id.*

11. *See* section IV.A, *infra.*

12. *See* section IV.B, *infra.*

13. Questions have seldom been raised about the meaning of "deprive." *See* Wilkinson, *Goss v. Lopez: The Supreme Court as School Superintendent,* 1975 SUP. CT. REV. 25, 51; *cf.* McMillan v. Board of Educ., 430 F.2d 1145, 1148–49 (2d Cir. 1970) (focusing on word "subjects" in 42 U.S.C. § 1983).

14. *See* Board of Curators v. Horowitz, 435 U.S. 78 (1978); Sweatt v. Painter, 339 U.S. 629 (1950).

15. *See* Goss v. Lopez, 419 U.S. 565 (1975); Brown v. Board of Educ., 347 U.S. 483 (1954).

16. *See* Monroe v. Pape, 365 U.S. 167 (1961); Screws v. United States, 325 U.S. 91 (1945).

17. *See, e.g.*, Jackson v. Metropolitan Edison Co., 419 U.S. 345 (1974); Moose Lodge v. Irvis, 407 U.S. 163 (1972).

18. *See* Evans v. Newton, 382 U.S. 296, 299 (1966); Burton v. Wilmington Parking Authority, 365 U.S. 715 (1961).

19. *See* Cannon v. University of Chicago, 559 F.2d 1063, 1069 (7th Cir.), *rev'd on other grounds*, 441 U.S. 667 (1979); Sanford v. Howard University, 415 F. Supp. 23, 29–30 (D.D.C.), *aff'd*, 549 F.2d 830 (D.C. Cir. 1977); Torres v. Puerto Rico Junior Col., 298 F. Supp. 458, 461 (D.P.R. 1969); *cf.* Johnson v. Southwest Detroit Community Mental Health Services, 462 F. Supp. 166, 168 (E.D. Mich. 1978) (pervasive state and federal regulation and funding insufficient to render acts of private nonprofit hospital state action). *But see* Braden v. University of Pittsburgh, 552 F.2d 948, 965 (3rd Cir. 1977); Newson v. Vanderbilt U., 453 F. Supp. 401, 419–22 (M.D. Tenn. 1978); Taylor v. Maryland Sch. For Blind, 409 F. Supp. 148, 151 (D. Md. 1976). *See generally,* cases cited at Braden v. University of Pittsburgh, 552 F.2d 948, 964 n. 79 (3rd Cir. 1977).

20. *See* Bright v. Isenbarger, 445 F.2d 412, 413–15 (7th Cir. 1971); Blackburn v. Fisk U., 443 F.2d 121, 123 (6th Cir. 1971). *But see* Brown v. Stickler, 422 F.2d 1000, 1002 (6th Cir. 1970); Newson v. Vanderbilt University, 453 F. Supp. 401, 419–22 (M.D. Tenn. 1978) (public function related to private university hospital's care for indigents constitutes state action).

21. *See* Greene v. Howard U., 412 F.2d 1128 (D.C. Cir. 1969); Pride v. Howard U., 384 A.2d 31 (D.C. App. 1978).

22. *See* Wright v. Arkansas Activities Ass'n, 501 F.2d 25, 27–28 n. 2 (8th Cir. 1974); Mitchell v. Louisiana High School Athletic Ass'n, 430 F.2d 1155, 1157 (5th Cir. 1970); Barnhorst v. Missouri State H.S.A.A., 504 F. Supp. 449, 457 (W.D. Mo. 1980). *See also* Yellow Springs Exempted Sch. Dist. v. Ohio H. Sch. A.A., 443 F. Supp. 753, 757 (S.D. Ohio), *rev'd on other grounds,* 647 F.2d 651 (6th Cir. 1981) (used four-part test to determine whether high school athletic association constituted state action).

23. Regents of U. of Minn. v. NCAA, 560 F.2d 352 (8th Cir.), *cert. dismissed,* 434 U.S. 978 (1977); Rivas Tenorio v. Liga Atlética Interuniversitaria, 554 F.2d 492 (1st Cir. 1977); Howard U. v. NCAA, 510 F.2d 213 (D.C. Cir. 1975); Parish v. NCAA, 506 F.2d 1028 (5th Cir. 1975); Associated Students, Inc. v. NCAA, 493 F.2d 1251 (9th Cir. 1974). *But see* McDonald v. NCAA, 370 F. Supp. 625 (C.D. Cal. 1974). *McDonald* appears to be a doubtful authority after the Ninth Circuit's *Associated Students* decision, *supra. See* Howard U. v. NCAA, *supra,* 510 F.2d at 218–19.

24. Parish v. NCAA, 506 F.2d 1028, 1033 (5th Cir. 1975).

25. *See* Stanley v. The Big Eight Conference, 463 F. Supp. 920, 927 (W.D. Mo. 1978); Kupec v. Atlantic Coast Conference, 399 F. Supp. 1377 (M.D.N.C. 1975) (implication).

26. *See* Jackson v. Metropolitan Edison Co., 419 U.S. 345, 351, 357 (1974); Burton v. Wilmington Parking Authority, 365 U.S. 715 (1961).

27. *See* Louisiana H.S.A.A. v. St. Augustine H.S., 396 F.2d 224, 228–29 (5th Cir. 1968) (private high school); Buckton v. NCAA, 366 F. Supp. 1152, 1157 (D. Mass. 1973) (NCAA membership among other factors); *cf.* United States v. Price, 383 U.S. 787, 794–95 (1966) (private person engaged in joint venture with state actors is also a state actor).

28. Howard U. v. NCAA, 510 F.2d 213, 222 n. 15 (D.C. Cir. 1975); Parish v. NCAA, 506 F.2d 1028, 1032 n. 10 (5th Cir. 1975).

29. *See* Regents of U. of Minn. v. NCAA, 560 F.2d 352, 363–64 (8th Cir.), *cert. dismissed,* 434 U.S. 978 (1977).

30. *See* Goss v. Lopez, 419 U.S. 565 (1975); Tinker v. Des Moines Independent Sch. Dist., 393 U.S. 503 (1969).

31. *See, e.g.,* Shelley v. Kraemer, 334 U.S. 1, 22 (1948).

32. *See* Santa Clara County v. Southern Pac. R. R., 118 U.S. 394 (1886). Until recently, corporations were regarded as having property but not liberty interests under the Constitution—*see, e.g.,* Hague v. C.I.O., 307 U.S. 496, 527 (1939); Western Turf Ass'n v. Greenberg, 204 U.S. 359, 362–64 (1907)—but a recent Supreme Court decision raises serious doubts about the vitality of this distinction—*see* First National Bank v. Bellotti, 435 U.S. 765, 775–80 (1978). *But see Bellotti, supra,* at 802–21 (White, J., dissenting); *id.* at 822–28 (Rehnquist, J., dissenting).

33. *See* Williams v. Baltimore, 289 U.S. 36 (1933); City of Trenton v. New Jersey, 262 U.S. 182 (1923); Hunter v. Pittsburgh, 207 U.S. 161 (1907). *See also* South Carolina v. Katzenbach, 383 U.S. 301, 323–24 (1966) (state is not a person under the Fifteenth Amendment).

34. *See* Williams v. Baltimore, *supra,* at 40; City of Trenton v. New Jersey, *supra,* at 189–90; Hunter v. Pittsburgh, *supra,* at 178–79; Santa Monica Community College v. P.E.R.B., 169 Cal. Rptr. 460 (Calif. 1980) (dictum).

35. *See* Township of River Vale v. Town of Orangetown, 403 F.2d 684, 686 (2d. Cir. 1968); Santa Clara v. Andrus, 572 F.2d 660, 675 (9th Cir. 1978); Sault Ste. Marie v. Andrus, 458 F. Supp. 465, 473 (D.D.C. 1978); United States v. Public Service Comm., 422 F. Supp. 676, 682 (D. Md. 1976).

36. In Regents of U. of Minn. v. NCAA, 560 F.2d 352, 362 (8th Cir.), *cert. dismissed,* 434 U.S. 978 (1977), the court considered but did not decide the question whether a state university was a "person" within the meaning of § 1983, the statutory vehicle for most Fourteenth Amendment cases. The court suggested that the university was not a "person" plaintiff because it was not a "person" defendant, relying in this respect on the law before it was changed by Monell v. Department of Social Services, 436 U.S. 658 (1978).

37. A distinct question might be raised concerning the standing to invoke the Article III power of the federal courts. Arguably, the plaintiff under any of these approaches would have to allege facts indicating that there was a reasonable probability that the judicial remedy requested would prevent the injury to the students claimed to be "caused" by the violation of the students' right. *See* Simon v. Eastern Kentucky Welfare Rights Organization, 426 U.S. 26 (1976); Warth v. Seldin, 422 U.S. 490 (1975).

38. *See* L. Tribe, American Constitutional Law §§ 3–23, 24, 25 (1978).

39. *See* L. Tribe, *id.,* § 3–26.

40. *See* Craig v. Boren, 429 U.S. 190, 195 (1976); Barrows v. Jackson, 346 U.S. 249, 257 (1953).

41. *See* Eisenstadt v. Baird, 405 U.S. 438, 446 (1972); Barrows v. Jackson, 346 U.S. 249, 257 (1953).

42. *See* Regents of U. of Minn. v. NCAA, 510 F.2d 352, 363–64 (8th Cir.), *cert. dismissed,* 434 U.S. 978 (1977) (university's duty not to violate right of student to procedural due process basis of right to be protected against NCAA order to declare student ineligible); *cf.* Brewer v. Hoxie Sch. Dist., 238 F.2d 91 (8th Cir. 1956) (school official's duty to desegregate schools basis of right to be protected from private harassment in carrying out duty).

43. *See* West Coast Hotel v. Parrish, 300 U.S. 379 (1937); Nebbia v. New York, 291 U.S. 502 (1934).

44. *See, e.g.,* Moore v. East Cleveland, 431 U.S. 494 (1977) (ordinance prohibiting grandmother from living with grandsons); Roe v. Wade, 410 U.S. 113 (1973) (abortions); Griswold v. Connecticut, 381 U.S. 479 (1965) (contraceptives).

45. Barnhorst v. Missouri State H.S.A.A., 504 F. Supp. 449, 458–64 (W.D. Mo. 1980); Kulovitz v. Illinois H.S.A., 462 F. Supp. 875, 879 (D. Ill. 1978); *cf.* Williams v. Hamilton, 497 F. Supp. 641, 645–46 (D.N.H. 1980) (holding, under equal protection clause, that classification of transfer rule is rationally related to legitimate state interest).

46. *See* Healy v. James, 408 U.S. 169 (1972). By the terms of the First Amendment, freedom of speech and, derivatively, freedom of association are rights protected only against Congress and, by implication, against the federal government, but speech is considered a "liberty" protected against state (and local) government as well by the Fourteenth Amendment. *See* Healy, *supra;* Gitlow v. New York, 268 U.S. 652 (1925).

47. *See* Belle Terre v. Boraas, 416 U.S. 1, 7 (1974); Griswold v. Connecticut, 381 U.S. 479, 484–85 (1965) (by implication, social association not protected).

48. *See* Tinker v. Des Moines Ind. Sch. Dist., 393 U.S. 503 (1969); Scoville v. Board of Educ., 425 F.2d 10 (7th Cir.), *cert. den.,* 400 U.S. 826 (1970).

49. *Cf.* Williams v. Eaton, 468 F.2d 1079 (10th Cir. 1972).

50. *Cf.* Fricke v. Lynch, 491 F. Supp. 381 (D.R.I. 1980).

51. Like the due process clause, the equal protection clause of the Fourteenth Amendment protects "persons" against "state action": "No state shall . . . deny to any person within its jurisdiction the equal protection of the laws."

52. The Fourteenth Amendment is not violated if the state can justify its sex classification on the ground that it "substantially" serves an "important" state interest. *See* Wengler v. Druggists Mutual Ins. Co., 446 U.S. 142 (1980); Craig v. Boren, 429 U.S. 190 (1976). Such a justification would be most unlikely in the hypothetical case in the text.

53. *See* Shapiro v. Thompson, 394 U.S. 618 (1969); *cf.* Vlandis v. Kline, 412 U.S. 441 (1973) ("irrebuttable presumption"); Doe v. Bolton, 410 U.S. 179 (1973) (article IV privileges and immunities).

54. *See* Sosna v. Iowa, 419 U.S. 393 (1975); Memorial Hospital v. Maricopa County, 415 U.S. 250 (1974); Starns v. Malkerson, 401 U.S. 985 (1971), *aff'g. without opinion* 326 F. Supp. 234 (D. Minn. 1970).

55. A high school transfer rule that flatly prohibited athletic competition for one year after transfer might be subject to a more serious equal protection challenge since it would be more likely to have an impact on interstate family migration.

56. Challenges could also be made asserting state constitutional violations, and such state challenges are sometimes more successful than their federal counterparts. *Compare* San Antonio Ind. Sch. Dist. v. Rodriguez, 411 U.S. 1 (1973) (equal protection challenge to educational financing scheme rejected), *with* Robinson v. Cahill, 62 N.J. 473, 303 A.2d 273, *cert. den.,* 414 U.S. 976 (1973) (challenge to educational financing scheme under state constitution successful).

57. *E.g.,* 1972 Education Amendments, Title IX, 20 U.S.C. §§ 1681–86

(federal prohibition of sex discrimination in education); § 601A.6, Code of Iowa (state prohibition of discrimination based on race, creed, color, sex, national origin, religion, disability in furnishing accommodations, advantages, facilities, services, or privileges).

58. *See* Gulf South Conference v. Boyd, 369 So.2d 553, 557–58 (Ala. 1979).

59. *See* 1980–81 NCAA Manual, Bylaws, Article 4, Secs. 1(j)(7)–(10), (k), (l), (m), (n).

60. *See* Greene v. Howard U., 412 F.2d 1128 (D.C. Cir. 1969); Gulf South Conference v. Boyd, 369 So.2d 553, 556 (Ala. 1979); Pride v. Howard U., 384 A.2d 31 (D.C. App. 1978); Buss & Novick, *The Detection of Cheating cn Standardized Tests: Statistical and Legal Analysis,* 9 J. L. & Ed. 1, 48–56 (1980).

61. It is very common to assert the substantive and procedural rights in the alternative. *See, e.g.,* Perry v. Sindermann, 408 U.S. 593 (1972).

62. *See* L. Tribe, American Constitutional Law, § 10–9, 11, 12 (1978); Monaghan, *Of "Liberty" and "Property,"* 62 Cornell L. Rev. 405 (1977); Van Alstyne, *Cracks in "The New Property": Adjudicative Due Process in the Administrative State,* 62 Cornell L. Rev. 445 (1977).

63. This disclaimer should not suggest, however, that "life" is incapable of broad construction. *See* Monaghan, *supra* note 62, at 410 n. 37.

64. Board of Regents v. Roth, 408 U.S. 564, 571, 572 (1972).

65. *See* Board of Regents v. Roth, 408 U.S. 564, 572 (1972).

66. *See* Goss v. Lopez, 419 U.S. 565, 575 (1975); Board of Regents v. Roth, 408 U.S. 564, 573–74 (1972).

67. *See id.*

68. *See* Goss v. Lopez, 419 U.S. 565, 575 (1975).

69. *See* Bishop v. Wood, 426 U.S. 341, 348–49 (1976); *cf.* Codd v. Velger, 429 U.S. 624, 628 (1977).

70. Paul v. Davis, 424 U.S. 693, 706 (1976).

71. Stanley v. The Big Eight Conference, 463 F. Supp. 920 (W.D. Mo. 1978).

72. Stanley, *supra,* at 930.

73. *Id.*

74. *Id.*

75. Board of Regents v. Roth, 408 U.S. 564, 573 (1972); *see* Paul v. Davis, 424 U.S. 693, 701–10 (1976); Cafeteria Workers v. McElroy, 367 U.S. 886, 898 (1961); Schware v. Board of Bar Examiners, 353 U.S. 232, 238 (1957); Joint Anti-Fascist Refugee Comm. v. McGrath, 341 U.S. 123, 184–85 (1951) (Jackson, J.).

76. *See* Albach v. Odle, 531 F.2d 983, 984–85 (10th Cir. 1976); Howard Univ. v. NCAA, 510 F.2d 213, 222 (4th Cir. 1975); Parish v. NCAA, 506 F.2d 1028 (5th Cir. 1975); Taylor v. Alabama H.S.A.A., 336 F. Supp. 54 (D. Ala. 1972) (opportunity of high school student obtaining college athletic scholarship).

77. *See* Parish v. NCAA, 506 F.2d 1028 (5th Cir. 1975); Kupec v. Atlantic Coast Conference, 399 F. Supp. 1377 (D.N.C. 1975); Williams v. Hamilton, 497 F. Supp. 641, 646 (D.N.H. 1980); Taylor v. Alabama H.S.A.A., 336 F. Supp. 54, 57 (M.D. Ala. 1972).

78. *See* cases cited note 75, *supra.*

79. 417 F. Supp. 885, 889 (D. Col. 1976).

80. For cases in which access to a legal career was foreclosed by bar ad-

mission requirements, *see* Willner v. Committee on Character, 373 U.S. 96, 103 (1963); Schware v. Board of Bar Examiners, 353 U.S. 232, 238 (1957).

81. Arguably, though, Board of Curators v. Horowitz, 435 U.S. 78 (1978), raises doubts about such a claim. *See* Buss, *Easy Cases Make Bad Law: Academic Expulsion and the Uncertain Law of Procedural Due Process*, 65 Iowa L. Rev. 1, 34–35 n. 227 (1979).

82. *See, e.g.*, Fluitt v. University of Nebr., 489 F. Supp. 1194 (D. Nebr. 1980). *But see* New York Times (October 27, 1981, Chicago Ed.), p. 23, col. 1 (Salazar, winner of New York marathon, arguing for under-the-table payments in lieu of placing money in trust with T.A.C.).

83. The contention that athletes need to pass through college competition is not belied by the occasional dramatic exception involving a superathlete who is able to enter professional competition without a full four years of college competition. *See* Des Moines Register (November 8, 1981), p. 11D (suggesting Herschel Walker of University of Georgia may attempt to become professional football player after second year in college); Chicago Tribune (July 8, 1981), sec. 4, p. 1 (David Wilson of University of Illinois drafted by New Orleans Saints of National Football League when Wilson became ineligible for an additional year of collegiate competition).

84. *See* Behagen v. Intercollegiate Conference of Faculty Representatives, 346 F. Supp. 602, 604 (D. Minn. 1972); J. Weistart & C. Lowell, The Law of Sports (1979), pages 22–25 & cases cited therein; *cf.* Kite v. Marshall, 454 F. Supp. 1347, 1349, 1351 (S.D. Tex. 1978) (emphasizing high school student's interest in obtaining college athletic scholarship).

85. In Howard U. v. NCAA, 510 F.2d 213, 222 n. 16 (D.C. Cir. 1975), the court speculated that there might be a property interest implicated by reason of the requirement to return trophies along with forfeiting a championship.

86. *See* Board of Regents v. Roth, 408 U.S. 564, 577 (1972).

87. *See* Board of Regents v. Roth, 408 U.S. 564, 577 (1972) ("independent source such as state law—rules or understandings").

88. 419 U.S. 565 (1975).

89. *Id.* at 573.

90. *See* Barnhorst v. Missouri State H.S.A.A., 504 F. Supp. 449, 465 (W.D. Mo. 1980); Pegram v. Nelson, 469 F. Supp. 1134, 1140 (M.D.N.C. 1979); Hunt v. NCAA, No. G76-370 C.A. (W.D. Mich., Sept. 10, 1976), slip opinion, p. 15; Kelley v. Metropolitan County Board of Educ., 293 F. Supp. 485, 492 (M.D. Tenn. 1968), *rev'd on other grounds*, 436 F.2d 856 (6th Cir. 1970).

91. *See* Ross v. Penn State U., 445 F. Supp. 147, 152–53 (M.D. Pa. 1978).

92. 397 U.S. 254 (1970).

93. *See* Hunt v. NCAA, No. G76-370 C.A. (W.D. Mich., Sept. 10, 1976), slip opinion, p. 4; Gulf South Conference v. Boyd, 369 So.2d 553, 556 (Ala. 1979). The contract or regulation may be implied. *See* Perry v. Sindermann, 408 U.S. 593, 601–03 (1972) (de facto tenure); Hennesey v. NCAA, 564 F.2d 1136, 1145–46 (5th Cir. 1977) (de facto tenure during tenure of head coach).

94. *See* 1980–81 NCAA Manual, Constitution, Article 3, sections 1(a), (e), (f), (g), (h); 4.

95. *See* Regents of U. of Minn. v. NCAA, 560 F.2d 352, 355–57 (8th

Cir.), *cert dismissed,* 434 U.S. 978 (1977); Hunt v. NCAA, No. G76-370 C.A. (W.D. Mich., Sept. 10, 1976), slip opinion, pp. 5–6.

96. *See* Michelman, *Formal and Associational Aims in Procedural Due Process,* in NOMOS 126 (J. Pennock & J. Chapman eds. 1977).

97. An especially troublesome problem is posed by a "state"-created property interest that includes a procedural limitation as an integral part of the created interest. Justice Rehnquist once advocated the validity of such a scheme in dissent, arguing that the grantee of the property interest had to take the "bitter with the sweet." Arnette v. Kennedy, 416 U.S. 134, 154 (1974). The rejection of the Rehnquist opinion was repeated recently in the majority opinion in Vitek v. Jones, 445 U.S. 480, 490–91 & n. 6 (1980). *See generally* Grey, *Procedural Fairness and Substantive Right,* in NOMOS 182 (J. Pennock & J. Chapman eds. 1977); Van Alstyne, *Cracks in "The New Property": Adjudicative Due Process in the Administrative State,* 62 Cornell L. Rev. 445 (1977).

98. *See generally,* J. Weistart & C. Lowell, The Law of Sports (1979), pages 20–22 & cases cited therein.

99. *See* Regents of U. of Minn. v. NCAA, 560 F.2d 352, 367 n. 22 (8th Cir.), *cert. dismissed,* 434 U.S. 978 (1977); Parish v. NCAA, 506 F.2d 1028, 1034 nn. 16 & 17 (5th Cir. 1975); Hunt v. NCAA, No. G76-370 C.A. (W.D. Mich., Sept. 10, 1976), slip opinion, p. 4; Colorado Seminary v. NCAA, 417 F. Supp. 885, 895 (D. Colo. 1976), *aff'd,* 570 F.2d 320 (10th Cir. 1978); Gulf South Conference v. Boyd, 369 So.2d 553, 556 (Ala. 1979).

With the exception of some dictum in *Parish* referring to NCAA regulations, these cases point to a contract source of property. In the *Colorado Seminary* case, the court speculated that an opportunity to participate in intercollegiate competition might have been part of the student's bargain in exchange for agreeing to attend the recruiting school and to participate in athletics. But the court rejected its own speculation, concluding that the student holding an athletic scholarship had "no more right to play than a walk on." *Id.* at 895 n. 5. The court should not have been so quick to reject its own suggestion. Of course, the athletic scholarship holder had no *right* to play. But it seems reasonable to construe the arrangement between student and college as contractual and to assume that one of the inducements to attract the student to the recruiting college was an *opportunity* to compete.

100. *See* Regents of U. of Minn. v. NCAA, 560 F.2d 352, 366 & n. 22 (8th Cir.), *cert. dismissed,* 434 U.S. 978 (1977); Howard U. v. NCAA, 510 F.2d 213, 222 (D.C. Cir. 1975).

101. *See* cases cited in notes 104, 107, 111, 115, *infra.*

102. 424 U.S. 693, 699–701 (1976); *see* Ingraham v. Wright, 430 U.S. 651, 676–78 (1977); *cf.* Arnette v. Kennedy, 416 U.S. 134, 154–55 (1974) (federal statute).

103. *But see* Hebert v. Ventetuolo, 638 F.2d 5, 6 (1st Cir. 1981).

104. *See* Hebert v. Ventetuolo, 638 F.2d 5 (1st Cir. 1981); Walsh v. Louisiana High School Athletic Ass'n., 616 F.2d 152 (5th Cir. 1980); Denis J. O'Connell H.S. v. Virginia H.S. League, 581 F.2d 281 (4th Cir. 1978), *cert. den.,* 440 U.S. 936; Albach v. Odle, 531 F.2d 983 (10th Cir. 1976); Barnhorst v. Missouri State H. S. Activities Ass'n., 504 F. Supp. 449 (W.D. Mo. 1980); Kulovitz v. Illinois H.S.A., 462 F. Supp. 875 (D. Ill. 1978); Dallam v. Cumberland Valley Sch. Dist., 391 F. Supp. 358 (M.D. Pa. 1975).

105. 431 U.S. 105, 114 (1977); *see* Codd v. Velger, 429 U.S. 624, 628 (1977).

106. *See* Regents of U. of Minn. v. NCAA, 560 F.2d 352, 368 (8th Cir.), *cert. dismissed*, 434 U.S. 978 (1977). *See also* text at notes 159–65, *infra*.

107. Dallam v. Cumberland Valley Sch. Dist., 391 F. Supp. 358, 362 n. 5 (D. Pa. 1975) (if property interest, *de minimis*); Hebert v. Ventetuolo, 638 F.2d 5, 6 (1st Cir. 1981); Walsh v. Louisiana H. S. Athletic Ass'n., 616 F.2d 152 (5th Cir. 1980); Blue v. University Interscholastic League, 503 F. Supp. 1030 (N.D. Tex. 1980); Pegram v. Nelson, 469 F. Supp. 1134, 1140 (M.D.N.C. 1979) (denial of one or several extracurricular activities may entail only *de minimis* property interest, but long-term exclusion from all extracurricular activities might trigger due process right).

108. *See* Goss v. Lopez, 419 U.S. 565, 576 (1975).

109. Local 761, Electrical Workers v. NLRB, 366 U.S. 667, 674 (1961).

110. *See* Dallam v. Cumberland Valley Sch. Dist., 391 F. Supp. 358, 361 (D. Pa. 1975).

111. *See* Colorado Seminary v. NCAA, 570 F.2d 320, 321 (10th Cir.), *aff'd*, 570 F.2d 320 (10th Cir. 1978); Albach v. Odle, 531 F.2d 983, 985 (10th Cir. 1976); Pegram v. Nelson, 469 F. Supp. 1134, 1140 (M.D.N.C. 1979); Dallam v. Cumberland Valley Sch. Dist., 391 F. Supp. 358, 361–62 (D. Pa. 1975).

112. *See* section IV.B, *infra*.

113. *See* Goss v. Lopez, 419 U.S. 565, 575–76 (1975).

114. The same point applies, perhaps even more clearly, to a decision that relies upon *de minimis* reasoning to conclude that athletic participation is never the source of a property interest. Occasionally, the opinions have narrowed the holding so that a more extensive ineligibility might lead to a different conclusion. *See, e.g.,* Parish v. NCAA, 506 F.2d 1028, 1034 (5th Cir. 1975).

115. *See* Denis J. O'Connell H. S. v. Virginia H. S. League, 581 F.2d 81, 84 (4th Cir. 1978); *cert. den.*, 440 U.S. 936; Parish v. NCAA, 506 F.2d 1028, 1034 (5th Cir. 1975); Mitchell v. Louisiana H.S.A.A., 430 F.2d 1155, 1158 (5th Cir. 1970); NCAA v. Gillard, 352 So.2d 1072 (Miss. 1977); Louisiana State Bd. of Educ. v. NCAA, 273 So.2d 912 (La. App. 1973); Tennessee Secondary Sch. A.A. v. Cox, 425 S.W.2d 597, 602 (Tenn. 1968.)

116. *See* Board of Regents v. Roth, 408 U.S. 564, 571 (1972); Bell v. Burson, 402 U.S. 535, 539 (1971); Goldberg v. Kelly, 397 U.S. 254, 262 (1970).

117. *See* Hebert v. Ventetuolo, 638 F.2d 5, 6 (1st Cir. 1981); Williams v. Hamilton, 497 F. Supp. 641, 645 (D.N.H. 1980), Pegram v. Nelson, 469 F. Supp. 1134, 1139 (M.D.N.C. 1979) (all mentioning the absence of an applicable *state* law).

118. *See* Friendly, *"Some Kind of Hearing,"* 123 U. PA. L. REV. 1267 (1975).

119. *See* Crampton, *A Comment on Trial-Type Hearings in Nuclear Power Plant Siting*, 58 VA. L. REV. 585, 593 (1972); Verkuil, *A Study of Informal Adjudication Procedures*, 43 U. CHI. L. REV. 739, 740–42 (1976).

120. Solesbee v. Balcom, 339 U.S. 9, 16 (1950) (Frankfurter, J., dissenting); *see* Hannah v. Larche, 363 U.S. 420, 442 (1960); Mullane v. Central Hanover Bank & Trust Co., 339 U.S. 306, 313–15 (1950).

121. 424 U.S. 319 (1976).

122. *Id.* at 335. *See* Buss, *Easy Cases Make Bad Law: Academic Expulsion and the Uncertain Law of Procedural Due Process,* 65 Iowa L. Rev. 1, 49–52 (1979) (suggesting that usual characterization of *Eldridge* test as a three-factor formula misleading).

123. *See* Buss, *Procedural Due Process for School Discipline: Probing the Constitutional Outline,* 119 U. Pa. L. Rev. 545, 639–40 (1971); Friendly, *"Some Kind of Hearing,"* 123 U. Pa. L. Rev. 1267, 1279–80 (1975); Kirp, *Schools as Sorters: The Constitutional and Policy Implications of Student Classification,* 121 U. Pa. L. Rev. 705, 789–91 (1973).

124. *See* Buss, Kuriloff & Pavlak, Disciplinary Due Process: An Empirical Feasibility Study of Procedural Due Process, School Discipline, and Educational Environment (a report prepared for the National Center for Administrative Justice, Washington, D.C., September 1981).

125. A notable exception is Hunt v. NCAA, No. G76-370 C.A. (W.D. Mich., Sept. 10, 1976), slip opinion, pp. 10–12, in which the court carefully articulated how each of the *Eldridge* variables influenced the determination of the process that was due.

126. Joint Anti-Fascist Refugee Comm. v. McGrath, 341 U.S. 123, 163 (1951) (Frankfurter, J., concurring).

127. 397 U.S. 254 (1970).

128. Aid for Families with Dependent Children.

129. *See* Verkuil, *A Study of Informal Adjudication Procedures,* 43 U. Chi. L. Rev. 739, 760 (1976), for a complete list of procedures required by *Goldberg.*

130. *See* K. Davis, Administrative Law of the Seventies (1976); Friendly, *"Some Kind of Hearing,"* 123 U. Pa. L. Rev. 1267, 1273 (1975); Kirp, *Proceduralism and Bureaucracy: Due Process in the School Setting,* 28 Stan. L. Rev. 841 (1976).

131. *See, e.g.,* Morrissey v. Brewer, 408 U.S. 471 (1972); Richardson v. Wright, 405 U.S. 208 (1972).

132. *See* Buss, *Easy Cases Make Bad Law: Academic Expulsion and the Uncertain Law of Procedural Due Process,* 65 Iowa L. Rev. 1, 39–56 (1979).

133. *See* Ingraham v. Wright, 430 U.S. 651, 680–82 (1975); Mathews v. Eldridge, 424 U.S. 319, 347–49 (1975); Wolff v. McDonnell, 418 U.S. 539, 566–72 (1974).

134. 419 U.S. 565 (1975).

135. *Id.* at 582.

136. *Id.*

137. *Id.* at 568 n. 2 & 583.

138. *Id.* at 584.

139. *See* Walsh v. Louisiana H. S. Athletic Ass'n, 616 F.2d 152, 159–60 (5th Cir. 1980); Colorado Seminary v. NCAA, 570 F.2d 320, 321 (10th Cir. 1978); Albach v. Odle, 531 F.2d 983 (10th Cir. 1976); Barnhorst v. Missouri State H.S.A.A., 504 F. Supp. 449, 465 (W.D. Mo. 1980); Fluitt v. University of Nebraska, 489 F. Supp. 1194, 1202 (D. Nebr. 1980); Kulovitz v. Illinois H.S.A., 462 F. Supp. 875, 878 (N.D. Ill. 1978); Dallam v. Cumberland Valley Sch. Dist., 391 F. Supp. 358, 361 (M.D. Pa. 1975).

140. *See* Regents of U. of Minn. v. NCAA, 560 F.2d 352, 368 (8th Cir.), *cert. dismissed,* 434 U.S. 978 (1977); Howard University v. NCAA, 510 F.2d 213, 222 (D.C. Cir. 1975); Barnhorst v. Missouri State H.S.A.A., 504 F. Supp. 449, 465 (W.D. Mo. 1980).

141. *See* Colorado Seminary v. NCAA, 570 F.2d 320, 321 (10th Cir.

1978); Albach v. Odle, 531 F.2d 983, 985 (10th Cir. 1976); Dallam v. Cumberland Valley Sch. Dist., 391 F. Supp. 358, 360–61 (M.D. Pa. 1975); French v. Cornwell, 276 N.W.2d 216, 218 (Nebr. 1979).

142. *See* Regents of U. of Minn. v. NCAA, 560 F.2d 352, 368 (8th Cir.), *cert. dismissed*, 434 U.S. 978 (1977) (right to counsel and fair and impartial hearing); Howard U. v. NCAA, 510 F.2d 213, 222 (D.C. Cir. 1975) (notice and full particulars of charge, right to defend against charge at three separate levels); Barnhorst v. Missouri State H. S. Activities Ass'n, 504 F. Supp. 449, 465 (W.D. Mo. 1980) (notice, opportunity to petition for hardship exception, appeal hearing); Fluitt v. University of Nebraska, 489 F. Supp. 1194 (D. Nebr. 1980); Braesch v. DePasquale, 265 N.W.2d 842, 845–46 (Nebr. 1978) (formal hearing, opportunity to present evidence, cross-examination, representation by counsel).

143. 501 F.2d 25 (8th Cir. 1974).

144. *Id.* at 29.

145. *See* Regents of U. of Minn. v. NCAA, 560 F.2d 352, 370 (8th Cir.), *cert. dismissed*, 434 U.S. 978 (1977); Fluitt v. University of Nebraska, 489 F. Supp. 1194, 1203–04 (D.C. Nebr. 1980); Taylor v. Alabama H.S.A.A., 336 F. Supp. 54, 56 (M.D. Ala. 1972).

146. *See* Hunt v. NCAA, No. G76-370 (W.D. Mich., Sept. 10, 1976); NCAA v. Gillard, 352 So.2d 1072, 1073–82 (Miss. 1972). In the *Hunt* case, the court did not simply equate the student and college interests but made an assessment to determine whether the student received due process *in light of* the college's participation. *See Hunt, supra,* slip opinion, pages 7–15.

In University of Nevada v. Tarkanian, 594 P.2d 1159, 1163–65 (Nev. 1979), holding that the NCAA was a necessary party in a suit against a university by a basketball coach who was suspended by the university pursuant to an NCAA rule, the court portrayed the university as being in a position potentially adverse to both NCAA and coach. *See also* Regents of U. of Minn. v. NCAA, 560 F.2d 352, 364 (8th Cir.), *cert. dismissed,* 434 U.S. 978 (1977) (university resisting order of NCAA to declare students ineligible or to suffer sanctions imposed by NCAA).

147. *See* 1980–81 NCAA Manual, Article 4, Sec. 1; Official Procedure Governing The NCAA Enforcement Program, Secs. 1–6, 8–9, 11–12 (indicating that educational institutions are "members," that a member is focus of NCAA enforcement, and that procedural protections are generally designed to safeguard members).

148. *See* 1980–81 NCAA Manual, Official Procedure Governing the NCAA Enforcement Program, Secs. 12(a)(4–9), (b)(3), (5), (6) (indicating limited participation and procedural protection for students).

149. *See* Regents of U. of Minn. v. NCAA, 560 F.2d 352, 364 (8th Cir.), *cert. dismissed,* 434 U.S. 978 (1977); University of Nevada v. Tarkanian, 594 P.2d 1159, 1163–65 (Nev. 1979); Note, *Due Process and Its Future Within the NCAA,* 10 CONN. L. REV. 290, 315 nn. 120 & 121 (1978); Note, *Judicial Review of Disputes Between Athletes and the National Collegiate Athletic Association,* 24 STAN. L. REV. 903, 908 & nn. 41, 42 (1972); New York Times (November 4, 1981, Chicago Ed.) p. 25, col. 7 (University of Miami's acceptance of violations resulting in ineligibility of athletes; coach expresses relief from pressure of investigation and president stresses importance of looking to future).

150. 346 F. Supp. 602 (D. Minn. 1972).

151. *Id.* at 932–33.

152. *Id.*

153. 463 F. Supp. 920, 932 (W.D. Mo. 1978).

154. *Id.* at 932–33.

155. *Id.* at 932.

156. *Id.*

157. *Id.* at 933.

158. *See* Tarkanian v. University of Nevada, at Las Vegas, No. A173498 (Nev. Dist. Court, 8th Judicial District, Oct. 3, 1977), *reversed on other grounds*, 594 P.2d 1159 (Nev. 1979).

159. *See* Dixon v. Love, 431 U.S. 105 (1977); Codd v. Velger, 429 U.S. 624 (1976).

160. *See* Codd v. Velger, 429 U.S. 624, 633–34 (1976) (Steven, J., concurring); Morrissey v. Brewer, 408 U.S. 471, 488 (1971); FCC v. WJR, The Goodwill Station, 337 U.S. 265, 274–76 (1949); 1 K. Davis, Administrative Law (1958) §§ 7.01, 7.07.

161. Regents of U. of Minn. v. NCAA, 560 F.2d 352, 368 (8th Cir.), *cert. dismissed*, 464 U.S. 978 (1977).

162. *See id.*

163. *See id.* at 368, 372.

164. 431 U.S. 105 (1977).

165. *See id.* at 112–14.

166. 435 U.S. 78 (1978).

167. *Id.* at 90.

168. *See* Mahavongsann v. Hall, 529 F.2d 448, 550 (5th Cir. 1976); Greenhill v. Bailey, 519 F.2d 5, 8 (8th Cir., 1975); 2 K. Davis, Administrative Law §§ 7.09, 8.14, 15.01 (1958); Buss & Novick, *The Detection of Cheating on Standardized Tests: Statistical and Legal Analysis,* 9 J. L. & Educ. 1, 32–33 (1980).

169. *See* Connelly v. University of Vermont and State Agricultural College, 244 F. Supp. 156, 159–61 (D. Vt. 1965).

170. This conclusion would also apply when the academic sanction, though not deliberately imposed, is an inevitable by-product of another sanction, as would be the case when a student is suspended for misconduct, and either a "zero" is assigned for unexcused absences or a test that cannot be made up is given on the day of suspension. *See* Minorics v. Board of Educ., N. Jer. Comm'n of Educ., Decision, March 24, 1972; S. Goldstein & E. Gee, Law and Public Education (2d ed. 1980), pp. 431–34. A challenge to the *appropriateness* of reducing a grade to punish misconduct also would not fall within the special *Horowitz* situation. But the appropriateness of the grade reduction might be challenged as a violation of substantive due process. *See* Ingraham v. Wright, 430 U.S. 651, 658–59, 679 n. 47 (1977); Hall v. Tawney, 621 F.2d 607, 611–15 (4th Cir. 1980).

171. *See* Buss, *Easy Cases Make Bad Law: Academic Expulsion and the Uncertain Law of Procedural Due Process,* 65 Iowa L. Rev. 1, 82–84 (1979).

172. It is arguable that a judgment concerning coaching "competence" would, like an academic judgment about students, entail subjective, professional, nonfactual considerations. If that argument prevailed, then, of course, the limitations of *Horowitz* would apply to cases involving dismissals or other sanctions of coaches for incompetence.

[2]

Liability for Injuries in Sports Activities

Cym H. Lowell

The area of the law of sports that has received the most frequent judicial analysis, and that has produced a correspondingly large body of decisional authority, is the liability that may result from injuries sustained in sports activities. The central technical questions raised by the liability cases are actually not very broad, and the questions presented by any given case are quite likely to fall within a very narrow range of applicable legal principles. While this might be viewed to indicate that a discussion of injury liability could be easily, and succinctly, presented, that is, unfortunately, not the case.

In this paper, we will consider liability for injuries to participants and spectators, enforceability of waivers and releases of liability, liability for injury in educational programs, liability of coaches, and liability relating to the provision of medical services. These subjects comprise many of the critical legal issues that arise in connection with injuries in sports activities, but they certainly do not exhaust the possibilities.

LIABILITY FOR INJURY TO PARTICIPANTS

The most direct type of liability resulting from sports activity is that which arises as a consequence of the injuries suffered by participants. Such injuries may be the result of the zeal of competitive activity at close quarters, but will more often be the product of other forces that are not an ordinary component of the sport. Regardless of the specific cause of injury, however, the basis upon which recovery will be sought by the injured participant will in most cases be the same. Thus, when a participant seeks to recover for his or her injuries, the most frequent

This chapter is drawn from a book entitled *The Law of Sports,* by John C. Weistart and Cym H. Lowell, published by the Michie/Bobbs-Merrill Co., 1979 ("LAW OF SPORTS").

allegation, and claim for relief, will be that the person from whom recovery is sought was "negligent."

Although this is certainly not the place for an exhaustive analysis of the law of negligence,[1] it is important, as a preliminary matter, to briefly review the basic principles. As a general proposition, "negligence" is conduct that falls below the standard established by law for the protection of others against unreasonable risks of harm.[2] In most cases, the standard against which any particular act or omission must be tested to determine whether it is negligent is the conduct expected of an ordinary, reasonable person under like circumstances.[3] In other words, negligence is either the failure to do something that would have been done by a reasonable person, guided by those considerations that ordinarily regulate the conduct of human affairs, or doing something that the prudent and reasonable person would not do.[4] The law of negligence is, thus, concerned with risk, and the circumstances in which a person must act to ameliorate risk or be prepared to accept responsibility for the harm that it visits upon others. The question, of course, is, when must a person recognize that a risk exists requiring action, or inaction, on his or her part? Again, the answer is that one must recognize that conduct involves a risk of injury to another if such would have been perceived by a reasonable person.[5] If a particular injury is unforeseeable or could not have been prevented by the exercise of reasonable caution, it may then be ân unavoidable accident, which will not be actionable.[6] The mere existence of risk, however, will not alone be the basis of negligence liability, since the law requires only that a person refrain from creating situations where there is an unreasonable risk of injuring others. There must, therefore, be an unreasonable risk that has not been eliminated.[7]

Even if a person has been "negligent," liability may be avoided in appropriate cases under either of two doctrines that bar recovery by the victim as a result of the latter's own conduct. The first of these doctrines provides that recovery will be denied if the injured party was engaged in "contributory negligence," which refers to conduct by the injured party that falls below the standard that is necessary for his or her own protection, and that is a legally contributing cause in bringing about the injury.[8] Contributory negligence is similar in all respects to ordinary negligence and thus requires proof of the same elements, except that ordinary negligence has reference to unreasonable risk to third parties, while contributory negligence involves an unreasonable risk created by the injured party himself. Contributory negligence may result from the victim's having intentionally or unreasonably "exposed himself to the danger created by the other person's negligence, of which the injured party knew or had reason to know, or from any other conduct that falls below that required by the reasonable person standard."[9] When proven to be a substantial factor in bringing about injury, contributory negligence will, in most cases, bar recovery by the injured party.[10]

A second doctrine precluding recovery by an injured party is the so-called assumption of the risk doctrine, which finds significant application to sports injuries. This doctrine states that a party who voluntarily assumes a risk of harm arising from the conduct of another cannot recover if harm in fact results.[11] Assumption of risk may arise in any of four separate circumstances. The first is where one by express consent relieves another of an obligation to exercise care for his or her protection and agrees to take the chance of injury from a known or possible risk.[12] Perhaps the clearest example of such undertakings in the sports world is the common contractual agreement between a participant and a sports promoter, whereby the former assumes the risks incident to a particular sports activity.[13] The second is where one enters a relationship with another that involves a known risk. In these circumstances, the party is deemed to have implicitly relieved the other of responsibility for that risk.[14] The clearest example of this in sports is the case of the spectator who is injured by the conduct of the activity being observed.[15] The third occurs when one is explicitly aware of a risk caused by the potential negligence of another, and yet proceeds to encounter it voluntarily.[16] Such assumption is made, for example, by athletes when they participate in athletic contests.[17] Finally, one may proceed to encounter a risk that is so unreasonably great as to render the party guilty of contributory negligence, so that recovery is barred both by assumption of the risk and contributory negligence principles.[18]

In an ordinary case involving the assertion of negligence liability, therefore, the courts will undertake a two-step process in determining whether the plaintiff may obtain a recovery from the defendant: the court will consider, first, the duty owed by the defendant to the plaintiff to ameliorate unreasonable risks to the plaintiff, and second, the duty owed by the plaintiff to himself. If the first duty has been violated, then the plaintiff should recover, unless the plaintiff has violated the second and thereby precluded such recovery. Although this same process is utilized in cases involving injuries to participants in sports activities, those cases are perhaps best analyzed by directing initial attention to the legal position of the participant. For these purposes, the term "participant" includes all persons who, in one way or another, take part in the activity (including actual participants, coaches,[19] managers, and umpires or referees,[20] as well as bat boys, caddies, sideline yardmark holders, scorekeepers, or any other party involved in the contest, whether or not taking human form.)[21]

From this point of reference, it may be stated as a general rule that voluntary, *sui juris*[22] participants in lawful sporting activity assume, as a matter of law, all of the ordinary and inherent risks in the sport, as long as the activity is played in good faith and the injury is not the result of an intentional or willful act.[23] The clearest statement of the general rule was made by Judge Cardozo in *Murphy v. Steeplechase Amusement Company, Inc.*,[24] where a vigorous young man had been injured when he voluntarily went upon an amusement device known as the "Flopper." The object of the amusement was to provide enjoyment through the tumbling of bodies and the accompanying screams and laughter. When the young man entered the "Flopper," however, he was injured when he was thrown from his feet and fractured a knee cap. In denying recovery, Judge Cardozo outlined the conditions upon which a participant may recover for injuries related to sporting activity:

> One who takes part in such a sport accepts the dangers that inhere in it so far as they are obvious and necessary, just as a fencer accepts the risk of a thrust by his antagonist or a spectator at a ballgame the chance of contact with the ball. The antics of the clown are not the poses of the cloistered cleric. The rough and boisterous joke, the horseplay of the crowd, evokes its own guffaws, but they are not the pleasures of tranquility. The plaintiff was not seeking a retreat for meditation. Visitors were tumbling about the belt to the merriment of onlookers when he made his choice to join them. He took the chances of a like fate, with whatever damage to his body might ensue from such a fall. The timorous may stay at home.
>
> A different case would be here if the dangers inherent in the sport were obscure or unobserved, or so serious as to justify the belief that precautions of some kind must have been taken to avert them. Nothing happened to the plaintiff except what common experience tells us may happen at any time as the consequence of a sudden fall. Many a skater or a horseman can rehearse a tale of equal woe. A different case there would also be if accidents had been so many as to show that the game in its inherent nature was too dangerous to be continued without change . . . . Some quota of accidents was to be looked for in so great a mass. One might as well say that a skating rink should be abandoned because skaters sometimes fall.[25]

Although these principles will preclude recovery by participants in many cases, they do not preclude the possibility that actionable negligence may be present in some situations. For example, the voluntariness of participation that is the basis for the general rule may in extreme situations be overcome by the pressures that are an implicit part of the competitive atmosphere.[26] More importantly, the general rule will be inapplicable where the injured participant can establish that the injuries were either the result of other than good faith competition or the product of risks that are not ordinary or inherent in the sport in question. Such factors may be present in several circumstances. The first might involve the acts of other participants. An unreasonable risk of injury may be created by the lack of skill or improper conduct of other participants or by the manner in which a particular activity is conducted. Such risks would not be assumed by the participant to the extent that they did not constitute the ordinary and inherent risks of the sport. For example, in *Bourque v. Duplechin*,[27] one Duplechin was on first base during a softball game when a teammate hit a ground ball. The ball was fielded by the shortstop, thrown to the second baseman (Bourque) and then to the first baseman for a double play. After his throw, Bourque stood five feet from second base toward the pitcher's mound. Although Duplechin was forced out by the throw, he continued to run toward Bourque, who was not in the basepath, at full speed. When he ran into Bourque, Duplechin delivered a blow under the former's chin with his arm, which caused a serious injury. Bourque then brought suit against Duplechin and the court found that he was entitled to recover for the injuries caused by Duplechin's blow. Although Duplechin alleged that Bourque had assumed the risk of the injury, the court found that such intentional misconduct was not a risk assumed by softball players:

> Bourque did not assume the risk of Duplechin going out of his way to run into him at full speed when Bourque was five feet away from the base. A participant in a game or sport assumes all of the risks incidental to that particular activity which are obvious and foreseeable. A participant does not assume the risk of injury from fellow players acting in an unexpected or unsportsmanlike way with a reckless lack of concern for others participating.[28]

In cases where intentional or reckless conduct is present, the courts in other recent cases have suggested that the assumption of risk doctrine may be less important than has typically been true when the conduct in question is less severe. In *Nabozny v. Barnhill*,[29] a soccer player invaded the defendant goalkeeper's penalty zone and kicked him as he was trying to receive a pass, causing permanent skull and brain damage. It was plainly a violation of the applicable rules for a player to make contact with a goalkeeper who has possession of the ball in the penalty zone. In holding that the trial court had erred in directing a verdict for the defendant, the court stated that "a player is liable for injury in a tort action if his conduct is such that it is either deliberate, wilful or with a reckless disregard for the safety of the other player so as to cause injury to that player. . . ."[30] Similarly, in *Hackbart v. Cincinnati Bengals, Inc.*,[31] an offensive football player (Clark) was severely injured when, after a pass was intercepted and the flow of play had gone in the opposite direction, an opposing player (Hackbart) blocked Clark to the ground and then, "acting out of anger and frustration, but without a specific intent to injure . . . stepped forward and struck a blow with his right forearm to the back of the kneeling [Clark's] head and neck . . . ." The trial court held that Clark could obtain no recovery for this intentional conduct, since "the game of professional football is basically a business which is violent in nature, and . . . the available sanctions are impositions of penalties and expulsion from the game."[32] The court of appeals reversed. It noted that there are no principles of law that allow a court to rule out certain tortious conduct merely because it occurs in a game that is generally rough, and that the conduct in question was specifically prohibited by the rules of the game. It also found that the appropriate standard was recklessness and concluded that the trial court had erred in determining that as a matter of social policy the game of professional football was so violent and unlawful that valid lines could not be drawn to separate actionable from nonactionable conduct. These cases have been viewed by some commentators as indicating that the courts may be withdrawing from the traditional assumption of risk principles,[33] but such an evolution is not yet firmly apparent.[34]

A second situation in which recovery would be possible involves risks created by the negligent acts of third persons. Such risks have frequently been created by the conduct of coaches. Thus, the courts have imposed liability where an injury is caused by the athlete's having been required by his or her coach to compete while injured;[35] by the failure of the coach or team physician to render proper medical attention;[36] by the failure of the coach to provide equipment;[37] and by the negligent instruction of a coach.[38] Liability has also been imposed when an injury is the result of the negligence of a referee in not detecting the use of an illegal wrestling hold[39] or failing to properly supervise a game.[40]

The participant may also suffer injury as a result of abuse from spectators excited by the events on the playing field. The chief difficulty in such cases will be the determination of who should be responsible for the injuries inflicted. If the spectator who throws the bottle, vegetable, or other missile is identifiable, there should be little difficulty in holding that person liable for the consequences of the proven acts. More difficult, however, are cases in which the plaintiff seeks to impose responsibility upon a participant who precipitated the spectator reaction that ultimately resulted in the injury. This difficulty is suggested by *Toone v. Adams*,[41] where an umpire at a minor league baseball game had made several calls that were adverse to the home team. After each call, the manager of the home team charged onto the field and engaged the umpire in a strident verbal exchange. During one of these confrontations, the manager stated that if another bad call were made he would behave in such a manner as to engender the partisan spectators' extreme hostility toward the umpire. During the ninth inning, there was another disputed call made against the home team, and, true to his word, the manager charged onto the field and behaved in a manner that engendered the spectators' hostility. After the game, the fans poured onto the field cursing and challenging the umpire to fight. Before he could get to the dressing room, the umpire was struck on the head by a spectator. He then brought suit against the manager, the home team, and the spectator who delivered the blow. In dismissing the claim against the manager and the home team, the court stated that the unsportsmanlike conduct of the manager was not contemporaneous with the assault, and the manager could not be held responsible for the acts of the spectators. To do so, the court said, would be "an intolerable burden upon managers" because they would then become responsible "for the actions of every emotionally unstable person who might arrive at the game spoiling for a fight and become enraged over an umpire's call which the manager had protested."[42] *Toone v. Adams* should not, however, be viewed to state that a manager or other participant would never be legally responsible for injuries incurred by another participant in such situations. For example, if a manager had reason to know that fans would shower an umpire with bottles, hot coins, or other missiles if he strongly protested a call against the home team, and he proceeded to so protest, and the umpire was in fact injured by such missiles from the stands, then the manager may be responsible for the injuries.

The most important risk that will not be assumed by participants is that posed by the negligence of others who have a specific duty of care toward them. Primary in this group are the operators of the sports facilities in which the activities take place. When actions are brought against operators for injuries suffered by participants, the legal issue will generally be whether they have met their duty to the participants utilizing their facilities. As business invitors, operators are subject to the same liability imposed on other possessors of land. They will be liable for conditions on their premises that cause physical harm to their invitees (the participants) if they know, or should reasonably have discovered, that the condition exists, that it poses an unreasonable risk of harm that the invitee-participants will not discover or protect themselves against, and fail to exercise reasonable care for protection of the invitee.[43] Thus, operators have the duty to exercise reasonable care to protect participants from injury caused either by the condition of the premises and equipment located thereon or by the conduct of the other invitee-participants or third parties, provided that the injury could have been prevented by the exercise of reasonable care.[44] This duty will include the duty to maintain the premises in a reasonably safe condition and to supervise the conduct of those on the premises. The operator is not, however, the insurer of the participants' safety, and to recover for injuries sustained on its premises, a participant must prove both that specific acts or omissions amount to a breach of the operator's duty of care and that the breach was the proximate cause of the injury sustained.[45] The operator may also assume that all participants will obey the rules and customs of the game.[46] Thus, liability will occur only when the participants have met their duty to exercise reasonable care for their own protection and the operator has defaulted on its own duty.

These principles are aptly illustrated by *Dawson v. Rhode Island Auditorium, Inc.*,[47] involving the Harlem Magicians basketball team. The players had assembled in a circle near the middle of the court to demonstrate their unusual dexterity and wizardry in the art of ball handling. At the completion of this demonstration, one player was to dash toward the basket, receive a softly thrown lead pass and then propel himself through the air and, at the height of his leap, "dunk" the ball through the hoop. When the player undertook this maneuver, however, he slipped on "something slick" and fell with a hard bang to the floor. The slick spot was actually a puddle of water, which was the result of a defective roof known by the owner to be riddled with leaks. As a result of the fall, the player sustained, in addition to doubtlessly crushing ignominy, serious injuries that terminated his career as a professional athlete. The player brought suit against the owner of the arena, and the appellate court upheld a verdict in his favor,[48] finding that the owner had notice of the condition and had failed to exercise reasonable care to correct it.[49]

LIABILITY FOR INJURY TO SPECTATORS

There is always danger that sports activity will cause injury to spectators when errantly hit or thrown balls escape the field of play, when improperly driven race cars or horses leave the track, when wrestlers are thrown from the ring, or when overeager tacklers pursue their game into the sidelines.[50] An injured spectator can be expected to seek recovery from the person who is responsible for those injuries.

In these cases, the inquiry of the court will be similar to that which has already been considered with respect to injuries to participants. Thus, although a court in a negligence case would normally analyze the duties and conduct of the defendant first, the spectator cases (like the participant cases) may be more easily analyzed by directing initial attention to the legal position of the spectator himself. From this point of reference, it should be noted first that most risks that attend athletic activities are normally readily apparent to any person of reasonable intelligence, even on the first visit to any given sport. In light of this apparent awareness of risk, the courts have evolved the general rule that spectators at sports activities assume, as a matter of law, all of the ordinary and inherent risks of the sport that they are observing.[51] This is frequently framed in terms of a "common knowledge" rule—that is, that the risks posed to spectators at sports activities are such a matter of common knowledge that any person of reasonable intelligence could not help but realize their potentiality and must, for that reason, be deemed to have accepted or assumed the risk of injury therefrom as a matter of law. Probably the most elaborate illustration of the rule was given by Lord Justice Greer in the classic English decision in *Hall v. Brooklands Auto Racing Club*.[52] In holding that a spectator at a sports car race could not recover for injuries suffered when a car hurtled into the spectator area, he stated that

> [a] spectator at Lord's or the Oval runs the risk of being hit by a cricket ball, or coming into collision with a fielder running hard to stop a ball from going over the boundary, and himself tumbling over the boundary in doing so. Spectators at football or hockey or polo matches run similar risks both from the ball and from collisions with the players or polo ponies. Spectators who pay for admission to golf courses to witness important matches, though they keep beyond the boundaries required by the stewards, run the risk of the players slicing or pulling balls which may hit them with considerable velocity and damage. Those who pay for admission or seats in stands at a flying meeting run a risk of the performing aeroplanes falling on their heads.[53]

Although most courts have applied the "common knowledge" rule, it has not found universal acceptance. This has been especially true where the risks of a given sport are found not to be a matter of common knowledge because it is a new activity in the locale in which the injury occurred. The difficulty in applying the "common knowledge" rule in such situations is best exemplified by the cases that have involved injuries suffered by spectators at hockey matches, where the primary cause of spectator injuries has been pucks propelled from the iced playing surface into the crowd surrounding the rink. With respect to such injuries, the courts have been unable to agree upon whether the "common knowledge" rule sh·uld apply to prevent recovery as a matter of law. The majority have concluded that the risks of watching a hockey match are not of such common knowledge as to hold that spectators assume, as a matter of law, the risks of injury therefrom.[54] Many other courts have, however, adopted the "common knowledge" rule invoked with respect to other sports.[55] Inasmuch as the basis for the assumption of risk doctrine is the plaintiff's voluntary consent to accept risk and look out for himself, it is entirely appropriate to inquire whether those in the locality of the injury would be aware of the risks and dangers of watching hockey matches. Where that inquiry shows that the risks and dangers are commonly known, then it will be appropriate to apply the "common knowledge" rule, but where they are not so known, then it should not be applied. Since it is this analysis that courts following each position have applied, their results are not inconsistent; they represent, rather, different conclusions as to the general level of knowledge in the localities in question. When hockey is as much a matter of common knowledge as is baseball, then the courts will surely implement the general "common knowledge" rule.

While the general rule will, thus, preclude the spectators from recovering for many injuries suffered while attending a sports activity, it does not by any means always prevent recovery. The spectator will be deemed to have assumed only the ordinary and inherent risks of attending a sports activity and will not assume other risks. The most important risk that the spectator will not assume is the risk that the owner or operator of the arena in which the sports event is conducted will fail to meet its duty of care. As business invitors, the operators of sports facilities will be liable for conditions on their premises that cause physical harm to invitee-spectators if they know, or should reasonably have discovered, that the condition exists, that it poses an unreasonable risk of harm that the invitee-spectators will not discover or protect themselves against, and fail to exercise reasonable care for their protection.[56] Thus, the operators have the duty to maintain the premises in a reasonably safe condition and to supervise the conduct of those on the premises to prevent injury.[57] Therefore, a spectator using an athletic facility may assume that the operator has exercised reasonable care to make the facilities safe for the purposes of the invitation. This will include the original construction of the premises, as well as any subsequent alterations, and will require that the premises be inspected to discover their actual condition, as well as any latent defects, and that all necessary repairs, safeguards, or warnings will be made for the spectators' protection.[58]

The operator will not, however, be the insurer of the spectator's safety, and to recover for injuries sustained on the premises, the spectator must prove both that specific acts or omissions amount to a breach of the duty of care and that the breach was a proximate cause of the injury sustained. As has been noted earlier, the operator will be obligated to take precautions to ameliorate only unreasonable risks. A risk will be considered unreasonable when the probability of injury outweighs the burden of taking adequate precautions to prevent its occurrence.[59] The amount of caution required by the operator will increase, then, in proportion to the probability that its activities will cause serious injury to others.[60] One of the classic examples of determining when a risk becomes unreasonable is the English decision of *Bolton v. Stone*,[61] where a member of a visiting cricket team drove a cricket ball out of the playing field and into an adjacent public roadway where it struck and severely injured a lady who stood in its path. Although the House of Lords found that such an occurrence was foreseeable, it having happened six times in twenty-eight years, it found the defendants blameless inasmuch as the risk was so small that a reasonable person would have been justified in disregarding it and taking no precautions to prevent its occurrence.[62] *Bolton v. Stone* thus involved a simple finding that the burden of precaution outweighed the probability of loss, and that reasonable people do not act to prevent the occurrence of largely speculative injuries. In other words, the risk of a cricket ball striking a person beyond the playing field boundaries was not an unreasonable risk, and when that event occurred, it would not be the result of negligent conduct.[63] The principle expressed in *Bolton v. Stone* appears to be sound, although contemporary courts might take a less tolerant view of what constitutes a reasonable risk than did the House of Lords in that case.

These several principles are perhaps best illustrated, again, by the decision in *Hall v. Brooklands Auto Racing Club*,[64] where a collision had propelled a sports car over a four-and-a-half-foot fence and into a spectator area, killing and injuring many of the spectators. Apparently no auto had ever entered the spectator areas before and the iron railing had always provided satisfactory protection. When an injured spectator then brought suit for his injuries, the court's first step was to determine the duty owed by the operator of race courses to paying spectators, who attend a spectacle the nature of which "is known to all people of ordinary intelligence who go to see it."[65] This duty, it said, was to exercise reasonable care for the safety of the spectators. The requirements of reasonable care "would depend on the perils which might be reasonably expected to occur, and the extent to which the ordinary spectator might be expected to appreciate and take the risk of such perils."[66] The duty would not, however, require the operator to warrant the safety of the spectators. Applying these principles to the case at hand, the court ruled that the defendants had fulfilled their duty and that the plaintiff-spectator had assumed the risk of the accident. Thus, Lord Justice Greer stated that

> a man taking a ticket to see motor races would know quite well that no barrier would be provided which would be sufficient to protect him in the possible but highly improbable event of a car charging the barrier and getting through to the spectators. The risk of such an event would be so remote that he would quite understand that no provision would be made to prevent its happening, and that he would take the risk of any such accident.[67]

A second risk that will not be assumed by the spectator, and that is distinct from the liability of owners or operators, is the risk of unreasonable conduct by participants, which is not an ordinary or inherent risk of any sport. Thus, a spectator has recovered for injuries caused by a baseball player's having intentionally thrown a ball into the stands in frustration after he dropped a crucial fly ball.[68] In most cases involving spectator injuries from participant conduct, however, recovery will be barred, since the risk producing the injury will be an ordinary and inherent risk of the sport, which will be assumed by the spectator. Thus, spectators will be held as a matter of law to have assumed the risk of injury caused by good faith and non-negligent competition.[69]

The classic exposition of the liability of participants to spectators is the decision of the English Court of Appeal in *Wooldridge v. Sumner*,[70] where a professional photographer had been injured by a horse during the course of a championship race. On the infield side of the grass racecourse was a low cement ridge with cables, and about two feet inside of that was a row of tubs, filled with rhododendrons and other shrubs, with benches between some of the tubs. The photographer was standing behind one of the benches. The accident occurred when the horses, which were "heavy hunters," rounded a turn and galloped toward a stretch in front of the grandstand. A horse, misnamed "Work of Art," was too close to the shrub-filled tubs, jumped two of them, knocked a third down, and then straightened its course and passed about four feet behind the benches. At the approach of the horse, the photographer, who was inexperienced with horses and was taking little interest in the race, took fright and stepped or fell into its path while trying to pull a lady friend off the bench. The impact caused the jockey to be thrown, but a sufficient recovery was made so that the horse won the race, becoming supreme champion of its class. The photographer then brought suit against the owner of the horse for the negligence of his jockey-agent, and the organizers of the race, who also owned the stadium. The trial court dismissed the suit against the organizers, but held the owner liable, finding that the jockey was negligent in causing the horse to take the turn too fast. The Court of Appeal, however, unanimously reversed.

The case presented, in the view of Lord Justice Sellers, the question of "whether liability should be placed on a competitor who is merely seeking to excel and to win, it being the very purpose on which he is engaged and the very endeavor which people have assembled to witness and applaud."[71] The standard to be applied in answering this question was best stated by Lord Justice Diplock to be that

> [a] person attending a game or competition takes the risk of any damage caused to him by any act of a participant done in the course

of and for the purpose of the game or competition, notwithstanding
that such act may involve an error of judgment or a lapse of skill,
unless the participant's conduct is such as to evidence a reckless
disregard of the spectator's safety.[72]

Applying this standard, Lord Justice Diplock then found that the jockey
had misjudged the speed at which "Work of Art" could take the turn,
and the centrifugal force of the horse caused it to come in contact with
the line demarcated by the tubs of shrubs. This showed at most, he
said, "an error or errors of judgment or a lapse of skill," which was "not
enough to constitute a breach of the duty of reasonable care which a
participant owes to a spectator."[73] The photographer had, furthermore,
caused his own injury by, in a moment of panic, stepping and stum-
bling out of his place of safety on the bench.[74]

WAIVER AND RELEASE OF LIABILITY

In light of the extensive liabilities inherent in the conduct of any
sporting enterprise, it is not surprising that those who sponsor sports
events posing a substantial risk of injury to participants or spectators
seek to acquire a release from any liability arising therefrom. Such releases will typically purport to release the promoter, or other party,
from any and all liability resulting from any loss that may be sustained
by the athlete during the event in question.

These provisions are known in the law as exculpatory agreements,
since their effect is to relieve the one party of all or a part of its responsibility to the other.[75] Exculpatory agreements are generally considered
as matters of contract law since they are, at least in theory, consensual
agreements, although their effect is to alter the ordinary negligence
principles that would otherwise apply. Such agreements, therefore,
create a tension between the fundamental tenet of contract law that all
persons should have freedom to contract as they wish and the fundamental principle of negligence law that one should be held responsible
for negligent acts that cause injury to others.[76] The difficulty created is
that when the freedom of contract "expresses itself in a provision designed to absolve one of the parties from the consequences of his own
negligence, there is danger that the standards of conduct which the law
has developed for the protection of others may be diluted."[77] The tension has been resolved in favor of the general enforceability of exculpatory agreements,[78] except where there is a strong public policy that
would be frustrated or where the party obtaining the agreement is in
a clearly dominant position to the party signing away his rights.[79] Some
courts have indicated that this result will follow even though one party
may claim not to have read or otherwise been aware of the release.

This is consistent with the general rule of contract law that a party is bound by contracts that he has signed, unless there is evidence of fraud, misrepresentation, or duress.[80] To be enforceable, however, the waiving party must have had an opportunity to know the terms of the release.[81] Thus, the waiver must be conspicuous,[82] result from free and open bargaining,[83] and its express terms must be applicable to the particular misconduct of the party whose potential liability is waived.[84] Moreover, exculpatory clauses will not be enforceable to insulate a party from liability for damage resulting from wanton, intentional, or reckless misconduct.[85] Finally, some courts have allowed recovery for the negligence of the operator of sports facilities, notwithstanding the presence of a waiver purporting to bar any recovery, where the release did not apply to the negligence of the operator.[86] Since the clauses are subject to contract principles, moreover, it has been held that they may be repudiated (disaffirmed) if signed by a minor.[87]

When exculpatory clauses have been signed by participants in athletic activities, they have, as a general rule, been upheld, with the courts considering and applying the same principles noted above. The application of these rules to athletic participants is illustrated by *Garretson v. United States*,[88] where an entrant in an amateur ski-jumping contest had been asked to sign an entry blank that contained a broad release clause. When the skier subsequently brought suit for injuries suffered as a result of an unfortunate landing, the court upheld the release as a bar to recovery. In reaching this result, it noted that the athlete had known what he was signing, the release was itself conspicuous on the entry form, and the operation of the release in the circumstances present was reasonable.[89]

Exculpatory agreements have been most frequently reviewed by courts in the area of automobile racing. As a general rule, when participants in such contests have signed the agreements, they have barred any recovery for injuries. Thus, in *Winterstein v. Wilcom*,[90] a drag-race driver was severely injured when he lost control of his racer when it struck a large engine component on the track. Before the race, however, he had executed a broadly worded exculpatory clause that stated that he knew the risks and dangers involved in drag racing and had inspected the premises. The clause also provided that the signer would assume all risks of injury to his person and property and release the owners, promoters, and sponsors from any liability. In upholding the validity of the agreement, the court observed that there is ordinarily no public policy to prevent parties from contracting as they see fit. Thus, they are free to provide that one party will undertake the responsibility of looking out for himself. Finding that there was nothing in the case before it to prevent application of the general rule of enforceability, the court stated that

> [t]here was not the slightest disadvantage in bargaining power be-
> tween the parties. Winsterstein [the driver] was under no compulsion,
> economic or otherwise, to race his car. He obviously participated in
> the speed runs simply because he wanted to do so, perhaps to
> demonstrate the superiority of his car and probably with the hope
> of winning a prize. This put him in no bargaining disadvantage.[91]

Similar results have been reached in many other cases.[92]

The general rule that exculpatory agreements will be enforceable
may not apply, however, in states where the legislature has established
a public policy requiring the application of a different rule. Thus, in
McCarthy v. National Association for Stock Car Auto Racing, Inc.,[93]
the driver was badly injured when his stock car burst into flames following the race. When he brought suit against the stadium owners, the
supervising racing association, and the track inspector, the defendants
set forth as their defense a release that had been signed by the driver.
Although the court noted the many decisions upholding such clauses
in racing situations, it held that such releases were not valid in New
Jersey because the legislature had undertaken to regulate the activity
involved and had enacted statutory provisions designed for the safety
of both participants and spectators. To allow these requirements to be
contracted away, the court said, would be to nullify "the salient protective features of the legislation."[94] This was especially clear in the case
before it, inasmuch as the statute specifically required an inspection of
all vehicles and such an inspection had not been made of the auto in
question. A contrary decision would, indeed, allow the parties to con-
tractually overrule the act of the legislature.

Although the majority of the cases have also enforced exculpatory
agreements against spectators at sports events,[95] the courts have demonstrated somewhat more reluctance to give them force than has been
the case with respect to agreements signed by participants. Perhaps the
best evidence of this reluctance is *Celli v. Sports Car Club of America,
Inc.,*[96] where three spectators had been injured when a sports car
skidded into the pit area of the track. Although the injuries were caused
by the failure of the promoter to provide adequate barriers to protect
spectators against such occurrences, the promoter sought to avoid
liability on the basis of an exculpatory clause contained on the pit pass
issued to the spectators. This clause provided that the spectator released "every claim, demand, action or right of action whatsoever kind
or nature . . . from or arising out of any accident or other occurrence
. . . ." In holding that the clause did not release the track owner or race
promoter from liability for the injuries caused by their negligence, the
court stated that the language of the pit pass must be construed against
the owner and promoter since it was a product of their draftsmanship
and sought to whittle the customer's ordinary rights. The basis of the

court's decision, however, was that the waiver did not purport to waive or release claims for negligence, so such claims were not affected thereby. Although the clause did not specifically mention negligence, its use of broad, general language could be interpreted to have implicitly included negligence.[97] Thus, the court's ruling seems to have been predicated on its reluctance to enforce the clause, not on the absence of the additional word. Indeed, the court went on to state that even if the clause had expressly mentioned negligence, it questioned "whether public policy . . . would permit judicial enforcement of a provision printed in such small type and designed to permit a tortfeasor to shift the risk of injury to the victims even where the release is sufficient to encompass defendant's own negligence."[98]

LIABILITY FOR INJURIES IN EDUCATIONAL PROGRAMS

Unquestionably the most common context in which sports activities take place is on the fields and in the gyms of public and private educational institutions. This is also the context in which a proportionately large number of sports-related injuries occur. Although the basic legal principles that govern the respective rights and liabilities of those involved in these predictable mishaps do not materially differ from those that apply in other contexts, the circumstances in which they will be applied present sufficiently distinct issues to require separate discussion.[99]

Before undertaking that inquiry, however, it will be useful to state several factors that bear upon the potential liability of those involved with education-related sports activities. The first is that schools are populated by young people who have a definite propensity for frolic and play. Thus, injuries in sports activities are probably inevitable, even when those in charge exercise due care in controlling and directing the activities. A second consideration is that the wide variety of factual situations that may be present in school-related activities precludes the articulation of precise standards of legally required conduct. Instead, the particular facts of each case will have to be evaluated in terms of the broad, general rules that have evolved. Finally, although the vast majority of the cases that will be reviewed are the result of activities in grammar or high schools, the principles considered are of equal applicability to the activities conducted or sponsored by institutions of higher learning.[100]

When actions are brought to seek compensation for school-related sports injuries, the first step will always be to ascertain the legal status of the entity that has responsibility for the school or activity in question. This will involve two basic inquiries. The first will be to determine whether the institution is subject to suit. In many jurisdictions, the institution may be immunized from liability by the doctrines of sovereign or charitable immunity,[101] and, where these doctrines are still viable, suit against that particular entity will be fruitless. If suit may be maintained against the institution, the second inquiry will be to ascertain the statutory requirements for the proper filing of such an action. Statutory provisions in particular jurisdictions may specify steps that must be taken before suit may be begun against an educational institution (such as presentation of claims to the institution within a specified period of time), and failure to comply therewith may well bar the action. Such procedural requirements will not be considered here, because the rules vary greatly among jurisdictions and do not directly relate to the present inquiry.

With respect to the athletic activities conducted under their auspices, educational institutions have the duty to exercise reasonable care to prevent reasonably foreseeable risks[102] and, where such risks are foreseen, to take sufficient precautions to protect the students in their custody.[103] This general duty can be translated into several specific obligations. Thus, the institution may be required to establish,[104] and enforce,[105] rules for the maintenance of discipline in sports and recreational activities (though they need not cover every possibility presented by the boundless natural instincts of children for self-amusement);[106] provide adequate supervision for the sports or recreational activities held under their auspices and exercise due care in the selection of supervisors;[107] and provide suitable equipment and facilities for the conduct of sports and recreational activities.[108] Although these responsibilities have primary application to endeavors that are part of the curriculum of the institution, they apply as well to extracurricular activities.[109]

Notwithstanding the doubtlessly correct statement that "[p]arents do not send their children to school to be returned to them maimed because of the absence of proper supervision or abandonment of supervision,"[110] educational institutions are not insurers of their students' safety[111] and will be held liable for injuries suffered by students only when the institution, or someone for whom it is legally responsible, fails to meet the prescribed duty of care. Thus, in *Underhill v. Alameda Elementary School District*,[112] the court stated that

> [baseball, basketball, volleyball and handball] contribute to the physical development of the pupils participating, and there is nothing inherently dangerous about any of them. They seldom result in injury to either the participants or spectators and are ordinarily played by school children of all ages without adult supervision. Nevertheless, it is also a matter of common knowledge that children

participating in such games and in fact in any form of play may injure themselves and each other, and that no amount of precaution or supervision on the part of parents or others will avoid such injuries. The injuries which may result from the playing of said games are ordinarily of an inconsequential nature and are incurred without fault on the part of anyone. In such cases there is no liability and, of course, the fundamental rules governing liability remain the same, even though the particular injury may prove to be of a more serious nature. The law does not make school districts insurers of the safety of the pupils at play or elsewhere and no liability is imposed upon a district under the above-mentioned section, in the absence of negligence on the part of the district, its officers or employees.[113]

Liability will, therefore, be denied for injuries that no amount of precaution, except elimination of the activity itself, could have prevented.[114] Liability will also be denied where the injury is solely the result of the unpreventable acts of fellow students[115] and where contributory negligence or assumption of the risk are present.[116]

Probably the most difficult issue present in this area is the extent to which an educational institution can be held liable for the negligent acts of its employees if its own duties have been satisfactorily performed. The traditional and majority rule is that, absent statutory provision to the contrary, an educational institution is not liable for the negligent acts of its teachers or instructors if they were selected with due care and the institution has met each of the other duties noted above.[117] The courts have relied upon a number of different considerations to support this rule. Thus, courts have reasoned that the institution's statutory duty is fully discharged if its own duties are satisfactorily performed;[118] that they are not subject to negligence liability as a result of the sovereign or charitable immunity doctrine;[119] or that teachers or instructors are not ordinary employees, so that the doctrine of respondeat superior, which makes a master responsible for its servant's negligent acts, is not applicable.[120]

The traditional, or majority, rule will not be applicable in states that have either expressly made educational institutions liable for the negligence of their teachers or instructors,[121] or where the state has simply waived its sovereign immunity.[122] The trend of states increasingly to fall into one or another of these patterns is well evidenced by *Domino v. Mercurio*,[123] which arose in New York, where schools had traditionally been immune from liability for the negligence of their teachers. When, however, the state waived soverign immunity by statute, the court held that public schools and school boards were no longer protected by that doctrine, so that they became liable for the negligence of their teachers and instructors under the general rule of respondeat superior.

Where educational institutions are charged with responsibility for their employees' actions, their duty toward their students is somewhat altered. They still have the duty to exercise due care to protect the students from unreasonable risks and dangers, but this duty will not be fulfilled simply by the use of reasonable care in delegating its performance to others. Rather, it will be satisfied only if the person to whom the duty of protection and supervision is delegated fulfills it in a non-negligent manner.[124] In other words, if the teacher or instructor fails to properly perform the supervisory duty, then the employer-institution will be vicariously liable under the doctrine of respondeat superior for all resulting injuries.[125] In the absence of any such employee negligence, the institution will be liable only for breaches of its own duties.[126]

Since the athletic facilities owned or maintained by educational institutions will inevitably be used by nonstudents for nonschool purposes, it is also necessary to consider the institutions' duties under such circumstances. In general, the duty of educational institutions to nonstudents using their athletic facilities is to exercise reasonable care under the circumstances. Thus, the institutions must keep equipment and facilities in a safe and suitable condition so that those using them will not be subjected to unreasonable risks of physical harm. If dangerous conditions do exist and cannot be immediately corrected, then the school must warn the nonstudents of the conditions so that they may avoid the danger.[127] This duty to nonstudents was considered in *Kelly v. Board of Education of the City of New York*,[128] where a public school had made its gymnasium available for use by a community center to provide recreation to neighborhood youths in the evening. On the evening in question, the youths moved a springboard to the center of the floor, for the purpose of propelling themselves over a gymnastic "buck" that was placed in front of the springboard. The springboard was defective, and the defects had existed for several weeks. One of the youths was injured when he attempted to use the device. On these facts, the court held the school district liable, stating that

> [t]he duty, therefore, rested upon the board of education to use reasonable care to keep the premises and appliances in a safe and suitable condition, so that invitees would not be unnecessarily and unreasonably exposed to danger. It was shown that this springboard had been out of repair for three or four weeks, and that such condition had been reported to the director. The duty of the [school] board was then to remove this defective apparatus, and not leave it in the gymnasium, or to take some means of notifying the invitees of its dangerous condition and prohibit its use.[129]

A similar result was reached where injury was the result of improper glass having been installed in a door directly under a basketball goal.[130] Educational institutions are not, however, the insurers of the safety of nonstudents using their facilities and will not be responsible for injuries caused by their own contributorily negligent conduct or for which they assumed the risk.[131] In addition, if the institution simply makes its facilities available for use by nonstudents and assumes no responsibility for conduct of the activities undertaken, it will have no duty to supervise those activities.[132] In short, the institution will owe no different duty to its nonstudent invitees than would any other landowner[133] and will not be burdened with the duties that are ordinarily owed to its students, unless it agrees to supervise the activities.

Apart from the liability of the institution that has overall responsibility for a sports program, it is also necessary to consider the potential liability of the teachers or instructors who are directly in charge of those programs.[134] The primary duty owed by teachers to their students is the duty to supervise the activities in which the students participate.[135] A teacher involved in physical education activity has the duty to supervise in a sufficiently diligent manner to prevent the students from confronting unreasonable risks of injury.[136] Perhaps the best statement of this duty is that

> [a] teacher occupies a position in relation to his pupils comparable to that of a parent to children. He has the duty to instruct and warn pupils in his custody of any dangers which he knows or in the exercise of ordinary care ought to know are present in the gymnasium; and to instruct them in methods which will protect them from these dangers, whether the danger arises from equipment, devices, machines, or other causes. A failure to warn students of such danger or to instruct them in the means of avoiding such danger is negligence.[137]

The teacher's duty of supervision does not, however, render the teacher the insurer of the safety of the students under his or her supervision. Even if the duty is properly performed, accidents will inevitably occur, and it is clear that a teacher will not be responsible in many cases. In *Nestor v. City of New York*,[138] for example, a teacher was supervising a group of children, most of whom were trying to catch fly balls. While the teacher was thirty feet away distributing milk, one of the children tried to hit a descending ball with a bat, rather than catch it as the others were doing. In the process, the batter struck the head of another child who was trying to catch the same ball. The court held the teacher's supervision to be free of negligence, since the injury was an unforeseeable accident. The court's language is instructive:

> Even if the teacher had had the game under steady observation and the measure of his supervision had been constant, an assumption

that he could have anticipated what ensued would be without justifiable warrant. The teacher would be required to be invested with a profound prescience to have foreseen that Michael would attempt, after batting the ball, to run to catch it and that Tony would suddenly run towards the ball with bat in hand and, without warning, swing with his bat at the descending ball while Michael was endeavoring to snare it.

To urge that the teacher should have anticipated each of the separate occurrences constituting the links in the chain of events hereinabove recited, or that a blast by the teacher on his whistle would have frozen the two boys into instant immobility and averted the accident which ensued, is indulgence in pure speculation. This reasoning is fortified by the fact that Anthony Occhuzzio said that he saw Michael at the last moment but that he could not check his swing. This was an accident that could occur equally in the presence or absence of the teacher.

In the context of all the foregoing, it would be without judicial sanction to conclude that the circumstances described were within the orbit of reasonable apprehension.[139]

The question involved in the duty of supervision, therefore, will be whether a reasonably prudent person in the position of the teacher should have had reason to believe that the situation presented the possibility of serious injury to anyone participating in the activity.[140] If such a basis for apprehension is present, then the supervising teacher will have the duty to undertake reasonable actions to prevent an injury from occurring. If such actions are not undertaken, then the teacher will be liable for the injuries caused thereby.[141] Even if a teacher is held liable for sports-related injuries, many states have enacted statutory provisions that will save the teacher harmless from personal liability.[142]

If, however, the teacher had no reason to believe that the situation presented the possibility of serious injury to anyone participating in the event, then, as suggested by *Nestor,* there will be no liability, because the teacher's duty of supervision would not have required the undertaking of any special procedures.[143] Similarly, if the students are properly instructed in the rules and procedures of the activity, the teacher will, absent special circumstances, not be required to observe constantly every phase of the activity as it is being conducted.[144] There will also be no liability where the injured student is contributorily negligent or assumes the risk of the act that caused the injury.[145]

In light of the potential liabilities that confront institutions that conduct sports activities, it may well be asked whether the assets of the institution may be insulated from sports-related liabilities.[146] As a traditional proposition, the most effective means of conducting relatively high-risk activities without subjecting all of one's assets to the liabilities thereof is to form a separate corporation through which the activities will be conducted. The corporation provides asset-insulation because it is a legal entity separate and distinct from its shareholders. Thus, when injury recoveries are awarded, the only assets available for their satisfaction are those of the corporation, and the shareholders are liable only for the limited amount of capital that they have exchanged for their shares of stock.

If an educational institution is authorized to form such a corporation, the basic legal question that it will present is whether the corporation will be a viable legal entity. As a general rule, a corporation will be recognized as a separate entity. If the facts in any given case, however, indicate that the corporation is merely the alter ego of its organizers and is not in fact operated as a separate entity, then it may be disregarded, with the result that there would then be no limited liability advantage to its shareholders.[147] A corporation formed to conduct athletic activities will normally be recognized as a viable entity so long as it has control of its own decision-making and is independent of the educational institution that is responsible for its initial organization.[148] To the extent, however, that the corporation is subject to the control, either financial or administrative, of the institution, or is set up with the evidently dominant purpose of avoiding specific tort liability, the corporation's separate identity will be more likely to be disregarded.[149] The provision of financial support or other services will not be determinative of the result, but it goes without saying that the more direct the financial support, the less likely it is that separate viability will be found.

In short, the separate incorporation of an entity to conduct educationally related athletic programs is an expedient means to *minimize the likelihood* of institutional tort liability. It must be borne in mind, however, that persuasive arguments may be readily mustered to pierce that corporate status, and the institution will seriously jeopardize its effort by retaining financial or administrative control. The further removed the institution is from the corporation, the more likely the avoidance of liability.[150]

LIABILITY OF COACHES

Since coaches normally have the most direct control of the activities of athletes, it is not surprising that they are frequently named as defendants in suits brought by injured athletes. In these cases, the critical inquiry will be whether the coach has fulfilled the duty to exercise reasonable care for the protection of the athletes under his or her supervision, which duty will be satisfied by providing proper instruction in how to play the game and by showing due concern that the athletes are in proper physical condition. The coach is not, however, an insurer of the athletes' safety, and the duty of care will be satisfied if the coach takes all reasonable steps to minimize the possibility of their injury in games that involve an inevitable amount of physical contact.[151] Thus, a coach who has properly instructed the players will not be liable for injuries caused when a first baseman hits another participant with a wildly thrown ball[152] or when a slightly injured player is sent home without first receiving medical aid.[153]

A pertinent case in this area is *Vendrell v. School District No. 26C, Malheur County*,[154] where a high school football player suffered a broken neck, and became a permanent paraplegic, when he charged head first into approaching tacklers. When the player brought suit alleging that several acts of his coach were negligent, the court absolved the coach and the school district of liability, holding that the duty of care had been fully satisfied. The court began its analysis by noting that all students on the football team had to be pronounced physically fit by a physician, and once fitness was determined they were put through a training program that included calisthenics, classes on physical conditioning and training rules, and instruction in the fundamental skills of the game, including the technique of using protective equipment to absorb blows. The coach had stressed these "fundamentals" as an essential aspect of successful play and self-protection. In short, the player had undergone extensive training and practice under competent supervision and instruction. In reaching its conclusion of nonliability, the court summarized the responsibility of an athletic coach by observing that

> [n]o one expects a football coach to extract from the game the body clashes that cause bruises, jolts and hard falls. To remove them would end the sport. *The coach's function is to minimize the possibility that the body contacts may result in something more than slight injury.* The extensive calisthenics, running and other forms of muscular exercise to which the . . . coaches subjected the . . . squad were intended to place the players in sound physical condition so that they could withstand the shocks, blows and other rough treatment with which they would meet in actual play.[155]

Where the coach does not conduct the activities, or the persons, under his or her direction in such a way as to minimize the possibility of injury, the coach will be liable for the injuries thereby caused. Thus, liability has been found where a coach requires a player to compete when he or she knows, or in the exercise of ordinary care should have known, that the player was already suffering from serious injuries to his back and spine;[156] directs that a severely injured player be carried from the field without awaiting the arrival of medical assistance;[157]

allows a team to compete against an opponent whose players are grossly disproportionate in size and ability;[158] allows spectators to congregate so closely to the playing field as to pose dangers to the players;[159] fails to properly instruct his wrestlers in the uses of, and defenses to, certain holds that may pose dangers of physical injury;[160] or instructs one team member to drive others home after practice, although the driver is known to be a reckless driver of an unsafe jalopy.[161]

The coach's duty to his players also encompasses activities that are not, as such, part of the sports activity. In *DeGooyer v. Harkness*,[162] for example, a coach was in charge of a high school lettermen's society. During an initiation ceremony, which was under the coach's direction, it was decided that each initiate should be subjected to a slight electrical shock. When it was found that the customarily used electrical apparatus was not available, the group decided to attach a cord to an electric light socket, pass the current through a rheostat (a glass jar full of water) and then to the initiate. Even though this procedure caused severe shock to the first several initiates, it was not stopped, and on a subsequent use one of the initiates was electrocuted. Inasmuch as the coach was in full control of the initiation proceedings, the court imposed personal liability upon him for the death, finding that he had failed to take proper precautions to prevent such an unfortunate occurrence.

LIABILITY FOR PROVIDING MEDICAL
TREATMENT FOR ATHLETIC INJURIES

When an injury occurs in a sports activity, it will frequently require medical treatment. In order to consider the legal principles that apply to such treatment, it is important to focus on two related issues. The first concerns the responsibility of those who conduct sports activities to provide medical care to persons who are injured in such activities, and will be considered in this section. The second issue involves the legal responsibilities of doctors who provide medical treatment to athletes, which will be considered in the discussion that immediately follows.

The persons and organizations in charge of sports activities will have a duty to secure or provide reasonable medical assistance to injured participants or spectators as soon as possible under the circumstances.[163] Whether the duty has been met in any given case will normally depend upon the quality of the treatment and the speed with which it is rendered. When satisfactory medical assistance is provided within a reasonable period of time, the duty will have been fulfilled. Thus, liability would presumably not be found where a doctor in attendance at a sports event provided immediate, and reasonable, medical assistance to an injured participant. When such assistance is not immediately available, the duty of care will require that the injured party be transported to a place where it can be rendered as quickly as reasonably possible.[164] It will also require that the injured party be properly cared for until medical attention can be obtained. Thus, a football coach was held liable for serious injuries suffered by one of his players when, despite suspicions that the player had suffered a severe neck or back injury, he directed that the player be carried from the field by eight of his teammates without awaiting the arrival of a physician.[165]

Liability will be denied, however, where the delay in summoning medical assistance does not cause or aggravate an injury.[166] Moreover, if the injuries do not reasonably appear to be serious, there may then be no need to summon medical assistance.[167] The circumstances of a particular injury may also indicate that transportation to a hospital is preferable to summoning a physician who would be ready and able to come to the scene of the injury.[168] If the person in charge of the activity is not possessed of medical training and undertakes, in the absence of an emergency, to render medical assistance, the acts may then be determined to be unnecessary or positively detrimental, in which event there may well be liability.[169] This will be especially clear if the injured person protests the profferred aid upon learning of the nonmedical status of the person offering the assistance.[170] Those in charge of sports activities are not, however, the insurers of the medical safety of the participants, and if the nature or seriousness of an injury could not reasonably be expected to have been discovered by a layman, then there may be no basis for liability.[171]

The leading case applying these principles is *Clark v. State*,[172] where a bobsled competing in the North American Championship failed to negotiate a reverse curve and hurtled over an almost perpendicularly banked curve into a snow-covered and wooded mountainside. Upon impact, Clark, one of the participants, sustained several injuries, including fractures of his left leg, collapse of his left lung, profound shock, and numerous cuts and bruises. Immediately after the accident, state employees carried Clark by stretcher to the first of several trucks used to transport him to a hospital, where, following X-rays, a cast was put on the leg. Between the time of the accident and admission to the hospital, a total of forty-three minutes had elapsed. After the cast had been applied, however, normal circulation did not return to the injured leg. When gangrene set in, the leg had to be amputated. Clark then brought suit against the state, which was the owner of the bobsled run, but not the sponsor of the event. He alleged negligence in the state's failure to provide sufficiently prompt medical care after the accident had taken place.[173] Clark conceded that the original accident was not due to any improper act of the state. On these facts, the court held that Clark could not prevail for three separate reasons. The first was that there was a lack of proof that the state's actions had caused the complications suffered by Clark. The second was that Clark, a participant in the bobsled contest, had assumed the risk of not only his injuries but the resultant complications as well.[174] Finally, the court found that the state had adequately discharged its duties to Clark after the original accident, inasmuch as it had promptly produced stretchers, blankets, and a doctor, and had caused him to be promptly transported to a hospital.[175]

LIABILITY OF DOCTORS IN TREATING ATHLETIC INJURIES

In considering the medical care that is provided for sports injuries, it is also important to analyze the legal responsibilities of the doctors who provide the care. Unfortunately, the specific nature of those responsibilities is less than clear. There have been very few reported decisions involving injuries that are allegedly the result of improper medical care of athletes, and those that exist provide little real guidance in resolving the many issues that appear to be present in the practice of sports medicine. The lack of such authoritative precedent makes discussion of the issues less certain than would otherwise be the case, but it certainly does not preclude an effort to develop the issues in terms of more general authority. There is a large body of law dealing with the legal duties of physicians generally, and the principles that have been developed in those cases should be equally applicable in the sports medicine context. In light of the lack of specific guidance in this area, the purpose of the following discussion is to identify the legal principles that would apparently be applied to cases when they arise and to suggest some of the issues that seem to have particular importance in sports medicine.

General considerations

The first step in considering the legal responsibility of the sports doctor is to identify the basic principles that would be utilized to determine liability in any given case. When it is alleged that a doctor has not treated a patient properly, the basis for the allegation will in almost all cases be that the doctor has been negligent.[176] The basic principles of negligence liability noted earlier will continue to be the touchstones of a doctor's liability, but they will be modified slightly to take account of the professional nature of the conduct in question (medical

treatment). As noted, the basic premise of the standard of care for negligence liability is that of the reasonable person under like circumstances.[177] Thus, when a doctor's conduct is alleged to be negligent,
the standard by which the conduct is to be judged must take into account the skill and knowledge of the medical profession as a whole.
The specific standard may vary from jurisdiction to jurisdiction, but it
may be said as a general rule that the doctor must practice with the
level of reasonable skill and knowledge that is common for members of
the medical profession in good standing.[178]

There are several aspects of this standard that should be emphasized.
The first is that it only requires a doctor to act reasonably, as measured
by what doctors with reasonable skill and knowledge would do or not
do in a similar situation. The doctor is not rendered an insurer of the
success of all treatment and procedures and will not be held liable for
honest mistakes of judgment where the proper treatment is open to
reasonable doubt. Liability will occur only when the doctor's conduct
has been unreasonable in terms of the general skill and knowledge of
the profession. The second is that the standard was traditionally limited
by a "locality" gloss, which required a doctor to act only in accordance
with medical practices in the locality in which he or she practiced.[179]
However, improvement in communications, facilities, training, and
availability of expert consultants and literature have led to an abandonment of the locality requirement as a fixed rule in many jurisdictions.
The community in which a doctor practices continues to have general
importance in those jurisdictions only as a factor to be considered in
applying the standard of care.[180] The third point to be mentioned is
that the components of reasonable skill and knowledge will normally
be established by the testimony of expert witnesses who are familiar
therewith.[181] If there is more than one school of thought on how a
given injury or disease should be treated, then the doctor's conduct will
be judged in light of the school that he or she follows, if its principles
can be established and the school is recognized by at least a respectable
part of the profession.[182] Finally, it should be noted that the standard
of care is not altered by the fact that the doctor is acting gratuitously,[183]
though good samaritan statutes have been enacted in some states that
would limit liability to situations involving intentional misconduct or
grossly negligent practice.[184]

When these principles are considered in the sports medicine context,
they essentially state that when a doctor in general practice undertakes
to treat a sports injury, he or she will have a duty to perform with the
degree of reasonable skill and knowledge that would be utilized by
members of the profession in good standing. Although this is, of course,
a rather general standard, it does carry the essential message that a
doctor's conduct will only be judged in terms of what is reasonable in

the profession generally. These basic principles are illustrated by one of the very few decisions in which a doctor was found to be negligent in treating a sports injury. In *Welch v. Dunsmuir Joint Union High School District*,[185] a high school football quarterback was participating in an interschool scrimmage and, on a "quarterback sneak" play, was tackled and thrown to the ground. After the play, he was unable to get to his feet. When the coach arrived at his side, the athlete was able to move his hands at the coach's direction. The athlete was then carried to the sidelines by teammates but with no supervision as to the manner of carriage. When he arrived at the sidelines, however, the athlete was unable to move either his hands or feet. Although there was a doctor in attendance at the scrimmage, the evidence was unclear whether he examined the injured player on the field or only on the sidelines. In any event, the boy was rendered a permanent quadriplegic by these events and brought suit against the school, coach, and doctor. Testimony at trial indicated that the spinal cord was not severed at the time of injury, since the athlete could move his hands, so that the severance could only have occurred when he was carried from the field. The jury returned a verdict for the athlete against all defendants (including the doctor). With respect to the doctor's conduct, the court found that the evidence sustained the jury's verdict. The apparent basis of the doctor's liability was his negligence in not treating the injury immediately and in allowing the injured athlete to be removed from the field via the hands of his teammates instead of by stretcher. In terms of the principles noted above, the court implicitly concluded that a doctor of reasonable skill and knowledge would have treated the athlete immediately to determine the nature of the injury and would have instructed that he be removed from the field in a manner that would not cause further injury.

If the doctor practices as a specialist in sports medicine or a more generic specialty (such as orthopedics), then the standard of care will be slightly altered. Since the doctor would then hold himself out as being a special expert in the field of treating sports injuries (or some other type of injuries), the standard will be adjusted to take account of this self-proclaimed expertise. The specialist will be held to a standard of care that is measured in terms of the speciality itself rather than the standard of the medical profession in general. In other words, the sports practitioner would be required to perform with the degree of reasonable skill and knowledge that would be utilized by sports medicine experts.[186] In light of this higher standard of care, it is possible that the conduct of a sports doctor treating a sports injury could be found to have been negligent even though the same conduct by a general practitioner might not have been negligent.

In considering the basic standards of care for sports doctors, it is also important to note that there may be other elements of an action for negligence that could be important in sports injury cases. One such element would be that a doctor will be held legally responsible for an injury only if some reasonable connection can be demonstrated between the conduct of the doctor and the injury that has been suffered. This is usually referred to as the need for establishing that an injury was proximately caused by the defendant's conduct. Although this is certainly not the place for a detailed analysis of legal causation,[187] several aspects of the problem may be considered. The basic issue in determining causation is to identify when a person's conduct will be a legal cause of an injury. The most appropriate response is that conduct will be the legal cause if it is a "substantial factor" in bringing the injury about.[188] This is an inherently factual issue, and the burden of establishing the connection between the conduct and injury will be upon the injured person.[189] In many situations, the burden may not be difficult to carry. For example, if a football player dropped dead of heart failure and the day before he had been given a physical examination that failed to disclose an obvious defect, it is quite possible that the legal cause of the injury would be the failure of the doctor to discover the defective condition.[190] In some situations, however, it may be much more difficult to establish causation, especially where the conduct of more than one person could potentially have been a factor in the injury. Under the "substantial factor" standard, it is possible that the conduct of more than one person could be a legal cause.[191] In the situation of the football player with the weak heart, for example, if the player had told his coach that he had severe chest pains and the coach continued to require the boy to participate in the summer heat, it seems likely that the coach's conduct would also be a "substantial factor" in bringing the injury about. In order for the conduct of more than one person to be a "legal cause," it must be shown that each was a substantial factor.[192]

In several of the sports medicine cases that have involved causation issues, the courts have held that the doctor's conduct, in the facts presented, was not a legal cause of the injury in question. Thus, in one case it was found that a doctor's conduct in taking and reading X-rays was not a legal cause of injury to a football player when it did not aggravate the injury,[193] and in another case several doctors were exonerated by the court's finding that an athlete's injury was a result of competition and not their conduct.[194] These cases obviously do not indicate that a doctor's conduct will not constitute a legal cause of an injury when more than one person's conduct is involved, but they do suggest that causation is implicitly a factual matter and that it may be quite difficult in some situations to prove the necessary connection between a doctor and an injury incurred in athletic competition.

In order to illustrate the application of these general standards of conduct, it is appropriate to consider some of the issues that seem to have special relevance to doctors engaged in a sports practice.

Relationship of doctor to athlete

The first issue that might be considered relates to the nature of the relationship between a sports doctor and the athlete. If a doctor is consulted by an athlete or an athlete's family for the purpose of acquiring treatment for a sports injury, the doctor will be under no legal duty to accept the athlete as a patient.[195] If the athlete is accepted as a patient, there will then exist a doctor-patient relationship, and the doctor will be obligated to treat the athlete in accordance with the standard of care noted above. These duties will not be affected by the fact that the doctor is acting gratuitously.[196]

Inasmuch as the reason for consulting the sports doctor will normally be to secure treatment for an injury that may require surgery, it is important to consider the extent to which the doctor must obtain consent for a specific type of treatment or surgical procedure. Under normal circumstances, it seems clear that a doctor must obtain the consent of an adult patient before medical care can be administered.[197] The situation with respect to minors is much less certain. Consent must still be obtained, and the question will frequently arise whether a minor may give valid consent or whether it must be obtained from the minor's parents or guardian. The general rule has been that consent for treatment of minors must be obtained from the parents or guardian, since the minor is deemed to be incapable of giving valid consent.[198] This general rule is, however, subject to several exceptions, which allow a minor to give valid consent when an emergency exists, the parent or guardian is inaccessible, or the child is near majority and able to give a knowingly informed consent.[199] The application of these exceptions is suggested by a recent case in which a seventeen-year-old girl injured her finger at a hospital, and her family doctor recommended minor surgery. The girl's mother was under sedation and her divorced father lived some 200 miles away. In holding that the girl's consent was lawful, the court observed that she was intelligent and capable for her age.[200] A similar result should follow when an athlete is treated under comparable circumstances.

In addition to the question of who may give consent, it may also be important to consider the type and scope of the consent that is to be obtained. The consent should always be in writing, if that is possible under the circumstances. This will insure that there is evidence of the fact of consent and the terms upon which it was given. The consent should be drafted so that its terms and scope are clear and should provide the doctor with both the general and specific authority to perform the necessary procedures in a particular case.[201] The consent should not, however, be written in such broad and ambiguous language as to purportedly provide blanket authority to do whatever the doctor deems appropriate, since it may then be invalidated on the grounds that it in fact authorized nothing.[202] The need for specificity is underscored by the view that a court may strictly construe consents in favor of the patient in light of the facts that consent forms are in almost all cases drafted by representatives of the doctor or hospital, and the patient will be required to "consent" as a condition precedent to treatment.

In order for a consent to be valid, it must also be shown that it is the product of the "informed" consent of the patient. The patient is said to be "informed" when the doctor has "imparted some quantum of medical information, relevant to a proposed treatment which is sufficient to enable the patient to make an *intelligent choice* as to whether he should undergo such treatment."[203] This would typically include a reasonable disclosure of the alternative procedures that are available to treat a given injury or disease and the dangers of each, as well as an indication of their relative advantages and disadvantages to the patient. The requirements of "informed" consent have attracted a rather large amount of attention.[204] The vagaries of its interpretation will not be summarized here, except to note that the general standard by which disclosure and subsequent consent appear to be analyzed is what good medical practice would require under the circumstances.[205]

If consent cannot be obtained from a patient, it may be implied from the circumstances in which treatment is given. This has especially been true in emergency situations where it has in some cases been concluded that a doctor was privileged to act because of the assumption that the patient would have consented to treatment if he had been competent to do so.[206]

An additional aspect of the doctor-patient relationship that may have particular importance in the sports medicine context involves the disclosure by the doctor of information relating to the physical condition of the athlete. It is apparently common for professional and college scouts (or team doctors) to contact a doctor who has treated an athlete to determine the condition of the athlete. When such contacts are made, the primary issue that the doctor will have to determine is whether he or she may make any disclosure or statement about the athlete's condition. This may in some cases be an exceptionally important issue. For example, if a star college football player had suffered a knee injury that was supposedly corrected by subsequent surgery, it seems almost certain that a professional team would seek some assurance of rehabilitation before signing the athlete to a substantial contract. It could, of course, have its own doctors test the athlete, but it may also seek the opinion of the attending surgeon. In this situation, the surgeon would be in a rather delicate position. Ethical and legal standards may preclude him from disclosing any information without the consent of the athlete, and a disclosure made with consent may subject him to potential liability if the team relies upon his statements that turn out, for one reason or another, to be inaccurate.

It is axiomatic that the doctor-patient relationship is a fiduciary relation,[207] in which the doctor will have a duty to maintain the confidence of disclosures made by the patient during the course of treatment. The purpose of the duty is to insure a free flow of information between patient and doctor, which will enable the doctor to learn all pertinent facts upon which a diagnosis may be based. The duty of confidentiality is indeed a part of the Hippocratic Oath, and is required by statutory provision in some states.[208] Although there was some doubt in early cases,[209] it now seems clear that a doctor may be held liable for the disclosure of confidential information relating to a patient. Thus, it has been held that "[t]he unauthorized revelation of medical secrets or any confidential communication given in the course of treatment, is tortious conduct which may be the basis for an action in damages."[210] In light of this potential liability for disclosure of medical information without consent from the patient, a sports doctor should give no information to a team that is interested in a patient-athlete without the specific written consent of the athlete.

If information is given in response to such an inquiry, it is also important to consider what is to be communicated. The doctor should normally restrict the disclosure to a statement of the nature of the injury and method of treatment. Such a disclosure is limited to the objective facts of the injury and leaves the team with the burden of determining the current fitness of the athlete. But if the doctor is asked to go further and state whether the athlete has fully recovered from the injury, then the doctor should exercise a high degree of caution. In such situations, the doctor would be asked to render his opinion on the physical condition of an athlete in circumstances where it is foreseeable that the team will to some extent rely upon the opinion in determining whether to sign the athlete. The danger in rendering such opinions is that, for example, a professional team might then sign the athlete to a substantial contract and if the athlete turned out to be physically disabled because of the injury said to have been corrected, the team could theoretically seek damages from the doctor for the erroneous opinion. It would be alleged that the doctor was negligent in making the disclosure. When one person makes a statement of opinion to another with knowledge that the other will rely upon it, that person may be responsible for damages incurred because of the inaccuracy of the opinion, even though it is rendered in good faith and gratuitously. The inaccu-

racy would constitute negligence if there was a failure to exercise reasonable care in determining the facts upon which it was based or an
absence of the skill and knowledge required by standards of the profession in formulating the opinion.[211] Although the specific parameters
of liability in this type of situation are less than clear, there is authority
that suggests that persons may be liable for damages caused by the rendering of gratuitous opinions in the course of professional activities
that fail to meet the standards noted above.[212] With such authority in
mind, a doctor should be rather circumspect in giving gratuitous opinions about the condition of athletes who have been treated by the
doctor.

Relationship of doctor to school or team

In many situations, a doctor treating sports injuries will be retained
by the educational institution for whom the athlete is competing. (Although an athlete may compete directly for a team—for example, a professional team—the legal issues would be essentially the same as in the
school situation, and for purposes of simplicity only the latter will be
specifically discussed herein.) When so engaged, the doctor will have
a duty to perform services in accordance with the express or implied
requirements of the contract and may be responsible for damages
caused by a failure to perform those requirements. This should pose
little real problem in most cases, since the duties of the doctor will be
relatively clear—for example, to provide medical care for a school's
athletic program—and the doctor will use his or her best efforts to perform those duties. Difficult issues may arise, however, if it is alleged
that the doctor performed the services required but did so in a negligent manner. When such allegations are made, it will be necessary to
determine who may be held responsible for the alleged negligence.
The initial candidate would be the doctor whose conduct is alleged to
have been negligent. In order for the doctor to be legally responsible
to the patient, it would be necessary to find that a doctor-patient relationship. As a means of avoiding such a relationship, it might be argued
that the doctor's only responsibility was to the school who had contracted for his services and that no relationship existed between the
patient-athlete and the doctor. Although the appropriate response to
the argument is certainly not clear, there is authority that holds that a
doctor-patient relationship exists between an employee and a doctor
who is hired to examine the employees by an employer.[213] This authority would appear to generally support a conclusion that a doctor-
patient relationship will exist when a doctor treats students pursuant
to a contract with the athlete's school. If the relation does exist, then
the doctor would be directly responsible to the athlete for negligent

conduct. This was, for example, apparently the result in *Welch v. Dunsmuir Joint Union High School District*.[214]

An additional candidate for liability would be the school who had undertaken to provide medical care. Such liability could be imposed on at least two theories. The first would be that the school has a duty to provide reasonable medical care to athletes who are injured in the course of school-related athletic programs, and that the duty would not be fulfilled by providing a doctor who in fact rendered negligent care. Although there is apparently no specific authority for this proposition, there are several cases holding that a school must provide reasonable medical care that have imposed liability when deficient care was rendered by persons who were not doctors.[215] While these cases are not dispositive of the issue, they do suggest that the theory is viable.[216] A second approach would be to argue that the school is responsible for the conduct since the doctor was acting under the school's authority—that is, that the school is vicariously liable for the conduct of the doctor.[217] In order to ascertain whether such liability could be imposed, it would be necessary to determine the specific nature of the relationship between the doctor and the school. Such liability may be imposed on a school only if the doctor is acting as an employee, as opposed to an independent contractor. The basis for distinction between these two categories is whether the school exerts control over the physical conduct of the doctor.[218] If such control exists, then the doctor will be an "employee" or "servant," and the school will be vicariously liable; but if it does not exist, then the doctor will be an "independent contractor," and the school will not be vicariously liable. In many situations, the school will contract with a doctor to provide medical care to one or more participants in its athletic program but will not retain a right to control the doctor's physical conduct in providing such care.[219]

Examination of athletes

One of the most frequent procedures that will be performed by the doctor who is retained to treat members of an athletic program will be to examine its participants. Such examinations are commonly required of all athletes who seek to participate in athletic activities to ensure that they are physically able to stand the rigors of competition. The scope of examination may vary substantially, depending upon the circumstances under which it is performed. It may constitute little more than a rapid perusal of all members of a junior football team, or it may require a thorough analysis of the physical condition of a single athlete. In light of the differing circumstances in which physical examinations may occur, it is difficult to articulate a precise standard by which a doctor's conduct would be evaluated. A court would inevitably apply the same basic standard noted earlier, which would require that in conducting physical examinations a sports doctor must act with the skill and knowledge that would be utilized by other members of the profession acting in similar circumstances.[220] In applying this standard, a court would consider the purpose of the examination, the nature of the conditions under which it was performed, the procedures generally utilized by the profession in conducting such examinations, and the requirements of good medical practice in responding to the results of the examination.

The situation in which a doctor's liability will most likely arise is when an athlete has been seriously injured and alleges that the injury could have been prevented by a reasonable medical examination. For example, if a football player died as the result of a heart attack, it might be alleged that a doctor who gave the player a physical exam before the season began was negligent, since death was the result of a defect or injury that should have been discovered in the examination. The approach that a court would take in determining liability in this type of situation is suggested by *Rosensweig v. State*,[221] in which a boxer died shortly after being knocked out in a professional fight. The evidence showed that the boxer had suffered technical knockouts (TKO's) in two previous fights within a three-week period. After the second fight, the boxer was examined by Doctor No. 1, who found nothing wrong. Ten days later, the boxer sought permission for another fight, but a sports commission representative required that he have an electroencephalogram (EEG) made before permission would be given. The boxer was then examined by Doctor No. 2; the EEG showed a "normal record"; and after Doctor No. 3 examined him permission was granted. Before the fight, Doctor No. 4 gave him an additional examination. Although this doctor thought that the boxer should not fight because of the two TKO's, he allowed the fight to proceed in light of the custom of boxing doctors to defer to the judgment of the doctor who examined a fighter after the most recent fight. Since Doctor No. 1 had found nothing wrong with the fighter, Doctor No. 4 certified him for the fight. As luck would have it, the boxer was knocked out and died shortly thereafter. An autopsy apparently showed that he had suffered brain injuries in the previous fights. Representatives of the boxer then filed suit and the trial court held that all of the doctors had been negligent for several reasons. The first was that a reasonable medical examination should have discovered the brain injury. The second was based upon its finding that good medical practice would require that a person who has received a severe beating to the head (as had this boxer) should be kept inactive for approximately two months to avoid the risk of further trauma. The failure of the doctors to follow this practice was also evidence of negligence.[222] Finally, the court found that the custom of boxing doctors to defer to the diagnosis of the doctor who examined a fighter after the last fight was no defense, since it required a doctor to disregard his or her own medical knowledge and experience.[223]

Although the court did not enunciate a clear doctrinal base for its conclusions, the essence of its reasoning would appear to be that good medical practice in this context required an examination that would discover an injury to the part of the boxer's anatomy that had suffered severe beatings (the head) and that the fighter be held out of further competition for a suitable period of recuperation. To this extent, the court's analysis is consistent with the general standard suggested above, since the court's findings are reflective of a failure of the doctors to perform with the skill and knowledge that is utilized by other members of the profession. The trial court decision was, however, reversed on appeal.[224] The appellate court obviously disagreed with the trial court's conclusion that there was negligence, but the doctrinal basis for disagreement is not clear. The court stated that a "standard examination" had revealed no injury, but it gave no indication of what such a standard examination required or what facts indicated that such an examination had been given in the present case. It also noted that the boxer had signed a medical history that disclosed no brain injury, but surely this fact could have little relevance to the negligence of the doctors. It also found that there was no duty to hold the boxer out of competition, since the state boxing commission had adopted no such rule. It did not suggest why a doctor would not have a duty to take such action if it was, as the trial court had concluded, required by the standards of good medical practice. Finally, the court stated that the actual cause of death was the blows received in the fatal bout. In short, the appellate court found no negligence but undertook almost no effort to indicate why it came to that conclusion. Its reasoning would appear to be that a doctor is required to give only a standard examination (which it did not define), and since such examinations had been given here (though it did not say why), there was no basis for a conclusion that the doctors had been negligent.

The *Rosenweig* case is important, because it is one of the few cases to focus specifically upon the potential liabilities of a sports doctor in conducting physical examinations of athletes.[225] Although the reasoning of the courts is not as clear as it could have been, the positions of the trial and appellate court suggest the parameters of how examination questions will be analyzed when they arise.

Prescription of drugs

One of the most interesting issues involved in the medical treatment of athletic injuries is the extent to which liability may be imposed for injuries caused by the administration of drugs to athletes.[226] It has been reported that drugs are in some situations administered to athletes in an attempt to increase their performance or delay the need for corrective surgery.[227] Suits have also been filed by some athletes. The basic allegation of such suits would be that a doctor was negligent in prescribing drugs that could cause, or worsen an existing, injury, or that the athlete could not validly consent to such prescription absent a clear disclosure of the dangers that the drugs might pose.[228]

Although there has apparently not yet been a reported decision involving these issues in the sports medicine field, the principles that a court would apply in such cases seem reasonably clear. The doctor's duty in prescribing drugs is the same as noted above: to utilize the level of reasonable skill and knowledge that is common for members of the medical profession (or for doctors practicing a given specialty).[229] The principal issue that would arise under this duty in the drug situation would be whether good medical practice would allow prescription of the drug in question to a given athlete in the manner and dosage utilized.[230] For example, if a football player were suffering from an injured knee and a doctor prescribed a pain killer to allow the player to continue competition, it would have to be determined whether good medical practice would allow use of such a drug in the circumstances that existed at the time of prescription for the particular athlete. This would be a factual question that would be resolved on the basis of testimony from experts in sports medicine (or whatever specialty of internal medicine would deal with the type of injury in question). Attention would also have to be given to whether the athlete had made an informed consent to the administration of the drug. As noted earlier, a doctor must make a disclosure to the athlete of the dangers of the drug prescribed and the existence of any procedures that would be alternatives to its administration. The necessity of such "informed" consent has been subsumed within the concept of good medical practice, and if it was not obtained prior to the prescription of a drug, the failure might itself constitute negligence by the doctor. Again, the resolution of this issue would be a factual determination that would be made on the basis of expert testimony as to what types of disclosure would be required by good medical practice.

NOTES

1. *See generally* RESTATEMENT (SECOND) OF TORTS ch. 12 (1965); 2 F. HARPER & F. JAMES, THE LAW OF TORTS ch. 16 (1956); W. PROSSER, THE LAW OF TORTS ch. 5 (4th ed. 1971).

2. RESTATEMENT (SECOND) OF TORTS § 282 (1965). Although it was once contended that these principles should not apply to the conduct of games, that contention has been rejected, and it is clear that ordinary negligence principles apply to the determination of liability for the injuries that arise as a consequence of sporting activity. *See* Cleghorn v. Oldham, 43 L.T.R. (n.s.) 465, 467 (K.B. 1927).

3. RESTATEMENT (SECOND) OF TORTS § 283 (1965).

4. RESTATEMENT (SECOND) OF TORTS § 284 (1965); Blyth v. Birmingham Water Works Co., 11 Ex. 781, 7, 156 Eng. Rep. 1047, 1049 (1856). In addition to the standard of the reasonable person, standards may also be established by league rules. Toone v. Adams, 262 N.C. 403, 136 S.E.2d 132 (1964) (rules for minor league baseball in case involving injury to an umpire). *But* cf. Barrett v. Phillips, 29 N.C. App. 220, 223 S.E.2d 918 (1976) (eligibility rule violation does not alone constitute negligence).

5. RESTATEMENT (SECOND) OF TORTS § 289 (1965). In Stewart v. D. & R. Welding Supply Co., 9 Ill. Dec. 596, 366 N.E.2d 1107 (1977), the court noted that "safety rules of the game define the limits of the consent given." *See also* LaVine v. Clear Creek Skiing Corp., 557 F.2d 730 (10th Cir. 1977) (ski instructor's handbook guidelines may be evidence of negligence). But violation of such a rule will not necessarily entitle the plaintiff to relief. *See* Oswald v. Township High School Dist. No. 214, 84 Ill. App. 3d 323, 406 N.E.2d 157 (1980) (cause of action not stated for kicking another in a basketball game in violation of National Federation of High School Association Rules).

6. Thus, in Curtis v. Portland Baseball Club, 1 Ore. 93, 279 P. 277 (1929), the court said it was an accident that a spectator had been injured by a foul ball that had curved around a protective screen, inasmuch as such an occurrence could not have been reasonably anticipated. *See also* Johnson v. Kreuger, 36 Colo. App. 242, 539 P.2d 1296 (1975) (unforeseeable that stump in adjoining lot would result in injury to football player).

7. The presence of an unreasonable risk is considered with respect to spectator injuries in LAW OF SPORTS § 8.03.

8. *See generally*, 2 F. HARPER & F. JAMES, THE LAW OF TORTS §§ 22.1–.11 (1956); W. PROSSER, THE LAW OF TORTS § 65 (4th ed. 1971).

9. RESTATEMENT (SECOND) OF TORTS §§ 465–66 (1965).

10. The contributory negligence doctrine may cause hardship when the injured party's negligence is only slight while the actor's negligence is great. As a result, some states have adopted so-called comparative negligence statutes. These statutes commonly provide that recovery will be determined by the relative negligence of the parties. Thus, if the actor's conduct is found to be twice as negligent as that of the injured party, the latter will recover only two-thirds of his damages. *See generally* W. PROSSER, THE LAW OF TORTS § 66 (4th ed. 1971).

11. *See generally* RESTATEMENT (SECOND) OF TORTS § 496A (1965); 2 F. HARPER & F. JAMES, THE LAW OF TORTS § 21.4–.8 (1956); W. PROSSER, THE LAW OF TORTS § 68 (4th ed. 1971); Bohlen, *Voluntary Assumption of the Risk*, 20 HARV. L. REV. 14 (1906); James, *Assumption of Risk*, 61 YALE L.J. 141 (1952).

12. RESTATEMENT (SECOND) OF TORTS § 496B (1965).

13. See notes 75–98 *infra*.

14. RESTATEMENT (SECOND) OF TORTS § 496C (1965).

15. *See* RESTATEMENT (SECOND) OF TORTS § 496C, illustration 4 (1965).

16. RESTATEMENT (SECOND) OF TORTS § 496D (1965).

17. *See, e.g.,* Thomas v. Barlow, 5 N.J. Misc. 764, 138 A. 208 (1927), *noted in* 26 MICH. L. REV. 322 (1928). It is this subject, of course, that will consume much of the remainder of this portion of this paper.

18. *See* Title v. Omaha Coliseum Corp., 144 Neb. 22, 12 N.W.2d 90 (1943).

19. McGee v. Board of Educ. of New York, 16 App. Div. 2d 99, 226 N.Y.S.2d 329 (1962).

20. Davis v. Jones, 100 Ga. App. 546, 112 S.E.2d 3 (1959) (official time-keeper at wrestling match); Toone v. Adams, 262 N.C. 403, 137 S.E.2d 132 (1964) (umpire may recover for assault by irate fan). *See generally* Annot., 10 A.L.R. 3d 446 (1966).

21. Thus, in Jolley v. Chicago Thoroughbred Enterprises, Inc., 275 F. Supp. 325 (N.D. Ill. 1967), the "participant" rules were discussed with regard to injuries suffered by a thoroughbred racing horse during a race at Arlington Park.

22. A "sui juris" person is one possessed of full legal capacity. If the participant is not so possessed—for example, if he or she is a minor—then the general rule will be applied on a much less strict basis, inasmuch as a minor would be less able to appreciate the risks of the sport. Diker v. City of St. Louis Park, 286 Minn. 461, 130 N.W.2d 113 (1964) (minor injured in hockey game apply general rule, but not as a matter of law).

23. A detailed list of cases applying this principle are cited in LAW OF SPORTS at 926 n.24. A higher standard of care may be required in some circumstances. For example, in Heldman v. Uniroyal, Inc., 53 Ohio App.2d 21, 371 N.E.2d 21 (1977), the court suggested that professional athletes may be subjected to a higher standard—"[a] higher degree of knowledge and awareness is imputed to professional tennis players than to average non-professional tennis players. . . ." *See* Tope v. Waterford Hills Road Racing Corp., 265 N.W.2d 761 (Mich. App. 1978) (professional race car drivers should be held to a higher standard of conduct).

It has also been suggested that participants in bodily contact games assume greater risks than do those involved in non–physical contact sports. Oswald v. Township High School Dist. No. 214, 84 Ill. App. 3d 323, 406 N.E.2d 157 (1980).

24. 250 N.Y. 479, 166 N.E. 173 (1929).

25. *Id.* at 482–83, 166 N.E. at 174–75 (citations omitted).

26. Thus, in Martini v. Olymphant Borough School Dist., 83 Pa. D. & C. 206 (1952), the court observed that "[i]t is also debatable whether or not the usual disciplinary authority of the coach, the presence of school spirit, the probable odium attached to refusal to play, both by his fellow-players and his schoolmates, might not have robbed him of volition under the circumstances." 83 Pa. D. & C. at 211.

27. 331 So.2d 40 (La. App. 1976).

28. 331 So. 2d at 42. *See also* Agar v. Canning, 54 W.R. 2 (1965), *aff'd* 55 W.W.R. 384 (1966) (not assume risk of retaliatory blow struck in anger).

29. 31 Ill. App.3d 212, 334 N.E.2d 258 (1975).

30. 334 N.E.2d at 261.

31. 601 F.2d 516 (10th Cir. 1979).

32. 435 F. Supp. 352 (D. Colo. 1977).

33. *See* Carbonneau, *The Liability for Injuries to Sports Participants and Spectators: A Consideration of Relevance of Assumption of Risk Principles in Sports Litigation,* 2 POTOMAC L. REV. 65, 78 (1979); Comment,

Assumption of Risk and Vicarious Liability in Personal Injury Actions Brought by Professional Athletes, 1960 DUKE L.J. 742.

34. There has been a considerable amount of attention focused on injuries caused by intentional conduct. Much of the attention has been spawned by the *Hackbart* case and by the return of a substantial verdict ($3.3 million) in a case involving an intentional assault in a professional basketball game. This case is discussed in Woolf, *Courts Coming Down Hard on Excessively Violent Players*, NATIONAL L. J. (Jan. 7, 1980); Kirshenbaum, *Scorecard*, SPORTS ILLUSTRATED, August 27, 1979, at 5. *See also* Underwood, *An Unfolding Tragedy*, SPORTS ILLUSTRATED, August 14, 1979 at 69.

One issue that these cases have brought to the forefront relates to the extent to which a team can be held liable for injuries caused by the intentional conduct of professional athletes. *See* Carbonneau, *supra* note 33, at 78–79; Comment, *supra* note 33, at 759–64.

35. Morris v. Union High School Dist. A, King County, 160 Wash. 121, 294 P.998 (1931). *But cf.* Hale v. Davies, 86 Ga. App. 126, 70 SE.2d 923 (1952) (assume such risk unless coach acts willfully or wantonly). Liability of coaches is considered at notes 151–62 *infra*.

36. Welch v. Dunsmuir Joint Union High School Dist., 326 P.2d 633 (Cal. App. 1958); Mogabgab v. Orleans Parish School Bd., 239 So.2d 456 (La. App. 1970). *But cf.* Duda v. Gaines, 12 N.J. Super. 326, 79 A.2d 695 (1951) (no liability where no immediate need to call medical assistance). Liability for medical treatment rendered for athletic injuries is considered at notes 163–75 *infra*.

37. Martini v. Olymphant Borough School Dist., 83 Pa. D. & C. 206 (1952).

38. Stehn v. Bernarr MacFadden Foundation, Inc., 434 F.2d 811 (6th Cir. 1970).

39. Carabba v. Anacortes School Dist. No. 103, 72 Wash. 2d 939, 435 P.2d 936 (1967) (the hold was a "full-nelson").

40. Rosensweig v. State, 208 Misc. 1065, 146 N.Y.S.2d 589 (1955), *rev'd on other grounds*, 5 N.Y.2d 404, 158 N.E.2d 229 (1959). *See also* Crohn v. Congregation B'nai Zion, 22 Ill. App.2d 625, 317 N.E.2d 637 (1974) (failure to supervise summer day camp baseball game).

41. 262 N.C. 403, 137 S.E.2d 132 (1964).

42. *Id.* at 412, 137 S.E.2d at 139.

43. RESTATEMENT (SECOND) OF TORTS § 343 (1965). *See generally* Lowell, *If the Suit Doesn't Fit*, 18 AUDITORIUM NEWS 8 (1980); Note, *Negligent Design of Sports Facilities*, 16 CLEV.-MAR. L. REV. 275 (1967).

44. Lincoln v. Wilcox, 111 Ga. App. 365, 141 S.E.2d 765 (1965).

45. Panoz v. Gulf & Bay Corp. of Sarasota, 208 So.2d 297 (Fla. App. 1968); Smith v. Village of Pine River, 232 N.W.2d 241 (Minn. 1975); Everett v. Goodwin, 201 N.C. 734, 161 S.E. 316 (1931); Juntila v. Everett School Dist. No. 24, 183 Wash. 357, 48 P.2d 613 (1935).

46. *See, e.g.*, Petrich v. New Orleans City Park Improvement Ass'n, 188 So. 199 (La. App. 1939); Schlenger v. Weinberg, 107 N.J. Law, 130, 150 A. 434 (1930); Everett v. Goodwin, 201 N.C. 734, 161 S.E. 316 (1931); Amon v. Schemaka, 419 Pa. 314, 214 A.2d 238 (1965).

47. 104 R.I. 116, 242 A.2d 407 (1968).

48. The actual-holding of the case was that the player should have a new trial, since error had been committed during the first trial, which had resulted in a jury verdict for the owner.

49. In reaching this conclusion, the court stated that the owner

owed a duty of care which required it to take such measures to provide a reasonably safe place for the purposes of the invitation extended to plaintiff, namely, the playing of basketball . . . . It seems to us, . . . that in order for defendant (the owner) to exculpate itself from a finding of negligence on its part, it had to show one of two things; first, that having become aware of the leaky roof, it had undertaken such action which would assure a reasonable auditorium owner that all the leaks in its building were corrected—in substance, to make certain that its building was watertight; or secondly, show, as an alternative to eliminating all the leaks, it had apprised plaintiff, before his scheduled performance on the court, of the actual conditions of the building and at the same time issued him a warning of the risk of harm which those conditions presented to anyone choosing to play basketball at defendant's auditorium.

Id. at 129, 242 A.2d at 415. *Compare* Nunez v. Isidore Newman High School, 306 So.2d 457 (La. App. 1975) (no liability for moisture on floor when it was found not to be an unreasonably dangerous condition).

50. The danger to spectators at sports events has been well summarized as follows:

A defect inherent in the nature of man is that perversity of spirit which attracts us to spectacles of danger in which our fellow men risk death for our amusement. Although the events in the coliseums of ancient Rome were somewhat different from those held in their modern counterparts, spectators were perhaps subject to similar risks for there must have been occasions when a lion escaped the arena to prowl among the patrons or a gladiator lost control of his weapon to the detriment of a front row observer.

Capital Raceway Promotions, Inc. v. Smith, 22 Md. App. 224, 322 A.2d 238 (1974).

51. *See* Law of Sports 951 n.52.

52. [1933] 1 K.B. 205, [1932] All E.R. 208. *See also* Murray v. Harringay Arena, Ltd., [1951] 2 K.B. 529, 534.

53. [1933] 1 K.B. at 209, [1932] All E.R. at 210.

54. *See* Law of Sports 954 n.55.

55. As representing the courts that have adopted the "common knowledge" rule, Sutherland v. Onondaga Hockey Club, 245 App. Div. 137, 281 N.Y.S. 505 (1935), is probably the most explicit. In affirming a verdict adverse to a spectator who had been struck by a flying puck, the court stated that she

occupied precisely the same status as a spectator at a baseball game and that the same rules should be applied in each instance. There was no obligation on the part of the respondents to protect appellants against a danger incident to the entertainment which any reasonable spectator could foresee and of which she took the risk. The risk of being hit by a baseball or by a puck at a hockey game is a risk incidental to the entertainment and is assumed by the spectators . . . . It is common knowledge that the puck may leave the ice when the players are shooting for a goal.

245 App. Div. at 319, 281 N.Y.S. at 508.

56. Restatement (Second) of Torts § 343 (1965); Hartzell v. United States, 539 F.2d 65 (10th Cir. 1967).

57. Law of Sports 957 n.60.

58. RESTATEMENT (SECOND) OF TORTS § 343, comment b (1965).

59. In United States v. Carroll Towing Co., 159 F.2d 169 (2d Cir. 1949), Judge Hand stated the proposition to be that "if the probability be called P; and the injury L; and the burden B; liability depends upon whether B is less than L multiplied by P; i.e., whether B is less than PL." Id. 173. In addition to the burden of taking precautions, the utility of the actor's conduct must also be considered. RESTATEMENT (SECOND) OF TORTS § 292 (1965).

60. 2 F. HARPER & F. JAMES, THE LAW OF TORTS § 16.9 (1956) (where all of these factors are considered at length).

61. [1951] A.C. 850, [1951] 1 All E.R. 1078.

62. Thus, Lord Justice Radcliffe stated that a reasonable man, "taking account of the chances against an accident happening, would not have felt himself called upon either to abandon use of the ground for cricket or to increase the height of his surrounding fences. He would have done what the appellants did; in other words, he would have done nothing." [1951] A.C. at 869, [1951] All E.R. at 1087. See also Hall v. Brooklands Auto Racing Club, [1930] 1 K.B. 205, 224 (risk that auto would plunge through a barrier and injure spectator remote).

63. See also Curtis v. Portland Baseball Club, 130 Ore. 93, 279 P. 277 (1929) (a reasonable man would not undertake to prevent a baseball from curving around a protective screen, it being a remarkable feat); Lee v. Tacoma Baseball Club, 38 Wash. 2d 362, 229 P.2d 329 (1951) (failure to provide overhead protection to fans behind home plate was not an unreasonable risk).

64. [1930] 1 K.B. 205, [1932] All E.R. 208, noted in 49 L.Q. REV. 156 (1933).

65. Id. at 214, [1932] All E.R. at 212.

66. Id. at 214, [1932] All E.R. at 213.

67. Id. at 224, [1932] All E.R. at 217.

68. Bonetti v. Double Play Tavern, 126 Cal. App. 2d 848, 274 P.2d 751 (1954) (liability imposed upon employer who sponsored the team upon which the participant played, on the basis of respondeat superior). See note 34, supra.

69. Wooldridge v. Sumner, [1962] 2 All E.R. 978. See also Douglas v. Converse, 248 Pa. 232, 93 A. 955 (1915); Davis v. Jones, 100 Ga. App. 546, 112 S.E. 2d 3 (1959).

70. [1962] 2 All E.R. 978. Although Wooldridge v. Sumner dealt primarily with negligence of the jockey, and not the assumption of risk by the spectator, it is illustrative of the approach that a court would take in analyzing this type of spectator injury case.

71. Id. at 981.

72. Id. at 989–99 (emphasis added). Lord Justice Diplock also noted that

[a] reasonable spectator attending voluntarily to witness any game or competition knows, and presumably desires, that a reasonable participant will concentrate his attention on winning, and if the game or competition is a fast moving one will have to exercise his judgment and attempt to exert his skill in what, in the analogous context of contributory negligence, is sometimes called 'the agony of the moment'. If the participant does so concentrate his attention and consequently does exercise his judgment and attempt to concentrate his skill in circumstances of this kind which are inherent in the game or competition in which he is taking part, the question whether any

mistake he makes amounts to a breach of duty to take reasonable care must take account of those circumstances.

Id. at 989. A similar standard was expressed by Lord Justice Sellers, who said that

> provided the competition or game is being performed within the rules and the requirement of the sport and by a person of adequate skill and competence, the spectator does not expect his safety to be regarded by the participant. If the conduct is deliberately intended to injure someone whose presence is known, or is reckless and in disregard of all safety of others so that it is a departure from the standards which might reasonably be expected in anyone pursuing the competition or game, then the performer might well be held liable for any injury his act caused.

Id. at 983. *See also* Barker v. Colorado Region–Sports Car Club of America, Inc., 35 Colo. App. 73, 532 P.2d 372 (1975) (participant liable for negligently responding to signal); Douglas v. Converse, 248 Pa. 232, 93 A. 955 (1915) (participants liable for *reckless* conduct).

73. [1962] 2 All E.R. at 991–92.

74. *Id.* at 991. Lord Justice Diplock also stated that while the photographer's own ignorance of horseracing and his concomitant panic may be understandable and excusable, they would not aid his case, inasmuch as "a reasonable competitor would be entitled to assume that spectators actually in the arena would be paying attention to what was happening, would be knowledgeable about horses, and would take such steps for their own safety as any reasonably attentive and knowledgeable spectator might be expected to take." [1962] 2 All E.R. at 991. This "assumption of the risk" element was also noted by Lord Justice Danckwerts. [1962] All E.R. at 984.

A similar result was reached in Davis v. Jones, 100 Ga. App. 546, 112 S.E. 2d 3 (1959), where a wrestler, trying to escape peril at the hands of an enraged opponent, dove through the rope and injured a timekeeper sitting at ringside. In denying the timekeeper's recovery, the court was of the opinion that the wrestler's duty was to warn spectators in proximity to their match of any "unusual dangers" which they may anticipate, a category that did not include their acts in question.

75. Note, *The Significance of Comparative Bargaining Power in the Law of Exculpation,* 37 COLUM. L. REV. 248, 248–49 (1937).

76. Morrow v. Auto Championship Racing Ass'n, 8 Ill. App. 3d 682, 291 N.E.2d 30 (1972).

77. O'Callagman v. Walter & Backwith Realty Co., 15 Ill. 2d 436, 155 N.E.2d 548 (1958).

78. RESTATEMENT OF CONTRACTS § 574 (1932).

79. RESTATEMENT OF CONTRACTS § 575 (1932). Thus, Professor Prosser has stated that "it is generally held that a contract exempting an employer from all liability for negligence to his employees is void against public policy. The same is true as to the efforts of public utilities. . . . A carrier who transports goods or passengers for hire, or a telegraph company transmitting a message, . . ." W. PROSSER, THE LAW OF TORTS § 68, at 442–43 (4th ed. 1971). *See generally* Note, *The Significance of Comparative Bargaining Power in the Law of Exculpation,* 37 COLUM. L. REV. 248 (1937); Annot., 175 A.L.R. 8 (1948); Annot. 8 A.L.R.3d 1393 (1966); Annot., 97 A.L.R. 582 (1935).

80. Theroux v. Kedenburg Racing Ass'n, 50 Misc. 2d 97, 269 N.Y.S.2d 789 (1965); *see also* Lee v. Allied Sports Associates, Inc., 349 Mass. 544, 209 N.E.2d 329 (1965).

81. Moore v. Edmonds, 384 Ill. 535, 52 N.E.2d 216 (1943).

82. Baker v. Seattle, 79 Wash.2d 198, 484 P.2d 405 (1971). *Cf.* UNIFORM COMMERCIAL CODE § 2-316 (1962).

83. Winterstein v. Wilcom, 16 Md. App. 130, 138–39, 292 A.2d 821, 824 (1972).

84. RESTATEMENT (SECOND) OF TORTS § 496B, comment *d* (1965); Phibbs v. Ray's Chevrolet Corp., 45 App. Div.2d 897, 357 N.Y.S.2d 211 (1974) (where waiver used only word "automobile," it did not include motorcycles).

85. Winterstein v. Wilcom, 16 Md. App. 130, 293 A.2d 821 (1972); French v. Special Services, Inc., 107 Ohio App. 435, 159 N.E.2d 785 (1958); W. PROSSER, THE LAW OF TORTS § 68 (4th ed. 1971).

86. Kaiser v. State, 55 Misc. 2d 576, 285 N.Y.S.2d 874 (1967) (based on special statutory provision).

87. Del Santo v. Bristol County Stadium, 273 F.2d 605, 607–08 (1st Cir. 1960).

88. 456 F.2d 1017 (9th Cir. 1972).

89. *Id.* at 1020–21. *See also* Hewitt v. Miller, 11 Wash. App. 72, 521 P.2d 244 (1974) (release by scuba diving student upheld).

90. 16 Md. App. 130, 293 A.2d 821 (1972).

91. *Id.* at 138, 293 A.2d at 825.

92. Rutter v. Arlington Park Jockey Club, 510 F.2d 1065 (7th Cir. 1975) (fire in horse stable); Gore v. Tri-County Raceway, Inc., 407 F. Supp. 489 (M.D. Ala. 1974); Cash v. Street & Trail, Inc., 136 Ga. App. 462, 221 S.E.2d 640 (1975); Morrow v. Auto Championship Racing Ass'n, 8 Ill. App.2d 682, 291 N.E.2d 30 (1972); Lee v. Allied Sports Associates, Inc., 349 Mass. 544, 209 N.E.2d 329 (1965); Gervasi v. Holland Raceway, Inc., 40 App. Div.2d 574, 334 N.Y.S.2d 527 (1972) (mechanic); Solodar v. Watkins Glen Grand Prix Corp., 36 App. Div.2d 552, 317 N.Y.S.2d 228 (1971); Theroux v. Kedenburg Racing Ass'n, 50 Misc.2d 97, 269 N.Y.S.2d 789 (1965); Seymour v. New Bremen Speedway, Inc., 31 Ohio App.2d 141, 287 N.E.2d 111 (1971); Hine v. Dayton Speedway Corp., 20 Ohio App.2d 185, 252 N.E.2d 648 (1969); French v. Special Services, 107 Ohio App. 435, 159 N.E.2d 785 (1958); Corpus Christi Speedway v. Morton, 279 S.W.2d 903 (Tex. Civ. App. 1955j). *But cf.* Del Santo v. Bristol County Stadium, 273 F.2d 605 (1st Cir. 1960) (release signed by minor not enforceable when disaffirmed by bringing suit within six months of reaching majority). *See generally* 2 BLASHFIELD AUTOMOBILE LAW & PRACTICE § 102.38 (3rd ed. 1965).

93. 48 N.J. 539, 226 A.2d 713 (1967).

94. *Id.* at 543, 226 A.2d at 715.

95. Lee v. Allied Sports Associates, Inc., 349 Mass. 544, 209 N.E.2d 329 (1965) (spectator in pits); Kotary v. Spencer Speedway, Inc., 47 App. Div.2d 127, 365 N.Y.S.2d 87 (1975); Church v. Seneca County Agricultural Society, 41 App. Div.2d 787, 341 N.Y.S.2d 45 (1973) (spectator in infield); Hine v. Dayton Speedway Corp., 20 Ohio App.2d 185, 252 N.E.2d 648 (1969) (owner in pits). A valid waiver need not bar recovery by others who have causes of action based on an injury to a spectator. *See, e.g.,* Barker v. Colorado Region–Sports Car Club of America, Inc., 35 Colo. App. 73, 532 P.2d 372 (1975) (loss of consortium by spouse); Kotary v. Spencer

Speedway, Inc., 47 App. Div.2d 127, 365 N.Y.S.2d 87 (1975) (father's medical expenses).

96. 29 Cal. App.3d 511, 105 Cal. Rptr. 904 (1972).

97. Thus, in Hine v. Dayton Speedway Corp., 20 Ohio App.2d 185, 252 N.E.2d 648 (1969), the court stated that

> The release does not specifically refer to the word "negligence," but there can be no doubt that its exculpatory language is thorough and comprehensive. Specifically, the plaintiff released the defendants from all causes of action and from all liability for injuries.
> Contracts purporting to relieve one from the results of his failure to use ordinary care must be strictly construed, but it is not necessary to use the word "negligence" if the intent of the parties is expressed in clear and unequivocal terms.

252 N.E.2d at 651.

98. 29 Cal. App.3d at 521, 105 Cal. Rptr. at 911.

99. *See generally* K. ALEXANDER & E. SOLOMON, COLLEGE AND UNIVERSITY LAW ch. 10 (1972); A. GRIEVE, THE LEGAL ASPECTS OF ATHLETICS (1969); H. LEIBEE, LIABILITY FOR ACCIDENTS IN PHYSICAL EDUCATION ATHLETICS RECREATION (1952); J. MOHLER & E. BOLMEIER, LAW OF EXTRACURRICULAR ACTIVITIES IN SECONDARY SCHOOLS 119–160 (1968); Franklin, *Tort Liability of Schools*, U. ILL. L.F. 327 (1958); Mancke, *Liability of School Districts of the Negligent Acts of Their Employees*, 1 J.L. & EDUC. 109 (1972); Miller, *Personal Injury Litigation in School Cases*, 20 LAW & CONTEMP. PROB. 60 (1955); Seitz, *Legal Responsibility Under Tort Law of School Personnel and School Districts as Regards Negligent Conduct Toward Pupils*, 15 HASTINGS L.J. 495 (1964); Annot., A.L.R.3d 908 (1971) (private school liability for lack of supervision); Annot. 160 A.L.R. 7 (1946); Annot., 56 A.L.R. 164 (1928); Annot. 24 A.L.R. 1070 (1923); Annot., 21 A.L.R. 1328 (1922); Annot. 14 A.L.R. 1392 (1921); Annot. 9 A.L.R. 911 (1920).

100. *See, e.g.*, Wells v. Colorado College, 470 F.2d 158 (10th Cir. 1973).

101. The sovereign and charitable immunity that may apply to the tort liability of public and private educational institutions is considered in detail at LAW OF SPORTS § 8.18.

102. Charonnat v. San Francisco Unified School District, 56 Cal. App.2d 840, 133 P.2d 643 (1943); Underhill v. Alameda Elementary School Dist. of Alameda County, 133 Cal. App. 733, 24 P.2d 849 (1933); Cambareri v. Board of Educ. of Albany, 246 App. Div. 127, 284 N.Y.S. 892, 127 (1936), *aff'd*, 283 N.Y. 741, 28 N.E.2d 968 (1940).

103. Carabba v. Anacortes School Dist. No. 103, 72 Wash.2d 939, 435 P.2d 936 (1967); Briscoe v. School Dist. No. 123, Grays Harbor County, 32 Wash.2d 353, 201 P.2d 697 (1949).

104. Selleck v. Board of Educ. of Central School Dist. No. 1, 276 App. Div. 263, 94 N.Y.S.2d 318 (1949); Garber v. Central School Dist. No. 1 of Sharon, 251 App. Div. 214, 295 N.Y.S. 850 (1937).

105. Tashjian v. North Colonie Central School District No. 5, 50 App. Div.2d 691, 375 N.Y.S.2d 467 (1974); Germond v. Board of Educ. of Central School Dist. No. 1, 10 App. Div.2d 139, 197 N.Y.S.2d 548 (1960).

106. Hoose v. Drumm, 281 N.Y. 54, 22 N.E.2d 233 (1939).

107. Brittan v. State, 200 Misc. 743, 103 N.Y.S.2d 485 (Ct. Cl. 1951) (providing nonqualified student as supervisor is an act of negligence).

108. Bush v. Norwalk, 122 Conn. 426, 189 A. 608 (1937) (failure to

provide mat under balance beam or to prevent its slipping on a greasy floor);
Fein v. Board of Educ. of New York, 305 N.Y. 611, 111 N.E.2d 732 (1953)
(failure to supply mat beneath chinning bar).

109. Albers v. Independent School Dist. No. 2 of Lewis County, 94 Ida.
2, 487 P.2d 936 (1971). These principles apply with equal force to public
and private institutions. See, e.g., Stehn v. Bernarr MacFadden Foundations,
Inc., 434 F.2d 811 (6th Cir. 1970).

110. Ohman v. Board of Educ., 300 N.Y. 306, 311, 90 N.E. 2d 474,
476 (1949) (Conway, J., dissenting).

111. Cambareri v. Board of Educ. of Albany, 246 App. Div. 127, 284
N.Y.S. 892 (1936), aff'd, 283 N.Y. 741, 28 N.E.2d 968 (1940); Read v.
School Dist. No. 211 of Lewis County, 7 Wash. 2d 502, 110 P.2d 179
(1941).

112. 133 Cal. App. 733, 24 P.2d 849 (1933).

113. Id. at 735–36, 24 P.2d at 851.

114. Kanofsky v. Brooklyn Jewish Center, 265 N.Y. 634, 193 N.E. 420
(1934) (a failure by an able student to complete a simple exercise); Gordon
v. Deer Park School Dist. No. 414, 71 Wash.2d 119, 426 P.2d 824 (1967)
(a baseball bat slipping from the hands of a teacher); Read v. School Dist.
No. 211 of Lewis County, 7 Wash.2d 502, 110 P.2d 179 (1941) (an injury
that could be explained only by the presence of many children playing a
game).

115. McCloy v. Huntington Park Union High School Dist. of Los Angeles
County, 139 Cal. App. 237, 33 P.2d 882 (1934).

116. See Wright v. San Bernardino High School, 121 Cal. App. 342, 263
P.2d 25 (1953) (contributorily negligent when run into flight of ball);
Albers v. Independent School District No. 2 of Lewis County, 94 Ida.
342, 487 P.2d 936 (1971) (assume risk of injury in pickup basketball game
in school gym on weekend). Since the participants in educational programs
will frequently be minors, a slightly different standard may be applied with
respect to both contributory negligence and assumption of risk. See RE-
STATEMENT (SECOND) OF TORTS §§ 464, 496D (1965).

117. Perkins v. Trask, 95 Mont. 1, 23 P.2d 982 (1933); Sherwood
v. Moxee School Dist. No. 90, 58 Wash.2d 351, 363 P.2d 138 (1961);
Read v. School Dist. No. 211, Lewis County, 7 Wash.2d 502, 110 P.2d 179
(1941).

118. Graff v. Board of Educ. of New York, 258 App. Div. 813, 15
N.Y.S.2d 941 (1939) (duty satisfied by provision of competent teacher).

119. Sawaya v. Tucson High School Dist. No. 1 of Pima County, 78
Ariz. 389, 281 P.2d 105 (1955); Hibbs v. Independent School Dist. of
Green Mountain, 218 Iowa 841, 251 N.W. 606 (1933).

120. Graff v. Board of Educ. of New York, 258 App. Div. 813, 15 N.Y.S.
2d 941 (1939); Katterschinsky v. Board of Educ. of N.Y., 215 App. Div.
695, 212 N.Y.S. 424 (1925).

121. See Dailey v. Los Angeles Unified School Dist., 2 Cal. 3d 741, 87
Cal. Rptr. 376, 470 P.2d 360 (19); Lee v. Board of Educ. of New York,
263 App. Div. 23, 31 N.Y.S.2d 113 (1941).

122. Rook v. State, 254 App. Div. 67, 4 N.Y.S.2d 116 (1938).

123. 17 A.D.2d 342, 234 N.Y.S.2d 1011 (1962), aff'd, 13 N.Y.2d 922,
193 N.E.2d 893 (1963).

124. Carabba v. Anacortes School Dist. No. 103, 72 Wash. 2d 939, 435
P.2d 936 (1968).

125. Rivera v. Board of Educ. of New York, 11 App. Div. 2d 7, 201

N.Y.S.2d 372 (1960) (teacher compelled students to use defective equipment); Lee v. Board of Education of New York, 263 App. Div. 23, 31 N.Y.S.2d 113 (1941) (teacher compelled children to play football in busy street); Rook v. State, 254 App. Div. 67, 4 N.Y.S.2d 116 (1938) (teacher compelled children to play with defective equipment); Keesee v. Board of Educ. of New York, 37 Misc. 2d 414, 235 N.Y.S.2d 300 (1962) (teacher failed to follow prescribed syllabus); Brooks v. Board of Educ. of New York, 29 Misc. 2d 19, 205 N.Y.S.2d 777 (1960), *aff'd*, 15 App. Div. 2d 495, 222 N.Y.S.2d 184 (1961) (teacher compelled children to compete in a dangerous sport where participants were unevenly matched); Carabba v. Anacortes School Dist. No. 103, 72 Wash. 2d 939, 435 P.2d 936 (1968) (wrestling referee, employed by the school board, negligently supervised match causing serious injury when an illegal hold was utilized).

126. Ostrowski v. Board of Educ. of Coxsackie-Athens School Dist., 31 App. Div. 2d 571, 294 N.Y.S.2d 871 (1968).

127. Fitzsimmons v. State University of New York at Stonybrook, 42 App. Div. 2d 636, 5 N.Y.S.2d 171 (1973); Kelly v. Board of Education of New York, 191 App. Div. 251, 180 N.Y.S. 796 (1920); Leahey v. State, 46 N.Y.S.2d 310 (Ct. Cl. 1944).

128. 191 App. Div. 251, 180 N.Y.S. 796 (1920).

129. *Id.* at 253, 180 N.Y.S. at 797.

130. Stevens v. Central School Dist. No. 1 of Town of Ramapo, 25 App. Div. 2d 871, 2 N.Y.S.2d 23 (1966), *aff'd*, 21 N.Y.2d 780, 288 N.Y.S.2d 475, 235 N.E.2d 448 (1968).

131. Chase v. Shasta Lake Union School Dist., 259 Cal. App. 2d 612, 66 Cal. Rptr. 517 (1968) (collision in adult evening softball game with an incinerator known to be close while chasing a fly ball); Iacona v. Board of Educ. of New York, 285 App. Div. 1168, 140 N.Y.S.2d 539 (1955) (participant in an informal boxing match simply dropping dead during the second round); Hanna v. State, 46 Misc. 2d 9, 258 N.Y.S.2d 694 (1965); Maltz v. Board of Educ. of New York, 32 Misc. 2d 492, 114 N.Y.S.2d 856, *aff'd*, 282 App. Div. 888, 124 N.Y.S.2d 911 (1953) (a collision with a brick wall located dangerously close to a basketball goal when the non-student had played upon the court frequently).

132. Orsini v. Guilderland Central School Dist. No. 2, 46 App. Div. 2d 700, 360 N.Y.S.2d 288 (1974); Bennett v. Board of Educ. of New York, 16 App. Div.2d 651, 226 N.Y.S.2d 593 (1962), *aff'd*, 13 N.Y.2d 1104, 246 N.Y.S.2d 634, 196 N.E.2d 268 (1963); Glatstein v. New York, 6 App. Div. 2d 824, 176 N.Y.S.2d 2 (1955).

133. Streickler v. New York, 13 N.Y.2d 716, 241 N.Y.S.2d 846, 191 N.E.2d 903 (1963).

134. The closely analogous question of the liability of coaches is considered at notes 151–62 *infra*.

135. Kerby v. Elk Grove Union High School Dist., 1 Cal. App. 2d 246, 36 P.2d 431 (1934).

See generally Proehl, *Tort Liability of Teachers*, 12 VAND. L. REV. 723 (1959); Seitz, *Legal Responsibility Under Tort Law of School Personnel and School Districts as Regards Negligent Conduct Toward Pupils*, 15 HASTINGS L.J. 495 (1965); Note, *Negligence Liability of Schoolteachers in California*, 15 HASTINGS L.J. 567 (1964); Annot., 32 A.L.R.2d 1163 (1953).

136. Pirkle v. Oakdale Union Grammar School Dist., 40 Cal. 2d 207, 253 P.2d 1 (1953); Albers v. Independent School District No. 302 of Lewis County, 94 Ida. 342, 487 P.2d 936 (1971); Luce v. Board of Educ. of

Johnson City, 2 App. Div. 2d 502, 157 N.Y.S.2d 123 (1956); La Valley v. Stanford, 272 App. Div. 183, 70 N.Y.S.2d 460 (1947); Reynolds v. State, 207 Misc. 963, 141 N.Y.S.2d 615 (1955).

137. Lueck v. Janesville, 57 Wis. 2d 254, 204 N.W.2d 6 (1973).

138. 28 Misc. 2d 70, 211 N.Y.S.2d 975 (1961).

139. *Id.* at 71–72, 211 N.Y.S.2d at 977 (citations omitted). *See also* Reithardt v. Board of Educ. of Yuba County, 43 Cal. App.2d 629, 111 P.2d 440 (1941) (student horse-play prior to start of class).

140. Reynolds v. State, 207 Misc. 963, 141 N.Y.S.2d 615 (1955).

141. Pirkle v. Oakdale Union Grammar School Dist., 40 Cal. 2d 65, 253 P.2d 1 (1953) (failure to warn about dangers in touch football); Bellman v. San Francisco High School Dist., 11 Cal. 2d 576, 81 P.2d 894 (1938) (failure to take into consideration the athletic aptitude and physical and emotional strength of a student, as well as the nature of the activity, in determining the kind of instruction to be given individual students); Darrow v. West Genesee Central School Dist., 41 App. Div.2d 897, 342 N.Y.S.2d 611 (1973) (failure to properly instruct about soccer); Armlin v. Board of Educ. of Middleborough Central School Dist., 36 App. Div.2d 877, 320 N.Y.S.2d 402 (1971) (failure to follow rule to have students and equipment in view at all times); Lee v. Board of Educ. of New York, 263 App. Div. 23, 31 N.Y.S.2d 113 (1941) (failure to refrain from "compelling a physical training class to engage in a game of football on Forty-Second Street, Manhattan, during a congested traffic hour").

142. *See, e.g.,* Kobylanski v. Chicago Bd. of Educ., 63 Ill. 165, 347 N.E.2d 705 (1976) (statute giving teachers in loco parentis authority, so that they will be liable only for wilful or wanton action).

143. Kerby v. Elk Grove Union High School Dist., 1 Cal. App. 2d 246, 36 P.2d 431 (1934) (teacher did not know of aneurism of student, so no duty to undertake special precautions); Stafford v. Catholic Youth Organization, 202 So.2d 333 (La. App. 1967) (no liability where teacher simply wrestled with students).

144. Lopez v. New York, 4 App. Div.2d 48, 163 N.Y.S.2d 562 (1957), *aff'd,* 4 N.Y.2d 738, 171 N.Y.S.2d 860 (1958); Nestor v. New York, 28 Misc. 70, 211 N.Y.S.2d 975 (1961) (teacher distributing milk thirty feet from accident); Chapman v. State, 6 Wash. App. 316, 492 P.2d 607 (1972) (teacher thirty to forty feet away supervising other students in physical education class); Lueck v. Janesville, 57 Wis.2d 254, 204 N.W.2d 6 (1973); Fagan v. Summers, 498 P.2d 1227 (Wyo. 1972).

145. Cox v. Barnes, 469 S.W.2d 61 (Ky. 1971) (student contributorily negligent at school outing and drowned); Stafford v. Catholic Youth Organization, 202 So.2d 333 (La. App. 1967) (assume risk of wrestling with teacher); Berg v. Merricks, 20 Md. App. 666, 318 A.2d 220 (1974) (improperly executed exercise); Sayers v. Ranger, 16 N.J. Super. 22, 83 A.2d 775 (1951) (assume risk when jumping over gymnastic horse with unconventional method known to be dangerous).

146. This result may, of course, be accomplished in most circumstances by the purchase of insurance. *See* A. GRIEVE, THE LEGAL ASPECTS OF ATHLETICS 111–16 (1969).

147. *See generally* 1 W. FLETCHER, CYCLOPEDIA OF CORPORATIONS § 41–46 (1963).

148. Scott v. University of Michigan Athletic Ass'n, 152 Mich. 684, 116 N.W. 624 (1908) (unincorporated association which conducted university's intercollegiate sports activities was indicated to be viably separate where it

was essentially independent of university control); Plattsburgh College Benevolent and Educ. Ass'n v. Board of Assessors of the Town of Peru, 43 Misc.2d 741, 252 N.Y.S.2d 229 (1964) (separate identity upheld where corporation operated entirely independently of the college); Faculty-Student Ass'n of the New York State College for Teachers, Albany, Inc. v. City of Albany, 17 Misc.2d 404, 191 N.Y.S.2d 120 (1959) (separate identity of corporation organized to conduct operation of dormitories, bookstores, and other student services upheld where it was completely self-governing and independent of the university).

Although it does not involve an educational institution, perhaps the strongest case indicating that separate incorporation of an athletic program may be viable is Klinsky v. Hanson Van Winkle Mining Co., 38 N.J. Super. 439, 119 A.2d 166 (1955), where an employer had separately incorporated an athletic association to conduct all employee athletic events. Hoping to get to the deeper pocket of the employer, the plaintiff, who had been injured by a bat that slipped from the hands of a batter at a family outing, alleged that the corporation was a mere instrument of the employer to maintain good labor relations. The court rejected this argument, however, and upheld the legal status of the athletic corporation, since the employer did not have or exercise ultimate control of its activities. Although the court noted that the employer provided financial support for the athletic corporation, it did not believe this fact to be of sufficient significance to alter the result.

149. Thus, in Rubtchinsky v. State University of New York at Albany, 46 Misc.2d 679, 260 N.Y.S.2d 256 (1965), suit was brought against a university for injuries suffered by a student in an athletic program sponsored by the Student Association, a separate unincorporated association in the university community. Although the university sought to defend on the ground that the association was a separate and distinct entity, the court rejected the defense. It found that under the constitution of the association, the president of the university had a final veto power, which the court believed to be "consonant with the effort to grant college students as much autonomy as possible in their extracurricular activities while still retaining final control in the hands of adult authority." 46 Misc.2d at 681, 260 N.Y.S.2d at 259. A similar result was reached in Carabba v. Anacortes School Dist. No. 103, 72 Wash.2d 939, 435 P.2d 936 (1968), where the court observed that

> [t]he fact that the wrestling matches were nominally staged by the student-body associations of the schools can afford no shield against liability on the part of respondent school districts under the facts appearing in this record, e.g. the participation of the faculty in the governing and operating of the student associations, and the full veto power possessed by the schools over proposed actions of the student associations.

Id. at 957 n.8, 435 P.2d at 947 n.8. *See also* T. BLACKWELL, COLLEGE LAW 186 (1961); Westbrook v. University of Georgia Athletic Ass'n, 206 Ga. 667, 58 S.E.2d 428 (1950) (not a separate entity for business competition purposes); People ex rel. Regents of University of Michigan v. Pommerening, 250 Mich. 391, 230 N.W. 194 (1930) (viability of corporation organized to conduct intercollegiate athletics not upheld where Board of Regents appointed its officers, and its control was to be in such officers as the governing body of the university should designate, since these facts indicated that it was but an operating agency of the Regents which was at all times under the Regents control); Wallace v. Weiss, 82 Misc.2d 1053, 372 N.Y.S.2d 416 (1975) (power to exercise control).

150. These same principles have been considered with regard to separate incorporation of student publications to protect the university from libel liability. Abbott, *The Student Press: Some First Impressions,* 16 WAYNE L. REV. 1, 13 (1969); Note *Tort Liability of a University for Libelous Material in Student Publications,* 71 MICH. L. REV. 1061, 1074–75 (1973).

151. McGee v. Board of Educ. of City of New York, 16 App. Div.2d 99, 226 N.Y.S.2d 329 (1962).

152. *Id.*

153. Duda v. Gaines, 12 N.J. Super. 326, 79 A.2d 695 (1951). Liability for medical treatment of athletic injuries is considered at notes 165–77, *infra.*

154. 233 Ore. 1, 376 P.2d 406 (1962).

155. *Id.* at 15, 376 P.2d at 413. *See also* Berg v. Merricks, 20 Md. App. 666, 318 A.2d 220 (1974) Lovitt v. Concord School Dist., 59 Mich. App. 415, 228 N.W.2d 479 (1975).

156. Morris v. Union High School Dist., A., King County, 160 Wash. 121, 294 P. 998 (1931). *But cf.* Hale v. Davies, 86 Ga. App. 126, 70 S.E.2d 923 (1952) (coach liable only if wanton or wilful act; very poor decision). The playing of injured athletes is discussed in H. SAVAGE, AMERICAN COLLEGE ATHLETICS 145 (Carnegie Fndn. 1929).

157. Welch v. Dunsmuir Joint Union School Dist., 326 P.2d 633 (Cal. App. 1958). *See also* Mogabgab v. Orleans Parish School Bd., 239 So.2d 456 (La. App. 1970) (failure to summon medical assistance).

158. This possibility was raised in Vendrell v. School District No. 26C, Malheur County, 233 Ore. 1, 376 P.2d 406 (1962).

159. Domino v. Mercurio, 17 App. Div.2d 342, 234 N.Y.S.2d 1011 (1962), *aff'd,* 13 N.Y.2d 922, 193 N.E.2d 893 (1963).

160. Stehn v. Bernarr MacFadden Foundations, Inc., 434 F.2d 811 (6th Cir. 1970).

161. Hanson v. Reedley Joint Union High School Dist., 43 Cal. App.2d 643, 111 P.2d 415 (1941). It has also been held that a hockey coach was negligent when he supplied helmets that he knew, or should have known, were not as safe as other models. Everett v. Bucky Warren, Inc., 380 N.E.2d 653 (Mass. 1978).

162. 70 S.D. 26, 13 N.W.2d 815 (1944). *See also* Sherwood v. Maxee School Dist. No. 90, 58 Wash.2d 351, 363 P.2d 138 (1961).

163. "Reasonable medical assistance" will require the provision of reasonable facilities and equipment as well as persons with the necessary degree of skill and experience. Clark v. State, 276 App. Div. 10, 93 N.Y.S.2d 28 (1949), *aff'd,* 302 N.Y. 795, 99 N.E.2d 300 (1951). *See generally* Ryan, *Medical Practices in Sports,* 38 LAW & CONTEMP. PROBS. 99 (1973).

164. Clark v. State, 2 App. Div. 10, 93 N.Y.S.2d 28 (1949), *aff'd,* 302 N.Y. 795, 99 N.E.2d 300 (1951). *See also* Mogabgab v. Orleans Parish School Bd., 239 So.2d 456 (La. App. 1970).

165. Welch v. Dunsmuir Joint Union High School Dist., 326 P.2d 633 (Cal. App. 1958) (interschool football scrimmage). *See also* Durham v. Commonwealth, 406 S.W.2d 858 (Ky. App. 1966) (swimmer fatally injured when he was improperly pulled from water).

166. Pirkle v. Oakdale Union Grammar School Dist., 40 Cal.2d 207, 253 P.2d 1 (1953) (junior high school touch football); Clark v. State, 276 App. Div. 10, 93 N.Y.S.2d 28 (1949), *aff'd,* 302 N.Y. 795, 99 N.E.2d 300 (1951).

167. Duda v. Gaines, 12 N.J. Super. 326, 79 A.2d 695 (1951) (high school football tackling practice). See note 173 *infra*.

168. Sayers v. Ranger, 16 N.J. Super. 22, 83 A.2d 775 (1951) (physical education class injury).

169. Mogabgab v. Orleans Parish School Bd., 239 So.2d 456 (La. App. 1970) (applying ill-advised treatment to football player who suffered heat stroke); Guerrieri v. Tyson, 147 Pa. Super. 239, 24 A.2d 468 (1942) (teacher held liable for rendering unnecessary medical aid).

170. Clayton v. New Dreamland Roller Skating Rink, 14 N.J. Super. 390, 82 A.2d 458 (1951).

171. Pirkle v. Oakdale Union Grammar School Dist., 40 Cal.2d 207, 253 P.2d 1 (1953) (spleen and kidney problems discovered several hours after time of injury when blood passed in urine). *See also* Cramer v. Hoffman, 390 F.2d 19 (2d Cir. 1968).

172. 195 Misc. 581, 89 N.Y.S.2d 132 (Ct. Cl. 1949), *aff'd*, 276 App. Div. 10, 93 N.Y.S.2d 28 (1949), *aff'd*, 302 N.Y. 795, 99 N.E.2d 300 (1951).

173. More specifically, Clark alleged that "he suffered undue exposure to cold through an unreasonable delay in removing him from the snow, lack of sufficient covering, and transportation in unheated open vehicles; and that such exposure greatly aggravated his shock condition, caused the failure of circulation, the ensuing gangrene and the resulting amputation." 195 Misc. at 583–84, 89 N.Y.S.2d at 134.

174. Specifically, the court stated that

> [a] person responsible for an injury must respond for all damages resulting directly from and as a natural consequence of the wrongful act accounting to common experience and in the usual course of events, whether the damages could or could not have been foreseen by him. [citation omitted]. This applies to aggravation of injuries through an error in treatment by a physician. [citation omitted]. While we find no case so asserting, we believe the converse is also true, namely that one who assumes the risk of injury assumes also the risk of consequential injuries or damages, whether or not he could have foreseen them. In this case severe shock, some exposure to cold, some delay in hospitalization, possible error in treatment, were natural consequences of the severe injury and the situation. We believe that failure of the circulation in the badly injured leg, and the resulting gangrene, while certainly uncommon results, were still direct and natural consequences of the injury, shock and other factors. [citation omitted]. They were included in the risk assumed, even though of course unforeseen.

195 Misc. at 589, 89 N.Y.S.2d at 139–40. The Appellate Division, however, disagreed with this statement to the extent that it required a participant to assume the risk of negligence. Thus, it stated "it may well be that known dangers of exposure to cold and the possibilities of delay in hospitalization were inherent in the risk assumed. However, such assumption would not cover delay and exposure due to negligence on the part of the State, had such been established." 276 App. Div. at 13, 93 N.Y.S.2d at 31.

175. In reaching this conclusion, the court stated that

> [t]he claimant concedes that the State violated no duty so far as the original accident is concerned. This being so, the State's subsequent position is most closely analogous to that of the volunteer, who, in no way responsible for the original accident, injury or occurrence,

assumes the care of an injured person. It is now well established that such a volunteer is charged with a duty of common or ordinary humanity to provide proper care and attention so that at least the injured party is made no worse. [citations omitted]. Unreasonable delay in securing medical attention for an injured person of whom one has taken charge can constitute a violation of this duty. [citations omitted].

We do not find any breach of this duty by the State in the present case. It promptly produced stretchers and blankets, and under the supervision of a physician, Dr. Bergamini, placed claimant and his teammates thereon, covered them, removed them with reasonable expedition to a vehicle, and transported them to a hospital without undue delay.

195 Misc. at 590, 89 N.Y.S.2d at 140. The court also noted that the state, as owner of the facility, had no duty to provide an ambulance and medical attendant on the scene, although the association had done so in the past, since the association, not the state, had assumed that responsibility in the past.

176. If a different basis of liability is alleged, it will probably be that the doctor has breached a contract or warranty. See W. PROSSER, THE LAW OF TORTS 162 (4th ed. 1971).

177. See notes 1–7 *supra*.

178. *See* W. PROSSER, THE LAW OF TORTS 162 (4th ed. 1971); McCoid, *The Care Required of Medical Practitioners*, 12 VAND L. REV. 549, 558–69 (1959).

179. *See, e.g.*, Small v. Howard, 128 Mass. 131 (18).

180. Speed v. State, 240 N.W.2d 901 (Iowa 1976); *see generally* D. HARNEY, MEDICAL MALPRACTICE § 3.3 (1973); A. HOLDER, MEDICAL MALPRACTICE LAW 53–55 (1975); W. PROSSER, THE LAW OF TORTS 164 (4th ed. 1971).

181. Such testimony will not be required, however, in those cases where the questions presented are within the common knowledge of laymen. *See, e.g.*, Corn v. French, 71 Nev. 280, 289 P.2d 173 (1955).

182. *See* D. HARNEY, MEDICAL MALPRACTICE § 3.2 (1973).

183. *See, e.g.*, Dubois v. Decker, 130 N.Y. 325, 29 N.E. 313 (1891).

184. *See* D. HARNEY, MEDICAL MALPRACTICE § 1.5 (1973).

185. 326 P.2d 633 (Cal. App. 1958).

186. *See, e.g.*, Lewis v. Read, 80 N.J. Super. 148, 193 A.2d 255 (1933); Belk v. Schweizer, 268 N.C. 50, 149 S.E.2d 565 (1966); Dinner v. Thorp, 54 Wash.2d 90, 338 P.2d 137 (1950). *See generally* Annot., 21 A.L.R.3d 944 (1966).

187. *See generally* W. PROSSER, THE LAW OF TORTS 161 (4th ed. 1971).

188. *See generally id.* §§ 41–45.

189. *Id.* at 240. An additional standard of causation that has been widely utilized is the "but for" test, which would say that a person's conduct is not the legal cause of injury if the injury would have occurred without the conduct of the defendant. The principal difficulty with this test is that it does not deal with the situation in which more than one person's conduct contributed to an injury.

190. A doctor's examination duties are considered at notes 222–27 *infra*. It should be emphasized that "causation" is only one element of the negligent action, and the plaintiff would still have to establish the other elements— for example, that the doctor had breached his or her duty of care to the athlete.

191. *See* W. Prosser, The Law of Torts 239–40 (4th ed. 1971).

192. *See, e.g.,* Fish v. Los Angeles Dodgers Baseball Club, 56 Cal. App.3d 620, 128 Cal. Rptr. 807 (1976); Welch v. Dunsmuir Joint Union High School District, 326 P.2d 633, 6 (Cal. App. 1958).

193. Cramer v. Hoffman, 390 F.2d 19 (2d Cir. 1968).

194. Rosensweig v. State, 5 App. Div.2d 293, 171 N.Y.S.2d 912 (1958), *aff'd on another ground,* 5 N.Y.2d 404, 158 N.E.2d 228 (1959). The court reached this conclusion as follows: "It is clear that the immediate proximate cause of the injury which resulted in death was the severe blow to the head which [the athlete] suffered in the final fight. [The representative of the athlete] has failed to establish that this blow alone, irrespective of previous condition, would not have produced the fatal result." 171 N.Y.S.2d at 914.

195. *See, e.g.,* Hurley v. Eddingfield, 156 Ind. 416, 59 N.E. 1058 (1901).

196. See note 183 *supra.*

197. *See, e.g.,* Schloendorff v. Society of New York Hosp., 211 N.Y. 125, 105 N.E. 92 (1914).

198. *See* D. Harney, Medical Malpractice ¶ 2.1(B) (1973).

199. Bakker v. Welsh, 144 Mich. 632, 108 N.W. 94 (1906); Lacey v. Laird, 166 Ohio St. 12, 139 N.E.2d 25 (1956); Smith v. Siebly, 72 Wash.2d 16, 431 P.2d 719 (1967). There are also statutes in some states specifying when a minor may give consent to medical procedures.

200. Younts v. St. Francis Hospital & School of Nursing, Inc., 205 Kan. 292, 469 P.2d 330 (1970).

201. Sample forms are reproduced in D. Harney, Medical Malpractice 44–46 (1973).

202. *Compare* Danielson v. Roche, 109 Cal. App.2d 832, 241 P.2d 1028 (1952) (upholding such general language) *with* Rogers v. Lumbermens Mutual Casualty Co., 119 So.2d 649 (La. App. 1960) (invalidating such language).

203. D. Harney, Medical Malpractice 58 (1973) (emphasis in original).

204. *See, e.g.,* Markham, *Doctrine of Informed Consent—Fact or Fiction,* 10 Forum 1073 (1975); Norton, *Contract Law as a Viable Alternative to Problems of Informed Consent,* 21 Catholic U. L. Rev. 122 (1975).

205. *See* Plant, *Informed Consent—A New Area of Malpractive Liability* in Medical Malpractice 29, 36 (Shapiro, Steingold & Needham eds. 1965).

206. *See, e.g.,* Dunham v. Wright, 423 F.2d 940 (3rd Cir. 1970); Kritzer v. Citron, 101 Cal. App.2d 33, 224 P.2d 808 (1950).

207. *See, e.g.,* Hammonds v. Aetna Casualty & Surety Co., 237 F. Supp. 96 (N.D. Ohio 1965); Berkey v. Anderson, 1 Cal. App.3d 790, 82 Cal. Rptr. 67 (1969).

208. The statutes are discussed in D. Harney, Medical Malpractice § 1.6(B) (1973), and generally provide that if a doctor violates the confidentiality of the relationship, his or her license may be revoked.

209. *See, e.g.,* Nelson v. Nederland Life Ins. Co., 110 Iowa 600, 81 N.W. 807 (1900).

210. Hammonds v. Aetna Casualty & Surety Co., 243 F. Supp. 793, 802 (N.D. Ohio 1965). *See also* Simonsen v. Suenson, 104 Neb. 224, 177 N.W. 831 (1920); Alexander v. Knight, 197 Pa. Super. 79, 177 A.2d 142 (1962); Barry v. Moench, 8 Utah 2d 191, 331 P.2d 814 (1958). *See generally* Note, 28 Okla L. Rev. 658 (1975).

211. *See* W. Prosser, The Law of Torts 704 (4th ed. 1971). If erroneous information is communicated to the athlete, the athlete may have an

action against the doctor. *See, e.g.,* Gambrell v. Kansas City Chiefs Football, Inc., 562 S.W.2d (Mo. App. 1978) (action brought against team doctor, among others, for fraud and deceit in connection with representation of physical condition, but court held that claim was merged into claim under Worker's Compensation Act.)

If the information is communicated to the press, it could produce other legal problems to the doctors on the team. *See* Chuy v. Philadelphia Eagles Football Club, 431 F.Supp. 254 (E.D. Pa. 1977) (evidence supported jury verdict that disclosure of erroneous information by team physician was an intentional infliction of mental distress).

212. *See, e.g.,* Virginia Dare Stores v. Schuman, 175 Md. 287, 1 A.2d 897 (1938). There are several additional aspects of the negligent misrepresentation question, and they are all considered in W. PROSSER, THE LAW OF TORTS 107 (4th ed. 1971).

213. *See* Hoffman v. Rogers, 22 Cal. App.3d 655, 99 Cal. Rptr. 455 (1972); Dubois v. Decker, 130 N.Y. 325, 29 N.E. 313 (1981); Beading v. Sirotta, 41 N.J. 555, 197 A.2d 857 (1964) (holding that the doctor owed a duty of reasonable care to the employee whether or not a doctor-patient relationship existed). *But cf.* Lotspeich v. Chance Vought Aircraft, 369 S.W.2d 705 (Tex. Civ. App. 1963). *See generally* McCoid, *The Care Required of Medical Practitioners,* 12 VAND. L. REV. 549, 554 (1959).

214. See note 185 *supra. See also* Fish v. Los Angeles Dodgers Baseball Club, 58 Cal. App.2d 620, 128 Cal. Rptr. 807 (1976).

215. See notes 164–75 *supra.*

216. One might view Welch v. Dunsmuir Joint Union High School District, 326 P.2d 633 (Cal. App. 1958), to stand for this proposition, but the court merely upheld a jury verdict against a doctor and a school district. The school district was apparently responsible for the negligent acts of the coach (its employee), but not for the acts of the doctor, since the court stated that there was no evidence that he was its employee.

217. *See generally* W. PROSSER, THE LAW OF TORTS § 69–71 (4th ed. 1971); Fahr, *Legal Liability for Athletic Injuries,* in D. MATTHEWS & R. THOMPSON, ATHLETIC INJURIES 219, 220–21 (1963).

218. RESTATEMENT (SECOND) OF AGENCY § 2 (1958).

219. In Cramer v. Hoffman, 390 F.2d 19 (2d Cir. 1968), for example, the evidence showed that a university had no discretion to control how a doctor treated injuries to its student-athletes, and the court held that he was an independent contractor whose negligence could not be imputed to the University. *See also* Fish v. Los Angeles Dodgers Baseball Club, 58 Cal. App.3d 620, 128 Cal. Rptr. 807 (1976) (issue not considered); Rosensweig v. State, 5 N.Y.2d 404, 158 N.E.2d 229 (1959) (doctors who examined boxers pursuant to statutory requirements were not employees of the state, and the state was not responsible for their conduct).

220. See notes 176–78, *supra. See also* Speed v. State, 240 N.W.2d 901 (Iowa 1976) (insufficient examination of member of basketball team). The examination may require that the doctor determine whether an athlete should be allowed to participate. *See* Colombo v. Sewanhaka Central High School Dist. No. 2, 87 Misc.2d 48, 383 N.Y.S.2d 518 (1976) (court upheld a doctor's decision that an athlete who was deaf in one ear should not be allowed to participate in contact sports).

For a discussion of the dilemma that team physicians face in determining whether to allow injured athletes to continue playing, *see* Wack, *Playing Hurt—The Doctor's Dilemma,* SPORTS ILLUSTRATED, June 11, 1979, at 31.

221. 208 Misc. 1065, 146 N.Y.S.2d 589 (1955).
222. 146 N.Y.S.2d at 596–97.
223. *Id.* at 597.
224. 5 App. Div.2d 293, 171 N.Y.S.2d 912 (1958). The decision of the appellate court was affirmed on subsequent appeal to the state's highest court, 5 N.Y.2d 404, 158 N.E.2d 229 (1959), but the court limited its consideration to whether the state could be held liable for the acts of the doctors. It did not address the question of whether the doctors' conduct was negligent. *Rosensweig* is noted at 14 SYRACUSE L. REV. 79 (1962).
225. *See also* Fish v. Los Angeles Dodgers Baseball Club, 56 Cal. App.3d 620, 128 Cal. Rptr. 807 (1976) (involving duties in examination of child hit by foul ball, but case remanded for proper instructions).
226. *See generally* R. GOODMAN & P. RHEINGOLD, DRUG LIABILITY: A LAWYERS HANDBOOK ch. 8 (1970).
227. Hearings Before the Senate Subcomm. to Investigate Juvenile Delinquency of the Senate Comm. on the Judiciary, 93rd Cong., 1st Sess. 9, 107, 124, 140–74 (1973) (Proper and Improper Use of Drugs by Athletes); *see also* H. SAVAGE, AMERICAN COLLEGE ATHLETICS 145 (Carnegie Fndn. 1929).
228. *See, e.g.,* N.Y. Times, September 14, 1976, at 50, col. 5 ($600,000 settlement of suit by former football star Dick Butkus, who made these allegations).
There has continued to be a significant amount of coverage in the sports press devoted to the problems that drugs, prescribed by team physicians and otherwise, may cause to athletes. *See* Reed, *A Miracle! Or Is It a Mirage?,* SPORTS ILLUSTRATED, April 20, 1981, at 71 (discussing the use of DMSO, which is allegedly taken by many amateur and professional athletes); Kirshenbaum, *Steroids: The Growing Menace,* SPORTS ILLUSTRATED, November 12, 1979, at 33; Papanek, *Off on a Wronged Foot,* SPORTS ILLUSTRATED, August 21, 1978, at 19 (discussing the dispute between professional basketball star Bill Walton and his team over alleged injuries resulting from the prescription of drugs by team physicians).
In Bayless v. Philadelphia National League Club, 472 F.Supp. 625 (E.D. Pa. 1979), a suit alleging negligent medical care, including the administration of pain-killing drugs, was found to be covered by the Worker's Compensation Act. *See also* Brickman v. Buffalo Bills Football Club–Division of Highland Service, Inc., 433 F.Supp. 699 (N.D.N.Y. 1977).
229. This issue has been considered in some nonsports drug cases. *See, e.g.,* Watkins v. United States, 589 F.2d (5th Cir. 1979) (prescription of large quantity of valium without taking an adequate medical history of the patient or checking existing medical records); Chrestman v. Kendall, 247 Ark. 802, 448 S.W.2d 22 (19); Talcott v. Holl, 224 So.2d 420 (Fla. App. 1969); Incollingo v. Ewing, 444 Pa. 263, 282 A.2d 206 (1971). *See generally* D. HARNEY, MEDICAL MALPRACTICE 9.6 (1973).
230. Failure to make such disclosure has been found to constitute negligence in some nonsports cases. *See, e.g.,* Koury v. Vollo, 272 N.C. 366, 158 S.E.2d 548 (1968); Sharpe v. Pugh, 270 N.C. 598, 155 S.E.2d 108 (1967). *But cf.* Challett v. Pirkey, 171 Colo. 271, 466 P.2d 466 (1970). *See generally* D. HARNEY, MEDICAL MALPRACTICE § 2.4(K) (1973).

[3]

Legal Approaches to Sex Discrimination in Amateur Athletics: The First Decade

Mark A. Kadzielski

This chapter concentrates on the two main approaches to sex discrimination in amateur athletics employed by litigants and judges during the past decade: equal protection under the Fourteenth Amendment to the United States Constitution and Title IX of the Education Amendments of 1972. The constitutional analysis of equal protection and Title IX's regulations and policy coincide on a number of issues in the area of sports. This chapter will describe the impact of these two approaches on sex discrimination in amateur athletics, identify some of the unanswered questions they raise, and suggest some future directions for the resolution of issues in this area.

I. INTRODUCTION

Today, a decade after Title IX was passed, it is universally agreed that great strides have been made by women in amateur sports in America. Prior to Title IX, even though college and high school populations were roughly half male and half female, women constituted only 5 percent of all high school athletes and 15 percent of all college athletes. Today, 33 percent of all high school athletes are female, an increase from 2.5 million to 7.5 million participants. At the college level, the female athlete now represents 30 percent of the athlete population, an increase from 100,000 to 250,000 participants.

Colleges and universities, which annually spend approximately half a billion dollars on intercollegiate athletics, were spending about 2 percent of this amount for women's sports prior to Title IX. They are now spending approximately 16 percent on women's athletics. Before Title IX, virtually no athletic scholarships were awarded to women; today,

over 20 percent of all athletic scholarship money goes to women athletes. More than five hundred colleges now offer athletic scholarships
to women. Before Title IX, the average number of women's varsity
sports teams was 2.5; today, the average is 6.48. During the same period, the average number of men's athletic teams held steady, increasing slightly from 7.3 to 7.4.[1]

In an age of declining school enrollments, the increased number of
women participants in amateur athletics is truly remarkable. More intercollegiate competition is available in more sports for women today
than ever before. Whether all or part of this change is due to Title IX,
or any other legal action, or due to the changing conditions and attitudes of society that occurred in the late sixties and early seventies
(highlighted by the passage of both the federal Equal Rights Amendment and Title IX in the Spring of 1972), is a question ultimately for
legal and social historians. What is important, however, is that these
changes have occurred.

On the other hand, whether all these changes constitute real "progress" can be and has been widely debated. Most school budgets are
still drastically skewed toward men's sports. While women make up
one-third of college athletes, they receive only about one-sixth of college athletic budgets. Second-class status in facilities, equipment, and
coaching is still accorded some female athletes, and the quandary of
the superior female athlete remains unsolved.

When Vice President Bush announced on August 12, 1981, the "hit
list" of the Federal Task Force on Regulatory Relief, it was perhaps
more than coincidence that among the thirty regulations and policies
picked for review and possible elimination or modification were one
regulation concerned with protection of endangered species and one
policy concerned with Title IX and intercollegiate athletics. Like the
snail darter, female athletes are, some would argue, an endangered
species that needs protection and not deregulation.

Whatever the outcome of this specific battle, the age-old issue of sexual equality in general has not come nearer to being resolved in the
past decade in America. Plato's *Republic* contained the comment that
"If women are to have the same duties as men, they must have the
same nurture and education. They must be taught music and gymnastics and also the art of war, which they must practice like the men."[3]
Significantly and recently on this last point, the United States Supreme
Court held in the summer of 1981 in *Rostker v. Goldberg* that Congress
did not offend the Constitution by excluding women from the draft and
thus, presumably, depriving them of the "opportunity" to learn and
practice the art of war.[4] The courts may not have addressed what the
Constitution has to say about music education, but they certainly have
discussed in detail its impact on "gymnastics" for women.

II. CONSTITUTIONAL APPROACHES
TO SEX DISCRIMINATION

Sex discrimination in athletics has been judicially approached under the due process clauses of the Fifth and Fourteenth Amendments as well as the equal protection clause of the Fourteenth Amendment. Both of the "due process" clauses prohibit the deprivation of "life, liberty or property without due process of law." The equal protection clause of the Fourteenth Amendment adds that no state shall "deny to any person within its jurisdiction the equal protection of the laws." Although the predominant challenge to sex discrimination in athletics has been under the equal protection clause, it is worth noting that due process claims are not totally disregarded by courts.

In a few instances, a substantive due process approach has led some courts to conclude that sex classifications create irrebuttable presumptions based on inappropriate criteria. Although the use of such presumptions has been judicially disfavored, this approach was employed by the federal district court in the case of *Yellow Springs v. OHSAA*, which dealt with an Ohio athletic association rule prohibiting mixed gender competition.[5] In finding that the rule was violative of due process, the district court judge held that it was based on a set of unwarranted conclusive presumptions that (1) girls are *uniformly* physically weaker and more injury prone than boys, and (2) girls are *uniformly* less proficient athletes than boys.[6] The district court judge ruled that both presumptions are unconstitutional because they can be rebutted by individualized ability determinations. The appellate court, in reversing and remanding this case to the district court, specifically disapproved the due process approach taken by the district judge.[7]

A. The equal protection clause and sex discrimination

The most traditional route for sex discrimination cases in recent years has been the equal protection clause. In cases that do not directly involve public institutions, it is necessary to demonstrate first that there is some "state action" or "nexus" between the discriminating entity and the state.[8] This state action must then be shown to have led to the denial of equal protection of the laws to an individual or a group of individuals. Although this approach has been favored in recent gender classification litigation, it yields somewhat mixed results.[9]

Traditional Fourteenth Amendment case law on equal protection has taken a two-tiered approach: the rational relation test and the strict scrutiny test. The rigidity of this twofold approach has been amply criticized in the literature, primarily because the results of the test depend upon which test is applied.[10] Under the rational relation test, the court gives a very superficial review to statutory provisions, while under the strict scrutiny test, involving fundamental interests or suspect classifications, a very thorough analysis of the challenged statute is conducted. Under the former test, the legislative determination is almost always upheld; under the latter test, it often is not.[11]

In the area of gender classifications, the courts historically applied the rational relation test. In fact, from 1868, when the Fourteenth Amendment was ratified, until 1971, no statute that discriminated on the basis of sex was held unconstitutional by the United States Supreme Court.[12] In 1971, the Supreme Court in *Reed v. Reed* struck down a statutory classification on the basis of a new test, an intermediate or "heightened rational relation" test.[13] The Court indicated that classifications under this test must be "reasonable, not arbitrary, and must rest upon some ground of difference having a fair and substantial relation to the object of the legislation, so that all persons similarly circumstanced shall be treated alike."[14]

Two years after the *Reed* case, the Supreme Court in *Frontiero v. Richardson* held that government regulations discriminating against women in the military were unconstitutional.[15] Four justices held that sex deserved suspect classification status and, on the basis of their strict judicial scrutiny, found the classification unconstitutional. Three justices followed the *Reed* test and held that the regulations were simply invalid under the test.[16] More recently, in 1976, the Supreme Court in *Craig v. Boren* crystallized the intermediate test of *Reed* by requiring that gender-based classifications "serve important governmental objectives and must be substantially related to the achievement of those objectives."[17] Subsequently, the Court has stuck to this intermediate test, leaving *Frontiero* as the high-water mark of strict scrutiny of sex discrimination by federal courts.

B. Equal protection and sex discrimination in athletics

How does all of this equal protection analysis apply in concrete situations in the area of education? Almost everyone is familiar with the case of *Brown v. Board of Education*, in which the Supreme Court held that "in the field of public education, the doctrine of 'separate but equal' has no place. Separate education facilities are inherently unequal."[18] However, because sex-based classifications do not fall into the strict scrutiny category applied to racial distinctions, the force of the Supreme Court decision in the *Brown* case does not provide much assistance in gender discrimination matters. Although there have been several cases regarding sex discrimination in the admission of women to educational institutions, the concept of separate but equal is very much with us in the realm of gender-based classifications.[19] In sum, because sex is not yet a suspect class, the courts have been reluctant to invalidate gender classifications simply because they exist.

Because of this judicial reluctance, cases on sex discrimination in athletics demonstrate that separate is still equal when it comes to sports. During the past decade, several cases involving sex discrimination in secondary school athletic programs have been brought against schools or interscholastic athletic associations. Factually, these cases can be grouped into two categories: (1) where one athletic team exists in a noncontact sport and is open only to one sex; and (2) where separate-sex athletic teams exist in a given sport but no coed team exists.[20]

In the first set of cases, courts have usually found violations of equal protection. However, in the second type of case, where separate-sex teams already exist in a given sport, the decisions have not generally overturned the categorization on the grounds of equal protection, despite the heightened rational relation test of *Reed v. Reed*. Such decisions seem to rest upon grounds that, while it is an important objective to encourage all students to participate in athletics, there is a corollary fear that mixed competition will result in male domination to the detriment of female participation. Of course, this analysis has been widely criticized by various commentators.[21]

Courts have generally had little trouble in finding a violation of equal protection in cases with the first fact pattern. In *Brenden v. Independent School District*, interscholastic athletic association regulations that prohibited athletic competition between male and female students were challenged by two female high school athletes. Their high school had no interscholastic athletic programs for female students and they wanted to participate on the men's team. In applying the *Reed* test, the Eighth Circuit held that the classification by sex did not have any "fair and substantial relation" to the objective of the interscholastic league rule, which was to ensure that similarly qualified student athletes would compete with one another. The court accordingly ordered an individualized determination of the plaintiffs' abilities.[22] In *Reed v. Nebraska School Activities Association* and *Gilpin v. Kansas State School Activities Association*, federal district courts upheld similar challenges to similar rules barring women from participation in interscholastic competition.[23]

On the state level, in *Haas v. South Bend Community School Corp.*, the plaintiff challenged an interscholastic athletic association regulation barring "mixed teams" and "mixed competition" in noncontact sports. The case went to the Indiana Supreme Court, which, on the basis of the *Reed* test, voted 3–2 in her favor. Significantly, four of the five justices indicated that if a comparable athletic program for female students had existed, they would have found the regulation valid under equal protection standards.[24]

In those cases where separate-sex teams were already established in a given sport, the modern equal protection analysis was less useful. In *Bucha v. Illinois High School Association,* the plaintiffs wanted to compete on the same swimming team with men despite the existence of a separate women's team. In applying a traditional rational basis test, the federal district court found that the association rules permitting this distinction were rationally related to the objective of encouraging the athletic participation of a maximum number of students. The court was particularly persuaded by the existence of a separate women's team as well as expert testimony that suggested that "mixed competition" would result in male domination, thus restricting female participation.[25] *Ritacco v. Norwin School District* was a class action challenge to sex-segregated teams in noncontact interscholastic athletics. Although the challenge was denied on procedural grounds, the *Ritacco* court pointed out that " '[s]eparate but equal' in the realm of sports competition, unlike that of racial discrimination, is justifiable and should be allowed to stand where there is a rational basis for the rule."[26] As in *Bucha,* the court found that the physiological differences between males and females that might lead to male domination of mixed teams constituted a rational basis for the challenged rules.

In *Hoover v. Meiklejohn,* the federal district court directly addressed the separate but equal doctrine in a case that involved a challenge to a Colorado High School Athletic Association rule that limited soccer participation to males. The court found that the complete denial to female student athletes of the opportunity to play interscholastic soccer violated the equal protection clause. However, the court specifically noted that the *Brown v. Board of Education* prohibition of separate but equal facilities in education did not apply to separate-sex athletic teams; the high school thus was left with options of fielding separate teams with substantially comparable programs, permitting both sexes to compete on the same team, or discontinuing soccer.[27]

The *Hoover* decision is interesting not only because of its holding but also because of the way it defined "equal" as meaning substantially equal support and substantially comparable programs. The court specifically stated that ". . . the standard should be one of comparability, not absolute equality." The very lack of athletic opportunity for female athletes was used by the court to justify the existence of separate sex teams, and " . . . may also justify the sanction of some sports only for females. . . ."[28]

On the state level, in *Ruman v. Eskew,* the Indiana Court of Appeals examined an interscholastic athletic association rule that prohibited mixed teams where separate teams existed. The case involved a female athlete's attempt to try out for the boy's tennis team, despite the existence of a women's team. The appellate court, relying on the dictum of the four *Haas* justices, found the rule to be reasonably related to the objective of providing athletic opportunities to both sexes and upheld its validity.[29]

The upshot of equal protection cases in the area of athletics is that the existence of separate programs, teams, and leagues for male and female students is not viewed as a denial of equal protection by the courts. Indeed, the argument that *Reed v. Reed* has given us a true heightened standard is often rebutted by pointing toward cases involving such separate programs. The critics indicate that, in reviewing classifications such as these, courts actually employ the old traditional rational basis test and find no violation of equal protection. The difficulty for the courts here, of course, is that case law on constitutional principles still permits the assumption that separate is equal when it comes to gender-based classifications.

C. The dilemma of the superior female athlete

This also brings us squarely to the quandary of the superior female athlete. Certainly we all have become aware during the past decade of the superior female athlete who has outdistanced both male and female competitors. She faces, however, a dilemma fostered by the separate-but-equal concept. If the women's team is the only team the superior female athlete can play on, she is being effectively prevented from fully developing her natural talents. Yet nonsuperior female athletes would arguably be prevented from any participation if the only opportunity afforded them was mixed competition.

While there are no easy solutions to this quandary, creative plaintiffs and administrators have been able to fashion some satisfactory remedies. For example, a first team–women's team approach may permit the superior athletes of both sexes to play on the "first" team, while preserving the opportunity for female participation. Some schools have also experimented with teams with fixed quotas of female players. However, neither of these options will perfectly accommodate all the interests of male or female athletes, and their legality can be questioned.[30]

The general result during the last ten years of these constitutional approaches to sex discrimination in amateur athletics has been an increased sensitizing of athletic administrators to the issues illuminated by the equal protection concept. Particularly during the first half of this past decade, the equal protection clause was the main battleground on which sex discrimination lawsuits were fought. However, as we have seen, the equal protection clause did not fully meet the heightened expectations of some litigants and did not permit a recategorization of sex as a suspect class requiring strict judicial scrutiny. Practically speaking, this meant that judicial review stopped once the existence of a separate athletic team in the challenged sport was demonstrated. This left many proponents of increased opportunities for women athletes unsatisfied and eager to find other approaches to combat the sex discrimination they perceived in amateur athletics.

III. STATUTORY AND REGULATORY APPROACHES UNDER TITLE IX

Title IX became law on June 23, 1972, three months after the Equal Rights Amendment was passed by Congress and submitted to the states for ratification. Congress presumably intended Title IX to be an intermediate measure to assure equality of opportunity in education for women on their way to full equal rights under the soon-to-be-new constitutional amendment. During the past decade, with the ratification of the ERA slowed and stalled, Title IX has taken on new meaning. Simply enough, Title IX provides that: "No person in the United States shall on the basis of sex be excluded from participation in, be denied the benefits of, or be subjected to discrimination under any education program or activity receiving federal financial assistance. . *l.* ."[31] Title IX was patterned after Title VI of the Civil Rights Act of 1964, which prohibited discrimination on the basis of race, creed, or national origin.[32] The Department of Education, as successor to the Department of Health, Education and Welfare, is responsible for enforcing Title IX pursuant to regulations and policy interpretations.[33]

A. Title IX's regulations

The long delays associated with the regulatory process under Title IX have been frustrating to individuals involved with education in the United States. The Department of Health, Education and Welfare, after much public comment, took more than three years to produce its final set of regulations. These regulations cover the three general areas of activity within educational institutions: admissions, treatment of students, and employment.[34] Athletic and sports-related programs are covered in several sections of the regulations dealing with the treatment of students.

The most important regulation of sports programs is now found in 34 C.F.R. § 106.41.[35] That section prohibits discrimination on the basis of sex in any intercollegiate, intramural, or club athletic programs offered at a covered educational institution. Separate-sex teams are permitted in contact sports or in other sports where team membership is based on competitive skills. In noncontact sports, where there only exists a single-sex team *and* where athletic opportunities for the other sex have previously been limited, members of the excluded sex must be allowed to try out for the team. Moreover, equal athletic opportunities for both sexes must be provided, as defined by a list of factors included in the regulations.[36]

These regulations allow for the complete exclusion of females from contact sports, even where only one team is provided by the school.[37] Since separate-sex teams are permitted where based on competitive skills, schools have avoided mixed competition by providing a women's team in a given sport and utilizing skill as a selection criterion. By exempting the traditionally male-dominated contact sports like football, basketball, rugby, wrestling, and ice hockey, Title IX leaves out a good chunk of male athletics.

These regulations, then, do not go much farther than case law in sex discrimination in athletics. The burden, of course, does shift from individual complainants to educational institutions. Enforcement of these regulations is now handled by the Office of Civil Rights of the Department of Education.

In the area of noncontact sports, the regulations depart only marginally from the case law. Only if an institution has one sex-segregated team and athletic opportunities have previously been restricted must members of that other sex be allowed to try out for the formerly single-sex team. There are some problems with this "try out" right, due to the historical lack of opportunity for women to develop competitive skills.[38] The creation of separate teams for women in noncontact sports has been the most visible response to this requirement and is borne out by the statistics at the beginning of this chapter.

In December 1979, after receiving more than 700 comments, the Department of Health, Education and Welfare also adopted a policy interpretation on Title IX and intercollegiate sports.[39] This policy interpretation goes into great detail concerning the requirements of equality and is the policy interpretation targeted for review by the Task Force on Regulatory Relief.

The only case concerning Title IX's athletic regulations to reach the United States Supreme Court was *O'Connor v. Board of Education of School Dist. 23*, in which Justice Stevens refused to vacate the Seventh Circuit's stay of the preliminary injunction won by the plaintiff, who was seeking the right to try out for the boy's basketball team despite the existence of a girl's team at her junior high school. In his opinion Justice Stevens noted:

> Without a gender-based classification in competitive contact sports, there would be a substantial risk that boys would dominate the girls' programs and deny them an equal opportunity to compete

in interscholastic events. The defendants' program appears to have been adopted in full compliance with the regulations promulgated by the Department of Health, Education & Welfare [citation to Title IX and its athletic regulations omitted]. Although such compliance certainly does not confer immunity on the defendants it does indicate a strong probability that the gender-based classification can be adequately justified.[40]

Subsequently, the Seventh Circuit followed Justice Stevens's analysis in dissolving the preliminary injunction and remanding the case to the trial court for further proceedings. The plaintiff attempted to have the United States Supreme Court review this decision but *certiorari* was denied on December 1, 1981.[41] The upshot of all of this, of course, is that the doctrine of separate but equal still reigns in American amateur athletics.

B. The scope of Title IX's coverage

There has been much comment and debate over the scope of the coverage of Title IX, although it is clear that this law is limited in its coverage to educational institutions, unlike Title VI, which is more broad in its scope. Of course, one of the reasons for increased debate on this issue was the movement by plaintiffs in sex discrimination cases away from the seemingly unhelpful equal protection analysis under the federal Constitution and toward the regulatory approach offered by Title IX. Recent cases in both the athletic area and the employment area revolved around the issue of what Congress intended to cover under Title IX.

Several district court decisions in the athletic area in 1981 focussed on the scope of Title IX's coverage. These cases are: *Othen v. Ann Arbor School Bd.*, 507 F. Supp. 1376 (E.D. Mich. 1981); *Bennett v. West Texas State University*, 525 F. Supp. 77 (N.D. Tex. 1981); and *Haffer v. Temple University*, 524 F.Supp. 531 (E.D. Pa. 1981). These cases referred to and relied for support on the interpretation of the employment cases under Title IX.

In *Othen*, District Judge Charles Joiner was asked only to rule on plaintiff's request for attorney's fees after the defendant school board had satisfied plaintiff's complaint by providing a separate girls' golf team. Judge Joiner, in ruling on this narrow question, went through an extended analysis of the legislative history of Title IX and held that plaintiff was not entitled to attorney's fees because Title IX regulations governing athletics were invalid. The basis for his holding was that none of the school district's athletic programs had directly received any federal funds and were thus not "infected" with federal monies to bring them within the program specific language of Title IX.

In *Bennett v. West Texas State University*, the federal district judge followed Judge Joiner's reasoning in holding that the Title IX regulations did not cover the challenged intercollegiate athletic programs because these programs did not receive direct federal funding. In granting summary judgment to the defendants, District Judge Robert W. Porter also found that the indirect aid received by the university's athletic program (which, the plaintiffs had argued, was made possible by federal funds for other school programs) did not suffice to bring West Texas State under the regulations.

Nevertheless, this issue is not fully decided. Recently, the federal district court in *Haffer v. Temple University* held that "logic supports a broad reading" of the Title IX statute and denied defendants' summary judgment on the issue that Temple's athletic programs were not covered by Title IX. In adopting an institutional as opposed to a programmatic approach, Judge Joseph S. Lord III explicitly distinguished the Temple situation from those in the *Othen* and *Bennett* cases.[42]

The impact of the *Othen* and *Bennett* decisions is not yet final. Plaintiff's counsel in *Othen* moved for summary reversal of that decision, based on the controlling Sixth Circuit holding in *Yellow Springs* that the athletic regulations of Title IX are valid, but that motion was denied. The case is currently on appeal to the Sixth Circuit on the issue that federal impact aid received by the school district could be traced to athletics and constituted "federal financial assistance" for purposes of Title IX. The *Othen* case may also be viewed as an anomaly, since the court did not have to go so far to decide the simple and sole issue of attorney's fees. Yet, the adoption of the *Othen* holding and reasoning in the *Bennett* decision suggests that this view of the scope of coverage of Title IX's athletic regulations may have some validity.

The coverage of employment in Subpart E of the regulations has also been the subject of much controversy. This subpart has been vigorously attacked by educational institutions during the past several years. In numerous court cases, the regulations on employment have been held to be overreaching and invalid on the ground that employees are not intended to be beneficiaries of Title IX. Four circuit courts of appeal, the First, Sixth, Eighth, and the Ninth, have reaffirmed this view.[43] One, the Second Court of Appeals, has rejected it, saying that such inclusion of employment is valid.[44] Another, the Fifth Circuit, has held that, while the current Subpart E regulations are invalid, Title IX might be used to regulate some employment practices of educational institutions under redrawn regulations.[45]

The Supreme Court of the United States granted *certiorari* in two consolidated Second Circuit cases, *North Haven Board of Education* and *Trumbell Board of Education*, to resolve this issue. Oral argument was held on December 9, 1981, and a decision affirming the validity of

Subpart E regulations was issued on May 17, 1982. 50 U.S.L.W. 4501. Prior to oral argument, the Department of Education considered the withdrawal of Subpart E from the Title IX regulations, although the Justice Department refused to permit such a withdrawal.[46]

The six-to-three decision by the Supreme Court in *North Haven* was not a complete victory for advocates of an enlarged view of Title IX's coverage. While the majority opinion by Justice Blackmun clearly held both that Title IX prohibits employment discrimination in educational institutions and that the Subpart E regulations are valid, it also emphasized that Title IX's authority regarding the promulgation of regulations and the termination of funding for sex discrimination was "program specific." By explicitly approving this "program specific" approach, the majority opinion stopped short of authorizing a remedy and remanded these cases to the district court for further factual findings. The opinion stressed, however, that the enforcement tool of fund termination under Title IX would be limited to a specific program or part of a program that receives federal financial aid. While this distinction may not be significant at the elementary and secondary school level, where federal funds pervade many programs, it may have great validity in certain school districts and particularly at the level of higher education, where federal funding is very often quite "program specific."

When coupled with the Bush press conference calling for review of the intercollegiate sports policy interpretations, the mixed result of the recent Supreme Court decision on employment regulations and the lack of enthusiasm for them by the agency enforcing them perpetuate the clouded picture for the enforcement of athletic regulations under Title IX. Although the Department of Education has adopted new complaint resolution approaches, it appears that, in the future, remedying sex discrimination in sports will be more up to the individual students and administrators than to government enforcers.[47]

C. A private right of action under Title IX

Because of these uncertainties involved with the government application and enforcement of Title IX, many potential complainants might feel abandoned. Yet, in 1979, in *Cannon v. University of Chicago*, the United States Supreme Court provided a way out.[48] It "discovered" an implied right of action under Title IX for individual plaintiffs while not requiring their prior exhaustion of administrative remedies. This right to sue in federal court under Title IX, especially given the unpredictable regulatory posture, appears to be the most likely vehicle for individuals seeking legal redress of athletic sex discrimination.

However, this private right of action is no guarantee of success. Upon remand in *Cannon,* the district court denied plaintiff's motion for pre-

liminary injunction and granted defendants' motions to dismiss. The
Seventh Circuit last year affirmed these decisions, holding that violation of Title IX requires not merely that the schools' policies have a
known disparate impact upon women, but that an "intentional discriminatory act" be committed. *Certiorari* was sought on this issue before the United States Supreme Court, but was denied on December
14, 1981.[49] Additionally, in *Lieberman v. University of Chicago,* the
Seventh Circuit recently held that Title IX does not implicitly provide
a remedy in damages to victims of sex discrimination.[50] These two decisions of the Seventh Circuit certainly indicate that there is still quite
a difference between being able to sue under Title IX and being able
to succeed in a Title IX lawsuit.

IV. CONCLUDING OBSERVATIONS

There are two concluding observations that can be drawn from this
chapter. First, there is a clear judicial reluctance to extend strict constitutional scrutiny to cases involving gender discrimination. Second,
attitudinal and not legal change will be the key for future resolution
of problems in this area.

A. Continued judicial reluctance

Chronic judicial vacillation on sex discrimination has been most visible in cases involving athletics. Our nation's highest court has repeatedly and recently refused to stretch equal protection principles to give
strict scrutiny to gender-based classifications. Lower federal courts
have gone much the same route in limiting the use of this constitutional
approach. On one level, it may be inferred that the courts are watching
and waiting to see the results of the Equal Rights Amendment ratification. Should that occur, there is no doubt that sex would become a suspect class, like race, and become subject to the strictest constitutional
scrutiny.[51] This is amply demonstrated in states where state equal
rights amendments have been added to state constitutions.[52]

On a second, more fundamental level, it appears that, in the general
area of civil rights law, courts are becoming increasingly reluctant to
impose remedies for inequality in a broad-based manner. This reluctance perhaps reflects only what we as a society are asking ourselves:
What does government imposed "equality" achieve? In the obvious
comparison, judicially imposed racial equality in education has pro-
voked backlash, white flight, imposition of quotas, forced busing, and
much resentment. Of course, much progress has been achieved since
Brown v. Board of Education, and no one would today disagree that
racial classifications are blatantly discriminatory and illegal. Yet the

courts, staffed by human beings who must make reasoned judgments, have become shell-shocked by the marathon litigation and the rampant politicization that have befallen educational racial discrimination matters. The judges reflect no more than the public ambiguity regarding appropriate methods for remedying racial discrimination. Given the fact that society has not been able to completely concur on *how* racial equality should be achieved in education, judges are reluctant, absent a public mandate like the Equal Rights Amendment, to add unilaterally sexual equality in education to the civil rights hopper.[53] Unless the federal Equal Rights Amendment is ratified before the 1982 deadline or unless the deadline is again extended, there is no resolution in sight for this situation on the federal judicial level.

Of course, Title IX, while potentially limited in the area of employment and intercollegiate athletics, still provides a private right of action to a complainant. Undoubtedly, this private right of action will be used by female athletes to challenge discriminatory classifications that limit their opportunities. There is not yet, however, enough case law on Title IX to make a reasoned judgment on a trend in this area. Whatever the future, the increased involvement of women in athletics and the increased opportunities for such involvement over the past decade indicate that the doors to the clubhouses and locker rooms of America's amateur athletics have been opened. Keeping them opened may now rest on the aggressive assertion by women of their interests and rights in athletic equality.

B. The importance of attitudinal change

More subtle, however, is the observation that attitudes inherent in society at large are the real bases for sex discrimination. Most of this chapter is devoted to legal approaches, all of which may have some effect on attitudes. Nevertheless, it is naïve to think that legal change can conclusively resolve these attitudinal problems.

This is most certainly the case in the area of amateur athletics. Significant public pressure, made effective through the threat of private rights of action under Title IX, even with watered-down regulations and enforcement, should lead to the resolution of such problems by educational institutions through acceptable administrative adjudication. Progress may also be made through the voluntary compliance approach adopted by the Office of Civil Rights. Even given tightened budgets, common acceptance of principles of sexual equality by educational institutions should permit equal treatment for female athletes. Changing public perceptions should also cause many of the so-called problems, such as the "safety" and "health" of the no longer "weaker sex," to vanish.

The mixed results of sex discrimination cases in the athletic area during the past decade show that, although women aren't winning, they haven't been losing, and they certainly have been gaining. Participation by women athletes in amateur sports is at an all-time high. Such increased female presence and prominence have done more to bring about an attitudinal change in favor of equality in athletics than have purely legal approaches to sex discrimination during the past decade.

NOTES

1. Most of these statistics were presented during the panel discussion at the Law and Amateur Sports Conference by Dr. Donna Lopiano, President of the A.I.A.W., and Women's Intercollegiate Athletic Director at the University of Texas, Austin. *See also Women Students Make Big Gains in U.S. Schools,* Washington Post, October 18, 1981, p. A1.

2. In fact, in academic year 1981–82, the NCAA planned to hold twenty-nine national championships for women in twelve sports. While this appears to be another expanded opportunity for women athletes, it may have the effect of reducing overall opportunities for women. *See* Banoff & Berscheid, *A Commentary on Women's Athletics,* 28 ON CAMPUS WITH WOMEN 2 (Fall, 1980).

3. PLATO, THE REPUBLIC, V, 451.

4. Rostker v. Goldberg, 101 S.Ct. 2646 (1981). Justice Rehnquist did not follow the reasoning of the three-judge District Court, which found male-only draft registration unconstitutional, nor did he follow the suggestions of commentators, such as the author of Note, *Women and the Draft: The Constitutionality of All-Male Registration,* 94 HARV. L. REV. 406 (1980), who, reminiscent of Plato's dictum, suggested that "[t]o exclude women from draft registration would be to uphold one of the most potent remaining public expressions of 'ancient canards about the proper role of women.'" *Id.* at 425.

5. Yellow Springs Exempted Village School Dist. v. Ohio High School Athletic Ass'n, 443 F. Supp. 753 (S.D. Ohio 1978).

6. *Id.* at 759. *But see* Note, 47 U.M.K.C. L. REV. 109, 120 (1978), for a critical view of this approach.

7. Yellow Springs Exempted Village School Dist. v. Ohio High School Athletic Ass'n, 647 F.2d 651 (6th Cir. 1981), in which both the majority and minority opinions disagree with the district court's due process approach. *Id.* at 657 and 661–62. In *Yellow Springs,* the Sixth Circuit reversed and remanded the district court decision that had held that part of Title IX's athletic regulation, now 34 C.F.R. § 106.41(b), was unconstitutional because it violated the due process clause. The majority opinion held that Section 106.41 was valid and had been violated by an Ohio High School Athletic Association rule that had been interpreted to *require* the prohibition of coed teams in contact sports. 647 F.2d at 656.

8. *See, generally,* WEISTART & LOWELL, THE LAW OF SPORTS, ¶ 1.14 (1979) and the cases cited therein.

9. Rostker, note 4, *supra.* It is important to note that in states where

state equal rights amendments have been adopted, courts have permitted challenges to sex discrimination in athletics on the basis that sex is a suspect class. Commonwealth v. Pennsylvania Interscholastic Athletic Ass'n, 334 A.2d 839 (Pa. Cmwlth, 1975); Darrin v. Gould, 85 Wash.2d 859, 540 P.2d 882 (1975).

10. The gist of the many criticisms is that, unlike a light switch, the equal protection clause is a dynamic and multifaceted analytical tool. *See generally* Karst, *The Supreme Court, 1976 Term—Forward: Equal Citizenship Under the Fourteenth Amendment,* 91 HARV. L. REV. 1 (1977).

11. Wilkinson, *The Supreme Court, The Equal Protection Clause, and The Three Faces of Constitutional Equality,* 61 VA. L. REV. 945, 948 note 5 (1975).

12. Muller v. Oregon, 208 U.S. 412 (1908); Goesaert v. Cleary, 335 U.S. 464 (1948); Hoyt v. Florida, 368 U.S. 57 (1961).

13. Reed v. Reed, 404 U.S. 71 (1971).

14. *Id.* at 76, citing Royster Guano v. Virginia, 253 U.S. 412, 415 (1920).

15. Frontiero v. Richardson, 411 U.S. 677 (1973).

16. Justice Brennan wrote the plurality opinion, in which he was joined by Justices Douglas, Marshall, and White. In finding the *Reed* test sufficient, Justice Powell, writing for the Chief Justice and Justice Blackmun, noted that state rejection or ratification of the Federal Equal Rights Amendment would settle this issue by giving sex suspect classification status. *Id.* at 692 (Powell, J. concurring).

17. Craig v. Boren, 429 U.S. 190, 204 (1976).

18. Brown v. Board of Education, 347 U.S. 483, 495 (1954).

19. Kirstein v. Rector and Visitors of University of Virginia, 309 F. Supp. 184 (E.D. Va. 1970); Bray v. Lee, 337 F. Supp. 934 (D. Mass. 1972); Berkelman v. San Francisco Unified School District, 501 F.2d 1264 (9th Cir. 1974); and Vorchheimer v. School District of Philadelphia, 532 F.2d 880 (3rd Cir. 1976), *aff'd by an equally divided court,* 430 U.S. 703 (1977).

20. For a detailed analysis of these categories and the cases thereunder, see Kadzielski, *Postsecondary Athletics in an Era of Equality: An Appraisal of the Effect of Title IX,* 5 J. COLL. & U. L. 123, 129–31 (1979).

21. *Id.* at 131, note 49.

22. 477 F.2d 1292 (8th Cir. 1973). The plaintiffs wanted to participate in cross-country running and skiing as well as tennis.

23. 341 F.Supp. 258 (D. Neb. 1972) (golf); 377 F.Supp. 1233 (D. Kan. 1974) (cross-country).

24. 259 Ind. 515, 289 N.E.2d 495 (1972); *see also* Stroud, *Sex Discrimination in High School Athletics,* 6 IND. L. REV. 661 (1973).

25. 351 F.Supp. 69, 75 (N.D. Ill. 1972).

26. 361 F.Supp. 930, 932 (W.D. Pa. 1973).

27. 430 F.Supp. 164 (D. Colo. 1977).

28. *Id.* at 170.

29. 333 N.E.2d 138 (Ind. App. 1975).

30. Kadzielski, note 20, *supra,* at 135–136; Hitchens, *A Litigation Strategy On Behalf of the Outstanding High School Female Athlete,* 8 GOLDEN GATE U. L. REV. [Women's Law Forum] 423 (1979).

31. P.L. 92-318 (1972), as amended by P.L. 93-568 (1974); codified as 20 U.S.C. § 1681, *et seq.* (1976).

32. 42 U.S.C. § 2000d (1976). *See also* note 42, *infra.*

33. Regulations were originally set forth at 45 C.F.R. Part 86 under HEW; they are now at 34 C.F.R. Part 106 under the Department of Edu-

cation. The intercollegiate athletics policy interpretation, enforced by the Office of Civil Rights (OCR), is at 44 Fed.Reg. 71413 (December 11, 1979).

34. Subpart C covers admissions, Subpart D deals with the treatment of students, and Subpart E covers employment.

35. 34 C.F.R. §§ 106.41(a) and (b) provide as follows:

> (a) *General.* No person shall, on the basis of sex, be excluded from participation in, be denied the benefits of, be treated differently from another person or otherwise be discriminated against in any interscholastic, intercollegiate, club or intramural athletics offered by a recipient, and no recipient shall provide any such athletics separately on such basis.
>
> (b) *Separate teams.* Notwithstanding the requirements of paragraph (a) of this section, a recipient may operate or sponsor separate teams for members of each sex where selection for such teams is based upon competitive skill or the activity involved is a contact sport. However, where a recipient operates or sponsors a team in a particular sport for members of one sex but operates or sponsors no such team for members of the other sex, and athletic opportunities for members of that sex have previously been limited, members of the excluded sex must be allowed to try out for the team offered unless the sport involved is a contact sport. For the purposes of this part, contact sports include boxing, wrestling, rugby, ice hockey, football, basketball and other sports, the purpose or major activity of which involves bodily contact.

36. 34 C.F.R. § 106.41(c) sets forth a nonexhaustive laundry list of factors that OCR may take into account in the determination of equal opportunity. This list includes:

> (1) Whether the selection of sports and levels of competition effectively accommodate the interests and abilities of members of both sexes;
> (2) The provision of equipment and supplies;
> (3) Scheduling of games and practice time;
> (4) Travel and per diem allowance;
> (5) Opportunity to receive coaching and academic tutoring;
> (6) Assignment and compensation of coaches and tutors;
> (7) Provision of locker rooms, practice and competitive facilities;
> (8) Provision of medical and training facilities and services;
> (9) Provision of housing and dining facilities and services;
> (10) Publicity.
> Unequal aggregate expenditures for members of each sex or unequal expenditures for male and female teams if a recipient operates or sponsors separate teams will not constitute noncompliance with this section, but the Assistant Secretary may consider the failure to provide necessary funds for teams for one sex in assessing equality of opportunity for members of each sex.

See also note 39, *infra.*

37. The distinction, however, between permissive exclusion and mandatory exclusion was the basis for Judge Kennedy's finding of a Title IX violation in the *Yellow Springs* appellate decision, 647 F.2d at 656.

38. Kadzielski, *Title IX of the Education Amendments of 1972: Change or Continuity?* 6 J. LAW & EDUC. 183, 199 (1977). *See also* the not so unique problem of defining "historical inequities" faced by the court in Gomes v. Rhode Island Interscholastic League, 469 F. Supp. 659 (D. R. I.),

vacated as moot, 604 F.2d 733 (1st Cir. 1979) and the comment on it at 24 Suffolk L. Rev. 1471 (1980).

39. 44 Fed. Reg. 71413 (December 11, 1979); for a good analysis of this policy, *see* Gaal, DiLorenzo & Evans, *HEW's Final "Policy Interpretation" of Title IX and Intercollegiate Athletics,* 6 J. Coll. & U.L. 345 (1980).

40. 101 S.Ct. 72, 76–7 (1980).

41. 645 F.2d 578 (7th Cir. 1981), *cert. denied,* 50 U.S.L.W. 3447 (December 1, 1981) No. 81-635.

42. 524 F.Supp. 531, 541 (E.D. Pa. 1981). This controversy is aptly analyzed in Comment, *Title VI, Title IX, and the Private University: Defining "Recipient" and "Program or Part Thereof,"* 78 Mich. L. Rev. 608 (1980).

43. Islesboro School Committee v. Califano, 593 F.2d 424 (1st Cir.), *cert. denied,* 444 U.S. 972 (1979); Romeo Community Schools v. HEW, 600 F.2d 581 (6th Cir.), *cert. denied,* 444 U.S. 972 (1979); Junior College Dist. of St. Louis v. Califano, 597 F.2d 119 (8th Cir.) *cert. denied,* 444 U.S. 972 (1979); and Seattle University v. HEW, 621 F.2d 992 (9th Cir. 1979), *cert. granted,* 101 S.Ct. 563 (1980).

44. North Haven Bd. of Education v. Hufstedler, 629 F.2d 773 (2nd Cir. 1980), *cert. granted sub. nom.* North Haven Bd. of Education v. Bell, 101 S.Ct. 1345 (1981) and Trumbull Bd. of Education v. HEW, 629 F.2d 773 (2nd Cir. 1980), *cert. granted,* 101 S.Ct. 1345 (1981) [consolidated on appeal]. A good analysis of these regulations in the athletic coaching area is Comment, *Equal Pay for Coaches of Female Teams: Finding a Cause of Action Under Federal Law,* 55 Notre Dame Lawyer 751 (1980).

45. Dougherty County School System v. Harris, 622 F.2d 735 (5th Cir. 1980), *cert. pending* No. 80-1023. The Fifth Circuit would let Title IX regulate employment where employees are paid through a program receiving direct federal funds. Note, *Eliminating Sex Discrimination in Educational Institutions: Does Title IX Reach Employment?* 129 U. Pa. L. Rev. 417 (1980).

46. This withdrawal has been widely reported and was, indeed, characterized at oral argument before the Supreme Court as a conflict between two departments of government. 50 U.S.L.W. 3497 (December 22, 1981). In a parallel vein, Senator Hatch has introduced Senate Bill 1361, which would limit Title IX to only those educational programs and activities that receive *direct* federal funds, and would exclude employment from Title IX. At any rate, the Department of Education has embarked on a wholesale regulation review process, which, whether hastened or hampered by the Bush press conference, will reconsider departmental regulations in order "to identify opportunities for de-regulation and possible alternative approaches to achieving program objectives, in accordance with Executive Order 12291." 46 Fed. Reg. 19000, 19001 (March 27, 1981); 46 Fed. Reg. 39882 (August 5, 1981). All of this, of course, occurs in the larger context of a presidential review of plans to abolish the Department of Education. *See Reagan Reviewing Plans to Abolish Education Agency,* Wall Street Journal, p. 10 (September 8, 1981).

47. The complaint resolution approaches of the Office of Civil Rights have historically met with criticism from civil rights groups who claim that Title IX enforcement is ineffective. *See* Kadzielski, note 20, *supra,* at 141, n. 80. The "new approach" taken by OCR is to meet with the leaders of an investigated institution and review proposed findings of fact prior to issuance of a letter of noncompliance. At three institutions where this

process has been employed (the Universities of Akron, Bridgeport, and Hawaii), OCR has been able to obtain a commitment for voluntary compliance within a reasonable time and thereby issued in each case findings of compliance with 34 C.F.R. § 106.41(c). Such voluntary attitudinal shifts seem to be more effective and productive in obtaining the desired result of equality than purely legalistic approaches.

48. Cannon v. University of Chicago, 441 U.S. 677 (1979). Note, *How to Cure Your Sex Discrimination Ills: Take One Title IX Private Action and Cannon v. University of Chicago, then Sue Them in the Morning*, 1980 UTAH L. REV. 629.

49. 648 F.2d 1104 (7th Cir. 1981), *cert denied*, 50 U.S.L.W. 3487 (December 14, 1981) No. 81-769.

50. 660 F.2d 1185 (7th Cir. 1981).

51. *See* note 16, *supra;* Kadzielski, note 20, *supra,* at 140–141.

52. *See* note 9, *supra.*

53. Part of the societal ambivalence regarding the ERA is caused by confusion about its goals. Professor Diane Ravitch, writing on *Why the Equal Rights Amendment Is Stalled* in the Wall Street Journal, July 20, 1981, p. 14, states:

> It never became clear whether the supporters of ERA wanted to achieve absolutely equal, gender-blind treatment for women or to win special preferences for them as a historically oppressed group. Sometimes, as in discussion about the draft, gender-blind treatment seemed to be the goal, but when affirmative action was at issue, the same people were quick to seek special treatment for women. Similarly, the surge of "consciousness-raising," which led to women's caucuses, to special facilities for women, and to something akin to separatism within institutions and organizations, contradicted the appeals to gender neutrality. This occasionally reached absurd proportions, as in professional women's meetings where men were barred or in the decision of a New England women's college to create a "women's center" in the middle of its all-female campus.

This societal ambivalence is one of the difficulties at the heart of the dilemma of the superior female athlete discussed in this chapter.

[4]

The Amateur Sports Act of 1978

James A. R. Nafziger

The Amateur Sports Act of 1978[1] culminated a tenacious and often tense effort to create a modern and competent Olympic program in the United States. Its impetus was a coincidence of administrative faux pas that beset the United States team in the 1972 Munich Olympics. For example, a team doctor failed to note that a swimmer's drug list contained a stimulant that was on the International Olympic Committee's (IOC) prohibited list; as a result, the swimmer lost his gold medal. Two sprinters failed to qualify because their coach gave them a wrong time for their trials. Two medal winners were disqualified from all future competitions because they refused to face the American flag during the awards ceremony. The final blow was the unprecedented defeat of a United States men's basketball team by the Soviets amid controversial calls by the referees, which were unsuccessfully and some maintained, incompetently appealed by U.S. officials.[2] In contrast, the Soviet Union seemed to compete with competence and class.[3] Sportswriters pondered why this country was unable to field teams with the apparent depth and polish of the Soviets and the East Germans.[4] These developments stirred public opinion and convinced authorities that the U.S. Olympic movement was buried in confusion and incompetence.

There were other problems, too. Critics charged that the United States Olympic Committee (USOC)[5] was an administrative "Tower of Babel" with a bloated committee structure, inadequate lines of authority, a great reluctance to change, and insufficient experience (only 30 percent of the team managers at Munich had had any Olympic experience).[6] Committee members were selected to satisfy internal politics and not on their merits.[7] USOC officials in general were said to be "hopelessly remote" from their respective sports and were "too casual and prestige-minded to be bothered with the legitimate concerns of athletes."[8]

On top of all this criticism, the National Collegiate Athletic Association (NCAA) withdrew from the USOC, vowing not to return until the Congress had reformed the USOC's organizational structure.[9] The

NCAA decision came amidst a vigorous campaign for the presidency of the USOC.[10] These internal problems alongside the unfortunate developments in Munich demonstrated that the USOC was in trouble.

Despite general agreement that something had to be done, there was disagreement on what changes should be made. The Congress repeatedly failed to pass legislation on the subject.[11] In 1975, President Ford appointed a study group, the President's Commission' on Olympic Sports (PCOS), to examine the United States Olympic program, identify the problems, and make recommendations.[12] During its deliberations the relative performance of U.S. athletes in the 1976 Games in Montreal underscored the perceived problems. The PCOS, not surprisingly, found the nation's amateur sports effort to be fragmented and uncoordinated.[13] Amateur sports organizations wasted valuable time, effort, and facilities by indulging in jurisdictional squabbles and by refusing to cooperate. These feuds unfortunately harmed the athletes themselves. For example, they were torn between the desire to compete internationally and the threat that doing so might jeopardize their eligibility for interscholastic athletics when they returned.[14] The feuds thus encouraged cynicism among athletes caught in the middle and caution among potential corporate donors,[15] who had difficulty determining which organization effectively represented a particular sport.

The PCOS recommended, among other things, that the Congress recharter the USOC, giving it a vertical structure of representative organizations and athletes and the following five powers:

(1) A means to settle organizational disputes over the right to be the recognized national governing body (NGB) in a sport,

(2) a means to induce all organizations with significant national programs in a sport to belong to the NGB so that their activities can be coordinated,

(3) a means to guarantee an athlete's right to compete,

(4) a means to finance amateur sports more effectively, and

(5) a central policy-making forum to identify U.S. sports problems and effect solutions.[16]

In response to the PCOS's recommendations and to a long history of failures to achieve a voluntary solution, the Congress passed the 1978 Act. It has something old, something new, something borrowed, and something red, white, and blue.

The purpose of this study is to analyze, evaluate, and identify problems in provisions of the Act. The study will briefly review its structure and definitions section and then analyze and evaluate its substantive provisions in terms of the objects and purposes that the Act assigns to the USOC.

STRUCTURE

The Act is divided essentially into six parts. The first provides definitions,[17] the second, the objects and purposes of the USOC,[18] and the third, the USOC's general corporate powers and obligations.[19] The fourth and fifth parts concern the establishment of national governing bodies (NGBs) in each Olympic/Pan-American sport. Specifically, the fourth part stipulates the requirements for an amateur sports organization to become an NGB and the responsibilities and authority of the NGBs.[20] The fifth part is particularly important to lawyers. It provides a mechanism for resolving complaints and determining among more than one contender which should serve as the recognized NGB.[21] The sixth part, the final paragraph in the Act, gives amateur sports organizations exclusive jurisdiction over "restricted competition," that is, competition limited to a specific class of amateur athletes. If the sports organization otherwise involved in restricted competition wishes to be involved in international competition, it must obtain a sanction.[22]

DEFINITIONS

In order to understand the Act, one must have some grasp of who the players are and what positions they play. The USOC is given the authority to establish one national governing body (NGB) for each Olympic or Pan-American sport.[23] An *NGB* is an organization recognized by the USOC according to detailed qualifications and authorized to grant a certificate of approval or *sanction*.[24] A *sanction* is required by any *amateur sports organization* or *international amateur athletic competition*.[25] An *amateur sports organization* is a not-for-profit organization that sponsors or arranges *amateur athletic competition*, that is, an event in which *amateur athletes* compete.[26] *Amateur athletes*, a term of legal art under the statute, are individuals who meet the eligibility standard established by the NGB for a particular sport.[27] *International amateur athletic competition* is any competition between athletes "representing the United States" and those from any foreign country.[28]

Generally, this definitional framework clarifies the scope of the Act. Thus, though it has other objects and purposes, the Act is primarily concerned with two sets of relationships: that between athletes eligible for international competition, on one hand, and amateur sports organizations, the USOC, and its authorized NGBs, on the other; and also the relationship among those organizations.

The definitions are broad, often necessarily so. For example, it would be counterproductive, in an Act designed to encourage and unfetter U.S. participation in international competition, to create a detailed definition of *amateur* that might be unacceptable either to the international sports federations that govern each Olympic or Pan-American sport or to the International Olympic Committee (IOC) and the Pan-American Sports Organization.[29] On the other hand, the definition of *international amateur athletic competition*, for example, is open textured to a fault, as will be discussed later.

OBJECTS AND PURPOSES

Congress assigns fourteen "objects and purposes" to the USOC. The remainder of this study will consider each of these by focusing in effect on several questions: What was the purpose of the Congress in establishing the objective, how well does the respective provision in the Act serve that objective, how has the USOC interpreted and acted upon the objective, and what problems remain under the Act, with consequences for amateur athletics in 1980s?

(1) National goals

> . . . establish national goals for amateur athletic activities and encourage the attainment of those goals.[30]

This requirement needs elaboration before it can be understood. What is meant by "amateur athletic activities"? How will the USOC "encourage the attainment" of the "national goals" it sets? For whom are these national goals to be established? Answers to these questions are important in order to understand not only this particular requirement but the Act as a whole.

Both the legislative history of the Act and ordinary canons of statutory construction suggest that it was designed to operate primarily by giving responsibility to the USOC for coordinating those sports which currently appear on the program of the Olympic or Pan-American Games, and no others.[31] There is other evidence to support this position: The Act defines "amateur athlete" as an athlete who meets the eligibility requirements established by an NGB.[32] The USOC may appoint only one NGB to govern each sport included on the program of the Olympic or Pan-American Games.[33] Inferentially, then, "amateur athletic activities" must be limited to Olympic or Pan-American sports because the USOC may only appoint NGBs in those sports and the Act's definition of "amateur athlete" is tied to the existence of eligibility requirements established by an NGB.[34] Thus, a competitor in marbles is not an "amateur athlete" under the Act, because the USOC cannot establish an NGB in marbles, so there is no NGB recognized by the USOC to establish eligibility requirements for competition in marbles.

An opposing argument can be made that "national goals" for "amateur athletic activity" are not limited to Olympic or Pan-American sports. After all, to the lay person, the word "amateur athlete" has a plain, easily understood meaning: an athlete who does not earn his living from competition. If the Act seeks to develop Olympic-class athletes, it may follow that, at the very least, its responsibility for early training ought to extend to youngsters in non–Olympic/Pan-American sports. Moreover, other objects and purposes in the Act suggest that the USOC must make a broad commitment to provide opportunities in amateur athletics to the handicapped and others whose access to amateur sport is limited.[35] Those provisions strengthen a broad reading of the Act to encompass non–Olympic/Pan-American sports as well.

The USOC has, however, taken the position that it must work principally through its NGBs.[36] Thus, it is unlikely to set "national goals" outside the arena of Olympic and Pan-American sports, because it is not designed to work independently of its NGBs. It is, after all, a small administrative body,[37] an organization of organizations. The NGBs do the actual grassroots work of organizing teams, instructing coaches and officials, preparing schedules, and developing young athletes. A major reason for this reliance on the NGBs can be found in the USOC's membership. The majority of the votes in the House of Delegates of the USOC is held by NGBs.[38] Since these NGBs have their own responsibilities and problems, it is understandable that the USOC should be primarily concerned with Olympic/Pan-American sports.[39]

Nevertheless, the USOC membership structure has a place for national amateur sports organizations in sports that are not regularly included on the program of the Olympic or Pan-American games but are widely practiced in other countries.[40] In order for an organization that is engaged in a non–Olympic/Pan-American sport to be accepted into this membership class, the sport must be eligible for inclusion into future Olympic or Pan-American games. The USOC therefore is more interested in having an organization ready to prepare an Olympic or Pan-American team than in seeking dominion over non–Olympic/Pan-American sports.

Despite the wide variety of popular sports that are currently not in the Olympic or Pan-American Games, the USOC has only one sport represented in this membership classification: the Tae Kwon Do division of the Amateur Athletic Union (TKD-AAU).[41] It is unclear why so many amateur sports organizations engaged in non–Olympic/Pan-American sports have failed to become participants in the USOC. It is somewhat clearer, however, why the Tae Kwon Do division of the AAU joined: The AAU, feeling comfortable enough within the USOC structure, would gain another vote in the USOC's house of delegates.[42]

Besides apparently limiting by definition the sports with which the

USOC is to be primarily concerned, the Act adds another restriction. Section 206 states that "amateur sports organizations" have exclusive jurisdiction over competition that is "restricted" to a specific class of amateur athletes competing within the United States, such as college students, Marines, or members of the downtown YWCA.[43] By contrast, international amateur athletic competition is considered "open," because it is not "restricted" to one class of athletes within a single country. The USOC and its NGBs have authority over "open" competition and competition leading up to the Olympics or Pan-American Games but not over "restricted" competition within the United States.[44]

Thus, for example, the conflict between the College Football Association (CFA) and the NCAA is, for the USOC, *ultra vires,* because U.S.-style football is not an Olympic or Pan-American sport, and the members of the two organizations represent institutions engaged in restricted competition among a single class of athletes, college students.

(2) Productive working relationships among sports organizations

> . . . coordinate and develop amateur athletic activity in the United States directly relating to international amateur athletic competition, so as to foster productive working relationships among sport-related organizations.[45]

Leaving aside the somewhat ambiguous phrase "amateur athletic activity," the intent of this objective is tied up in the meaning of the words "coordinate and develop." In order to understand this phrase, it is important to know what language was not included. The original phrase was "coordinate, develop, and direct." The Senate Commerce Committee removed the word "direct" at the insistence of the NCAA.[46] This change suggests that the Congress did not want the USOC to have the authority to dictate to an amateur sports organization how to conduct its activity. The language that the Committee approved suggests a less authoritative role for the USOC. The word "coordinate" implies communication and cooperation among independent groups, and "develop," simply promotion of growth. Implicit in the call to "coordinate and develop," but not "direct," is the conclusion that the USOC must be able to encourage amateur sports organizations to join the USOC and its member NGBs if it expects to develop or coordinate anything.

An important element in the USOC's working relationship with amateur sports organizations is a simple membership structure that allows for meaningful participation. By contrast, prior to the PCOS report, the USOC had a complicated and curious nine-level membership structure.[47] Group A members were the NGBs. Group B members were national organizations that convened national championships and had a substantial number of their athletes on Olympic or Pan-American

teams, for example, the NCAA. Group C members were national organizations that sponsored sports recognized only in the Pan-American
Games. Group D members were representatives from the USOC fund-
raising groups in each state. Group E members were organizations carrying on regional competition, for example, the Big Ten Conference.
The last four groups were made up of various patriotic groups, past
presidents and officers of the USOC, representatives from the International Olympic Committee and the Pan-American Sports Organization,
and the current officers and directors. Conspicuously absent was any
provision for representation by current athletes. This gap was especially
noticeable in an athletic organization that managed to find a place for
thirty-six organizations of a "patriotic, educational, cultural, civic, or
benevolent character."[48]

Despite the long list of membership categories, the appearance of a
broadly based organization was a façade. Group A members, the NGBs,
held two-thirds of the votes and could automatically receive extra votes
if the number of NGB votes at a meeting slipped below two-thirds of
the total. Within Group A membership, aquatics and track and field enjoyed twice the representation of any other sport on account of the
success, popularity, and relative importance in the Olympics of these
programs.[49] On the lower membership rungs, the system took some
peculiar twists. All members in Group E had the same number of votes,
so that large national sports groups were encouraged to pile their sub-
groups into Group E.[50] Consequently, the Alaskan AAU and the Pacific
Eight Conference, for example, were Group E members of equal
standing. The same problem existed in Group B. The Catholic Youth
Organization (CYO) had the same number of votes as the National
Federation of State High School Associations (NFSHSA), despite the
immense difference in size and scope between the high school programs
and the CYO. The USOC, therefore, had a voting structure that failed
properly to balance the participation of amateur sports organizations in
this country and favored a relatively small group of NGBs.

In its comparative simplicity, only one section of the Act directly
addresses the membership structure of the USOC.[51] A lot is packed into
that section, however. It requires the USOC to establish provisions in
its constitution and by-laws for the "reasonable representation" of
NGBs, as well as amateur athletes who are actively competing or have
competed within the last ten years, and individuals not affiliated with
any sports group who represent the interest of the American public.
The Act does not provide any guidance on the meaning of "reasonable
representation."

Despite such ambiguities, the USOC has amended its constitution to
reform its membership structure. The overall voting power of the NGBs
has been reduced to a simple majority.[52] At least twenty percent of the

delegates from each NGB must be current athletes or have represented the United States in international amateur athletic competition within the last ten years.[53] The total number of membership groups has been reduced to the following five:[54] Group A—the NGBs; Group B—amateur sports organizations that conduct a national program or a regular national competition in two or more Olympic/Pan-American sports; Group C—national amateur sports organizations that serve as NGBs in non–Olympic/Pan-American sports; Group D—representatives of the Olympic fund-raising committees in each state; Group E—amateur sports organizations that conduct a national competition for athletes possessing physical or mental limitations that preclude participation in unrestricted competition. Each of the members of Group A is allocated five delegates and fifty votes, except for aquatics and track and field, which each get ten delegates and one hundred votes.[55] Group B members are each allotted five delegates and fifty votes.[56] Group C and E members are each allotted one delegate and one vote.[57] Group D members are allotted delegates based on the number of congressional districts in their respective states and have one vote per delegate.[58]

The formal changes in the USOC voting structure have reduced the voting superiority of the NGBs, required athlete participation, and reduced the number of membership classes. Even though the CYO, the NCAA, and the Amateur Athletic Union (AAU), as Group B members, all have the same number of votes, despite having programs of varying scope,[59] the apparent inequity of granting a large Group B member the same number of votes as a small Group B member must be seen in a larger context. The Act requires an NGB to provide a place on its board of directors for each amateur sports organization that has a national program of competition in the NGB's sport.[60] A large Group B member will, therefore, not only have its own votes but will have a strong voice in each sport in which it competes. Through representation on multiple NGBs, an amateur sports organization can expand its influence on the USOC without being directly assigned more votes. This should encourage national amateur sports organizations to join the USOC and its member NGBs.

Major amateur sports organizations have not always had such influence in their NGBs, because of the latters' symbiotic relationship with the international sports federations that had granted them membership.[61] On this basis, the AAU, an NGB in eight sports, repeatedly told the Congress that the AAU's position as an NGB in a particular sport was non-negotiable.[62] The AAU's argument was that only an international sports federation could designate an NGB. There was, consequently, no point in the Congress's or the USOC's even discussing the question of the appropriate NGB in a sport.

Understandably, the other unrecognized organizations saw the problem in a different light. The NCAA, in particular, would not accept the idea that an organization could have a very weak competitive program and still be an NGB.[63] This was most apparent in basketball, where AAU-member basketball teams have been of relatively minor importance. In response, the NCAA joined other organizations in encouraging the formation of new federations in basketball, track, and wrestling to displace the AAU.[64] Much of the pain and confusion that led to the passage of the Act resulted from the struggles between the NCAA-sponsored federations and the AAU to control a particular sport.[65] The system had no principled procedure for selecting an NGB from competing organizations or for removing an NGB that no longer did the job.[66] As an umbrella organization, the USOC was understandably reluctant to become involved in selecting and evaluating NGBs. Each NGB effectively possessed a sphere of influence or autonomy over decisions by the USOC concerning the NGB's sport. Thus, outside its sphere of influence, an NGB in hockey was likely to be indifferent about the selection of an NGB in basketball: it was simply someone else's sport and problem.

The Act responds to this jurisdictional imbroglio by giving the USOC the authority to select NGBs based on detailed procedures and criteria. These criteria require the NGB to be responsive to the actual participants in its sport, and only in its sport. The NGB must belong to only one international sports federation; be free from restraint and control by any larger parent organization; be open to membership by any individual or amateur sports organization active in the sport; protect the opportunity of athletes, coaches, trainers, managers, or officials to participate; include active athletes on the board of directors and grant them at least 20 percent of the board's votes; provide for direct representation on its board of directors for any amateur sports organization that conducts a national program of competition from which world-class athletes might be selected; and ensure that each organization's representation on the board reflects the "nature, scope, quality and strength" of that organization's program.[67]

The PCOS argued that the best way to make the NGBs a viable and credible part of the amateur sports structure would be to ensure that each NGB is a creature of a single sport.[68] In other words, wrestlers should decide what is best for wrestlers, and gymnasts for gymnasts. The Congress accepted the recommendation of the PCOS, stipulating that an NGB must have both the capacity to represent a sport abroad and the backing of the sport's participants at home.

The Congress provided a grace period though 1980 for those organizations subject to displacement which were NGBs when the Act was passed.[69] During this grace period the USOC could not enforce the new NGB criteria, but afterward, if the NGB failed to bring its organization into compliance, the USOC could suspend or revoke recognition of the NGB.[70] The USOC could also choose to grant a one-year extension if there was "clear and convincing" evidence that the NGB was unable to comply through no fault of its own.[71] If, at the end of this extension, the NGB still had not met the criteria, the USOC would have to revoke recognition of the NGB.

Since the grace period ended, there have been changes in the affiliations and organizational structure of the NGBs.[72] The NGB in track and field, for example, had been the Athletics Division of the AAU. In September 1979 that entity was reorganized to become independent of the AAU, at first maintaining its offices within the AAU building but later establishing separate offices.

The membership of the new track-and-field NGB, The Athletics Congress of the U.S.A. (TAC), is a good illustration of the positive results achieved under the Act.[73] The members of the NCAA and the NFSHSA organize the lion's share of the track-and-field teams in this country.[74] Neither of these groups belonged to the AAU-sponsored NGB because, in their opinion, AAU membership did not provide sufficient representation.[75] Thanks to the Act, TAC's board of directors is broadly based.[76] Thus, indispensable groups that conduct track-and-field competition at the high school, college, and postcollegiate level are represented, as they had not been before, in the decision-making structure of the new track-and-field NGB.

So far, with one major exception,[77] the structural reforms in sports previously administered by the AAU have gone smoothly.[78] The new NGBs have been formed out of the old AAU committee structure with remarkably little fuss. In sum, the Act seems to be working well in accomplishing the objectives of productive working relationships among amateur athletic organizations in the United States.

(3) Areas of exclusive jurisdiction: Olympic and Pan-American Games

> . . . exercise exclusive jurisdiction, either directly or through its constituent members of committees, over all matters pertaining to the participation of the United States in the Olympic Games and in the Pan-American Games, including the representation of the United States in such games, and over the organization of the Olympic Games and the Pan-American Games when held in the United States.[79]

How "exclusive" is the USOC's authority? Although the Act does not explicitly define the term, it does reserve a range of specific tasks for the USOC, as a chosen instrument. Thus, the USOC serves as the coor-

dinating body for amateur athletic activity in the United States directly
relating to international amateur athletic competition, represents the
United States in its relations with the International Olympic Committee and the Pan-American Sports Organization; organizes, finances, and
controls the U.S. teams in the Games; recognizes eligible NGBs; and
facilitates the resolution of conflicts arising in trials, the Games, or competitions preliminary to the Games.[80]

Within the USOC framework, the NGBs are authorized to sanction
international competition in their sport between U.S. and foreign athletes, whether in or outside the Olympic or Pan-American Games.[81]
Each NGB is authorized also to be the official representative of its sport
in its international sports federation.[82] The NGBs also have the authority to recommend athletes to the USOC for participation in the Olympic and Pan-American Games and to select national teams for other
competitions.[83]

While the Act gives the USOC and its NGBs the authority to select
Olympic and Pan-American teams, others may effectively decide
whether an athlete actually competes. Hence, a first chink appears in
the armor of the USOC's "exclusive jurisdiction." For example, many
state high school associations are reluctant to allow student athletes to
compete in nonschool competition.[84] The effective jurisdiction of the
USOC is arguably not "exclusive" if a gifted athlete could be dissuaded
from entering even the Olympic trials for fear, if selected to the team,
of not being able to compete in high school competition after the
games.

Given such threats to individual athletes and the possibility of friction between amateur sports organizations and the USOC, cooperation,
rather than insistence by the USOC on its "exclusive" prerogatives,
may offer a *modus vivendi*. A good example is a model eligibility rule
recommended by the NFSHSA for adoption by state high school athletic associations.[85] The model rule prohibits participation in organized
nonschool sports competition while a student is a member of a high
school team. The rule does, however, make an exception for participation in an NGB-selected national team or in a USOC-sponsored "Olympic Development Program." Thus, although its model rules are discretionary, one national amateur sports organization has chosen to
cooperate with the USOC in order to protect athletes and to prevent
conflict. In sum, the more the USOC is able to inspire and retain the
confidence of important non-NGB amateur sports organizations such as
the NFSHSA, the NCAA, and the Association for Intercollegiate Athletics for Women (AIAW), the more exclusive the USOC's jurisdiction
will in fact become.

Retaining the confidence of non-NGB amateur sports organizations
will not, however, by itself ensure exclusive jurisdiction for the USOC

over the participation of U.S. nationals in the Games. When the United States hosts the Olympic or Pan-American Games, the Act grants the USOC exclusive jurisdiction over the organization of the Games.[86] In fact, the USOC's jurisdiction in this area is far from exclusive. As a practical matter, the host city and state governments help organize and supervise the Games.[87] The IOC rules may also require the USOC to share authority with the host city's Olympic organizing committee.[88]

The federal government also challenges the exclusiveness of USOC jurisdiction over amateur athletics. As it turns out, the federal government, which mothered the Act, is also its Godfather. This role should not be surprising, insofar as the Congress chartered the USOC and identified the USOC as its chosen instrument to implement a broad range of sports policy. Many facets of this policy have significant political implications, even though "[t]he corporation shall be nonpolitical."[89] The federal government has been substantially involved in amateur sports for a long time,[90] and, indeed, the need and rationale for such involvement are clear.[91] The Act explicitly stipulates that the USOC must report annually to the Congress and the president[92] and reserves to the Congress, somewhat perfunctorily but also potently, "[t]he right to alter, amend or repeal this Act at any time."[93]

The Congress and the president poignantly demonstrated their own jurisdiction over amateur athletics by effectively compelling the USOC to boycott the 1980 Olympic Games in Moscow.[94] Indeed, President Carter's campaign to convince the USOC to boycott the 1980 Moscow Olympics is an example of how the USOC's "exclusive" authority may be compromised. The president backed up his campaign by threatening lawsuits, withdrawal of tax exempt status, and other sanctions against the USOC and any individual athletes who participated in the Moscow Games.[95] The Congress responded to the president's campaign and public opinion by overwhelmingly supporting a resolution urging the USOC to boycott the Games.[96]

In order to implement this policy, the Carter administration apparently realized that, under the Act, it needed to obtain the support of the USOC, although later statements by the president indicated that he was prepared to take legal action, if necessary, to prohibit participation by U.S. nationals in the Games. The administration, including the president himself, therefore began to persuade or compel the USOC to boycott the Games.

The pressure from Washington raised serious legal questions by compromising the statutorily mandated "nonpolitical" character of the USOC. The pressure also tore at the fabric of the USOC. As a creature, or at least an integral part, of the Olympic Movement, subject to the Olympic Charter, rules, and decisions, the USOC has first and foremost an international character.

While the USOC may cooperate with the government, Rule 24c of the Olympic Charter proscribes any association with an undertaking that would conflict with the principles of the Olympic Movement. Among these principles, Rule 24c specifically cites the obligation of a National Olympic Committee to be autonomous and to resist all political, religious, and economic pressure.

The USOC also has a national character. It is chartered by the Congress as a patriotic society.[97] The success or failure of the USOC's amateur athletes is typically greeted, respectively, with flag-waving or national soul-searching. It would be hard for an organization so deeply anchored in the national psyche to ignore the lobbying efforts of the president and the Congress. The USOC was clearly in a very awkward, if not impossible, position.

The USOC agreed to the boycott by a 2–1 margin. Several athletes and one member of the executive board of the USOC promptly filed a civil action to enjoin it from barring the athletes' opportunity to compete in the Games. In *De Frantz v. United States Olympic Committee*,[98] the court held that under the Rules of the IOC and the 1978 Act, the USOC not only had authority to decide not to send a team but could do so for geopolitical reasons unrelated directly to sports considerations. In reaching its decision, the court ruled that the Act did not provide individual athletes with a bill of rights, including the right to compete.[99]

A pivotal, and very controversial, legal issue before the court was whether the federal government's involvement in promoting the boycott was state action. The court held that it was not, and therefore the USOC's decision did not give rise to an actionable claim for infringement of the plaintiff's constitutional rights under the First, Fifth, and Ninth Amendments.

In defining "state action," the court addressed two guidelines. The first concerned whether the state " . . . has so far insinuated itself into a position of interdependence with [a private entity] that it must be recognized as a joint participant in the challenged activity."[100] Citing *Burton v. Wilmington Parking Authority*,[101] the court emphasized that the USOC received no federal funding, which has turned out to be incorrect, and that it existed and operated independently of the federal government, which is also incorrect, simply in view of the substantial intermingling between the USOC and the government stipulated in the Act, even though technically the two entities may not be involved in a "symbiotic relationship" of "joint participation"[102] in the governance of amateur athletics.

The second guideline to define state action involved an inquiry whether " . . . there is a sufficiently close nexus between the state and the challenged action of the regulated entity so that the action of the latter may be fairly treated as that of the state itself."[103] The plaintiffs argued "a novel theory," in the court's words,

> . . . that the campaign of governmental persuasion, personally led by President Carter, crossed the line from "governmental recommendation," which plaintiffs find acceptable and presumably necessary to the operation of our form of government, into the area of "affirmative pressure that effectively places the government's prestige behind the challenged action," and thus, results in state action.[104]

Citing two opinions, the court disagreed. It seemed to rely particularly on language in one of the cases that would require plaintiffs ". . . to show that the Government exercises some form of control over the actions of the private party."[105] The court concluded that the government exercised neither *de jure* nor *de facto* control over the USOC. In regard to factual compulsion, the court characterized the involvement of the federal government in the boycott decision as one of *persuasion.* As a matter of policy the court wrote that it could not

> . . . equate this with control. To do so in cases of this type would be to open the door and usher the courts into what we believe is largely nonjusticiable realm, where they would find themselves in the untenable position of determining whether a certain level, intensity, or type of "Presidential" or "Administration" or "political" pressure amounts to sufficient control over a private entity so as to invoke federal jurisdiction.[106]

The court then concluded that, even if the requisite state action had been shown, the plaintiffs had no constitutionally protected rights, such as liberty, self-expression, travel, and pursuit of their chosen occupation or avocation of athletics.[107] The court held that the plaintiffs' argument would unreasonably expand the concept of due process and particularly the right to travel simply to cure one of life's disappointments. A final paragraph offered sympathy to the plaintiffs but, in a dubious analogy to military service by government fiat, characterized the plaintiffs' plight as one of the "simple, although harsh facts of life" and concluded that these facts were "immutable."[108]

The facts here seem mutable, however. First, the analogy between nonparticipation in the Olympics and military service is strained. More importantly, the president's threat of legal action for noncompliance with his boycott campaign goes well beyond "persuasion" to *de facto* control. Finally, the president's actions, backed up by resolution of the Congress, with its power to repeal the USOC Charter, arguably "insinuated" the government "into a position of interdependence" with the USOC so far as to become "a joint participant" in the boycott.[109]

De Frantz ignored a second issue of state action. Aside from direct governmental intervention, it is arguable that the USOC necessarily acted on behalf of, or in concert with, the state, as defined by public institutions that comprise the membership of such constituent organizations of the USOC as the NCAA and the NFSHSA. Courts have repeatedly found that the conduct of these organizations constitutes state action.[110]

At the very least, the *De Frantz* opinion and the entire Moscow boycott episode leave several unanswered questions concerning the meaning of the phrase "exclusive" jurisdiction. Can federal involvement in the USOC's corporate affairs ever constitute state action? To what extent, precisely, is the federal government obligated to respect the "exclusive" jurisdiction of the USOC? Under what conditions must the federal government respect the emerging international legal authority of the IOC, where political intervention would defeat the obligation of the USOC to remain nonpolitical under the 1978 Act and IOC Charter alike?

This latter question merits special attention. The issue of the IOC's authority[111] was badly distorted by the court in *De Frantz*, when it noted

> . . . that on April 23, 1980 the IOC Executive Board reviewed the actions of the USOC and concluded that they were not in violation of IOC Rule 24(C), which requires that NOC's "must be autonomous and must resist all pressures of any kind whatsoever, whether of a political, religious or economic nature." To the extent that plaintiffs are alleging that defendant has violated any provision of its Constitution and Bylaws requiring it to be autonomous, *we adopt the conclusion of the IOC and find that this resolves any such allegations in favor of defendant.* [Emphasis added.][112]

In fact, the IOC publicly came to no such conclusion. Instead, the IOC was very concerned about the possibility of a rule infraction and decided on April 23, 1980, that "[t]he position of all National Olympic Committees which have declined the invitation to the Games of the XXIInd Olympiad will be reviewed after 24th May 1980." (That is, the court decided *De Frantz* six days before the scheduled final review of the matter by the IOC).[113]

After *De Frantz*, injunctions in the Act and the Olympic Charter against political activity by the USOC will create tension and potential conflict between private and public domestic authority and between the national and international characters of the USOC. In the distressing case involving the 1980 boycott of the Olympic Games, the public authority prevailed, and the national athletes stayed home on what proved to be an incorrect premise: that the boycott would enhance

national security by effectively challenging the Soviet Union and perhaps compelling a withdrawal of its troops from Afghanistan. This did
not happen. The Soviets remained mired in Afghanistan. Once again,
amateur athletes were a pathetic pawn of power politics. Moreover, in
terms of the Act, the incident put a cloud over the Act's clear reservation to the USOC of "exclusive jurisdiction" over amateur athletics.[114]

The boycott experience demonstrates that any legal argument by the
USOC for exercising its authority on the basis of "exclusive jurisdiction"
is built on quicksand. The constitutional ground upon which that provision in the Act rests has been adjudicated in *De Frantz*. Though
somewhat unsettled, the USOC's jurisdiction appears to be less than
exclusive in the face of governmental intervention; after *De Frantz*, it
will be difficult to find state action so as to test the constitutionality of
governmental restraints on the actual freedom of the USOC. In the face
of challenge by other organizations, the USOC is likely to find more
effective authority in the confidence and good will of its members than
under the "exclusive jurisdiction" language of the Act. The cooperative
rather than legalistic stance of the USOC vis-à-vis the NFSHSA, discussed earlier, is a good example of productive cooperation.

(4) Competent representation

> . . . obtain for the United States, either directly or by delegation to
> the appropriate national governing body, the most competent ama-
> teur representation possible in each competition and event of the
> Olympic Games and of the Pan-American Games.[115]

As a clarion call to greater amateur athletic success, the phrase "most
competent amateur representation possible" seems modest. The Act
does not require the USOC to become competitive in all Olympic and
Pan-American sports but merely "competent" and only as competent
as possible. While the phrase may not be inspiring, the tone of the requirement reflects the desire of the Congress to improve the U.S. position in international amateur athletics.[116]

The Congress assumed that if it cleared away the organizational
problems, U.S. amateur athletes could achieve success without further
government involvement or expense.[117] It is too early to tell whether
this assumption is correct. It is, however, clear that many positive steps
have occurred that should improve the competitive position of U.S.
amateur sport. For example, as will be discussed later, the NGBs are
becoming more open and responsive to participants in their sport, training facilities have been constructed, fund-raising has improved, sports
medicine programs have been initiated, and more money is being spent
on developing young athletes and minor sports.

(5) Promotion of international amateur athletic competition

> . . . promote and support amateur athletic activities involving the
> United States and foreign nations.[118]

The Act seeks to implement this object by reforming the sanctioning
process to provide detailed criteria, by establishing a means for mini-
mizing conflicts between organizations, and by minimally correlating
the amateur status requirements of each NGB with those of its international federation. The USOC has also contributed by establishing
programs to assist post- and noncollegiate amateur athletes to continue
their involvement in sport.

Amateur athletes may compete in only those international competitions sanctioned by an NGB. Before the Act, NGBs used their sanctioning power as a weapon to keep amateur athletes and sports organizations in line.[119] If an amateur athlete failed to secure a sanction from
an NGB before participating in a competition, the NGB might rule the
athlete ineligible for further competition. The NGB exercised complete,
unreviewable discretion in denying, approving, or ignoring requests for
sanctions.[120]

The Act seeks to prevent arbitrariness by specifying a procedure for
requesting and issuing sanctions.[121] An amateur sports organization
planning to hold an international competition in this country must
demonstrate to the appropriate NGB that the competition will comply
with the requirements of § 202(b)1. These requirements include payment to the NGB of any "reasonable and nondiscriminatory" sanctioning fee as may be required; a financial report of similar events, if any,
conducted by amateur sports organizations; and a showing that "appropriate measures" have been taken to protect the competitor's amateur
status, to validate records of the competition, to comply with any specific amateur athletic requirements of the competition, to employ qualified officials, to provide medical supervision, and to protect the safety
of athletes and spectators. An amateur sports organization wishing to
participate in competition outside of the United States must meet the
§ 202(b)1 requirements and must provide the NGB not with a financial
report of similar events but with a report of its most recent foreign trip,
if any, involving the sponsorship of amateur athletes.

While the Act requires the amateur sports organization to submit information to show compliance with § 202(b)1, an NGB is not restricted
to the requirements of that section alone in deciding whether to grant
a sanction. The test is whether holding or sponsoring a competition,
according to "clear and convincing evidence," would be "detrimental
to the best interests of the sports."[122] On that standard, NGBs, for reasons of human rights, refuse to sanction competition between U.S. and
South African athletes.[123]

Under the Act, an NGB is unlikely to abuse its sanctioning authority. First, under the USOC Constitution, an organization denied a sanction may appeal the decision to the USOC and, if still dissatisfied, to an arbitration board.[124] In reviewing requests for sanctions, the burden of proof is on the NGB to show by "clear and convincing" evidence that granting the sanction would be detrimental to the sport.[125] The NGB knows, therefore, that an unreasonable denial of a request for a sanction is likely to be reviewed and reversed. Second, the NGB comprises amateur sports organizations who will want sanctions for their events. Thus, for political reasons, a member of an NGB is not likely to vote arbitrarily to deny a sanction to another member when it needs to secure a sanction for its own future competition. Finally, an NGB that arbitrarily refuses to grant sanctions may be replaced by another group: the Act explicitly provides for the replacement of NGBs that do not meet their duties, one of which is to review sanction requests with fairness.[126] For these three reasons, an NGB is likely to be evenhanded in its sanctioning process.

This leaves an even more basic question: Who, precisely, needs a sanction? While the question is simple, the answer is not. An NGB has the authority to sanction "international amateur athletic competition" both inside and outside the country.[127] The Act defines "international amateur athletic competition" as "any amateur athletic competition between any athlete or athletes representing the United States, either individually or as part of a team, and any athlete or athletes representing any foreign country."[128] Given the private character of the USOC and NGBs, what does it mean to "represent the United States"? The legislative history discloses that the phrase is "not intended to be limited to athletes or teams known as 'national' teams of the United States."[129]

If the sanction requirement is not limited to designated national teams, to what is it limited? Must a bush league team representing a tavern in Detroit secure a sanction in order to challenge a team across the border in Windsor to a basketball game? The legislative history discloses that the sanctioning requirement is not intended for normal high school and college competition with Mexican and Canadian teams.[130] There is, however, no similar exemption for other cross-border competition. Common sense, one would hope, will prevail. The American Basketball Association of the USA (ABAUSA) has already indicated that it would be foolish for it to punish athletes who engage without formal sanction in a basketball game with Mexican or Canadian teams.[131]

The Act seems to rely upon the NGBs for this and other interpretations of the breadth of sanction requirements; the USOC does not have the authority to grant sanctions, although it does have the authority to review an NGB's sanctioning decision.[132] Also, because the USOC may appoint NGBs in only Olympic and Pan-American sports, neither the USOC nor its NGBs has authority to review sanction decisions by groups governing non–Olympic/Pan-American sports.[133]

The incapacity of the USOC and its NGBs to review sanction decisions by groups governing non–Olympic/Pan-American sports poses a serious threat to the USOC and the Olympic Movement when other members of the movement threaten to retaliate against the USOC for its failure to govern such groups. A good example was the threat of many Olympic committees either to withdraw from the 1984 Los Angeles Games or to favor their relocation abroad in retaliation against competition in the United States between U.S. and South African rugby teams.[134] Although rugby is not an Olympic or Pan-American sport and is therefore beyond the USOC's competence to govern directly under the Act, the threat posed a serious crisis for the USOC in its dual capacity as the national organizing committee of the 1984 Games and as the protector of U.S. amateurs whose eligibility for future international competition was implicitly threatened.

Despite this problem and others, the sanctioning process required by the Act is working. The Act will have rendered a great service, indeed, if it has changed the authority to grant a sanction from a weapon to defend an NGB's territory into a tool to protect amateur athletes.

The Act also requires NGBs to minimize scheduling conflicts.[135] Prior to the Act, they sometimes authorized major competitions at awkward times. For example, the AAU, the then NGB in track and field, scheduled participation in a meet in China at the same time the NCAA was scheduled to hold its conference championships.[136] This dilemma forced top college athletes to choose between competing for their schools and passing up a rare opportunity in China, or competing there and, most likely, losing their scholarships.[137] The scheduling provision requires the NGB to "minimize" scheduling conflicts "through coordination with other amateur sports organizations."[138] Arguably, an NGB's authority under this provision extends beyond offering its good offices to actually resolving scheduling conflicts whenever possible. At the very least, the language of the provision, couched in terms of a duty, seems capable of dissuading amateur sports organizations from noncompliance if they expect to elicit the future cooperation of an NGB.

The Act also furthers participation by preventing an NGB from establishing amateur status requirements that are more restrictive than those of the sport's international federation.[139] This provision is a response to the AAU's policy of having uniform amateur status requirements for all the many sports it governed.[140] The President's Commission discovered that in many cases the AAU's standard was higher than that of the international federations.[141] By requiring that amateur status rules be no more restrictive than the international rules, the Act encourages participation by excluding fewer athletes and preserving the morale of American athletes. They now know they may take advantage of any liberal eligibility provision of the international federations, just as foreign athletes may.

The USOC has gone beyond the specific provisions in the Act to initiate other programs enhancing opportunities for amateur athletes to engage in international competition. The President's Commission discovered that many post- or noncollegiate athletes were forced to give up participation in their sport because they could not find permanent work that would allow them to train and participate in international competition.[142] As a consequence, many athletes were retiring from amateur sports before they had reached their physical peaks.[143] In response, the USOC has adopted an Olympic Job Opportunities Program, broadened "broken time" payments to reimburse athletes for financial hardships they may have suffered while in pre-Games training camps, and encouraged state governments to let their employees have time off with pay while the employees are engaged in international competition.[144] By helping with financial and scheduling difficulties, these programs are designed, according to the USOC, to encourage a mature amateur athlete to continue participation in international competition, without violating international definitions of amateur status.[145]

The USOC Olympic Job Opportunities Program seeks to match athletes with employers who are sympathetic to the athlete's training schedule and will allow the athlete to take time off with pay to train and compete.[146] An athlete is provided a career position that is expected to continue even after the athlete retires from sport.[147]

Where the USOC is unable to persuade an employer to allow someone time off with pay to train and compete, the "broken time payment" program may assist the athlete. In accordance with IOC rules, the USOC may not only compensate an athlete for expenses directly related to competition, but provide the athlete with money to cover lost wages as well.[148] The USOC has also persuaded thirteen state governments to allow their employees to have time off with pay to compete in international competition.[149]

Although this financial assistance is consistent with both the Act and the Olympic Rules, the growing problem of more substantial assistance to amateur athletes casts a shadow on the path to Mount Olympus. Sports organizations, edging toward the "open" competition for professionals and amateurs alike in tennis, have become increasingly lenient toward remuneration of expenses incurred by amateur athletes, well beyond the USOC and Olympic provisions for assistance to amateurs.[150]

Whatever the emerging problems affecting amateurism, financial aid programs have served to extend athletic careers and improve athlete morale.[151] Combined with sanctioning reforms and the provisions requiring scheduling coordination, the USOC through the Act has significantly resolved many difficulties that had hindered international competition.

(6) Physical fitness and public participation

> . . . promote and encourage physical fitness and public participation in amateur athletic activities.[152]

The Act establishes the USOC as a chosen instrument not only for international amateur athletic competition but, to a degree, for purely domestic competition as well. Even if the phrase "amateur athletic activities" is interpreted to include only those in the Olympic/Pan-American programs, "physical fitness" clearly contemplates a much broader range of activity.

The USOC promotes physical fitness and public participation primarily through its NGBs.[153] It has also begun implementing that goal by staging a National Sports Festival.[154] Members of an NGB may represent many levels of a sport. In swimming, for example, NGB members represent amateur swim clubs, high schools, colleges, YMCA/ YWCA organizations, and city recreation programs.[155] Taken together, these programs provide a wide range of opportunities for participation related only indirectly to major international competition.

Of course, many of these programs are so competitive as to exclude less skilled or noncompetitive participants. If, because of the Act, competitive programs in Olympic/Pan-American sports come to claim a much greater share of available facilities, such participants may end up with less than they had before the Act.[156] It is imperative, therefore, that the USOC concern itself with general physical fitness, the public's need to participate in amateur sports, and the concomitant turf problems of access to adequate facilities. The USOC and NGBs must understand that encouragement of top competitors is not necessarily synonymous with the encouragement of public participation, as mandated by the Act.

(7) Development of amateur athletic programs

> . . . assist organizations and persons concerned with sports in the development of amateur athletic programs for amateur athletes.[157]

As already noted, the term "amateur athlete" is generally interpreted to refer to a person who meets the eligibility standards set by a USOC-recognized NGB.[158] This means that the USOC's development responsibilities are limited to sports that appear on the program of the Olympic and Pan-American Games.

Regardless of whether "amateur athlete" is defined in this way or more broadly, the key word in any development program is "money." How should the USOC raise and spend it?

The Act does not provide an ongoing commitment by the federal government to finance USOC activities. Instead, the Act adopted the viewpoint of the President's Commission that private corporations would be willing to help if the USOC could be reworked into an organization that could achieve its goals, inspire confidence, and become a more aggressive fund-raiser.[159] The PCOS did, however, recommend that Congress authorize a $215 million "one time only" appropriation for developing amateur sports and an annual appropriation of $83 million for general operating expenses.[160] These sums would have constituted an astounding increase in the USOC's financial resources.[161] The Congress, however, chiseled the recommended amount down to $16 million.[162] Even this money was not appropriated as expected; instead, the USOC received $4 million directly and $6 million as matching funds.[163] Public money thus far has been restricted in amount and applicability for use primarily to offset the costs of hosting Olympic competition in the United States.[164]

Despite this lack of public funding, the USOC's fund-raising efforts have been successful. From $12.6 million for the 1976 Olympiad, the USOC's revenue has grown to $22.3 million in 1980.[165] Altogether the USOC raised over $49 million for the 1980 Olympiad.[166] To be sure, this impressive fund-raising effort cannot be attributed solely to the Act: in 1977 alone, before the Act was passed, the USOC raised more money from corporations than it had over the entire four-year Olympiad of 1976.[167]

The USOC and its membership have been courting corporate sponsorship for some time. For example, in 1974, the AAU swim committee persuaded Phillips Petroleum Co. to sponsor the senior swimming program for the 1976 Olympiad.[168] As the 1980 Olympics approached, fifty corporations had exchanged gifts or cash for the right to declare that their product was used or approved by the U.S. Olympic team, leading to the wry observation that "[i]n 776 B.C. Greek Victors in the first Olympic games wore only a crown of laurel leaves. In 1980, when U.S. athletes march in Moscow, they'll be wearing Levi Strauss clothing, Timex watches, and Coppertone tans."[169]

Outside the Act itself, both the Congress and the USOC have been helpful. The Congress has encouraged the growth of amateur athletics through the federal tax code, which provides tax exempt status to any entity that is organized to "foster national or international amateur sports competition (but only if no part of its activities involve the provision of athletic facilities or equipment)."[170] As further support, a bill before the 1981 session of the Congress would have enabled taxpayers to donate one dollar to the U.S. Olympic Committee by means of a check-off on their federal income tax returns.[171]

The USOC has also improved its method for using some of this money for programs of sports development. The problem here is that the USOC must take into account other factors involved in athletic development. For example, academic institutions in the United States play a critical role in training young athletes[172]—at once an advantage and a potential problem. On one hand, it means that almost every child is exposed to sports through gym classes and interscholastic competitions. On the other hand, schools often have interests that diverge from those of the USOC. To an academic sports director, many Olympic sports, unlike football, for example, are often regarded as "minor" or "nonrevenue" sports.[173] When times are tough, these are typically the first to be cut from the school's athletic program.[174]

The USOC's assistance for the development of world class athletes had a checkered past before the Act. Instead of emphasizing underdeveloped programs, the USOC allocated development money on the basis of what amounted to a spoils system. The more successful and popular the sport, the more development money it received.[175] This left minor sports, which most needed the development programs, in the flats below Mount Olympus.

Even those sports on the Olympic heights did not receive much. For the 1976 Olympiad, men's track and field received the most development money, $216,500, whereas, at the bottom of the appropriations list, synchronized swimming received only $17,060.[176] The total amount allocated for the four-year period of that Olympiad was estimated to be $2.8 million.[177]

The USOC has greatly improved its sports development program. The USOC Development Committee now conducts a survey every four years to rank the development of each event on the Olympic or Pan-American program.[178] The events are classified as "developed," "emerging," or "underdeveloped," based on the pool of world class athletes capable of representing the United States in the event. This committee requires each NGB to indicate its intended use of funds to build up weak events in its sport. Each NGB is then responsible for meeting the goals laid out in its plan. Future receipt of developmental funding depends upon an NGB's ability to attain its goals.

Not only has the mechanism for distributing developmental funding changed, but the amount of money involved has changed as well. In the 1980 Olympiad, the USOC spent $10.4 million on sports development,[179] over three times the amount spent on development during the 1976 Olympiad.[180]

The USOC has introduced a National Sports Festival, which is designed to help develop amateur athletic talent by encouraging actual participation in less popular Olympic/Pan-American sports, by exposing more spectators to these sports, by broadening the numerical and geographic base of the sport, and simply by drawing young athletes to a contest that gives them an opportunity to show off their talent under a national spotlight.[181] The festival can be seen as an athletic recital. The festival's regionally organized structure encourages an NGB in an underdeveloped sport to draw athletes from many parts of the country and not merely from areas where the sport is prominent. Speed skating, ice hockey, archery, and men's field hockey are examples of sports that are prominent in very specific regions of the country that could benefit from broader geographical exposure.[182]

In sum, while the Act seems to require the USOC to raise money for sports in which the United States has a small pool of world class athletes, the federal government is not, and many would say should not be, a sugar daddy. The USOC has established, however, an impressive fund-raising apparatus and a better method for funneling money to sports that appear to need it most.

(8) Conflict resolution and athletes' rights

> . . . provide for the swift resolution of conflicts and disputes involving amateur athletes, national governing bodies, and amateur sports organizations, and protect the opportunity of any amateur athlete, coach, trainer, manager, administrator, or official to participate in amateur athletic competition.[183]

The Act requires that the USOC, in its constitution and bylaws,

> shall establish and maintain provisions for the swift and equitable resolution of disputes involving any of its members and relating to the opportunity of an amateur athlete, coach, trainer, manager, administrator, or official to participate in the Olympic Games, the Pan-American Games, world championship competition, or other such protected competition as defined in such constitution and bylaws.[184]

More directly, the Act specifies two procedures for settling conflicts. The first involves an amateur sports organization or an eligible person seeking to compel an NGB to comply with the organizational and sanctioning criteria in the Act. The second procedure involves an amateur sports organization seeking to replace an incumbent as an NGB.

While the provisions for resolving conflicts are very detailed, an athlete's "opportunity" to compete is poorly defined. The Congress apparently believed that an athlete's opportunity to compete, at least, is best secured by creating an accountable and responsive NGB structure with a well-oiled process for conflict resolution rather than by establishing a statutory "bill of rights" for athletes.

Complaint Mechanism:
Enforcing Compliance with the Organizational Criteria

The Act establishes certain criteria that an NGB must meet in order to become an NGB.[185] If an NGB fails to satisfy the criteria, any person eligible to belong to the NGB or an amateur sports organization may file with the USOC a complaint against the NGB.[186] The complainant may take this action only after having "exhausted all available remedies" within the NGB. The USOC must waive this requirement if the complainant can show by "clear and convincing" evidence that complying with it would result in "unnecessary delay." The USOC must rule within 30 days after the filing date on whether the complainant's remedies within the NGB have been exhausted or, if they have not been exhausted, whether following the remedies within the NGB would result in unnecessary delay. If the USOC rules that the complainant is entitled to bring the complaint before the USOC, it must schedule a hearing within 90 days of the filing date. After the hearing the USOC may either dismiss the complaint, place the NGB on probation for up to 180 days, or revoke its recognition of the NGB. If the NGB is placed on probation and fails to bring itself into compliance with the Act in the required time, the USOC must revoke recognition of the NGB unless the latter can show by clear and convincing evidence that it needs more time through no fault of its own. Either party may appeal the USOC's decision to a regional office of the American Arbitration Associaiton (AAA).[187] The demand for arbitration must be filed within 30 days of the USOC's decision.

These procedures have curtailed formal complaints within the USOC. The USOC, at least, is satisfied, proudly noting that all of the very few complaints have been resolved "amicably" without arbitration.[188]

NGB Challenge Mechanism: Replacing an Incompetent NGB

While the complaint mechanism has worked quite smoothly, the challenge mechanism was itself seriously challenged as the result of a dispute between the United States Wrestling Federation (USWF) and The Wrestling Division of the AAU, Inc. (WD-AAU). That dispute is instructive in several ways. First, though, it is essential to understand the challenge mechanism. It is like the complaint mechanism, except that instead of seeking to compel an NGB to comply with organizational criteria under the Act, the complainant, an amateur sports organization, seeks itself to replace an existing NGB.[189] In order for an organization to succeed in its challenge, it must first appear in a hearing to show by a preponderance of the evidence that it meets the criteria for recognition as an NGB. The challenger must also show either that the current NGB does not meet those criteria or that the challenger does, and will do, a better job of meeting the criteria and provides or is capable of providing a more effective national program of competition than the current NGB.

Within 30 days after the hearing the USOC must decide whether to retain the existing NGB, revoke recognition of the existing NGB and declare a vacancy (in other words, recognizing neither party to a challenge), replace the existing NGB with the challenger, or place the existing NGB on probation.[190] The USOC has 61 days to recommend and support a new NGB to the appropriate international sports federation.[191]

Any party aggrieved by a USOC decision on a challenge has a right to review by any regional office of the AAA if it files a demand within 30 days of the decision.[192] The arbitral decision is binding and may be enforceable against nationals of states that are parties to the Convention on the Recognition and Enforcement of Foreign Arbitral Awards.[193]

Shortly before the Act was passed, the USWF challenged the WD-AAU under the USOC Constitution. The executive board of the USOC, after a hearing, denied the USWF's application. It immediately filed a Demand for Arbitration with the AAA. On September 7, 1978, the three arbitrators unanimously found that the USWF had successfully established its claim for recognition as the wrestling NGB and was therefore entitled to replace the WD-AAU as a group A member of the USOC.[194] On September 23, 1978, the USOC legal counselor advised the committee that while the arbitral award purported to establish the USWF as the NGB, the international wrestling federation (FILA) still had to recognize the USWF before it could be seated as a group A member of the USOC. That is a required step because the Olympic Charter specifies that national committees can recognize only members of appropriate international federations.[195] Therefore, the USOC president promptly wrote to FILA recommending "as strongly as we can" that FILA recognize the USWF as the NGB "as soon as possible."[196] On October 17, 1978, FILA replied that any application by the USWF for membership in FILA could only be determined by its Congress, which would not meet until 1980. The USOC president repeated his request that FILA take action before then.

The USWF, encouraged by this support from the USOC president, filed an application with FILA on December 5, 1978, which included an affidavit from the USOC executive director stating that the USOC recognized the USWF as the U.S. wrestling NGB. Four days after the USWF had filed its application with FILA, however, the executive board of the USOC repudiated its decision of September 23 by restoring its recognition of the WD-AAU.[197]

In response to the USOC's decision to let the matter rest until 1980, the USWF, which had already fought off a court challenge to the arbitration award,[198] brought an action against the USOC. The USWF sought an order compelling the USOC to recognize it as a Group A member. On April 19, 1979, the court held that the USWF had acquired the status of an NGB contingent upon its recognition by FILA.[199] Thus, until then, the WD-AAU was required to give its "full recommendation and support" to USWF efforts to be recognized by FILA.

At its 1980 Congress, FILA rejected the USWF's application for recognition. The USWF was not allowed to present its case before FILA. Instead, the USOC presented the USWF's application to the FILA Congress, with a recommendation that, some time after the 1980 Games, the USWF should replace the WD-AAU.[200] A recent amendment to the FILA Constitution facilitated its decision to reject USWF by eliminating a prior presumption in favor of any candidate supported by a national Olympic Committee.[201]

The U.S. Congress, in order to prevent the Act from being undermined, responded by passing the Bellmon rider to a bill appropriating assistance to the USOC.[202] This provision forbids the USOC from allocating any of the appropriation to an NGB when another amateur sports organization has been designated the NGB by binding arbitration and prohibits any NGB so displaced from exercising its powers under § 203 of the Act. The USWF brought an action against the WD-AAU, the essence of which was to request a determination that the Amateur Sports Act, newly armed with the Bellmon rider, was applicable to the dispute and had been constitutionally applied.[203] The court's failure to render a prompt decision and the likelihood that any decision would be appealed by the losing party evidence the capacity of a successfully challenged but stubborn NGB (the WD-AAU) to obstruct the challenge mechanism of the Act.

The wrestling controversy concerned a challenge under the USOC Constitution and not under the Act because it predated the latter. Nevertheless, that brouhaha is instructive in understanding the Act and its problems. First, FILA, in flagrantly ignoring an arbitral award, set a bad precedent for other international federations. If this precedent becomes more general practice, an amateur sports organization challenging an NGB under the Act would no longer be able to rely upon the Act to seek review before a disinterested arbitral body free from sports politics and less protective of the status quo than the USOC executive board is likely to be. Second, the Act, apparently assuming that the international federations would recognize any organization that the USOC recommended, provides only that the latter must do so within 61 days after the new NGB has been selected. The Congress, prior to passage of the Bellmon rider, failed to provide for enforcement of either the USOC determination or an arbitral award in the face of a contradictory decision by an international federation.

Even without the Bellmon rider, the wrestling dispute put a hammerlock on the USOC. On one hand, it is bound by the Act and its own constitution to honor the results of an arbitration by seating the prevailing party as a Class A member. On the other hand, it is obliged to follow IOC rules, which prohibit the USOC from recognizing an NGB that is not a member of an international federation.[204] In such a situation, the USOC must depend upon the goodwill of the international federations to defer to the reasonable provisions of the Act, the supremacy of national means for resolving such jurisdiction disputes, and the paramouncy of arbitral and judicial awards.

The wrestling dispute brought one last problem to light: the sheer delay and expense of the elaborate legal procedures for dispute settlement stipulated in the Act. The expense of litigation, or even arbitration, may discourage an amateur sports organization from seeking to complain against or challenge an NGB. It may also encourage an incumbent NGB to delay a challenge process in order to drain the resources of a challenger. To preserve the intent of the Act, the USOC must consider ways to prevent the NGB challenge mechanism from becoming a test of financial strength instead of merit.

USOC Review of NGBs

The USOC does not have to wait for a complaint or challenge before it takes action. On its own initiative, the USOC may review the performance of an NGB.[205] If the USOC is not satisfied, it may take whatever action it deems appropriate.

Protecting the Opportunity of an Athlete to Compete: A Structural Approach

The President's Commission on Olympic Sports (PCOS) recommended that the Congress enact an "athlete's bill of rights" to include a right to compete internationally.[206] In the face of NCAA opposition, the Congress chose not to enact those rights but provided instead for an "opportunity to compete."[207] The USOC satisfies its obligation to protect the opportunity to compete by implementing an athlete's bill of rights in its constitution.[208] This bill of rights is enforceable against all USOC members, including the NGBs.

The Congress deliberately left a loophole in placing restricted competition beyond USOC competence. To return to an earlier issue, the NGBs and the USOC have no statutory authority over amateur sports organizations that are not NGBs, for example, the NFSHSA and the NCAA, to prevent them from denying an athlete the right to compete in restricted competition after participation in unrestricted international competition.[209] The NCAA's argument supporting this loophole is that because its members expend a great deal of money on their athletic programs, they must come first.[210] Also, high school competitors may be minors who need special supervision, or an academic institution may be legitimately concerned that too much classwork would be lost if an athlete should choose to participate in both interscholastic and international competition. Finally, academic institutions want to protect young athletes from being exploited by unscrupulous promoters.[211] For these reasons some state high school associations, faced with unclear distinctions, simply proscribe participation of students in any nonschool athletic programs during the school year.

Despite this loophole, it appears that the Congress, wittingly or unwittingly, was on the right track. By seeking to establish responsive and broad-based NGBs, the Act creates an atmosphere where the fears and concerns of the academic institutions are more likely to be heard and dealt with in a mutually satisfactory manner. An NGB that seeks to encourage college and high school participants will be disinclined to schedule major competitions during final exams or interscholastic seasons, so as to pose conflicts with academically oriented sports organizations:[212] an NGB simply cannot ignore the special status of student athletes.[213]

The USOC's obligation under the Act to ensure athletes an "opportunity" to compete is primarily implemented under its constitution, which forbids a member from denying an amateur athlete the opportunity to compete in "protected" competition.[214] That term refers to international amateur athletic competition between foreign and U.S. athletes who have been officially designated by the sport's NGB to "represent" the United States. To return to earlier discussion, this provision[215] may conflict with section 206 of the Act, which grants an amateur sports organization "exclusive jurisdiction" over restricted competition. This exclusive jurisdiction might be interpreted to prevent the USOC from taking actions that interfere with an amateur sports organization's authority over restricted competition. The USOC should nevertheless be able to claim powers to enforce the opportunity to compete whenever an athlete is participating in competition within the larger Olympic or Pan-American framework.[216] Since the USOC has exclusive jurisdiction over U.S. participation in these competitions, to allow an amateur sports organization to prevent an athlete from returning to restricted competition after participating in these competitions might well affect the capacity of the USOC, within its exclusive jurisdiction, to "obtain for the United States . . . the most competent amateur representation [in the Games]."[217] Perhaps this issue may be resolved best by common law accretion on a case-by-case basis.

The statutory enactment of an athlete's "bill of rights" without the other reforms in the Act would not have readily resolved pesky denials of athletic opportunity to compete internationally. A bill of rights would have given them just that, perhaps enforceable in court, but without a framework for developing a set of relationships that would promote harmony within the arena of U.S. amateur athletics. The resolution of problems concerning membership in the USOC and the NGBs, the establishment of responsive and accountable NGBs, and the provisions relating to sanctions and complaints all work to promote an atmosphere in which an athlete is less likely to be the victim of a jurisdictional feud.

(9) Development of athletic facilities

> . . . foster the development of amateur athletic facilities for use by amateur athletes and assist in making existing amateur athletic facilities available for use by amateur athletes.[218]

The turf problem that inspired this requirement is that access to training facilities is spread unevenly throughout society, particularly between students and nonstudents. The best facilities frequently belong to educational institutions. Thus, an athlete who is attending school usually has greater access to equipment. A nonstudent unable to join an athletic club oriented to major competition may be left with either no training facilities or inadequate ones.

Since the USOC may not be able to find new facilities for postcollegiate athletes, it must "foster development," presumably by persuading its members, such as colleges and universities, who do have facilities to accommodate serious athletes. Even if the USOC had the money to build training facilities for postcollegiate athletes throughout the United States, such an effort might be wasteful, given existing facilities built with public funds that are idle for long stretches of time.

By its use of a contemplated data processing system for use by the NGBs,[219] the USOC could foster development by collecting information on the availability of training facilities in particular regions of the country. In this way, an amateur athlete might be able to secure necessary information concerning access to them. The USOC has also developed a successful national training center at Colorado Springs for athletes designated by NGBs and financially supported while at the center by the USOC, but has had difficulty in establishing regional centers.[220]

(10–11) Research and distribution of information

> . . . provide and coordinate technical information on physical training, equipment design, coaching, and performance analysis.[221]

> . . . encourage and support research, development, and dissemination of information in the areas of sports medicine and sports safety.[222]

Prompted by criticism from the PCOS, the USOC established the Sports Medicine Council to serve as a central depository for information on sports medicine and to provide continuing education on sports medicine to persons concerned with amateur athletic training.[223] The council has developed a highly sophisticated sports medicine program at its Sports Medicine Clinic and Research Center at Colorado Springs.[224] Its name belies its active involvement in testing and training young athletes.[225] The USOC also owns a Mobile Fitness Van, which is equipped for cardiovascular testing of athletes at their own training facilities. In the first year of the USOC's sports medicine program over seven hundred athletes from seventeen different sports were tested by members of the Sports Medicine Council.[226] As a USOC official explained, "[f]or the first time, the USOC has decided to rely on scientific evaluation in training rather than simply talent."[227] Although these measures have their origins before the Act, the latter nevertheless serves as a continuing impetus.

(12–14) Encouragement of women, the handicapped, and minorities

> . . . encourage and provide assisitance to amateur athletic activities for women.[228]

> . . . encourage and provide assistance to amateur athletic programs and competition for handicapped individuals, including, where feasible, the expansion of opportunities for meaningful participation for handicapped individuals in programs of athletic competition for able-bodied individuals.[229]

> . . . encourage and provide assistance to amateur athletes of racial and ethnic minorities for the purpose of eliciting the participation of such minorities in amateur athletic activities in which they are under-represented.[230]

The commitment to women athletes reflects the heightened global awareness of women as participants in all social processes. Since women in different sports face different specific problems, each individual NGB is required to initiate and execute its own program. The USOC admits to very little supervision or review of these programs.[231]

With regard to the handicapped, in 1978 the USOC organized the Handicapped In Sports Committee, which serves to represent the USOC in five nationally recognized organizations that conduct athletic competition for the handicapped. The USOC helps to underwrite travel and other costs for handicapped athletes who wish to participate in competitions like the Special Olympics. In 1981, the USOC evidenced the seriousness of its commitment to the handicapped by creating a special membership group for organizations that directly conduct a national program or a regular national competition for "individuals possessing physical or mental limitations which preclude participation in unrestricted athletic competition."[232]

As to minorities, some sports where they are underrepresented, such as figure skating and gymnastics, require expenditures at the world class level beyond the capacity of most. The USOC delegates to the NGBs its responsibility for developing programs to help promising young minority athletes to meet the expense of competing in those sports where they are underrepresented.[233]

CONCLUSION

The Amateur Sports Act of 1978, with the United States Olympic Committee as its chosen instrument, has met most expectations to provide a comprehensive structure for promoting and coordinating amateur athletic activity in the United States and for enhancing participation by United States amateurs in international competition. In order to pursue these aims, the Act has already eliminated most, though not all, of the jurisdictional blood feuds among amateur sports organizations that had seriously handicapped the performance of United States teams in the international arena.

The Act defines a simple governing structure for the robust new USOC that relies upon national governing bodies (NGBs), one for each sport in the Olympic and Pan-American Games. Other organizations and individuals supplement the decision-making structure. Detailed provisions in the Act address a range of troublesome issues, from eligibility of individual athletes for international competition to organizational review, complaint, and challenge procedures, subject in large part to binding arbitration. Although the exigencies of major international competition and its roster of sports are paramount, the Act, directly or indirectly, has the capacity to nurture the growth of all organized amateur athletic activity in the United States.

Despite this favorable climate, four clouds appear on the horizon of the 1980s. First, USOC governance of participation by U.S. nationals in the Olympic and Pan-American Games, ostensibly within its "exclusive jurisdiction," is uncertain. The open texture of that term exposes a latent ambiguity that ironically allows the USOC both to base decisions on considerations unrelated to sports and to be compelled to make such decisions, as the questionable boycott of the 1980 Games in Moscow confirmed. Even apart from blatant governmental intrusion into the exclusive jurisdiction of the USOC, the most serious social issues of the day may generate tensions within the USOC framework between the private and public, as well as national and international, characters of amateur athletic activities. Most acutely, the issue of the extent to which amateur athletics involving U.S. nationals ought to assist in implementing global human rights, even if it means nonparticipation, looms large on the horizon of the 1980s. As the rugby crises evidence, the USOC may become deeply engaged even when Olympic sports are not involved.

Second, because the NGBs are creatures of both the USOC and international federations and because the USOC is a creature of both the Olympic Movement and the 1978 Act, varying standards of organizational recognition, not entirely reconciled by the Act, may be dissonant. Thus, for example, a pesky dispute became a tug-of-war between two wrestling organizations for recognition as the appropriate NGB. On one side was one of the organizations, the USOC, federal courts, and an arbitral tribunal; on the other side was the other organization and the international wrestling federation.

Two other clouds, although somewhat wispy, cast shadows over the road to Mount Olympus. These are the allocation of USOC funds between elite and mass development, and financial support of amateur athletes by private sources and of amateur athletics by the government. Although the tension between elitist and nonelitist objectives of the Act is minimal today, it may intensify if school programs atrophy and thereby prompt budding sandlot athletes to seek more support from organizations within the USOC framework. Although limited financial support may well promote both elite and mass development, substantially greater support of individual athletes from private sources outside the USOC framework poses a possible threat to the integrity, quality, and appeal of amateurism. The question of public revenue for amateur athletics arises, despite a given traditional reliance on the private sector, as appeals are made for remuneration of host site expenses and for other specific projects. Fortunately, the Act seems to have invigorated private support as a fairly dependable alternative for amateur sports organizations. If the financial cloud is not yet gold-lined, it nevertheless appears to more silver-lined than before the Act.

Although amateur athletes, sports organizations, the government, and lawyers may view the 1978 Act differently, these clouds seem to be the most obvious on the horizon of the 1980s. The 1984 Games in Los Angeles will, in a sense, put both athletes and the Act to the test.

NOTES

The author is grateful for the research assistance of Conrad Hutterli.
1. 36 U.S.C. §§ 371–396 (Supp. III 1979) [hereinafter cited as the Act].
2. The tales of the swimmer, the two sprinters, and the basketball defeat

were repeated in the Congress and elsewhere as evidence of the need for reform. *See, e.g.,* 120 Cong. Rec. 15,896 (1974) (remarks of Sen. Pearson). On some unruly applications of the Olympic Rules in Munich, *see* Nafziger, *On the Rules of the Games,* Olympic Rev., No. 70–71, at 449 (1973).

3. The West Germans described the American delegation as the most arrogant and the worst led of all the delegations. The West German officials contrasted the American's behavior with the "gentility" of the Russians and East Germans. For example, the Russians treated the West German officials to a cocktail party complete with caviar and also presented the officials with gifts. N.Y. Times, Sept. 2, 1972, at 10, col. 1.

4. Further prowess of Soviet and East German teams in the 1976 Olympics deepened concern about the status of amateur athletic performance by U.S. teams. *See, e.g.,* N.Y. Times, July 11, 1976, § 5, at 15, col. 1; N.Y. Times, July 11, 1976, § 5, at 15, col. 2; N.Y. Times, July 11, 1976, § 5, at 15, col. 4; N.Y. Times, July 11, 1976, § 5 at 15, col. 6; N.Y. Times, July 30, at 16, col. 7; *How Russia wins Olympics—Why U.S. Falls Behind,* 80 U.S. News & World Rpt., June 28, 1976, at 56–57.

5. The USOC, a nongovernmental, national organ of the International Olympic Committee, was chartered by the Congress in 1950 with the responsibility for U.S. participation in the Olympic and Pan-American Games. 36 U.S.C. § 373(3) (1950). It is governed by its members through a House of Delegates. For a discussion of how the USOC's members are now represented in the House of Delegates, *see* text at notes 51–58, *infra.* Members of the House of Delegates elect the majority of the executive board. The board is charged with carrying out the "business, affairs and activities" of the USOC. USOC Const. art. XIV, §§ 1–2 (1981). The administrative committee oversees the day-to-day management of the USOC pursuant to the policy guidelines established by the executive board. USOC Const. art. XV, § 1 (1981).

6. N.Y. Times, Nov. 5, 1972, § 5 at 4, col. 3.

7. N.Y. Times, Nov. 6, 1972, at 40, col. 1.

8. *Id.*

9. N.Y. Times, Oct. 27, 1972, at 47, col. 4. *See* N.Y. Times, Oct. 28, 1972, at 24, col. 2.

10. Robert J. Kane, Cornell University official, opposed Phillip O. Krumm, retired Wisconsin businessman. Krumm had put together a coalition of independent National Governing Bodies to oppose candidates supported by the Amateur Athletic Union (AAU) and National Collegiate Athletic Association (NCAA). Kane was backed by the NCAA. Krumm won the election. N.Y. Times, Dec. 6, 1972, at 57, col. 2; N.Y. Times, Nov. 7, 1972, at 41, col. 4.

11. The Amateur Athletic Act of 1975, which failed in the Congress, provided for an independent federal agency, The Amateur Sports Board, which would have implemented several legislative objectives designed to rectify the problems that were becoming acute during the 1970s. *See* Comment, *Administration of Amateur Athletics: The Time for an Amateur Athlete's Bill of Rights Has Arrived,* 48 Fordham L. Rev. 53, 66–67 (1979).

12. N.Y. Times, June 20, 1975, at 15, col. 1. President Ford instructed the PCOS to find a way out of the "quagmire" of American amateur sport. *Id.*

13. President's Commission on Olympic Sports, The Final Report 1975–1977, Executive Summary, at 1 [hereinafter cited as PCOS Report].

14. The PCOS noted a variety of instances where athletes were hurt as a result of jurisdictional squabbles. *Id.* vol. 1, at 59–60.

15. For examples of the attitudes of some athletes as a result of the infighting and incompetence, *see* N.Y. Times, Nov. 18, 1972, at 46, col. 5; N.Y. Times, Aug. 11, 1974, § 5 at 1, col. 4. The PCOS Report gives an example of the kind of incident that undermined the confidence of U.S. amateur athletes in their administrators. In 1973, the U.S. cycling team was stranded in Barcelona, Spain, for four days while airplane tickets for the trip home were being arranged. When help finally arrived, there was money for the airplane tickets but not for the hotel bill. The team was advised to "leave inconspicuously." PCOS Report, *supra* note 13, vol. 2, at 41. A less comfortable fate befell a U.S. biathlon team member stranded in Minsk, Russia. *Id.* at 17. The commission concluded that many businessmen who might want to contribute were unwilling because of jurisdictional disputes and perceived managerial incompetence. *Id.* Executive Summary, at 3–4.

16. PCOS Report, *supra* note 13, Executive Summary, at 2.

17. Act, *supra* note 1, at § 103.

18. *Id.* at § 104.

19. Act, *supra* note 1, §§ 105–09. The corporate powers and obligations not specifically addressed in this study include the following:

§ 105 . . .
    (6) sue and be sued;
    (7) make contracts;
    (8) acquire, hold, and dispose of real and personal property as may be necessary for its corporate purposes;
    (9) accept gifts, legacies, and devices in furtherance of its corporate purposes;
    (10) borrow money to carry out its corporate purposes, issue notes, bonds, or other evidences of indebtedness therefor, and secure the same by mortgage, subject in each case to the laws of the United States or of any State;
    (11) provide financial assistance to any organization or association, other than a corporation organized for profit, in furtherance of the purposes of the Corporation;
    (12) approve and revoke membership in the Corporation;
    (13) adopt and alter a corporate seal;
    (14) establish and maintain offices for the conduct of the affairs of the Corporation;
    (15) publish a newspaper, magazine, or other publication consistent with its corporate purposes; and
    (16) do any and all acts and things necessary and proper to carry out the purposes of the Corporation.

§ 108. The Corporation shall have no power to issue capital stock or to engage in business for pecuniary profit or gain.

§ 109. The Corporation may acquire any or all of the assets of the existing unincorporated association, known as "The United States Olympic Association", upon discharging or satisfactorily providing for the payment and discharge of all the liabilities of such unincorporated association.

[Section 111 provides for corporate filing].

Also, the Act grants the USOC an exclusive right to the Olympic insignia, motto, and the words "Olympic," "Olympiad," and "Citius Altius Fortius." Act, *supra* note 1, § 110. Anyone who uses these trademarks and related symbol, emblem, and words without permission of the USOC is subject to civil liability under the Trademark Act of 1946. Prior to the Act, a criminal penalty was levied for unauthorized use of these trademarks. This penalty was unworkable as it required proof of criminal intent. H.R. REP. No. 95-1627, 95th Cong. 2nd Sess. (1978), *reprinted in* [1978] U.S. CODE CONG. & AD. NEWS 7478, 7488.

20. Act, *supra* note 1, at §§ 201–03. Also, § 106 spells out the requirements and procedures for formation of the USOC membership structure.

21. *Id.* at §§ 204–05.

22. *Id.* at § 206.

23. *Id.* at § 201(a).

24. *Id.* at § 103(6).

25. *Id.* at § 103(7).

26. *Id.* at § 103(3).

27. *Id.* at § 103(1).

28. *Id.* at § 103(5).

29. The USOC, each NGB, each international sports federation, and the IOC itself all have a hand in defining the phrase "amateur athlete."

30. Act, *supra* note 1, at § 104(1).

31. H.R. REP. No. 95-1627, 95th Cong., 2nd Sess., *reprinted in* [1978] U.S. CODE CONG. & AD. NEWS 7478, 7482, 7486.

32. Act, *supra* note 1, at § 103(1).

33. *Id.* at § 201(a).

34. *Id.* at § 103(1), § 201(a).

35. The Act suggests a broad scope in a number of sections. *E.g.*, at § 104(6) (encouragement of physical fitness and public participation in amateur sport); § 104(7) (development of amateur athletic programs); § 104(10) (provision of technical information on training and equipment); § 104(11) (encouragement of research in sports medicine); § 104(12) (encouragement of amateur athletics for women); § 104(13) (assistance in creating athletic programs for the handicapped); and § 104(14) (assistance to racial and ethnic minorities who are underrepresented in certain amateur sports).

36. Telephone interview between Conrad Hutterli and Ronald T. Rowan, In-House Counsel for the USOC (June 15, 1981) [hereinafter cited as Rowan interview].

37. The USOC has seventy-four salaried employees. Twenty-one of these work to direct and maintain the Olympic Training Center. For the 1976–80 Olympiad the USOC had a $49 million budget. USOC, Report to the President of the United States to the President of the Senate to the Speaker of the House for the Calendar Year 1980, at 3 (June 1, 1981) [hereinafter cited as 1980 USOC Report].

38. USOC Const. art. IV, § 4(a) (1981). This provision in the USOC Constitution is required by the International Olympic Committee [IOC]. Olympic Charter rule 24(D) (1980).

39. *But see* discussion, text at note 134, *infra*, of USOC's relationship with non–Olympic/Pan-American sports competition where it affects principal functions and responsibilities of the USOC.

40. USOC Const. art. IV, § 6(a) (1981).

41. *Id.* at appendix (1981).

42. The AAU is one of the oldest members of the USOC and one of the strongest; it had been the NGB in a large number of sports. *See* PCOS Report, *supra* note 13, vol. 2, at 277. Such Group C members are allotted one vote. USOC Const. art. IV, § 6(b) (1981).

43. Act, *supra* note 1, at § 206.

44. *See*, S. REP. No. 93-380, 93d Cong., 1st Sess. 2 (1973).

45. Act, *supra* note 1, at § 104(2).

46. Hearing on S. 2727 before the Senate Committee on Commerce, 2nd Sess. 178–79 (1977) (statements of Philip Brown and Sen. Stevens) [hereinafter cited as Hearings].

47. PCOS Report, *supra* note 13, vol. 2, at 404–06.

48. *Id.* at 406. For example, a group like the Daughters of the American Revolution could have been a Group F member of the USOC.

49. *Id.* at 407.

50. *Id.* at 406–407.

51. Act, *supra* note 1, at § 106.

52. USOC Const. art. IV § 4(a) (1981). The NGBs are allwed two-thirds of the vote in the House of Delegates when constitutional amendments are being considered. *Id.* at § 4(d).

53. *Id.*

54. *Id.* at §§ 4(a), 5(a), 6(a), 7(a), 8(a).

55. *Id.* at § 4(d).

56. *Id.* at § 5(b).

57. *Id.* at §§ 6(b), 8(b).

58. *Id.* at § 7(c).

59. USOC Const., appendix (1981).

60. Act, *supra* note 1, § 201(b)9.

61. Address by Michael Scott, counsel to NCAA, Syracuse University (Sept. 19, 1980) [hereinafter cited as Scott address]:

> As private bodies, NGBs have historically been responsible to their respective parent international sport federations. Efforts over the years in this country to subject their often arbitrary conduct to judicial scrutiny have been singularly unsuccessful. Challenges to NGB conduct on a "due process" or "equal protection" theory have been unavailing . . . attempts to apply the anti-trust laws have normally foundered . . . . So, in effect, these NGBs have been permitted to operate over the years in this country as unregulated mini-monopolies, free to use their enormous power over athletes and others in their domain without regard for substantive or procedural fairness.

62. S. REP. No. 89-753, 89th Cong., 1st Sess. 7 (1965).

63. The crux of the NCAA's argument can be demonstrated by comparing the financial commitment being made by The Wrestling Division of the AAU (WD-AAU) with that of NCAA members. PCOS reported that the WD-AAU spent about $62,696 annually for "competition." PCOS Report, *supra* note 13, vol. 2, at 293. In 1975, the NCAA-member host of the NCAA wrestling championships spent $93,054 on that event alone. *Id.* at 347. The NCAA's position is that its members, given the large financial commitments they have made in many Olympic and Pan-American sports, deserve highly placed representation in the NGBs that oversee these sports.

64. *Id.*, vol. 1, at 47–48. One of the organizations, the United States Track and Field Federation, explained its opposition to AAU leadership in the following manner: "The AAU has no track facilities of its own, few meets of its own, few athletes who are not already recruited and trained through the school system, and almost no coaches except those involved with educational institutions. The AAU has just a piece of paper—its international franchise." *Id.*, vol. 2, at 227.

65. *Id.*, vol. 2, at 400. The Olympic House coalition agreement, the

MacArthur arbitration decision, and the Kheel Commission were all unsuccessful attempts in the 1960s to reconcile the AAU and the NCAA and to prevent jurisdictional struggles from preventing U.S. athletes from competing. *See generally*, Moore, *The Campaign for Athletes' Rights*, 445 ANNALS 59 (Sept. 1979).

66. PCOS Report, *supra* note 13, vol. I, at 47.

67. Act, *supra* note 1, § 201(b).

68. PCOS Report, *supra* note 13, Executive Summary, at 2. The PCOS also recommended that an organization could have more than 20 percent of an NGB's votes in only one NGB. *Id.* vol. 1, at 235. This proposal, removed from the Act in the Senate Commerce Committee, was designed to prevent large multisport organizations from taking over a number of NGBs. Hearings, *supra* note 46, at 165 (statement of Sen. Stone). If Congress had included the provision, it would have enhanced the "single sport" concept by making it more difficult for one organization to corral effective control over a group of NGBs. The failure to approve this provision is not crucial to the success of the Act, because there are many organizations that sponsor competition in more than one sport. It is therefore unlikely that one organization could dominate a large number of NGBs (*e.g.*, there are twelve Group B members of the USOC that by definition must conduct competition in more than one Olympic or Pan-American sport).

69. Act, *supra* note 1, at § 201(c)(1).

70. *Id.* at § 201(c)(1), A and B.

71. *Id.* at § 201(c)(1)C.

72. Primarily in sports originally governed by committees of the AAU, for example, track and field.

73. *See also* discussion of the new USOC structure in the House of Delegates, text at notes 51–60, *supra*.

74. In 1974, the NFSHSA reported that 897,189 high school athletes participated in track and field. In 1973, the NCAA reported that 20,579 college athletes participated in its members' track and field programs. PCOS Report, *supra* note 13, vol. 2, at 230.

75. Both the NCAA and the NFSHSA belonged to the U.S. Track and Field Federation, which was organized to unseat the Athletics Division of the AAU as the track-and-field NGB. *Id.* at 225.

76. The Athletes Congress of the U.S.A., 1981 Directory, at 6, 21–23.

77. The exception is the case of the disputed position of the wrestling NGB. *See* text at notes 194–201.

78. This is particularly noteworthy with respect to track and field and aquatics, traditionally the AAU's strongest sports. This harmony may be ruptured if the NCAA and other organizations become dissatisfied with the openness of the reorganized NGBs. The NCAA expects a "thoroughgoing and enlightened reevaluation of the composition of several NGB Boards." Scott address, *supra* note 61.

79. Act, *supra* note 1, at § 104(3).

80. *Id.* at § 105(a) 1–5.

81. *Id.* at § 202(4).

82. *Id.* at § 203(1).

83. *Id.* at § 203(6),(7).

84. Eleven states substantially restrict nonschool participation during the school year and would probably not permit an athlete to participate in a USOC-sponsored development program. Telephone interview with Warren Brown, Assistant Director of NFSHSA (June 11, 1981).

85. NFSHSA, 1980–81 Handbook, at 48–49.

86. Act, *supra* note 1, at § 104(3).

87. For a discussion of the various actors involved in hosting the Olympic Games, *see* Galante, *The Olympic Games: Legal Hurdles and Lawsuits,* 4 L.A. Law 19 (June 1981).

88. Olympic Charter Rule 47 (1980). The USOC has greater authority over the upcoming Los Angeles Olympics than it has had in the past. At the Lake Placid Olympics, the USOC served a "liaison and coordination" role but was never part of the "day-to-day planning and supervision of operations." The USOC has five representatives on the Los Angeles Olympic Organizing Committee (LAOOC) and 25 percent of the members of the LAOOC board of directors. The USOC therefore has effective veto power over the organization of the Los Angeles games. 1980 USOC Report, *supra* note 37, at 6–7.

89. Act, *supra* note 1, at § 107.

90. *See* Nafziger, *Legal Aspects of a United States Foreign Sports Policy,* 8 Vand. J. Transnat'l L. 837, 841–45 (1975). In 1980, a member of a team selected by the Taiwanese National Olympic Committee brought a civil action to enjoin the local Organizing Committee of the 1980 Winter Olympic Games in Lake Placid to use the flag, emblem, name, and anthem of the Republic of China and, in effect, to allow the Taiwanese to participate in the Games. The opinion of the Court of Appeals of New York, affirming the decision of a lower court to refrain from exercising jurisdiction to resolve the dispute, reads as follows:

> PER CURIAM:
>   In view of the statement of interest submitted by the Attorney General of the United States on behalf of the Department of State pursuant to section 517 of title 28 of the U.S. Code, we are persuaded that the courts of our State must refrain from the exercise of jurisdiction to resolve a dispute which has at its core the international "Two Chinas" problem.
>   Accordingly, the order of the Appellate Division should be affirmed, without costs.

Ren-Guey v. Lake Placid 1980 Olympic Games, Inc., 49 N.Y.2d 771, 403 N.E.2d 1978 (1980).

91. *Id.* at 845–55; Nafziger, *The Regulation of Transnational Sports Competition: Down from Mount Olympus,* 5 Vand. J. Transnat'l L. 180, 199–206 (1971), *reprinted in* B. Lowe, D. Kanin, & A. Strenk, Sports and International Relations 160 (1978); Nafziger & Strenk, *The Political Uses and Abuses of Sports,* 10 Conn. L. Rev. 259 (1978).

92. Act, *supra* note 1, at § 113.

93. *Id.* at § 112.

94. *See* Nafziger, *Diplomatic Fun and the Games: A Commentary on the United States Boycott of the 1980 Summer Olympics,* 17 Willamette L. Rev. 67 (1980) [hereinafter cited as Diplomatic Fun].

95. *See* DeFrantz v. USOC, 492 F. Supp. 1181, 1184–85 (1980). For a bizarre interpretation of international law to justify the president's action, "that a host-state for the Games was under a duty not to invade another nation," see Address by Lloyd N. Cutler, Counsel to the President, 74 Proc. of the Am. Soc. Int'l L. 43 (1980); *contra,* Remarks of Alfred Rubin, *id.* at 274. *See also* Diplomatic Fun, *supra* note 94, at 79. *Inter alia,* "the President apparently contemplated involving the sanctions of the Interna-

tional Emergency Economic Powers Act." 492 F. Supp. 1181. For a brief discussion of this questionable legal technique for inducing compliance, as well as that of the Export Administration Act of 1979, *see* Diplomatic Fun, *supra* note 94, at 79.

96. H. R. Con. Res. 249, 96th Cong. 2nd Sess. (1980).

97. The USOC Charter appears in Chapter 36 of the United States Code, dealing with "patriotic" societies recognized and incorporated by the Congress.

98. 492 F. Supp. 1181 (1980). The plaintiffs stated three causes of action in their complaint: that the USOC violated the 1978 Act, that it engaged in unconstitutional state action, and that it violated is own constitution, by-laws, and governing statute.

With respect to the statutory claim that the defendant violated the 1978 Act, the plaintiffs claimed as follows:

> a. Defendant exercised a power it does not have—to decide that no United States amateur athletes shall participate in the 1980 Games.
> b. Defendant breached a duty to organize, finance and control participation in the events and competitions of the Olympic Games by United States athletes.
> c. Defendant denied to United States amateur athletes the opportunity to compete in these Games on a basis other than their want of athletic merit, or for a sports related reason.
> d. Defendant yielded its exclusive jurisdiction over Olympic matters to the political leaders of the nation.
> e. Defendant acted in a political manner.
> f. Defendant yielded its autonomy and has succumbed to political and economic pressure.

Id. at 1185.

99. *Id.* at 1190–91. *See generally* Comment, *supra* note 11.

100. *Id.* at 1193.

101. 365 U.S. 715, 725 (1961).

102. 492 F. Supp. 1181, 1193 (1980).

103. *Id.*

104. *Id.*

105. *Id.* at 1194.

106. *Id.*

107. Although the court's preliminary conclusion on state action seems incorrect, its determination that the plaintiffs had no constitutionally protected right to compete seems more reasonable. The USOC's boycott of the Moscow Olympics, while it was a bitter pill for the participants, did not preclude the athletes from engaging in other competition. In other words, even if the court had found a constitutionally protected "liberty" or "property" interest in competition, it is unlikely that the boycott was at a level of constitutional concern to create an actionable violation of due process or equal protection. *See* Board of Regents v. Roth, 408 U.S. 564 (1972). In Roth, the Court held that "[i]t stretches the concept too far to suggest that a person is deprived of 'liberty' when he simply is not rehired in one job but remains free as before to seek another." *Id.* at 575. If the Court, the ultimate arbiter, was unwilling to recognize a liberty interest in Roth where the interest was employment, it is unlikely that it would hold that the USOC could not bar U.S. athletes from attending one competition, even if that competition was the Olympics.

108. *Id.* at 1195.

109. *Id.* at 1193, under the principle in *Burton v. Wilmington Parking Authority*, 365 U.S. 715, 725 (1961).

110. *See, e.g.*, Howard Univ. v. NCAA, 510 F.2d 213 (D.C. Cir. 1975); Wright v. Arkansas Activities Assoc., 501 F.2d 25 (8th Cir. 1974); Assoc. Students, Inc. v. NCAA, 493 F.2d 1251 (9th Cir. 1974); Mitchell v. Louisiana High School Assoc., 430 F.2d 1155 (5th Cir. 1970). It is important to note that not all of these cases involved racial discrimination. The *De Frantz* court consequently erred in declaring that state action had been found in NCAA activities only in cases of alleged racial discrimination. Williams v. Hamilton, 497 F.Supp. 641, 644 (D.N.H. 1980), stated the following reasons why state action had been found in NCAA activities: Fifty percent of the NCAA's members are state or federally supported, the vast majority of the NCAA's capital is provided by public schools, the public schools dominate policy-making, and the NCAA extensively regulates and supervises its member schools. It is arguable that some NGBs include and are dominated by public organizations like the NCAA, the military, or state high school associations. These organizations provide the NGBs with membership and sanctioning fees. The NGBs in turn scrutinize and control the international amateur sports activities of these members. Consequently, the NGBs, like the NCAA, could be seen as state actors.

111. 492 F. Supp. 1181, 1192 (1980).

112. *Id.* at 1192, n. 23.

113. USOC, *Olympic Focus on Lausanne*, Olympic Rev., No. 151, at 228 (1980).

114. Act, *supra* note 1, § 104(3).

115. *Id.* at § 104(4).

116. The comments of Senator Long and Congressman Kemp in support of the proposed Amateur Athletic Act reflect the concern and wounded pride of many Americans. Senator Long was "sick and tired" of seeing "America beaten" and declared that such humiliation should not be visited on the "richest nation on earth." 120 CONG. REC. 22,459 (1974). Congressman Kemp argued that while people in this country may understand the reasons behind its amateur athletic shortcomings, these were unclear to our "Indonesian, Kenyan, or Venezuelan friends" vis-à-vis the Soviets. 120 CONG. REC. 15,753 (1974).

117. The Congress chose not to make the USOC an agency of the federal government and refused to appropriate money to support the operating budget of the USOC. Instead, it focused on the USOC's organizational structure and procedures. The Congress did not believe that the USOC needed federal money or management to be successful; rather, it simply needed to be reorganized. H.R. REP. No. 95-1627, 95th Cong., 2nd Sess. (1978), *reprinted in* [1978] U.S. CODE CONG. & AD. NEWS 7478; 7483–86, 7491, 7498–99, 7501–04.

118. Act, *supra* note 1, at § 104(5).

119. PCOS Report *supra* note 13, vol. 1, at 59–61.

120. *Id.* vol. 2, at 443.

121. Act, *supra* note 1, at § 202(b).

122. The operating phrase is "[i]f an (NGB) does *not determine* by clear and convincing evidence that holding an international amateur athletic competition would be detrimental to the best interest of the sport, the (NGB) shall promptly grant . . . a sanction" (emphasis added). Act, *supra* note 1, at § 202(b). The NGB must produce the "clear and convincing" evidence of the detrimental impact. *Id.*

123. *E.g.*, the WD-AAU recently refused to allow Oregon State University wrestlers to compete against South African wrestlers. Statesman-Journal (Salem, Or.), July 21, 1981, § D, at 1, col. 5. The current circumstances of athletic apartheid have been summarized as follows:

> Sport, in the forefront of change due to foreign pressures, continues to be a sensitive subject. The government has lifted all the legal restrictions against multiracial sport, and blacks are now playing on some South African international teams. But at the club level integration remains discretionary and a huge row broke out recently when a white Pretoria high school fielded two black boys on its rugby team.

de St. Jorre, *South Africa: Is Change Coming?* 60 FOR. AFF. 87, 108 (1981); *cf.* Tyler, *South Africans Told To Ignore Race Laws On The Playing Field*, Christian Sci. Monitor, Oct. 16, 1981, at 13, col. 3.

124. Act, *supra* note 1, §§ 205(a)(1), (c).

125. *Id.* at § 202(b).

126. *Id.* at § 205(b).

127. *Id.* at § 203(4).

128. *Id.* at § 103(5).

129. H.R. REP. No. 95-1627, 95th Cong., 2nd Sess., *reprinted in* [1978] U.S. CODE CONG. & AD. NEWS 7478, 7487.

130. *Id.*

131. Telephone interview between Conrad Hutterli and Tom McGrath, Asst. Dir., ABAUSA (July 2, 1981).

132. Act, *supra* note 1, §§ 204, 205(a)1.

133. *Id.* at § 201(a). The USOC under the Act may appoint NGBs in only Olympic and Pan-American sports. The Act therefore does not provide for sanctioning non–Olympic or Pan-American sports.

134. Kilborn, *Storm brewing over South African Rugby team's U.S. tour*, Christian Sci. Monitor, Aug. 10, 1981, at 13, col. 1; *Soviets to use rugby tour as ammo against LA Games*, Statesman-Journal (Salem, Or.), Sept. 12, 1981, at 2D, col. 2. On the importance to U.S. amateurs of staging the Games in Los Angeles, *see* Eldridge, *An Olympian peers at 1984 games and perceives 'winners' everywhere*, Christian Sci. Monitor, Aug. 10, 1981, at 16, col. 1.

135. Act, *supra* note 1, at § 202(a)2.

136. Hearings, *supra* note 45, at 179 (statement of Mr. Neinas).

137. *Id.* at 179–82.

138. Act, *supra* note 1, at § 202(a)2.

139. *Id.* at § 201(b)12.

140. PCOS Report, *supra* note 13, vol. 1, at 85, 88.

141. *Id.*

142. *Id.* at 69–70.

143. *E.g.*, fencers generally do not reach their peak until well after the normal eighteen to twenty-two collegiate age bracket, but there are very few postcollegiate programs in the United States. Hockey players frequently have to give up their sport at age eighteen or nineteen because of the lack of any organized program. Nearly 85 percent of the 11,000 teams registered with the hockey NGB are for boys under fifteen. *Id.* vol. 2, at 67 and 109–10.

144. 1980 USOC Report, *supra* note 37, at 1–2.

145. *Id.*

146. N.Y. Times, Feb. 24, 1978, at 22, col. 4.

147. *Id.*
148. Olympic Charter Bye-laws § VII(A)2b (1980).
149. 1980 USOC Report, *supra* note 37, at 2.
150. Yerkey, *Amateur athletes and the forbidden fruit-money*, Christian Sci. Monitor, Sept. 3, 1981, at 2, col. 2.
151. Athletes involved in these programs seem to be enthusiastic about them. N.Y. Times, Feb. 24, 1978, at 22, col. 4. There are critics who favor a nonelitist approach to athletics and would oppose cradle-to-grave nurturing of world class athletes. *See, e.g.,* Lipsyte, *Varsity Syndrome: The Unkindest Cut,* 445 ANNALS 15 (Sept. 1979).
152. Act, *supra* note 1, § 104(6).
153. Rowan interview, *supra* note 36.
154. 1980 USOC Report, *supra* note 37, at 4. *See* text at notes 181–82, *infra.*
155. United States Swimming, The Best the World has to Offer (no date) (brochure explaining the organizations and nature of the new aquatics NGB).
156. For example, if more pool time is devoted to training and competition, there obviously is less time for noncompetitive swimmers to use a pool for improving their physical fitness. For a view of a national program that is very successful in terms of developing elite athletes but is delinquent in providing athletic facilities for the masses, *cf.* commentary on Soviet athletics, N.Y. Times, July 11, 1976, § V, at 15, col. 2; Willis, *Moscow amasses medals but sport's not for masses,* Christian Sci. Monitor, Aug. 12, 1980, at 3, col. 1.
157. Act, *supra* note 1, at § 104(7).
158. *See,* text at notes 32–38, *supra.*
159. PCOS Report, *supra* note 13, vol. 1, at 3–4.
160. *Id.*
161. The USOC's projected revenue for the four years of the 1976 Olympiad was $12.6 million. *Id.* vol. 2, at 422.
162. Act of Oct. 18, 1978, § 113, 36 U.S.C. § 384 (1978). The Act itself does not provide for any funding; a separate provision authorizing $16 million for the USOC was passed as part of a larger appropriation package.
163. The original $16 million appropriation was to be released to the USOC in fiscal year 1980. In 1980 Congress did not include the $16 million in the budget. Senator Ted Stevens did manage to persuade the Congress to expend $4 million immediately and $6 million in matching funds to be disbursed by the Secretary of Commerce. Act of July 8, 1980, Pub. L. No. 96-304, § 203, 94 Stat. 898. The USOC maintains that the $10 million appropriated in 1980 had nothing to do with the Amateur Sports Act but was emergency money the Congress approved to cover loans the USOC had taken out to finance U.S. participation in the Moscow Olympics. *See* 1980 USOC Report, *supra* note 37, at 3.
164. The government finds it easier to justify reimbursing the USOC and related organizations for hosting international competition in this country than to provide federal funds more broadly to develop amateur athletics. The Department of Commerce, for example, was able to slip the Olympic Winter Games Authorization Act, which made federal money available for the Lake Placid Olympics, into a program administered by the Economic Development Administration, because Lake Placid is in a depressed area. Commerce was uncomfortable, however, with an appropriation to "finance the development and operation of programs to assist in

the restructuring of amateur sports" because it has no similar program to which the appropriation could be tied. Letter from C. L. Haslam, Gen. Counsel of U.S. Dept. of Com. to Hon. Peter W. Rodino, Chairman of the House Committee on the Jud. (June 20, 1978), *reprinted in* [1978] U.S. CODE CONG. & AD. NEWS 7478, 7497–98. After the tremendous expense associated with the Munich, Montreal, and Lake Placid Olympics, city governments are reluctant to sponsor the Olympic Games. Galante, *The Olympic Games: Legal Hurdles and Lawsuits,* 4 L.A. LAW 19, 20, 28 (June 1981). Congressmen have also become less willing to allow the federal government to become the sugar daddy for money necessary to hold Olympic Games. *See, e.g.,* N.Y. Times, Sept. 16, 1972, at 14, col. 3. *See also* N.Y. Times, April 4, 1976, § V, at 2, col. 1. After Denver withdrew its bid to host the 1976 Winter Olympics, the USOC changed its procedures for determining potential U.S. Olympic sites. The new procedures require the potential host city to show that substantial funding and facilities already exist and to present the USOC with surveys showing public support in the city. N.Y. Times, July 15, 1973, § V, at 1, col. 5.

165. USOC, Financial Statements and Supplemental Schedules for the Year and Four Year Period Ended December 31, 1980 and Auditor's Opinion (June 1, 1981) [hereinafter cited as 1980 Audit].

166. *Id.*

167. N.Y. Times, Aug. 14, 1977, § V, at 4, col. 1.

168. N.Y. Times, Aug. 11, 1974, § V, at 5, col. 2.

169. Wall St. J., April 13, 1979, at 1, col. 1.

170. I.R.C. § 501(c)3, *as amended.* The denial of relief to organizations that provide athletic facilities or equipment is intended to exclude "organizations which, like social clubs, provide facilities for their members. This provision is not intended to adversely affect the qualifications for charitable tax exempt status or tax deductible contributions of any organization which would qualify under the standards of the existing law." [1981] 815 STAND. FED. TAX REP. (CCH) ¶3001. The Tax Court has held that an amateur baseball league can be granted tax-exempt status. Hutchinson Baseball Enterprises, Inc. v. Comm'r, 73 T.C. 144 (1979). For other pertinent decisions, *see* Rev. Rul. 365, 1977–2 C.B. 192 (tax-exempt status granted to a nonprofit organization which held clinics, workshops, lessons, and seminars on popular amateur sports); Rev. Rul. 2, 1965–1 C.B. 227; Rev. Rul. 215, 1980–32 I.R.B. 9 (tax-exempt status granted to an organization designed to develop, promote, and regulate an amateur sports league for children.)

171. Statesman-Journal (Salem, Or.), Sept. 11, 1981, at C-1, col. 1.

172. In 1971–72, the NCAA's 663 members had over 5,300 full-time coaches, $1.5 billion in facilities, and a total annual operating budget of $535 million, of which $154 million went for athletic scholarships. PCOS, *supra* note 13, vol. 2, at 331. The statistic on NFSHSA members is even more impressive. Over 20,000 high schools are members of the NFSHSA, and their programs involve over three million athletes. *Id.* at 359.

173. *E.g.,* the NCAA maintains that there is not a single college track and field program in the country that does not lose money. Hearings, *supra* note 46, at 160–61 (remarks of Mr. Byers). Football and ice hockey are the only sports that make money; basketball breaks even. *Id.*

174. PCOS Report, *supra* note 13, vol. 1, at 70.

175. Six criteria were used to determine how much development money an NGB should receive. The criteria were medal production, world rank,

participation (number of amateur athletes engaged in the sport), NGB activities (that is, the activity level of the NGB—for example, how many training clinics does the NGB hold?), team size (number of athletes on an Olympic team), and public interest (popularity of the sport in the United States). These criteria were weighted as follows:

Medal Production	15%
World Rank	27%
Participation	20%
NGB Activities	13%
Team Size	10%
Public Interest	15%

Id. vol. 2, at 423.

176. *Id.* at 425.

177. *Id.* at 422.

178. USOC Const. By-Laws, ch. XVI, § 7 (1980).

179. 1980 Audit, *supra* note 165.

180. PCOS Report, *supra* note 13, vol. 2, at 422.

181. USOC, The Olympic Games, at 9 (1979); Atkin, *U.S. festival emerges as showcase for Olympic hopefuls,* Christian Sci. Monitor, July 31, 1981, at 14, col. 1.

182. PCOS Report, *supra* note 13, vol. 2, at 5, 76, 109, 201.

183. Act, *supra* note 1, at § 104(8).

184. *Id.* at § 114.

185. *Id.* at § 201(b).

186. *Id.* at § 205(a).

187. *Id.* at § 205(c).

188. Rowan interview, *supra* note 36.

189. Act, *supra* note 1, at § 205(b).

190. *Id.* at § 205(b)4.

191. *Id.* at § 205(b)5.

192. *Id.* at § 205(c).

193. *Done* June 10, 1958, 21 U.S.T. 2517, T.I.A.S. No. 6997, 330 U.N.T.S. 3.

194. *See* United States Wrestling Fed'n v. USOC, No. 13460-78, Findings of Fact, at 6 (Super. Ct. D.C., April 19, 1979). [Hereinafter cited as D.C. Decision.]

195. Olympic Charter Bye-laws, § V(5) (1980).

196. *See* D.C. Decision, *supra* note 194.

197. *Id.* at 7.

198. For a reference to this decision, upholding it on other issues, *see* United States Wrestling Fed'n v. Wrestling Div. of the AAU, Inc., 605 F.2d 313, 315 (7th Cir. 1979).

199. D.C. Decision, *supra* note 194, at 8–9.

200. *See* 1980 USOC Report, *supra* note 37, at 8–9.

201. USWF's, Statement of Position, at § VI (undated release explaining the USWF's position in the USWF–WD-AAU conflict. FILA did not respond to the author's request for information concerning its decision).

202. Act of July 8, 1980, Pub. L. No. 96-304, § 203, 94 Stat. 898.

203. United States Wrestling Fed'n v. Wrestling Div. of the Amateur Athletic Union, Inc., No. C80-1322 (N.D. Ohio 1980).

204. Olympic Charter Bye-laws, § V(5) (1980).

205. Act, *supra* note 1, § 204.

206. PCOS Report, *supra* note 13, vol. 1, at 139–40. *See also* Comment, note 11.

207. Act, *supra* note 1, §§ 201(b)(6), 202(a)(5). On the legislative history, *see* Hearings, *supra* note 46, at 159–61 (statement of Mr. Byers).

208. USOC Const. art. IX (1981).

209. High school and college associations have exclusive jurisdiction over their "restricted competition." Act, *supra* note 1, § 206. By its broad language in § 206, the Congress ignored the PCOS recommendations that would have explicitly limited the ability of an amateur sports organization to prevent an athlete from reentering its restricted competition after participating in unrestricted competition. PCOS Report, *supra* note 13, vol. 1, at 139–40.

210. *See* text at notes 63, 172–73, *supra.*

211. These fears are expressed in the NFSHSA's explanation of its model rules for nonschool participation. NFSHSA, 1980–81 Handbook, at 39–45 (1980).

212. As the AAU did for its track and field meet with China. Hearings, *supra* note 46, at 179.

213. Three years before the Act, Houston McTear, then a promising high school student unable to travel without a chaperone, was unable to compete in the 1975 AAU National Championships because the AAU failed to send enough money for McTear's coach to accompany him. Neither McTear nor his high school could fund travel to the championships for McTear's coach. The travel expense policy of the Athletics Division of the AAU failed to anticipate that a 100-yard dash star might be a minor requiring a chaperone. N.Y. Times, June 20, 1975, at 16, col. 6.

214. USOC Const. art IX, § 1 (1981).

215. Act, *supra* note 1, § 103(5).

216. The USOC should be able to enforce the "opportunity to compete" in the context of competition relating to the Olympic or Pan-American Games because the Congress gave the USOC "exclusive jurisdiction" over U.S. participation in those games. *Id.* at § 104(3).

217. *Id.* at §§ 104(4).

218. *Id.* at § 104(9).

219. 1980 USOC Report, *supra* note 37, at 2.

220. 1980 USOC Report, *supra* note 37, at 5; Eldridge, *Olympic training site given big boast to US athletes,* Christian Sci. Monitor, Sept. 17, 1981, at 10, col. 1. The USOC established one regional center at Squaw Valley but had to close it during the fall of 1980 because of high operating costs.

221. Act, *supra* note 1, § 104(10).

222. *Id.* at § 104(11).

223. PCOS recommended that the USOC establish a sports medicine program. PCOS Report, *supra* note 13, vol. 1, at 123–25. The Sports Medicine Council is authorized in the USOC By-Laws. USOC Const. By-Laws, ch. XXVII, §§ 1, 2 (1981).

224. 1980 USOC Report, *supra* note 37, at 5.

225. The program is designed to "maximize the individual skills, techniques, health, and physiological parameters of our athletes." *Id.*

226. N.Y. Times, Oct. 4, 1977, at 45, col. 1.

227. *Id.* An example of the kind of work done by the center is the help American kayakers received. Even though American kayakers seem to be bigger and stronger than their European rivals, the Americans continued to have limited success in the sport. Computer analysis of European and

American teams revealed that the Americans were emphasizing their strokes in the wrong place and as a consequence were working harder and achieving less than their European counterparts. *Id.*

228. Act, *supra* note 1, § 104(12).

229. *Id.* at § 104(13).

230. *Id.* at § 104(14).

231. Letter from Ronald T. Rowan, In-House Counsel for the USOC (July 20, 1981).

232. USOC Const. art. V, § 8 (1981). The five current group E members are the American Athletic Association of the Deaf, the National Association of Sports for Cerebral Palsy, National Wheelchair Athletic Association, Special Olympics, Inc., and the U.S. Association for Blind Athletes. *Id.* at appendix.

233. *Supra* note 231.

[5]

The Regulation of Academic Standards in Intercollegiate Athletics

Ronald J. Waicukauski

Incidents of cheating have been periodic if not common occurrences in intercollegiate athletics almost since its inception in 1852, when Yale first met Harvard in a rowing contest on New Hampshire's Lake Winnipesaukee.[1] It was not then particularly surprising when Arizona State University declared eight of its football players ineligible in November 1979 because they had received credit for an extension course they did not attend.[2] There ensued, however, a rash of reports of violations at other universities, including New Mexico, Utah, Oregon, Oregon State, UCLA, and Southern California.[3] The result was a national scandal, the proportions of which, in the words of an official report of the University of Southern California, were "substantially larger and far less innocent"[4] than earlier scandals.

The recent scandal received extensive coverage in the national news media. *Newsweek*[5] and *Sports Illustrated*[6] published lengthy cover-page articles that were sharply critical of intercollegiate athletics. *Newsweek* quoted Indiana Basketball Coach Bobby Knight calling the situation "a monumental swamp"[7] and *Sports Illustrated* spoke of a "student-athlete hoax," concluding that college sports had become "an abomination to the ideals of higher education."[8] CBS News was equally critical in a "60 Minutes" segment that included an interview with a young man who, after four years of attending college and playing intercollegiate football, could neither read nor write.[9] These reports suggested that there is an epidemic of corruption in college sports involving a variety of legal, ethical, and rule violations. The focus of most of the criticism has been on the lack of academic integrity that allegedly pervades intercollegiate athletics. Specifically, the nation's colleges and universities were called to task for recruiting and admitting into their schools athletes who patently lacked the intellectual tools to succeed academically; forging and altering transcripts; giving credit for courses not attended; giving grades not warranted by the athlete's academic performance; channeling athletes into courses that are not meaningful;

161

and failing to provide the education or grant the degrees that the athletes were promised.

Historically, the nation's colleges and universities have relied primarily on action by individual institutions to correct abuses of this sort. In 1948, this reliance on institutional control was supplemented by a code of conduct adopted by the National Collegiate Athletic Association.[10] This code has evolved into an elaborate scheme of regulation designed in part to protect academic standards. Recently, courts have been asked to step in to recognize legal rights in pursuit of similar ends.[11] This article examines the regulatory scheme of the NCAA in light of the legal initiatives under way and the recent scandal, finds the scheme deficient in several respects, and proposes specific reforms to remedy the deficiencies.

I. THE REGULATORY SCHEME

The NCAA was formed in 1906 to regulate and supervise college athletics throughout the United States.[12] It is a voluntary association dedicated to the objective, as described in its first constitution, of maintaining athletic activities "on an ethical plane in keeping with the dignity and high purpose of education."[13] Almost all the major colleges and universities in the United States are members.[14] There are other national associations regulating intercollegiate sports, including the National Association of Intercollegiate Athletics (NAIA), composed of approximately 500 small four-year colleges and universities,[15] the National Junior College Athletic Association (NJCAA), with a membership of about 600 two-year colleges in its men's division,[16] and the Association of Intercollegiate Athletics for Women (AIAW), controlling women's sports for almost 800 colleges and universities.[17] The NCAA, however, is the oldest, wealthiest, and most powerful of the national associations, governing the largest, richest, and most popular sports programs in higher education.[18] Accordingly, it is regulation by the NCAA that is the focus of this inquiry.

Not all NCAA members engage in big-time college sports; the majority in fact do not.[19] To accommodate the differing sports interests and activities of its members, the NCAA is divided into three divisions:[20] Division I consists predominantly of universities supporting big-time programs, while Divisions II and III are composed of universities that maintain more modest programs.[21] NCAA regulations vary in some respects among these divisions. For example, Division II is more restrictive than Division I in the number of athletic grants-in-aid that may be awarded,[22] and Division III, unlike Divisions I and II, prohibits awarding financial aid to any student athlete except upon a showing of financial need.[23]

All divisions are subject to the principal NCAA rules governing academic standards in intercollegiate athletics. These rules are guided by the constitutionally prescribed "Fundamental Policy" of the association to maintain intercollegiate athletics "as an integral part of the educational program and the athlete as an integral part of the student body."[24] This policy is implemented initially through Article Three, Section 3 of the Constitution. This provision, entitled the "Principle of Sound Academic Standards," imposes four requirements for a student athlete to be eligible to represent his institution in intercollegiate athletic competition.[25] First, the student athlete must be admitted in accordance with the regular published entrance requirements of the institution. Second, he must be in good academic standing with the university in accordance with the standards applied to all students. Third, he must be enrolled in a minimum full-time program of studies. And fourth, he must be making satisfactory progress toward a degree.

These constitutional requirements are supplemented by provisions in the NCAA bylaws, designed to insure that college athletes are genuine students. Bylaw 5-1-(c) requires that an athlete be registered in a minimum of twelve hours of courses to be eligible to participate in an NCAA championship in any sport.[26] Bylaw 5-1-(j)-(2) adds that a freshman will not be eligible for Division I competition unless he has graduated from high school with a minimum 2.000 grade-point average on a 4.000 scale.[27] Student athletes transferring from a junior college to an NCAA institution are subject to a myriad of restrictions designed to insure that a minimal level of academic competence has been demonstrated before they may participate in NCAA competition.[28] Most notable among these restrictions is the recently enacted requirement that the athlete graduate from junior college to be eligible during his first year at a Division I institution if he did not achieve a 2.000 grade-point average in high school.[29]

Another recently enacted bylaw strengthens the constitutional requirement that a student athlete make satisfacory progress toward a degree by specifying that he complete twelve semester or quarter hours for each term he has been enrolled to remain eligible for competition after his freshman year. Academic standards are protected by the NCAA not only through these constitutional provisions and bylaws that have been adopted by the full NCAA membership at the annual NCAA convention but also through official interpretations adopted by the NCAA Council, the body that governs in the interim between conventions,[30] or by the president, secretary-treasurer, and executive director, in the interim between meetings of the council.[31] One such interpretation, Official Interpretation 8, seeking to avoid a repetition of the recent scandal, excludes the use of correspondence and extension courses taken from other institutions in determining "academic standing" or "satisfactory progress," rendering such courses useless for maintaining eligibility.[32]

In addition to these regulations that directly control academic standards, the NCAA has myriad other regulations having the purpose or effect of protecting academic standards in college sports. Article 3 of the NCAA bylaws limits playing and practice seasons in football, soccer, and basketball.[33] It also limits the number of games that may be played in these sports.[34] The effect of these limitations is to reduce the time some student athletes must spend away from studies.

Probably the most complex and detailed rules of the NCAA regulate recruiting. Among other things, these rules limit the financial aid or benefits that may be offered to an athlete, his relatives, or his friends as an inducement to attend a particular school.[35] Presumably, the athlete will then make his decision based on appropriate educational concerns rather than considerations unrelated to his educational goals. The rules provide that representatives of an institution may contact a student in person only three times at his high school and three times at sites away from the school.[36] An institution may finance only one visit to its campus for a given prospect, which may not exceed forty-eight hours.[37] Prospects are limited to making six paid visits to NCAA institutions.[38] No tryouts are permitted.[39] These restrictions all serve to reduce the disruption to the athlete's high school studies caused by the recruiting process.[40]

NCAA regulations exclude from eligibility in a sport any athlete who has received pay for participating in that sport.[41] Institutions may provide financial aid to a student athlete, but such aid is limited essentially to tuition and fees, room and board, and required course-related books.[42] The intent is to limit intercollegiate sports to genuine amateurs —students who participate in sport as an avocation.[43] Presumably, their principal activity is not athletics but getting an education.

In a similar vein, NCAA bylaws 5-1-(d) and 4-1 limit eligibility for a student athlete to four seasons of intercollegiate competition during five calendar years, beginning with the term in which he first registers.[44] Bylaw 5-1-(d)-(3) adds that participation in any organized competition in a sport during any twelve-month period after the student's twentieth birthday and prior to matriculation at an NCAA institution shall count as one year of competition.[45] The net result of these three provisions is to restrict NCAA competition to individuals who at least have certain credentials associated with real students—they are only temporarily engaged in the college sport (no more than four seasons in five years) and are relatively inexperienced, not having engaged in the organized sport for more than four years after reaching age twenty.

Considered collectively, these regulations present an extraordinary set of detailed requirements. Indeed, no other area of higher education

is as heavily controlled by extrainstitutional regulation as intercollegiate sports.[46] In addition to the regulations of the NCAA, which constitute the bulk of a 300-page manual, most universities are members of
athletic conferences that prescribe additional rules. For example, the
Big Ten Conference has an elaborate regulatory system, described in
a 163-page conference handbook, which is in many respects more strin-
gent than the NCAA.[47]

These NCAA and conference regulations are not mere window dressing, simply to be ignored; at least in some cases, institutions must follow them to the letter or risk substantial penalties. The NCAA has an
elaborate enforcement program, which in 1978 and 1979 was the subject of a congressional investigation, not because it was too weak, but
because it was, allegedly, too harsh and unfair.[48] The NCAA employs
a full-time staff of thirteen in its enforcement division, including eight
investigators.[49] This staff assists the NCAA Committee on Infractions
in developing information about violations of the NCAA's academic
and athletic standards.[50] If a violation is found, the Committee on Infractions is empowered to impose a variety of penalties ranging from
a private reprimand and censure to closing down an institution's intercollegiate sports program for a specified period.[51] The NCAA Council
has similar power, acting essentially in the capacity of an appellate tribunal.[52] The most severe penalty that the association can impose is to
expel a member; that action may only be taken by the full membership
at its annual convention.[53]

During its first twenty-five years in operation, from 1952 to 1977, the
NCAA enforcement machinery considered 993 cases and took disciplinary action in 548.[54] In most cases, the penalty was mild, but there are
numerous instances in which punitive action was substantial.[55] The
most severe was the penalty imposed in 1973 on the University of
Southwestern Louisiana for numerous willful violations of rules governing recruiting, financial aid, and admission requirements. For these
offenses, the university's basketball team was excluded from all competition for two years, all sports were placed on probation for four years,
and for that period, the university was denied voting and membership
privileges on NCAA committees.[56] The NCAA has strong enforcement
tools available and has demonstrated the will to use them.

The athletic conferences also have enforcement authority and are
using it. On August 11, 1980, The Pacific Ten Conference declared five
of its members ineligible for the league's 1980 football championship
and postseason games, including the Rose Bowl.[57] The penalties were
imposed for "violations of conference rules and standards in the areas
of unearned credits, falsified transcripts, and unwarranted intrusion of
athletic department interests into the academic process of the respective universities."[58] The Big Ten was recently enmeshed in a compli-

cated controversy with quarterback David Wilson and the University of Illinois. The crux of the dispute was that the conference was unwilling to soften its academic standards for the benefit of Wilson and, based on certain actions by Illinois personnel in handling the Wilson matter, believed that the university was not adequately dedicated "to conference principles which place academic standards ahead of athletic interests."[59] Accordingly, the conference placed the university on probation, prohibited its participation in postseason football contests for one year, and excluded it from sharing certain conference revenues, resulting in a loss to the university of an estimated $500,000.[60]

From this cursory review, it would appear that the regulatory scheme of the NCAA and its member conferences should be adequate to protect the academic integrity of intercollegiate sports. Regulations, supported by powerful enforcement machinery, purport to insure that the athletes who represent the nation's colleges are academically qualified to be genuine students and that they are successfully pursuing a full-time course of study toward a degree. The reality, though, is that they fail to achieve either objective.

II. REGULATING ADMISSIONS

The preponderance of the evidence available demonstrates that many institutions are enrolling athletes who are not academically qualified for college. Consider the case of the University of Southern California. Over the years it has won sixty-three NCAA team titles, far more than any other school, seventeen Rose Bowls, and eight national football championships.[61] At least some of these honors were achieved by athletes who were admitted to the university by the department of athletics. The USC admissions office was told by USC's former president, Dr. John Hubbard, "to keep hands off."[62] Between 1970 and 1980, the athletics department exercised its admission authority to enroll 330 students although academically they "fell below normal USC standards of admission."[63] It may be, as the late Red Smith, dean of American sportswriters, stated, that the cheating at USC has been "more widespread, more brazen, more cynical than elsewhere,"[64] but there appears little reason to believe that USC is unique in enrolling athletes unqualified to be students.

Some institutions have admitted athletes who were, at the time of admission, functionally illiterate. Fred Butler was an outstanding high school football player at Morningside High School in Englewood, California. He graduated 190th out of 355 students in his high school class and then went to El Camino Junior College, where he led the football team to a conference championship. He moved on to California State University at Los Angeles, where he completed the remaining years of his college athletic eligibility. At the time of his admission, and even after four years of attending college, Fred Butler could not read or write. He is unable even to read a menu in a restaurant but must rely on pictures or the assistance of a friend.[65]

Illiterate statements from student athletes in NCAA files demonstrate vividly that Fred Butler is not an isolated example.[66] Sports sociologist Harry Edwards estimates that 20 to 25 percent of black athletes at four-year colleges are functionally illiterate,[67] and, clearly, the problem of illiteracy is not restricted to blacks. The reason why universities seek to admit such students is obvious—to better compete on the athletic field and thereby reap the enormous rewards that now accrue to those who are successful in intercollegiate sports.[68] What is not so obvious is how such students are admitted consistent with NCAA regulations.

As outlined above, to be eligible for NCAA competition, a student athlete must have "been admitted in accordance with the regular published entrance requirements of that institution"[69] and if a freshman in Division I, must have accumulated a 2.000 high school grade-point average on a 4.000 scale.[70] In practice, these requirements have not proved to be a significant obstacle to the enrollment of academically deficient athletes. The requirement that athletes be admitted in accordance with regular published entrance requirements is of almost no force, for the simple reason that the "regular published entrance requirements" of most universities are sufficiently flexible so that persons with little or no academic ability may qualify. Even the extraordinary admission practices of the University of Southern California are probably in compliance since, as representatives of the university have explained, the athletes were enrolled under a special program designed for disadvantaged students who fail to meet the usual requirements for admission.[71] As it turned out, approximately 25 percent of USC's total undergraduate special admissions were scholarship athletes.[72] Other schools have also not hesitated to abuse similar programs to serve athletic ends.[73] The NCAA investigated one school in the Southwest and found that half the special admissions were scholarship athletes.[74] Stephen Morgan of the NCAA's enforcement division reported, "We've seen some academic records for athletes that were almost laughable. But when we approach the school, they say, 'we have no minimum standards.' "[75] Consequently, the NCAA has yet to find its first violation of the rule requiring application of regular published admission standards.[76]

The 2.000 Rule has more teeth but not many. If high school transcripts were accurate and if satisfactory grades in high school really meant that a student had demonstrated some academic competence, the rule would be meaningful; often, however, neither of these requisite conditions is met. Some high schools today "grant a 2.0 average if a warm body appears in class without slugging the teacher."[77] Even in those schools which maintain real standards for normal students, outstanding athletes who have the opportunity to receive an NCAA athlete grant-in-aid are often the recipients of gratuitous grades. The NCAA reports seeing transcripts of outstanding athletes who go into their final year of high school with a 1.7 average and, without attending class, receive a 3.0 average or better in their senior year to finish with the requisite 2.0.[78] If the teachers fail to "help the kid out" by inflating his grades, school administrators and athletic departments sometimes step in to falsify transcripts "so that young athletes turn up with A's and B's where they originally had D's and F's."[79] The result is that high school grades are now seldom a factor in schools with big-time sports.[80]

There are, of course, some athletes who are unable legitimately or illegitimately to obtain the requisite high school transcript with a 2.0 average and their name on it. For such athletes, the junior colleges offer a viable route to big-time college sports. Usually, a high school degree is not needed, and, once enrolled, the athlete can often achieve sufficient academic success to move on to a four-year NCAA institution without any real demonstration of academic competence. Witness the Fred Butler case; likewise, the case of David Wilson, the Illinois quarterback. Wilson was a nonqualifier in high school, having received a 1.81 grade-point average.[81] In junior college he accumulated a much improved 2.63 grade-point average, largely by virtue of excellent grades in basketball, raquetball, body development, weight training, and seven courses in football, which served to overshadow poor grades in such courses as reading and composition, philosophy, and American literature.[82] This academic performance fully satisfied NCAA requirements.

A few years ago NCAA requirements were somewhat tougher, at least for incoming freshmen. From 1966 to 1973, to be eligible a freshman had to "predict" an ability to maintain a 1.600 grade point average (C−) in college, based upon (1) high school grades or rank in class and (2) a score on a scholastic aptitude examination.[83] The rule was intended to accomplish three objectives: to reduce the possibility of exploiting young athletes by recruiting those who would likely be unable to meet the necessary academic requirements for a degree; to foster the concept that college sports are engaged in by athletes who were first and primarily students; and to encourage the student who could not meet the requirements of the rule to devote his full freshman year to study and not engage in athletics.[84] Notwithstanding such noble purposes, the rule proved too restrictive for the NCAA membership and was thrown out in 1973 in favor of the more relaxed 2.000 rule.[85] One effect of the change is that a substantial percentage of present major college athletes fail to meet even the relatively low 1.600 test.

In fairness, the problem of maintaining academic standards in admissions is not limited to athletes. With the advent in recent years of affirmative action programs, declining college enrollments, open admission policies, decreasing SAT scores, and increasing illiteracy among high school graduates, many young men and women are being admitted into college who are unequipped by training and intellect to do college-level work.[86] In a sense, the academic deficiencies of athletes are merely one part of a much larger problem afflicting higher education in America.[87] It is, however, a part with special attributes that may be analyzed and addressed separately.

The rewards for success in intercollegiate athletics to schools, coaches, and athletes present unique incentives for abusing the admissions process. That such abuses are occurring is clear. Universities may be admitting other poor students but athletes have on the average lower school records, test scores, and academic prediction at the time of admission than their nonathlete classmates.[88] Moreover, unlike most other students of limited academic ability, they are intensely recruited to attend college and awarded grants-in-aid for virtually all their college expenses. A regulatory response to athletic abuses of the admissions process has already begun with the existing NCAA rules. As written, however, in the circumstances of contemporary American education, they are inadequate. Perhaps a complete cure must await resolution of the broader issues in education, but more can and should be done to address directly the separable problem of bending admission standards for athletic purposes.

III. REGULATING ACADEMIC PERFORMANCE

Admission is just the first point in an athlete's college career at which the NCAA may seek to protect academic standards. Further opportunities are presented during the athlete's years of possible eligibility. As described above,[89] the NCAA Constitution and bylaws provide a variety of regulations that apply to this period and that are designed to insure that the athlete is performing satisfactorily as a student. Their success in achieving that goal is uncertain at best.

One potential measure of that success would be the percentage of athletes that graduate. If an athlete earns a degree, that is strong (though not conclusive) evidence that his academic performance was adequate and that he was a genuine student. Unfortunately, there are no good and comprehensive statistics about this basic fact. Various limited studies have been done that suggest that a large percentage of student athletes fail to graduate. For example, a study of the Southwest Conference indicates that only one-third of black athletes graduate, although approximately three-quarters of the white athletes do.[90] Harry

Edwards surveyed the graduation rate of black scholarship athletes at the University of California from 1971 to 1978 and found that "between 70% and 80% didn't graduate—even the ones who came to Berkeley with two years of junior college."[91] An older study at Michigan State University found that for students entering between 1960 and 1964, 82.3% of the white athletes and 46.5% of the black athletes had graduated by 1970.[92] A recent survey of professional athletes, the majority of whom participated in college athletics for four years, disclosed that 70% of professional basketball players do not have college degrees and 80% of football players coming into the NFL in 1981 had failed to earn college degrees.[93]

On May 1, 1981, the NCAA released a report of the largest study yet done on graduation rates of student athletes.[94] It indicates that of male athletes entering forty-six colleges in Fall 1975, 52 percent had graduated by spring 1980 (within five years) and that among the forty-six colleges the median graduation rate for athletes was 36.9 percent.[95] Another 13.5 percent of the athletes were still enrolled in their institutions, apparently continuing to pursue a degree.[96] The graduation rates for athletes in football (42.9 percent) and basketball (41.9 percent) were lower than in other sports.[97] Comparing these data with the graduation rate of nonathletes, the study reported that the athletes had done better: 52 percent graduating v. 41.5 percent.[98]

Although these data may be the most comprehensive yet produced, they must be interpreted with caution. Initially, two hundred institutions were randomly selected for the study; usable data were ultimately gathered from a less-than-random forty-six, or 23 percent.[99] No doubt, many of the institutions with the least impressive graduation rates were among those who failed to cooperate with the study. In addition, the study fails to disclose how many of these forty-six colleges engage in big-time intercollegiate competition and to what extent the final figures are affected by the success of athletes at Division II and III institutions, where it is generally recognized that the academic problems of athletes are less severe.

In any event, the finding that 52 percent of athletes graduate within five years is hardly comforting. It may exceed the graduation rate for nonathletes, but the comparison is not entirely apt, since nonathletes rarely receive full grants-in-aid for, effectively, their entire college career. In view of such aid, one would expect a substantially higher graduation rate for scholarship athletes in comparison with nonathletes, many of whom must drop out of school for lack of funds. A more revealing comparison would be between those athletes who compete in college sports for four years and scholarship nonathletes who attend college for four years. The relative dearth of respectable unbiased graduation rate data, combined with the lack of cooperation the NCAA has received in its efforts to survey the area, even though the data should be readily available in the files of NCAA institutions, suggests that for many schools the statistics are embarrassing.[100] Whatever the percentage, there are clearly a large number of college athletes, recruited with a promise of an education, who are not receiving degrees.

For many of these athletes, there may be no harm done as a result of this failure. For those few who go on to successful careers in professional sports, the absence of a degree may be no liability.[101] For others, the fact that they earned no degree may mean that they are no better off by virtue of their college athletic experience, but they are probably no worse off either. They are not likely to have fewer or poorer employment opportunities than would otherwise have been available to them. To the extent that participation in athletics may have obstructed educational opportunities by interfering with essential study time, inducing them to schedule useless courses, or removing incentives to learn by being assured of satisfactory grades regardless of performance, then they have been hurt, but the available evidence indicates generally no negative correlation between participation in athletics and the academic success of individual athletes.

The principal and pervasive harm resulting from the educational inadequacies of college athletes is to the integrity of our academic institutions. If athletes are not doing the work of genuine students, then a sham is being perpetrated. Institutions of higher education, which should be bastions of high ideals, are party to a hoax in which they are representing to the American public that the young men playing on their teams are real students, when the reality too often is that they are paid professional athletes, not remotely engaged in the full-time pursuit of scholarly objectives. The colleges and universities that contribute to this hoax may succeed on the playing field but are worthy of little respect in the community of scholars.

The NCAA has long sought to avoid such a hoax by mandating in its constitution that to remain eligible an athlete must be "maintaining satisfactory progress toward a baccalaureate or equivalent degree." Until recently, the determination of "satisfactory progress" was left solely to the individual institutions. As a result, athletes have not infrequently completed four years of eligibility, making "reasonable progress" in each year as defined by the institution, and yet, when their eligibility is exhausted, remain far short of a degree.[102] There is usually no problem with the athlete registering for that requisite twelve hours each term that bylaw 5-1-(c) requires. Completing those courses, though, presents more difficulties. Some athletes, particularly in their last term of competition, register for the requisite hours, never attend class, and then drop out after the final game.[103]

At the January 1981 Convention, the NCAA adopted a normal progress rule requiring that an athlete, in essence, complete twelve hours of credit each term to remain eligible.[104] This will not solve the problem, but it is a significant step in the right direction. It will still be possible for an athlete to accumulate the requisite credits each term in courses at the introductory level and in subject areas that will not fulfill degree requirements. Thus, we may still see an O.J. Simpson complete his college football career while fifty-six credit hours short of a degree, but the frequency of such cases should be diminished.[105]

One continuing problem affecting the academic performance of student athletes is the time and energy required for practice and participation in major college sports. There is little doubt that to compete in sports at the highest college levels requires such a substantial investment of the athlete's time and energy as to seriously detract from his studies. Some athletes have even found it "next to impossible to be a legitimate student and a football player too."[106] NCAA regulations of practice and playing seasons in basketball, football, and soccer may curb but do not eliminate the problem. Moreover, no effort has yet been made to control other sports, where the problem is now, perhaps, most severe. In college baseball, athletes are now expected to play up to one hundred game schedules or more and still fulfill their duties as students.[107]

The reality is that in big-time intercollegiate sports, as Alabama Coach Bear Bryant has said, "The boy is really an athlete first and a student second."[108] Befitting this secondary status, NCAA regulations serve to guarantee only minimal performance of student responsibilities —primarily the taking, and now completion, of twelve credit hours of courses each term. Other regulations prescribing that the student be in "good academic standing" and make "satisfactory progress toward a degree"[109] rely on the autonomous standards of individual institutions to give them meaning. Recent experience indicates that institutions involved in the intense competition of intercollegiate athletics, when acting alone, are unlikely to impose on themselves standards that might hinder their ability to compete. As a result, such regulations, relying on autonomous action, are frequently ineffective.

The uncomfortable truth is that the academic performance of athletes has become "a national disgrace."[110] The forces contributing to the erosion of academic standards in intercollegiate athletics are powerful and will not be warded off by the relatively weak regulatory shield now imposed by the NCAA. Stronger rules and novel approaches are required if the academic integrity of college athletics is to be restored.

IV. LEGAL INITIATIVES

One novel approach is now being pursued by seven former student athletes in a California court.[111] They are suing officials of California State University at Los Angeles for, among other things, failing to provide the higher education that had been promised when they agreed to bring their athletic talents to the university.[112] The athletes assert that this failure to educate breached contractual duties owed by the university to them under individual oral and written agreements and under NCAA rules.

The complaint alleges that a contract existed between each of the student athletes and the university, pursuant to which the student athletes agreed to provide their athletic services to the university for two to four years in exchange for an equal number of years of tuition-and-cost-free education.[113] The complaint was careful to define what was required by the promise of an education in terms of access to specific university services and resources, rather than in terms of educational attainment.[114] The achievement of an education is influenced by a host of factors, physical, neurological, emotional, cultural, and environmental, which "affect the student subjectively, from outside the formal teaching process, and beyond the control of its ministers."[115] Thus, a university might do everything within its power for an athlete who nonetheless fails to become educated.[116] Thus, any deficiencies by the university will ordinarily have to be measured in terms of access to specific services or resources rather than achievement.

California State University at Los Angeles was allegedly deficient in providing the requisite access as follows: (1) It denied the athletes access to adequate counseling services by instructing them "to seek counseling *solely* from the coaches in the athletic department" and prohibiting them "from seeking counseling services from the traditional counseling offices" of the university.[117] (2) The athletes were instructed by coaches "not to enroll in certain degree-requirement courses because such courses might jeopardize their eligibility status."[118] (3) They were "instructed to repeat their enrollment in certain physical education courses even though such courses would be a total waste" to them, having been satisfactorily completed in prior terms.[119] (4) Unlike other students, they were never advised of the academic and course requirements for graduation. (5) They were never given individual course programs reasonably constructed to allow normal progress toward a degree. (6) They were counseled to accept grades for courses they never attended, removing incentives for learning. (7) They were denied access to remedial courses that were fundamental to their overcoming educational handicaps.[120] Because of this conduct by representatives of the university, the athletes assert that they failed to make reasonable progress toward a degree and to receive the higher education that had been promised.[121]

Whether this course of conduct will be legally significant depends at the outset on whether there is a contractual relationship between the athlete and the institution. The few courts that have considered the question have concluded that the recipient of an athletic grant-in-aid has contracted with the institution.[122] The terms of the contract may vary, depending on the specific representations that have been made, but typically, the essence of the transaction is the exchange of the promise of athletic services by the student for the reciprocal promise of educational services by the institution. Weistart and Lowell have urged that the relationship should ordinarily be viewed not as contractual but as a traditional academic relationship, in which the institution makes a conditional gift to a promising student.[123] The analysis, however, does not adequately account for the reality that the student is recruited and the scholarship granted only because of the expectation that he will perform in an extracurricular activity. If he fulfills the expectation, the university may reap substantial rewards, including increased revenues, alumni support, and national publicity. If, however, he chooses not to perform, the grant may be cancelled.[124]

The Internal Revenue Service has ruled, consistent with the notion urged by Weistart and Lowell, that in the absence of an explicit requirement of athletic performance, an athletic scholarship is not regarded as compensation for tax purposes.[125] The conclusion has been aptly criticized as "rather naive,"[126] since athletic awards "are made to secure the athlete's services and generally are maintained subject to his participation in college athletics."[127]

Even if one accepted the characterization of the arrangement as a conditional gift, the promise of educational benefits would likely still be legally enforceable on an estoppel basis. The law recognizes that "[a] promise which the promisor should reasonably expect to induce action or forbearance of a definite and substantial character on the part of the promisee . . . and which does induce such action or forbearance is binding if injustice can be avoided only by enforcement of the promise."[128] When a university promises to provide educational services to an athlete if he will go to the school and play football, the promise will be legally binding if the athlete, relying on the promise, attends the school and plays football.[129] Accordingly, if the California State student athletes are able to prove the allegations of their complaint, the law should provide a remedy, most likely under the contract theory asserted, but if not, under a promissory estoppel theory.

One other legal basis for the claim merits only brief mention. The athletes assert a cause of action as third-party beneficiaries of a contract between California State University at Los Angeles and the NCAA.[130] That such a contract exists has support in the case law. Indeed, in a case involving the university's sister school, California State University at Hayward, the California Court of Appeals found that the relationship between the NCAA and its member institutions is determined by contract, the terms of which find expression in the constitution and bylaws of the association.[131] California State University at Los Angeles allegedly violated the NCAA Constitution and bylaws in several respects: by failing to adhere to admission standards, by arranging for third parties to take standardized admission tests on behalf of plaintiffs, by maintaining unofficial funds for disbursement to plaintiffs and other team members, by failing to provide academic counseling, by failing to provide plaintiffs with course plans that could realistically be used in making reasonable progress toward a degree, and by requiring plaintiffs to spend more than the allotted time in practice sessions.[132]

If these allegations are true, there is no doubt that NCAA rules that express the terms of the contract between the university and the NCAA have been violated. It does not follow, however, that the plaintiffs' claim as third-party beneficiaries has merit. On the contrary, the claim is probably not sustainable, because the "contract" sets forth the means by which the rules are to be enforced and violations to be remedied. The Committee on Infractions considers charges of violations and metes out punishment satisfactory to the NCAA.[133] Like a party bound by an agreement for arbitration[134] or reasonable liquidated damages,[135] the NCAA would be limited to the remedies to which it and its member institutions have agreed: the enforcement system prescribed by the NCAA constitution and bylaws. No greater remedy would be available to a third-party beneficiary, since such a person's rights are limited by the terms of the contract.[136]

Moreover, only "intended beneficiaries" are entitled to sue as third parties to a contract.[137] Student athletes are most reasonably regarded as "incidental beneficiaries" who have no right to sue since they fail to meet one of the conditions to be an "intended beneficiary": that recognition of a right to performance in the beneficiary be appropriate to effectuate the intentions of the parties.[138] In view of the elaborate enforcement system established by the NCAA, it is doubtful that the intentions of the NCAA and its member institutions would be effectuated by giving student athletes a supplemental judicial remedy.

The student athletes should thus be limited to a remedy for breach of the promises expressly made to them by representatives of the university. Although courts have been reluctant to interfere in the academic affairs of universities,[139] they have recognized on numerous occasions that promises made by universities to students are legally enforceable.[140] For example, in *Zumbrun v. University of Southern California*,[141] after citing ten cases in support of the proposition that "the basic legal relation between a student and a private university or college is contractual in nature," with the "catalogues, bulletins, circulars, and regulations of the institution" being "a part of the contract,"[142] the court found that a cause of action for breach of contract had been stated when the school failed to provide the normal lectures and examinations in a sociology course. Similarly, if California State University at Los Angeles, contrary to official representations, failed to provide adequate counseling to its athletes, denied them access to advertised remedial courses, and refused to allow them to enroll in courses necessary to earn a degree, then a legal remedy should be available.

The remedy the athletes seek is specific enforcement of the contract and damages of $5,000 for each quarter of schooling lost. It seems doubtful that they will be able to prove damages of that magnitude, but if they are able, for example, to establish reasonably calculable lost earnings attributable to the contract breach, then a substantial monetary award is possible.[143] The more likely and appropriate remedy would be to remit the athletes back to the university with an order requiring the school to provide the promised educational services along with necessary financial assistance.

Whether such relief is ever granted in the *Echols* case, the potential for similar judicial action exists whenever a school fails in meeting its academic obligations to student athletes. Such obligations are self-imposed and could be minimized by a university through appropriate language in the tender of the athletic grant-in-aid narrowly stating the academic promises of the institution and disclaiming all others. It should not, however, be able to evade its legal obligation to provide athletes, like other students, meaningful access to faculty, courses, and books that could lead to a degree and a genuine education.

Civil liability for breach of contract is not the only legal sanction potentially available for abuses in intercollegiate athletics. Ben Apuna, a former linebacker at Arizona State University, has filed a lawsuit against his academic adviser and other officials of the university for fraud, negligence, and interference with contract because of circumstances arising from the 1979 scandal.[144] Apuna had registered for a summer course at Rocky Mountain College. Allegedly on the advice and with the assistance of his academic adviser, he attended no classes, did no work, and received a B for the course.[145] He was subsequently suspended, along with seven fellow Arizona State football players, for receiving academic credits illegitimately. He now seeks $2.4 million in damages because of the alleged adverse impact the suspension and scandal have had on his professional football career.[146]

Another lawsuit premised on academic abuses but raising different concerns has been brought by Curtis Jones, a former prep basketball star in Detroit.[147] He has sued the University of Michigan, North Idaho Junior College, and various high school and college coaches and officials for contributing to his mental breakdown through, *inter alia*, the following alleged course of conduct: arranging his transfer when he was fifteen years old from a school for slow learners to a regular junior high school, where he could not and did not receive the special help he needed, for the sole purpose of exploiting his basketball talent; passing him through junior and senior high school although he did not do passing work in class, solely to maintain his basketball eligibility; inducing and assisting him to attend North Idaho Junior College, though he could not read or write well enough even to fill out the application (his high school coach did it for him); and permitting cheating on examinations and otherwise improperly maintaining his junior college eligibility.[148] During Jones's second year in junior college, large segments of the student body learned that he could not read or write and began to insult and taunt him mercilessly. In the face of this psychological pressure, he suffered a complete mental breakdown, triggering psychosis and schizophrenia, for which he has required constant medical supervision since 1970. He seeks to recover damages exceeding $15,000,000 on several legal theories, including educational malpractice, breach of fiduciary duty, fraud, intentional infliction of mental distress, and denial of the right to an education.[149]

In addition to such civil actions,[150] it may occasionally be possible to pursue criminal penalties for certain misconduct in the administration of intercollegiate athletics. The University of New Mexico's former basketball coach, Norm Ellenberger, was tried in 1981 in a New Mexico state court on twenty-two counts of fraud and filing false public vouchers.[151] Ellenberger billed the university for several thousand dollars of nonexistent travel expenses and then used the "extra money," he said, to help support the school's basketball program.[152] He was convicted of twenty-one of the twenty-two counts and could have received up to 105 years in prison; what he got was one year of unsupervised probation without having to make restitution.[153] In explaining the light sentence, Judge Phillip Baiamonte said:

> I'm being asked to sentence a man who was only one cog in the entire machine called college ball. I'm being asked to sentence a man because he got caught, not because his conduct was unacceptable. The question is how fair is it to incarcerate a man for doing what almost everyone in the community wanted him to do—namely win basketball games at whatever cost. Naturally, rules and laws were broken. Is anyone really surprised? This is a problem that probably exists at every major college and university in the country.[154]

The judge urged "the nation's colleges and universities to get out of the business of conducting professional athletics and go back to the academics for which they were established."[155]

The "feathery tap on the wrist"[156] given to Ellenberger has been much criticized. Regardless of its wisdom, it serves to illustrate the limitations of the criminal justice system in responding to misconduct in college sports. Such misconduct will rarely offend the criminal law, and even in those relatively few instances when it does, punishment is by no means assured.

Intercollegiate athletics are not and should not be immune from the constraints imposed by civil and criminal law on the rest of society. The reality, though, is that those general laws are unlikely to be fully enforced against popular coaches and universities. And even if they were, because they are general and do not directly address the most serious problems in intercollegiate athletics, they would do little to improve the situation. What is needed is not more civil and criminal litigation but enforceable NCAA regulations that specifically respond to the special circumstances of college sports.

V. REMEDIAL REGULATION

The first regulatory step that should be taken toward returning academic integrity to intercollegiate athletics is to tighten admission requirements to preclude enrollment of students who are illiterate or otherwise unqualified to do academic work. This could be accomplished by replacing the 2.000 Rule with something stronger and by eliminating the loophole of special admissions. Instead of being satisfied with a mere 2.000 high school grade-point average, the NCAA should require that a freshman who receives an athletic grant-in-aid to a Division I university demonstrate real academic competence through a high school transcript with at least a 2.50 average, or performance on the SAT or ACT that, considered in combination with the high school average, would predict satisfactory performance in college academic coursework.[157] In other words, the NCAA should return to something similar to, but stronger than, the old 1.600 Rule. Simultaneously, the NCAA should end the abuse of affirmative action programs in the service of athletic ends by making the percentage of athletes admitted under such standards proportionate to the percentage admitted by the school for the entire incoming class. For example, if the university limits special admissions to 4 percent of the incoming class, then only 4 percent of the incoming scholarship athletes should be admitted under these more lenient standards.[158]

If implemented, one impact of these changes would probably be to reduce athletic scholarships available to disadvantaged black youth.[159] This may seem harsh but is in the long-run best interest of both the athlete and NCAA institutions. Experience demonstrates that the athlete, black or white, who fails to meet the ordinary entrance requirements of a college will usually fail to earn either an education or a degree. He is, in reality, being exploited by the institution for his athletic talent and receiving nothing of real consequence in return. There is, of course, the possibility of using college as a steppingstone to professional sports, but the chances are so remote that it is an illusion for all but the truly exceptional athletes.[160] If such athletes are unable to meet these standards, minor leagues are now available in all sports but football, and even there, the aspiring athlete may hone his talents in junior college while attempting to raise his grades for the big-time. The institution, of course, will benefit from these tougher standards by the enhancement of perhaps its most precious asset, the integrity of its academic program.

Beyond strengthening admission standards, the NCAA should act, second, to mandate further proof that an athlete is making real progress toward a degree. Specifically, the NCAA should supplement its new normal progress rule with the requirement that the athlete progress in a program of studies through which he can qualify for a baccalaureate degree within no more than five years.[161] Language should be included to insure that notwithstanding a change in an athlete's major, he will still be on course to receive a degree within five years. Experience in the Big Ten has demonstrated that such qualitative requirements are effective in raising the graduation rate of student athletes.[162]

The NCAA should also act to reduce the control that athletic departments now have over the student athlete's academic life. Academic counseling for athletes should be removed from the athletic departments, where the dominant interest is in the athlete's eligibility for sports competition. Accordingly, he is often channeled into courses that serve the end of eligibility but are not necessarily consistent with the athlete's educational needs or goals. Counselors outside the athletic department's domain would be more likely to give these educational concerns higher priority.[163] In addition, the NCAA should strive to further limit the demands of athletics to leave more time for the athlete's academic pursuits.

These relatively modest reforms would be helpful but are no panacea. A regulation that offers the potential for real change in the conduct of intercollegiate athletics is one that would restrict athletic scholarships in accordance with the percentage of athletes who graduate. If athletic departments were penalized by taking away scholarships when athletes fail to graduate, a powerful incentive would be added to encourage the enrollment of only athletes who had demonstrated the potential to graduate and to make sure that they progress toward a degree during their years of athletic eligibility.[164] Such a proposal would have to be carefully framed, since it could prove in practice to be counterproductive if, for example, the penalty were imposed only as to athletes who had completed four years of eligibility. To avoid the penalty, coaches might employ the various means at their disposal to induce the mediocre athlete to leave school before his fourth year.[165] If crafted with care, though, such a proposal could dramatically alter the academic character of intercollegiate athletics.

The effectiveness of each of these proposals depends not only on the soundness of its content but also on the adequacy of its enforcement. An unenforceable rule is probably worse than no rule, because only the honorable will comply and will be disadvantaged by their compliance.[166] Accordingly, any expansion of the protection to be afforded to academic standards should be accompanied by an enforcement plan and an infusion of enforcement resources adequate to insure compliance. This may require, for example, regular sworn reports to the NCAA disclosing the admissions credentials, courses, and grades of every athlete receiving an NCAA grant-in-aid. Any misrepresentations in such reports would subject the athlete and institution to severe sanctions.

A few serious observers of intercollegiate sports have suggested that any effort to impose real academic standards is hopeless and that the only solution is to end the hypocrisy by acknowledging and approving of professionalism at least in big-time college football and basketball.[167] In other words, cut the tie between athletes and academics; pay the players and make no effort to require that they be students, although give them the opportunity to take courses if they wish. But treating the athletic department "as if it were a Burger King franchise"[168] serves no legitimate goals of a university. It may make money, but that is not the object of higher education. A university's primary function is to educate. Only if college athletics involve genuine students in an activity having educational merit should the universities be involved.

CONCLUSION

Intercollegiate sports possesses significant educational potential for the athlete. From it, he may learn how to work with a group, to discipline himself, to pick himself up after being knocked down, and to develop competitive desire. He may experience the sense of fulfillment from giving his best effort in the pursuit of excellence and the freedom to express intense emotions in the thrill of victory or the agony of defeat. He may learn to appreciate the importance of commitment, of hard work and of perseverence, and may acquire specific knowledge and skills to be used in a career as a physical educator, coach, or professional athlete. While serving these educational ends, intercollegiate sports can also entertain and inspire thousands of spectators, yielding immense revenues and prestige to the successful university. When it does, the temptation is great, perhaps irresistible, to lose sight of the educational goals in the pursuit of such laurels. Some colleges and universities have yielded to that temptation with the consequent denigration of academic standards in their athletic programs. Other institutions, in order to compete effectively, have felt compelled to do likewise. For the same reason, it is unrealistic to expect institutions on their own to raise academic standards for their athletes. To succeed, the remedy must be collective, through regulation by the NCAA. The present regulatory scheme is inadequate to the task; it must be significantly strengthened and supplemented if we are to achieve academic integrity in college athletics befitting America's great institutions of higher education.

NOTES

1. Harvard won in a contest the character of which is suggested by a remark of one of the Harvard crew, "that they had only rowed a few times for fear of blistering their hands." H. Savage, *American College Athletics* (Bulletin No. 23; The Carnegie Foundation For The Advancement of Teaching), 16–17 (1929). For an historical treatment of scandals in intercollegiate sports, see also J. BENAGH, MAKING IT TO NUMBER ONE: HOW COLLEGE FOOTBALL AND BASKETBALL TEAMS GET THERE (1976).

2. N.Y. Times, Oct. 26, 1979, at 27, col. 3.

3. Underwood, *The Writing Is on the Wall,* Sports Illustrated, May 19, 1980, at 38–39.

4. University of Southern California, Academic Conduct, Admission, Advisement and Counseling of Student-Athletes at the University of Southern California: A Report to the USC Community, October 12, 1980, at 2, excerpt in N.Y. Times, Oct. 19, 1980.

5. *The Shame of College Sports,* Newsweek, Sept. 22, 1980, at 54.

6. Sports Illustrated, note 3, *supra.*

7. Newsweek, note 5, *supra.*

8. Sports Illustrated, note 3 *supra,* at 38 and cover page.

9. Broadcast on February 3, 1980; segment entitled, "Losers."

10. E. SHEA & E. WIEMAN, ADMINISTRATIVE POLICIES FOR INTERCOLLEGIATE ATHLETICS 16 (1967).

11. *Infra* Part IV.

12. The NCAA was formally organized on March 31, 1906, following a conference convened late in 1905 by President Theodore Roosevelt. Roosevelt was concerned in particular about brutality in intercollegiate football and what he perceived as an increasingly pervasive win-at-any-cost philosophy. He told the colleges to take remedial action, or he would put an end to the whole enterprise. In response, the NCAA was formed "to codify, promulgate, and enforce rules and regulations which would ensure proper behaviors on and off the field. . . ." Hanford, *Controversies in College Sports,* ANNALS AMER. ACAD. POL. & SOC. SCI. 66, 68 (1979); Lewis, *Theodore Roosevelt's Role in the 1905 Football Controversy,* RESEARCH QUARTERLY 40 (1969).

13. The first NCAA Constitution provided: "Its object shall be the regulation and supervision of college athletics throughout the United States, in order that the athletic activities of the colleges and universities of the United States may be maintained on an ethical plane in keeping with the dignity and high purpose of education. The method of control selected was that the Colleges and Universities enrolled in this Association severally agree to take control of student athletic sports as far as may be necessary to maintain in them a high standard of personal honor, eligibility and fair play, and to remedy whatever abuses exist." SHEA & WIEMAN, *supra* note 10, at 14.

14. As of October 1980, the NCAA had 883 members consisting of 740 colleges and universities who are active members and 143 other allied, associate, and affiliate members such as conferences and other athletic organizations.

15. *The Final Report of the President's Commission on Olympic Sports 1975–1977*, Vol. II, 325 (1977).

16. *Id.* at 383.

17. The AIAW active membership for 1981–82 includes 772 institutions. Complaint, AIAW v. NCAA, Civil No. 81-2473 (D.D.C. October 1981). This represents a 20 percent decline from the 970 members reported in the AIAW Handbook for 1980–81. The principal reason for the decline is that beginning in the 1981–82 school year the NCAA is offering championships in women's sports, and many institutions have elected to drop their membership in the AIAW and pursue women's sports solely under NCAA regulation.

18. It has been judicially noted that the NCAA is the "dominant" intercollegiate sports organization. College Athletic Placement Service, Inc. v. NCAA, 1975 Trade Cas. P60,117 (D. N.J.), *aff'd*, No. 74-1904 (3d Cir., Nov. 25, 1974).

19. In 1980, of 740 NCAA colleges and universities participating in intercollegiate athletics, 271 were classified in Division I, 188 in Division II, and 281 in Division III. NCAA Annual Reports 1979–80.

20. For purposes of intercollegiate football, the NCAA is also divided into Divisions I-A and I-AA, further separating the truly big-time institutions from the others. Pursuant to legislation passed at a special convention held on December 4–5, 1981, in order to be a member of Division I-A, an institution must have had an average home football attendance of 17,000 over the last four years or a home stadium capacity of 30,000. Approximately 94 institutions should qualify (down from 137), leaving 90 schools in Division I-AA (up from 50). St. Louis Post-Dispatch, Dec. 6, 1981, at 8.

21. Sections 1, 2, and 3 of NCAA Bylaw Article 10 describe respectively the criteria for membership in Divisions I, II, and III. 1981–82 Manual of the National Collegiate Athletic Association, 108 (1981) [hereinafter cited as NCAA Manual].

22. NCAA Bylaw 6-5, NCAA Manual 90.

23. NCAA Bylaw 10-3-(a), NCAA Manual 111.

24. NCAA Constitution, Article Two, Section 2: *"Fundamental Policy.* (a) The competitive athletic programs of the colleges are designed to be a vital part of the educational system. A basic purpose of this Association is to maintain intercollegiate athletics as an integral part of the educational program and the athlete as an integral part of the student body and, by so doing, retain a clear line of demarcation between college athletics and professional sports." NCAA Manual 7–8.

25. NCAA Constitution, Article Three, Section 3. *"Principle of Sound Academic Standards."*

    (a) A student-athlete shall not represent an institution in intercollegiate competition unless the student-athlete: (1) Has been admitted in accordance with the regular published entrance requirements of that institution; (2) Is in good academic standing as determined by the faculty of that institution, in accordance with the standards applied to all students, and (3) Is enrolled in at least a minimum full-time program of studies and is maintaining satisfactory progress toward a baccalaureate or equivalent degree as determined by the regulations of that institution, except that a student-athlete who is enrolled in less than a minimum full-time program of studies and has athletic eligibility remaining may participate if the student-athlete is carrying for credit the courses necessary to complete degree requirements as determined by the faculty of the institution. Further, a student-athlete who has received a baccalaureate or equivalent degree and who is enrolled in the graduate or professional school of the institution attended as an undergraduate, or who is enrolled and seeking a second baccalaureate or equivalent degree at the same institution, may participate in intercollegiate athletics provided the student-athlete has athletic eligibility remaining and such participation occurs within five years after initial enrollment in a collegiate institution.

NCAA Manual 16.

26. NCAA Bylaw 5-1-(c):

    The student-athlete must, at the time of competition, be registered for at least a minimum full-time program of studies as defined by the institution, which, in any event, shall not be less than 12 semester hours or 12 quarter hours (or a similar minimum academic load as determined by the NCAA Eligibility Committee in an institution which determines registration other than on a traditional semester or quarter hour basis or conducts a cooperative education program; or a minimum full-time graduate program as defined by the institution and approved by the NCAA Eligibility Committee in the event fewer than 12 hours are required, but which may be no fewer than eight hours); further, if the competition takes place between terms, the student-athlete must have been so registered in the term immediately preceding the date of competition.

NCAA Manual 70.

27. NCAA Bylaw 5-1-(j)-(2): "An entering freshman with no previous college attendance who matriculates as a 2.000 nonqualifier in a Division I institution and whose matriculation was solicited per O.I. 100 shall not be eligible for financial aid, regular-season competition and practice during the first academic year in residence." NCAA Manual 73.

28. *E.g.*, NCAA Bylaws 5-1-(j)-(8) & (10), 5-1-(k), and 5-1-(n).

29. NCAA Bylaw 5-1-(j)-(9): "A transfer student from a junior college who was a 2.000 nonqualifier is not eligible in Division I institutions for financial aid, practice, regular-season competition and for any NCAA championships the first academic year in residence unless the student has graduated from the junior college." NCAA Manual 76.

30. NCAA Constitution 6-2; NCAA Manual 38. Article Six of the NCAA Constitution also speaks of "Executive Regulations" and "Resolutions." Neither of these appear to be of consequence in the regulation of academic standards and are therefore not treated herein.

31. *Id.*

32. NCAA Manual 17.

33. NCAA Bylaw 3-1 prohibits preseason practice as follows: In basketball —before October 15; in football—nineteen days before the first game or twenty-two days before the next-to-last Saturday in September or on that date which will permit no more than twenty-nine "practice opportunities" prior to the first game; and in soccer—before September 1 or on the first day of classes or nineteen days prior to the first game. NCAA Bylaw 3-2 limits the playing seasons as follows: In basketball—to the period from the last Saturday in November for Division I and the next-to-the-last Saturday for Divisions II and III to the date of the championship game in the NCAA Basketball Tournament; in football and soccer—"to the traditional fall season," with provision for a spring football game and one postseason contest.

34. NCAA Bylaw 3-3 limits the number of games in basketball to twenty-seven in Divisions I and II, twenty-six in Division III; in football to eleven; and in soccer to twenty-two. For purposes of these restrictions, football bowl games, postseason tournament basketball games and games in Hawaii and Alaska are not counted.

35. NCAA Bylaw 1-1-(b); NCAA Manual 43.

36. NCAA Bylaw 1-2; NCAA Manual 43–44.

37. NCAA Bylaw 1-8-(a); NCAA Manual 50.

38. NCAA Bylaw 1-8-(e); NCAA Manual 51.

39. NCAA Bylaw 1-6-(a); NCAA Manual 48.

40. These restrictions also serve other purposes, including, perhaps most importantly, "to reduce recruiting and operating costs by restraining competition." Koch, *A Troubled Cartel: The NCAA,* 38 LAW AND CONTEMP. PROB. 135, 138 (1973).

41. NCAA Constitution 1-(a). It is possible for a student to be a professional in one sport and participate in NCAA competition in another.

42. NCAA Constitution 3-1-(g) and 3-4; NCAA Manual 12, 18.

43. This idea is expressed in the "Principle of Amateurism and Student Participation," NCAA Constitution, Article Three, Section 1: "An amateur student-athlete is one who engages in a particular sport for the educational, physical, mental and social benefits derived therefrom and to whom participation in that sport is an avocation."

44. NCAA Manual 69–70.

45. NCAA Manual 70–71.

46. Gerber, *The Legal Basis for the Regulation of Intercollegiate Sport,* 60 EDUC. REC. 467, 481 (1979); *see* Weistart, *Foreword,* 38 LAW & CONTEMP. PROB. 1 (1975).

47. Handbook of the Intercollegiate (Big Ten) Conference (1980).

48. *NCAA Enforcement Program: Hearings Before the Subcomm. on Oversight and Investigations of the House Comm. on Interstate and Foreign Commerce,* 95th Cong., 2d Sess. and 96th Cong., 1st Sess. (1978–79) [hereinafter cited as *NCAA Enforcement Hearings*].

49. NCAA Manual 190.

50. Official Procedure Governing the NCAA Enforcement Progam, Sections 2 & 3 [hereinafter cited as NCAA Enforcement]; NCAA Manual 166–67.

51. NCAA Enforcement 7-(b) lists twelve disciplinary measures available to the Committee on Infractions and the NCAA Council. NCAA Manual 166–67.

52. NCAA Enforcement, Sec. 5-7: NCAA Manual 165–67.

53. NCAA Constitution 4–6; NCAA Manual 29–30.

54. *NCAA Enforcement Hearings, supra* note 48, at 1512.

55. *See* NCAA Enforcement Summary in *NCAA Enforcement Hearings* following p. 1512.

56. *Id.*

57. Chron. Higher Educ., Aug. 25, 1980.

58. *Id.*

59. Report, "April 27, 1981 Decision of the Intercollegiate Conference of Faculty Representatives Concerning the University of Illinois," at 19.

60. Chicago Tribune, Aug. 6, 1981, Sec. 3, at 1.

61. Sports Illustrated, Oct. 27, 1980, at 19.

62. N.Y. Times, Oct. 15, 1980, at 8.

63. "Academic Conduct, Admission, Advisement and Counseling of Student-Athletes at the University of Southern California, A Report to the USC Community," Oct. 12, 1980.

64. N.Y. Times, Oct. 26, 1980, at 4, Col. 1.

65. Chicago Tribune, Nov. 5, 1978, Sec. 1, at 1.

66. Sports Illustrated, May 19, 1980, at 39: "I think he (a coach) did visied me a school one . . . Since I have been at (the school), Coach (name deleted) have not give me any money, period. But he have lend me five to tin dollars but I have paid it back to." And, "Coach (name deleted) give me a 5 or 6 dr. to do my clothis with but other than that he have not give me any money."

67. The Progressive, April 1979, at 48.

68. Fordham Basketball Coach Tom Penders observes, "Unfortunately, board scores are usually inversely proportionate to a kid's athletic ability." N.Y. Times, Feb. 8, 1981, Sec. V, at 2, Col. 4. He laments that only 5 percent of quality high school players qualify for admission at his institution. *Id.* Obviously, if he cannot get that 5 percent, he will be at a tremendous competitive disadvantage unless the institution's admissions standards are lowered.

69. NCAA Constitution 3-3-(a)-(1).

70. NCAA Bylaw 5-1-(j)-(2).

71. N.Y. Times, Oct. 17, 1980, Sec. B, at 5.

72. Sports Illustrated, Oct. 27, 1980, at 19.

73. Jim Benagh reports in his book, MAKING IT TO NUMBER ONE: How COLLEGE FOOTBALL AND BASKETBALL TEAMS GET THERE, at 60 (1976), that for many years, Rutgers University had difficulty competing in big-time intercollegiate sports because of its academic entrance requirements. That, however, changed when the university opened the doors of its Livingston College to underprivileged youth with the potential to benefit from higher education though lacking the necessary academic background. "Before long, Livingston College was filled with black athletes. Good ones." *Id.*

74. J. UNDERWOOD, DEATH OF AN AMERICAN GAME 248 (1979).

75. Chron. Higher Educ., Dec. 15, 1980.

76. Sports Illustrated, Oct. 27, 1980, at 19.

77. J. MICHENER, SPORTS IN AMERICA 198 (1976).

78. *Id.* The gift of unearned grades is one illustration of what Robert Lipsyte calls "The Varsity Syndrome," in which athletes are granted privileges denied the rest of us. "Those privileges begin with favors and gifts in grade school, little presents like an unearned diploma, perhaps a college

scholarship. Athletes are waved, as it were, through the toll booths of life."
Varsity Syndrome: The Unkindest Cut, ANNALS AMER. ACAD. POL. & SOC.
SCI. 15, 19 (Sept. 1979).

79. J. MICHENER, SPORTS IN AMERICA 198 (1976). Michener adds, "I
have six such cases on my desk as I write." This activity is not a recent
phenomenon. Savage noted in his 1929 report for the Carnegie Foundation:
"Grades assigned by school teachers for particular courses are known to
have been raised by certifying officers on solicitation of college coaches or
alumni in order to enable boys to slip easily into college. The complaints of
not a few college officials, verified by field agents of this study, indicate
that these dishonest practices are far more extensive than is generally
realized."

80. J. BENAGH, MAKING IT TO NUMBER ONE 70 (1976).

81. Faculty Representatives Report, *supra* note 59, at 4.

82. Wilson's junior college transcript was incorporated in the complaint
in *David Wilson v. NCAA et al.*, No. 80-C-801, Illinois Circuit Court, 6th
District, Champaign County.

83. Note, *Judicial Review of Disputes Between Athletes and The National
Collegiate Athletic Association*, 24 STAN. L. REV. 903, 905 (1972), citing
to NCAA Manual 1971–72 at 40–44, 45–48.

84. Associated Students Inc. v. NCAA, 493 F.2d 1251, 1255 (9th Cir.
1974).

85. *See* Cross, *The College Athlete*, 38 LAW & CONTEMP. PROB. 151, 159
(1973) (explaining that pressure for special admissions and concern for institutional autonomy were the principal reasons given for the change).

86. *See* T. GROSS, ACADEMIC TURMOIL: THE REALITY AND PROMISE OF
OPEN EDUCATION (1980) (noting, *inter alia*, that open admissions at The
City College of New York meant opening college doors to "excessive numbers of poorly trained students," at 11, and that "the most dramatic reason
why literacy became a national problem was the opening of admissions
everywhere," at 60); S. BLUMENFELD, THE NEW ILLITERATES (1973) ("In
the last twenty years the United States has undergone a staggering degenera-
tion of its literary skills, on all levels of society, affecting small children
in school, high school students, college students, factory workers, corporation
executives, from ghetto dropouts to suburban middle-class youths").

87. *See* The Carnegie Council on Policy Studies in Higher Education: A
Summary of Reports and Recommendations (1980).

88. G. Hanford, Report to the American Council on Education on an
Inquiry Into the Need for and Feasibility of a National Study of Intercollegiate Athletics, 131 (1974) [hereinafter cited as The Hanford Report].

89. *Supra* Part I.

90. Burwell, *Scholarship Athletes: Is There Life After Football?* Chron.
Higher Educ., Nov. 26, 1979, at 21.

91. Sports Illustrated, May 19, 1980, at 65. An official study was undertaken by the University of California to determine its graduation rates. A
short oral report was made concerning this study to the NCAA Convention
in January 1981, in which it was indicated that the graduation rate for
California athletes was roughly equal to that for nonathletes. The actual
data, however, have not been made public, and requests by the author for
the data have been denied.

92. R. Brown, Race, Sport, and Academe, Report of the Task Force on
the Black Athlete, Appendix to The Hanford Report at 67. The report also
disclosed the following: At the University of Washington between 1957 and

1967, seven black football players graduated, thirteen did not; at the University of Oregon between 1965 and 1968, six black athletes graduated, five did not; at the University of Utah only twelve of forty-six black athletes eventually received degrees; and at Utah State only nine of forty black athletes graduated. *Id.*

93. H. Edwards, "Exploitation and the NCAA," Presentation at the Second Annual Conference of the North American Society for the Sociology of Sport, Nov. 15, 1981. J. Durso reports in THE SPORTS FACTORY (1975), at 81, the results of an earlier survey indicating that 63 percent of NBA players and less than 50 percent of NFL players had earned college degrees.

94. NCAA News Release, "Graduation Rate Higher for College Athletes Than for Nonathletes," May 1, 1981.

95. National Collegiate Athletic Association—Survey of Graduation Rates After Five Years for Males First Entering College in Fall 1975, Prepared By Institutional Services Department, Research and Development Division, American College Testing Program, Iowa City, Iowa, April 1981, at 5 and 13.

96. *Id.* at 11.

97. *Id.*

98. *Id.* at 5 and 9.

99. *Id.* at 1. Significantly, the report noted an earlier survey done by the ACT for the NCAA in which usable data were obtained from 25 percent of the institutions solicited. The ACT remarked, "Because of the poor response rate, the statistics had to be interpreted with caution since data from responding colleges may have differed from non-responding colleges." Although no similar note of caution was sounded concerning the results of the current study, it is clearly warranted.

100. Some institutions appear to have relied on the Buckley Amendment as an excuse for failing to produce this information. As long as the data relate solely to graduation, and particularly if they do not identify individuals, concern with provisions of the Act are unjustified. *See* Family Educational Rights and Privacy Act of 1974, 20 U.S.C. Sec. 1232(g).

101. George McGinnis, for example, left Indiana after his sophomore year to play in the ABA and has prospered without a degree. He concluded "College did me no good whatsoever. . . . I got a right to earn a living, and I don't have to be a college grad to do it." Of course, for the average pro athlete, the rewards are not as great and are available over only a few years. For such pros, the lack of degree may well be a handicap over the long term. J. BENAGH, MAKING IT TO NUMBER ONE, at 129 (1976).

102. Underwood reports that a University of Cincinnati basketball player, after competing for four years, had accumulated approximately fifty credits, barely 25 percent of the number required by the school for graduation. Sports Illustrated, May 19, 1980 at 44.

103. Bob Knight, Transcript of *Forum, The Scandals in Intercollegiate Sports: How Should the Universities Respond,* Indiana University, Bloomington, Nov. 7, 1980, at 15.

104. NCAA Bylaw 5-1-(j)-(6); NCAA Manual 74.

105. *Student-Athletes: Tackling The Problem,* Phi Delta Kappan, Sept. 1980, at 12 (comment by J. Underwood in discussion edited by B. Hammel).

106. Dave Meggyesy, *Football and Education,* in J. SCOTT, THE ATHLETIC REVOLUTION (1971).

107. The 1981–82 Arizona State baseball team, defending NCAA national champion, has a fall and spring combined schedule of 105 games plus conference and NCAA tournaments.

108. J. MICHENER, SPORTS IN AMERICA 203 (1976).

109. NCAA Constitution 3-3-(1) and (2); NCAA Manual 16.

110. Sports Illustrated, May 19, 1980, at 40.

111. Echols v. Board of Trustees, California State University and Colleges, No. C 266 777 (Ca. Superior Ct., L.A. County, filed Oct. 22, 1979).

112. The complaint recites ten causes of action. In addition to the breach of contract claims that are discussed in the text, the complaint asserts claims for cancellation of loans for fraud and failure of consideration, misrepresentation, conversion, and assumpsit, and seeks injunctive relief against state loan collection procedures on due process grounds.

113. Complaint, *Echols, supra* note 103, at 11–12.

114. *Id.* at 12.

115. Peter W. v. San Francisco Unified School District, 60 Cal. App. 3d 814, 131 Cal. Rptr. 854, 861 (1976) (rejecting complaint for educational malpractice by high school graduate who could read only at the fifth grade level). Accord, Donohue v. Copiague Union Free School Dist., 47 N.Y. 2d 440, 391 N.E. 2d 1352 (1979); Hoffman v. Board of Educ. of City of N.Y., 49 N.Y. 2d 121, 400 N.E. 2d 317 (1979).

116. To paraphrase an old saying about a horse, you can lead a jock to class, but you can't make him think.

117. Complaint, *Echols, supra* note 111, at 12 (emphasis in original).

118. *Id.* at 12–13.

119. *Id.* at 13.

120. *Id.*

121. *Id.*

122. Taylor v. Wake Forest University, 16 N.C. App. 117, 191 S.E. 2d 379 (1972); Begley v. Corp. of Mercer Univ., 367 F. Supp. 908 (E.D. Tenn. 1973).

123. J. WEISTART & C. LOWELL, THE LAW OF SPORTS 11–12 (1979).

124. NCAA Constitution 3-4-(c)-(2) authorizes the cancellation of an athletic scholarship if the athlete "voluntarily withdraws from a sport for personal reasons." Other rules limit the period of any scholarship grant to one year (NCAA Const. 3-4-[d]), and the only restriction on nonrenewal is procedural—the athlete is entitled to a hearing if he believes the grant has not been renewed for "questionable reasons." NCAA Const. 3-4-(g). No attempt is made to define "questionable reasons" and thereby give substance to the hearing requirement. AIAW rules are stricter, specifically prohibiting the withdrawal or nonrenewal of financial aid because of "skill performance, illness or injury." AIAW Handbook 1980–81 at 51. AIAW rules still permit terminating aid to any student who voluntarily withdraws from the sport or for any other reason fails to participate for a year. *Id.* at 49, 50.

125. Rev. Rul. 77-263, 1977-2 Cum. Bull. 47.

126. Kaplan, *Intercollegiate Athletics and the Unrelated Business Income Tax*, 80 COLL. L. REV. 1430, 1462 (1980).

127. *Id.*

128. RESTATEMENT, SECOND, CONTRACTS Sec. 90 (1981).

129. The Restatement provides an appropriate illustration: "A, knowing that B is going to college, promises B that A will give him $5,000 on completion of his course. B goes to college, and borrows and spends more than $5,000 for college expenses. When he has nearly completed his course, A notifies him of an intention to revoke the promise. A's promise is binding and B is entitled to payment on completion of the course without regard to whether his performance was 'bargained for' . . . ."

130. Complaint, *Echols, supra* note 111, at 19–21.

131. California State University, Hayward v. NCAA, 47 Cal. App. 3d. 533, 121 Cal. Rptr. 85, 89-90 (1975); Trustees of State Colleges and Universities v. NCAA, 82 Cal. App. 3d 461, 147 Cal. Rptr. 187, 192 (1978).

132. Complaint, *Echols, supra* note 111, at 20.

133. NCAA Constitution 4-6; NCAA Bylaw 8-5; NCAA Manual 29–30, 100–01.

134. *See* RESTATEMENT, SECOND, CONTRACTS Sec. 345 (1981).

135. *Cf.* RESTATEMENT, SECOND, CONTRACTS Sec. 345(f) (1981).

136. WILLISTON ON CONTRACTS 3d Ed. Sec. 364 A (1959): "Where the contract contains an arbitration clause which is legally enforceable, the general view is that the beneficiary is bound thereby to the same extent that the promisor is bound."

137. RESTATEMENT, SECOND, CONTRACTS Sec. 304 (1981).

138. *Id.* Sec. 302.

139. *See* University of Missouri v. Horowitz, 430 U.S. 964 (1978); Connelly v. University of Vermont, 244 F. Supp. 156 (D. Vt. 1965); Keys v. Sawyer, 353 F. Supp. 936, 940 (D. Tex. 1973).

140. *E.g.*, DeMarco v. University of Health Sciences, The Chicago Medical School, 40 Ill. App. 3d 474, 352 N.E. 2d 356 (1976); Lowenthal v. Vanderbilt, Chancery Court, Davidson County, Tennessee, No. A8525, Aug. 15, 1977, summarized in H. EDWARDS & V. NORDIN, HIGHER EDUCATION AND THE LAW 430–32 (1979).

141. 25 Cal. App. 3d 1, 101 Cal. Rptr. 499 (1972).

142. *Id.* at 504.

143. In *Lowenthal v. Vanderbilt, supra* note 140, the court recognized that, if proved, lost earnings may be recoverable from a university that fails to meet its academic obligations to students.

144. Chron. Higher Educ., Nov. 25, 1981, at 9.

145. *Id.*

146. *Id.*

147. Complaint, Jones v. Snowden, No. 81–131648 (Wayne County Circuit Court, Mich.).

148. *Id.*

149. *Id.*

150. The problem of protecting academic standards was addressed in early 1982 in an unusual civil suit that, in effect, saw the court intervene against the imposition of academic requirements for an athlete. Mark Hall, a senior guard on the Minnesota Gophers basketball team, was rejected for admission to a degree-granting program at the university on the reported grounds that his academic performance had not been adequate. He sought and obtained a temporary restraining order from U.S. District Judge Miles Lord on the theory that his rights to due process had been violated. N.Y. Times, Jan. 4, 1982, Section C, at 11, col. 1.

152. Sports Illustrated, July 20, 1982, at 7.

153. *Id.*

154. N.Y. Times, *supra* note 151.

155. *Id.*

156. Sports Illustrated, *supra* note 152.

157. The American Football Coaches Association has suggested a related proposal, known as the "triple option." It would begin initially with a 2.25 grade-point-average requirement, instead of the present 2.0. If a high school graduate did not have that, he could qualify for a scholarship by

having either a combined verbal and math SAT score of 750 or a 17 on the ACT. Sports Illustrated, May 19, 1980, at 71.

158. See *Id.*

159. In fact, Harry Edwards contends that earlier NCAA legislation reducing the limits on athletic scholarships was unfair to blacks, because its impact was greatest on those perceived as "academic risks." *Sport within the Veil,* ANNALS OF THE AMER. ACAD. POL. & SOC. SCI. at 122, (Sept. 1979).

160. Each year only about 150 football players (out of 41,000 on NCAA varsity rosters) and 50 basketball players (out of 15,000 on NCAA varsity rosters) go to the pros from college. On the average, they play respectively 4.2 seasons in football and 3.4 seasons in basketball. Sports Illustrated, May 19, 1980, at 60.

161. Legislative Proposal No. 30, NCAA 1981 Convention Program; proposed by universities in the Big Ten Conference.

162. Comments of Gwendolyn Norell, Faculty Athletic Representative, Michigan State University, on the floor of the NCAA Convention, Jan. 13, 1981.

163. See Hanford Appendix at 141.

164. It is conceivable that some institutions might respond to this change by more readily granting degrees to undeserving athletes with the result that corruption is extended rather than reduced. The reluctance of institutions to do so in the past indicates that there would be considerable resistance to such a development. It is precisely the power of that resistance which is needed to bolster academic standards for athletes.

165. *See* G. SHAW, MEAT ON THE HOOF (1972) (explaining how football coaches at the University of Texas used various techniques to induce athletes to quit football early in their careers and give up their scholarships so that the scholarship could be committed to others).

166. G. Lueschen, a distinguished sports sociologist, has observed, "[T]he rewards that are at stake in a contest will determine the amount and severity of cheating." SOCIAL PROBLEMS IN ATHLETICS (D. Landers ed. 1976), 70. Given the sizable rewards now available to the successful big-time college athletic programs, it is not surprising that some institutions have not only exploited the inadequate rules that now exist but have cheated as well and can be expected to continue to cheat unless enforcement is effective.

167. *E.g.,* J. MICHENER, SPORTS IN AMERICA 199 (1976); J. ROONEY, THE RECRUITING GAME 159–85 (1980).

168. Sports Illustrated, May 19, 1980, at 72.

[6]

Unsportsmanlike Conduct: The Student Athlete, the NCAA, and Agents

Robert H. Ruxin

The popular hero did the unthinkable, in the eyes of many—including his coach, Bob Zuppke—when he brought his enormous prestige to the cause of professional football. On November 22, 1925, the day after he had played his last college game, [Red] Grange signed a contract, *negotiated by his manager,* Charles C. Pyle, guaranteeing him at least $100,000 to play with George Halas's and Dutch Sternaman's Chicago Bears.[1]

Although Red Grange retained a manager or agent more than a half century ago, it is only during the last decade that agents have assumed a pervasive role in professional sports and among student athletes[2] with pro career ambitions.[3] One sportswriter has observed, "Surely, the growing power of sports agents was never more graphically shown than during the ceremonies. [Pitcher Frank]Tanana's best man was his agent."[4]

A good agent can help a professional athlete attain financial and mental stability during and after his career. An incompetent or dishonest agent can ruin an athlete's playing career and threaten his financial security for years afterward.[5] An agent can also jeopardize an undergraduate athlete's collegiate eligibility and cause his university to forfeit athletic contests and television revenue.[6]

The rise of agents can be attributed to the athlete's increased bargaining power since the mid-1970s.[7] Two factors primarily account for the athlete's stronger position: (1) In the 1970s competition from new leagues against the established leagues in football, basketball, and hockey pushed up salary levels[8] and other benefits.[9] (2) The opportu-

This chapter is published with the permission of the National Association of College and University Attorneys.

nity to enter the open market as a free agent—won by arbitrators' decisions,[10] legal suits,[11] and collective bargaining drawing on the leverage obtained from those decisions and suits[12]—has given athletes an alternative to accepting a team's final offer. Moreover, major league teams have been willing to pay higher salaries because of lucrative television contracts[13] and the promise of cable television revenues.[14]

Agents can help individual athletes take advantage of their bargaining power.[15] Unfortunately, too often agents instead take advantage of the athlete.[16] Consider, for example, the plight of Dennis Duval, an all-American basketball player at Syracuse University and briefly a guard with two National Basketball Association teams. "I'm the victim of a crime and I'm being asked to pay for it," Duval told a federal court as he filed for bankruptcy.[17] His agent, Richard Sorkin, handled his money and supposedly paid his bills, Duval said. But he allegedly lost $30,000 to Sorkin, who was later sentenced to three years in prison for taking at least $300,000 (and possibly as much as $1.3 million) from thirteen athletes.[18]

Sometimes, both the athlete and the university suffer. Another basketball player, Jeff Ruland, lost his eligibility for his senior year at Iona College because he was "sweet-talked" into signing a contract with an agent in violation of National Collegiate Athletic Association (NCAA) rules.[19]

One long-time participant in the college sports scene, Al McGuire, former Marquette University basketball coach, has blamed many of the problems in professional sports on agents. "It's a lot like a bouncer in a bar. If there's not a fight, the bouncer will create one and throw somebody out. It seems like athletes find an agent and all of a sudden they get into a turmoil type of thing."[20]

This article will review NCAA rules relevant to student athletes and agents and suggest several approaches to reduce the abuses associated with agents, protect and enhance the student athlete's rights and interests, and preserve the university's substantial educational and financial interest in ensuring that its student athletes and athletic officials comply with NCAA eligibility rules. It suggests that each university that awards athletic scholarships has an obligation to educate its student athletes as to the realities of the business of professional sports and the student athlete's obligation to the university to comply with NCAA rules governing amateur status. The article also recommends that the NCAA members review and modify those rules with the aim of balancing the long-standing goal of preventing excessive professionalism against an athlete's need for and pressures to retain competent advisers *before* completing his college athletic eligibility. It raises the possibility of pursuing tort actions against agents who violate the NCAA rules.

I. NCAA RULES[21]

A. Prohibitions

NCAA rules forbid:

1. an athlete to agree, either orally or in writing, to be represented by an agent or organization in the marketing of his athletic ability or reputation until after completion of his last intercollegiate contest;[22]
2. an athlete or any representative of the athlete to *negotiate* or *sign* a playing contract in any sports in which he intends to compete or from marketing the name or image of the athlete;[23] it makes no difference whether or not the contract is legally enforceable;[24]
3. an athlete to ask to be placed on a professional league's draft list,[25] whether or not he withdraws his name before the draft,[26] whether or not he is actually drafted,[27] and whether or not he signs a professional contract.[28] This rule applies only to sports that require an undergraduate to declare his desire to be drafted prior to completion of his eligibility (primarily basketball);
4. an athlete to accept expenses or gifts of any kind (including meals and transportation) from an agent (or anyone else) who wishes to provide service to the athlete; such payment would represent compensation based on athletic skills and a preferential benefit not available to other students;[29]
5. an athlete to receive preferential benefits or treatment (e.g., loans with deferred pay-back basis) because of the athlete's reputation, skill, or pay-back potential as a professional athlete;[30]
6. an athlete to retain professional services for personal reasons at less than the normal charge from a representative of an institution's athletic interests;[31]
7. a member of the athletic staff to represent, directly or indirectly, a student athlete in the marketing of his athletic ability or reputation to a professional sports team or organization and to receive any compensation or gratuities for such activity.[32]

B. Allowances

NCAA rules allow:

1. an athlete to compete professionally in sports in which he does not participate for the university;[33]
2. an athlete to retain an agent specifically limited in writing to representing him in those sports in which he competes as a professional;[34]
3. an athlete to retain an attorney for matters of a personal nature, including evaluating the terms of a proposed professional contract, providing the attorney does not represent the athlete in negotiating such a contract[35] and the student athlete pays normal fees;[36]
4. an athlete to talk to an agent, providing he neither agrees to be rep-

resented nor accepts anything of value from the agent;[37]
5. an athlete to inquire about his eligibility to be drafted.[38]

C. Discussion

The NCAA rarely enforces its rules relating to agents and student
athletes.[39] Part of the problem is that the rules are largely unenforceable. Usually, the NCAA and the university will be unaware that an
athlete has entered a prohibited agreement with an agent. Only if the
athlete or agent becomes disenchanted, or possibly if the athlete flaunts
the monetary benefits bestowed by the agent, is the agreement likely
to become known.[40]

One notable recent exception involved Jeff Ruland. The *Washington
Post* described what it termed "a sequence of bizarre and contradictory
events" that began the day after Ruland announced he would return to
Iona College for his senior year:[41]

> • Iona's president and the school's basketball coach called a press
> conference the next day to announce that Ruland had forfeited his
> college eligibility by signing a personal management contract a year
> earlier with a professional agent, Paul Corvino of Mamaroneck.
> Ruland, declared Brother John Driscoll, Iona's president, had been
> "sweet-talked" into the agreement for which he had received cash
> and other favors in violation of NCAA rules.
> • Ruland applied for the National Basketball Association's draft
> pool as an underclassman. . . .
> • Corvino announced he had no contract at all with Ruland. . . .
> • Ruland repudiated Corvino as his agent.
> • Corvino met with writers for Basketball Times. . . . In fact, there
> was an agreement with Ruland, Corvino declared, and under its
> terms he was entitled to 10 percent of Ruland's gross earnings over
> the next four years.
>
> In exchange for his signature, Corvino asserted, he had, in the
> last year, given Ruland cash totaling $9,000, purchased shares of
> oil stock in Ruland's name, opened a bank account containing
> $2,500 for him and lavished several other "gifts" on the gifted basket-
> ball star. "These kids need security while they are still in school,"
> said Corvino. The lawyers [for Corvino] made it clear that any at-
> tempts to displace Corvino as Ruland's agent would be met with a
> court challenge.
>
> Ruland served formal notice that he considered any arrangements
> with Corvino null and void.

More than a year later, when asked what advice he had for college
athletes concerning agents, Ruland replied, "Don't talk to any of them.
. . . [T]oo many agents are out there for themselves."[42] While conced-

ing, "what I did was wrong," Ruland said 150 other guys did the same thing.[43]

A few of the dilemmas created by the NCAA rules can be illustrated by examining a situation that dozens of athletes go through each spring. The most talented undergraduate (nonsenior) college basketball players face a major decision: whether to place their name on the National Basketball Association (NBA) draft list and negotiate an NBA contract or return for another year of college basketball (and, presumably, schooling).[44] At stake for the athlete may be hundreds of thousands of dollars—or even a million—and his college degree. At stake for the agent who becomes that athlete's representative may be as much as 10 percent of that amount. At stake for the college coach may be the difference between playing in the final four of the NCAA tournament and a losing season; i.e., his job.[45] At stake for the university are the potential hundreds of thousands of dollars that an all-American basketball player may help generate through gate receipts, television revenue, and tournament revenues. At stake for the NBA team or teams that think they may be able to draft the player may be the ability to win a division title or even keep the franchise solvent. In sum, the student athlete's decision may have a cumulative multimillion dollar impact.

Where can the athlete, a relatively unsophisticated teenager with only a year or two of college education, turn for help in reaching his decision? What help can he receive? He can talk to agents, but he can't agree to retain one. As one college coach noted, the agent will probably encourage the athlete to leave school, because that is the only way the agent gets paid.[46] He can hire a lawyer, but only if the lawyer charges his normal fees. The lawyer can review any offers; he can return the contract; but he cannot make any counteroffers. He can ask his coach to help, but the coach probably is not experienced in making major business deals, may be leery of violating NCAA rules, and has a vested interest in the athlete's staying in school.

One of the most respected college basketball coaches, Dean Smith of the University of North Carolina, recently told a reporter:

> I think any young man making a decision like that should have the advice of counsel. I don't think it has to be an agent. It can be a family attorney or longtime friend who genuinely has his best interests in mind. The players who left school early and had problems are, for the most part, the ones who left without really knowing what they could get.[47]

Unfortunately, the NCAA rules are not structured to maximize the unbiased information available to a student athlete. If, for example, an undergraduate basketball player retains an agent who contacts professional teams on his behalf to sound out his value, the student will be forced into turning professional, because he either retained an agent, allowed someone to negotiate on his behalf, or both—unless the NCAA does not find out.[48]

The National Basketball Association will no longer permit its teams to contact an undergraduate before he applies for the draft. The change, announced in June 1981, was ostensibly "a gesture not to encourage undergraduates to leave college," and an attempt to improve relations with the NCAA. In explaining the change, Jerry Colangelo, general manager of the Phoenix Suns, alleged that agents had contacted NBA teams and claimed to be in a position to represent particular college stars. "They then ask for financial commitments and when and if they get them, they go back to the kids and get them to try and leave school." Colangelo called on the NCAA "to find a better way of policing the agents. Things are getting out of control."[49]

Although some agents have induced student athletes to violate NCAA rules and have made false representations to professional teams and to athletes, the NBA's rule change may be motivated more from a desire to reduce salaries paid to undergraduate stars than from a desire to help the NCAA police agents. If the teams cannot contact an athlete before he asks to be drafted (and thereby loses his collegiate eligibility), his bargaining power will be reduced substantially, because he will not have the option of spurning their offers and staying in college.

Proposals for modifying the NCAA rules are discussed below.

II. WHAT COULD BE DONE

A. Educate the athletes

Dr. George Hanford, President of the College Board, has proposed that universities with big-time sports programs offer a Bachelor of Athletics degree. There would be two mandatory requirements for graduation: first, that the student has read and understands the NCAA Manual; second, that each student athlete be counseled about sports agents and other issues related to the business aspects of playing professional sports.[50]

Few students are likely to meet the first requirement, since it is beyond the capabilities of most coaches and athletic administrators and probably most law professors at the student athlete's university. As a prominent university administrator told a congressional committee investigating the NCAA, the complexity of the NCAA Manual is directly related to the difficulties in controlling college athletes:[51]

> . . . I submit that when you need a book of more than 289 pages to tell you how to conduct intercollegiate athletics, you are no longer talking about "sport."

> And the rules themselves are a patchwork quilt, with one added
> on to the last to the point where even the most dedicated coach or
> athletic administrator can run afoul of them without even knowing it.

But Dr. Hanford's counseling proposal—including an explanation of
the NCAA rules—should be implemented by every university that
awards athletic scholarships, at least in regard to its students with professional athletic potential.

Set out below is a synopsis of the information, in *addition* to the
NCAA rules, that should be conveyed to student athletes and to their
families and personal advisers. The university may present the information in a speech (perhaps by an alumnus who has played professionally, a law or business school professor, a university attorney, an academic counselor, the athletic director, or a coach), a film, a pamphlet,
or by a combination of methods.

What is an agent? Since there are no prerequisites to calling oneself
an agent, an agent is anyone who says he is an agent and has a client.
Except in California, agents are subject only to general principles of
agency law.[52] Agents have a variety of backgrounds: accountants, real
estate brokers, dentists, coaches, used car salesmen, ex-professional athletes, dry cleaners, and even a kosher caterer. Many agents have stud-
ied law but are not necessarily practicing lawyers or admitted to the
bar.

The term agent covers a broad range of relationships with a professional athlete. An agent may simply be a personal friend—a family lawyer, teacher, or high school coach—who offers advice on a contract
negotiation. At the other extreme, an agent may be part of an international conglomerate that handles financial matters for the athlete. Or,
as Penn State football coach Joe Paterno recently said, "anybody who
is a fast talker, who can get a kid who might be a little naive, slip him
a few bucks and get him to sign something can be an agent."[53]

What do agents do? The term agent is most commonly used to refer
to persons who are involved in negotiating playing contracts. A good
agent can help a player in several ways, including: determining the
value of his services; convincing a team to pay him that value; shaping
the package of compensation to suit the player's needs; protecting the
player's rights under his contract and the sport's collective bargaining
agreement and rules; counseling the player about postcareer security,
both financially and occupationally; finding a new team for a free
agent; generally, allowing the athlete to concentrate on playing. An
agent may also obtain product endorsement contracts, speaking engagements, and generally help the athlete capitalize on his name and
athletic reputation. Agents are often associated either directly or indirectly with financial management and investment firms.[54] Most pro-

fessional athletes will also require the services of a lawyer (unless the agent is part of a law firm), an accountant, and often an independent financial adviser.

How does an athlete find an agent? The problem is not finding an agent, but finding the right one at the right time. The agents find the athlete. Freeman Williams, a two-time NCAA basketball scoring leader, stated in April of his senior year, "Just about every day there's another guy who tells me he's the guy to be my agent. That's the usual line, that he'll do what's best for me."[55] More than one hundred would-be agents contacted all-American quarterback Neil Lomax before the 1981 NFL draft. A recent Seattle Seahawks' early-round draft choice received more than ninety letters from people who wanted to represent him. Many of those letters came while he was still playing college football, despite the NCAA rule that forbids an athlete from retaining an agent until after his playing season ends.[56]

Some of the more competent agents who are practicing lawyers may have more difficulty than nonlawyers in making their services known to student athletes. This is primarily because of the traditional bar limitations on solicitation of new clients.[57]

An approach some student athletes have used is to set up a screening committee in the community where the university is situated.[58] The athlete and his family can refer inquiries from agents to the committee. The committee can also invite agents, including attorneys who feel constrained from soliciting, to submit proposals for representing the athlete. The utility of this procedure varies according to the qualifications of the committee members and their commitment to the athlete's best interests.

How should an athlete select an agent? First, *get help.* The combination of the athlete's lack of business experience and the knack of many agents to sweet-talk a prospective client often makes it wise for the athlete to ask his parents or a coach to help screen the agents. After the athlete narrows his choices, a hometown lawyer may be valuable in interviewing these agents and in reviewing any contract between the athlete and an agent *before* the athlete signs anything. This adviser can also help the athlete determine what services he will require and whether they should be provided by one agent or firm or by a combination of agent, lawyer, accountant, or other specialists. Some athletes are represented by two independent lawyers—a personal lawyer and a specialist in their sport.

Don't rely solely on titles (lawyer, financial consultant) or educational background. Incompetence among agents spans the educational and occupational horizons.

Ask a prospective agent for *proof* of his educational background, training, work experience—particularly in the sports field—and character and professional *references* from other clients and persons such as a lawyer not involved in sports or an accountant.

Inquire about a particular agent's *reputation* through a players association, other players, and even other agents.

If the agent will handle any of the athlete's funds, find out if he is *bonded*. While bonding is not essential and may not indicate anything about the agent's ability, it is an important factor to consider in evaluating the safety of trusting an agent with substantial amounts of money.

Question him in detail about his fees, his relationships with club management, the likely impact of his other clients on the athlete's interests, his policy on renegotiating a contract, circumstances under which the athlete can dismiss him, whether he feels bound by any code of ethics, and any other topic that seems at all relevant. The athlete should not hesitate to continue asking questions about any conceivably relevant matter.

If the agent is not a practicing attorney, make sure he is amenable to having the athlete's lawyer review any playing contracts or any investment agreements. Even if such a review is not necessary, a reputable agent should not object to consultation with an attorney before the athlete signs any legal documents.

Choosing an agent is one of the most important decisions an athlete ever makes. It is a process that an athlete cannot afford to take lightly. The athlete has a wide choice of agents—both competent and incompetent—competing for a few available clients and the prospect of glamor, glory, and riches. The athlete should not rush into a decision; he should decide only after consulting parents, coaches, other players, his players association, and a nonagent lawyer.

Is a written contract necessary? It is crucial for the athlete and agent to reach a precise and clear understanding of the services the agent will provide before the athlete authorizes the agent to act on his behalf. For example, will the agent do more than negotiate the player's contract? Will he try to obtain product endorsements, speaking engagements, a writer to do a biography? If he seeks endorsements, will he be the exclusive agent for the player and therefore entitled to a fee for all endorsements, even those obtained by another agent?

First, the athlete and the agent should agree orally about the nature and extent of their relationship.[59] Then consider a written contract. A written agreement may protect the player in case he later believes the agent is not fulfilling his duty. An athlete normally will have a better chance of winning a legal dispute over the rights of the athlete and the obligations of the agent if he has a written contract.[60]

But a written agreement is no guarantee of satisfactory service. It could be useless against a fly-by-night agent or an agent who goes bankrupt. Moreover, the contract could hurt the athlete. For example, if a contract is for a period of several years, it could prevent a player from changing agents despite having a legitimate reason to do so. A written agreement may contain an exclusivity clause under which a former agent will claim a percentage of all the player's endorsement contracts, including ones that he had no part in arranging.[61]

Some respected agents, including many lawyer-agents, reject the idea of a contract between player and agent. Bob Woolf, for example, has never had a written agreement with any of his more than three hundred clients. Richard Moss considers a long-term representational contract abhorrent to the nature of representing someone. He likened it to a doctor refusing to treat a patient unless he agreed not to see any other doctor for three years. However, even a lawyer's fee arrangement should be in writing. While this does not bind the athlete to the lawyer, it sets forth the basis for determining compensation of the lawyer.

In summary, two points are essential in formalizing a relationship with an agent. First, an athlete should not agree to any representational arrangement until he has a precise understanding of his relationship with the particular agent. Second, the agent may require the athlete to sign a contract with him, or the athlete may decide he wants a written agreement. In either case, the athlete should ask an uninvolved attorney to review the contract before he signs it. But the student athlete must remember that he cannot accept any agreement—oral or written, formal or informal—if he wishes to retain his collegiate eligibility.

How much will the agent charge? "There are hundreds of people constantly running after players. They sign them to outrageous kinds of agency contracts—7½ to 10 per cent of all earnings for extraordinary lengths of time. People are pigs, taking advantage of fairly innocent players."[62] Not all agents are pigs, but all do charge for their services— even those who offer gifts to college athletes who agree to be represented by them. The four most commonly used methods of calculating fees for negotiating a contract are as follows: (1) *percentage* (contingent fee): the agent takes a percentage of the total dollar value of the contract; (2) *time:* the agent, typically an attorney, charges a set hourly rate for the time he spends working for the player; (3) *flat fee:* the agent agrees to negotiate the contract in return for a predetermined fee regardless of the time spent or the amount of the contract; (4) *combination:* the agent, for example, considers the time he spent and makes a subjective judgment of what he accomplished[63] and then limits his fee to a maximum of three, four, or five percent of the contract's dollar value.

No consensus exists as to the relative merits of each method of fee calculation.[64] The percentage is the most widely criticized but probably the most popular method. Since the athlete usually can negotiate with only one team and has his prior salary as a base (or the minimum salary if he is a rookie), the agent's primary job is to negotiate an increase in the salary. For this reason some critics of the percentage method suggest that a contingent fee would more closely reflect the agent's performance if the fee were calculated as a percentage of the increase over the present contract. For example, if a player earning $100,000 signs a new contract for $150,000, the agent would collect a percentage of the $50,000 increase rather than of the $150,00 total. But this approach might encourage the agent to negotiate a shorter term contract with a higher salary to maximize his immediate benefit. The contingent method also encourages an agent to exchange nonmonetary benefits desired by his client (such as restrictions on being traded) for a higher salary or bonus.

Proponents of the percentage system cite three advantages: an economic rather than moral incentive for the agent to negotiate for more money; an incentive for the athlete to consult the agent more frequently because it will not cost him more, as it would if the agent charged on a time basis; and ease of accounting for the agent, particularly if he does more for the client than negotiate his contract.

The athlete should discuss in detail an agent's method of fee calculation before agreeing to retain the agent. Many agents will agree to an approximate fee before the negotiations begin and will be willing to negotiate their fee. Regardless of how the agent calculates the fee, most reputable agents consider about five percent of the contract's value to be the maximum appropriate fee. This amount may be greater in unusual situations—for example, to cover the costs of additional specialized tax advice used in drafting the contract. An agent who provides services in addition to contract negotiation usually will charge an additional fee. Most important, all compensation arrangements should be in writing, signed by the agent.

When does the athlete pay the agent? Fees should be collected as the player earns the compensation negotiated by the agent. The agent should not take a fee up front—one payment, often taken out of the player's bonus. Consider an agent who negotiates a two-year contract with annual salaries of $40,000 and $45,000 and a $15,000 signing bonus; the agent takes his 10 percent of the total $100,000—*$10,000*. If the athlete does not make the team, he's left with only *$5,000*. Up front collection cheats a player in two ways: primarily because he may be cut and not receive part or all of the salary; secondarily, because of inflation, a dollar todays buys more than today's dollar will buy next year and much more than today's dollar will buy in twenty years, when the player may be collecting deferred compensation. But an agent who collects up front receives his entire fee in present dollars rather than in the inflated dollars the player will earn.

Expect an agent to collect up front for his out-of-pocket expenses for the negotiations, such as telephone calls and airplane fares. The player should ascertain in advance whether or not such expenses are included in an agent's fee, be it percentage, hourly, flat, or combination.

How might the agent's other clients impede his ability to represent additional clients? Most athletes are represented by agents who represent more than one client. Since an agent's work for his other clients may affect how well he serves any other client, the athlete should question prospective agents about their other clients and how their interests may affect his interests. Several potential problems arise when an agent represents more than one client. They include conflicting demands on the agent's time, his ability to represent the interests of one client without compromising the interests of any other client, and his ability to take advantage of multiple representation to benefit each client.[65]

Since few, if any, agents are likely to admit they are overcommitted, the athlete must make his own assessment of the agent's ability to spend sufficient time on his behalf and weigh it as one factor in his choice of agents.[66] To protect himself against the possibility that the agent will not devote enough time to his interests, a player may want a written promise from the agent that such neglect will permit the athlete to end their relationship. Of course any agent—whether he represents one athlete or fifty—will have other demands on his time.[67]

A more complex issue involves the agent's responsibilities when he represents several players drafted by a particular team.[68] Will the agent be less hard-nosed in negotiating any particular contract in order to cultivate the goodwill of the owner for his other clients and for himself? If he represents several players who play the same position, will he play favorites? Will he even realize he is favoring one client over another?

Each athlete should try to determine if he would be better off with a different agent. For example, a high-round football draft pick may suffer if his agent refuses to agree to terms offered until the team sweetens its offer to a lower-round pick, whom the agent also represents.[69] The athlete should consider whether the agent will be capable of meeting this test: can the agent separate and carry out his function as if the players were represented by different agents?[70]

Finally, the athlete should insist that any potential agent "disclose" any possible conflicts to the clients involved.[71] Disclosure should mean a full and clear explanation. Unfortunately, this does not always happen. It is the athlete's responsibility to question the agent closely to try to understand how the conflict may affect his own interests. He should ask the agent for a list of his clients. In some cases, the athlete may want to accompany his agent to a crucial negotiating session as an observer, in part to force the team to deal with him as an individual rather than as one of a group represented by the same agent.

The points discussed above are intended only to suggest some of the areas in which the university should educate the student athlete. Other topics include legal obligations that flow from a contract, the role of players associations, and data about salaries and average career duration in professional sports. While a degree in athletics might be difficult for most college faculties to accept, an interdisciplinary course that deals with the business of professional sports could be educationally sound for athletes and other students. The course could draw on the talent of various professors, including those specializing in labor relations, business/finance, law, journalism, history, sociology, and economics.

B. Reevaluate the NCAA rules and enforcement

"The best thing for everyone involved would be just to bring the thing out of the closet. That way, if the player wants to come back and consult with his coach, he can. As it is now, we don't want to know what the agents are telling them because, in effect, that makes us accessories to a crime."[72] That suggestion, by Joey Meyer, DePaul University assistant basketball coach and an unofficial, unpaid adviser to Mark Aguirre (who left DePaul after his sophomore year to play in the NBA) should be the touchstone by which the member schools of the NCAA review all its rules relating to agents. [73] No one seriously doubts that the rule against agreeing to representation prior to completion of eligibility is frequently violated. [74] But as Meyer's comment implies, if an athlete tells his coach that an agent is advising him to leave, the coach's hands are tied because of possible violations of NCAA rules. Moreover, the agent will probably tell the student athlete not to discuss anything about turning professional with his coach, because he risks losing his eligibility.

The result is to force the student athlete to make crucial decisions without sufficient information and opportunity to discuss the matter with trusted advisers. The rule such as the one that forbids an athlete from receiving services at less than normal fees,[75] if strictly interpreted and enforced,[76] could even shut off an athlete from legal advice allowed by the NCAA rules. If an athlete cannot afford to pay the going rate for the attorney's services, then he would not be allowed to retain an attorney.

The "[f]undamental [p]olicy" of the NCAA, explicitly stated in its constitution, is "to maintain intercollegiate athletics as an integral part of the educational program and the athlete as an integral part of the student body and, by so doing, retain a clear line of demarcation between college athletics and professional sports."[77] But there is a fundamental tension between this policy and the ever-increasing commercialism attached to college athletics, particularly football and basketball.[78] The beneficiaries and the victims of this tension are the persons most responsible for the multimillion dollar television contracts—the outstanding student athletes.[79]

Without altering its fundamental policy, the NCAA should help its student athletes develop the ability and capacity to protect and enhance their postcollegiate opportunities—whether in professional sports or elsewhere.[80] One important means of achieving this responsibility is to maximize the athlete's ability to make informed decisions. Among the possible ways to do so, in addition to educating the student athlete (generally and specifically in regard to agents and other aspects of the business of professional sports) are the following:

1. Provide an information clearing house and career counseling by someone associated with the university,[81] its sports conference,[82] or the NCAA[83] who has a working knowledge of the professional sports industry. This service need not violate current strictures against preferential treatment for student athletes if it would be available to any student, including those interested in nonplaying jobs in professional sports. In fact, not providing such a service may discriminate against student athletes, because students receive counseling and placement services for almost any other field. While such a service should not recommend particular agents, it should help the student athlete decide how to obtain representation and provide data on the compensation and terms for comparable professional prospects so that the athlete can measure the promises of prospective agents against more impartial data. Presumably the professional players associations and leagues[84] could be persuaded to cooperate in providing contract data to the counseling services.

2. Allow student athletes to retain agents under strictly regulated conditions,[85] such as: (a) the athlete could accept no compensation, gifts, or favors in return for the agency agreement; (b) a copy of the agency agreement or a memorandum describing the relationship (if there is no contract) would be filed with the university and its athletic conference office.[86] While this proposal would not solve all problems—for example, how to enforce the no-compensation rule—it would enable anyone associated with the university and the more reputable agents to participate in the process without fear of sanction. It will be opposed by some as counter to the NCAA's amateur creed and likely to encourage athletes to play for themselves rather than for the college team.[87] Realistically, such a change is unlikely to occur soon: "That means the clandestine negotiations will go on. Coaches with outstanding players will be left wondering what is going on as the [NBA draft] deadline approaches and they find it

more and more difficult to get in touch with the player to learn what he is thinking."[88]

3. Enforce the present rules. If under-the-table agency agreements and payoffs are as prevalent as they appear to be, it should not be difficult for the NCAA, with the cooperation of its members and the professional leagues, to discover some of the agents who induce the athletes to violate the rules and make them prominent examples.[89]

4. Bring suit against agents who enter agreements in violation of NCAA rules. For example, consider the situation after the 1971 basketball tournament involving Howard Porter, who had signed an agency agreement (and a professional basketball contract) while he was still playing for Villanova. The NCAA forced Villanova to forfeit its runner-up position in the national championship tournament and return its tournament share of $68,318.84.[90]

Hypothetically, the university has at least two potential grounds for a tort action. The first is interference by the agent with the contractual relationship (a) between Porter and Villanova and (b) between Villanova and the NCAA.[91] Although at least one court has held that the student athlete/university relationship is contractual,[92] and student's rights advocates argue that a contract exists,[93] a university might hesitate to adopt such a position because of potential legal implications that flow from an employer-employee relationship.[94] However, a claim based on interference with the university-NCAA relationship would not pose such a problem but might threaten the voluntary association status of the NCAA.[95]

The second grounds would be interference with prospective economic advantage. This theory has the advantage of not requiring a prior contractual relationship but rather is more inclusive.[96] A leading California case sets out the elements of this tort as applied in the real estate brokerage context:

> (1) an economic relationship between broker and vendor or broker and vendee containing the probability of future economic benefit to the broker, (2) knowledge by the defendant of the existence of the relationship, (3) intentional acts on the part of the defendant designed to disrupt the relationship, (4) actual disruption of the relationship, (5) damages to the plaintiffs proximately caused by the acts of the defendant.[97]

The athlete-agent situation seems to meet all of these elements. (1) Even if the relationship between student and college does not rise to the contractual level, the scholarship and the revenues associated with successful football and basketball programs certainly make the relationship an economic one. Similarly, the television contracts make the

NCAA-university relationship economic. Assuming the athlete retains his eligibility, there is a strong probability of future economic benefit to the university. (2) Certainly the agent and the athlete know of both relationships. (3) Entering an agency agreement would be an intentional act to disrupt the relationships (and certainly the agent and, one would hope, the athlete would know that the agency agreement violated the rule and if discovered would jeopardize the relationship). (4) The actual disruption is clear: the athlete is declared ineligible; the university is required to forfeit past wins or to suffer other sanctions, including loss of television revenues. (5) Loss of television revenues clearly would be an act proximately caused by the defendant and easily valued; other acts proximately caused, such as forfeits and other sanctions, could be valued with additional evidence. The goal of bringing suit, besides compensating the university for its losses, would be to chill future violations by agents and athletes.

III. CONCLUSION

> Under the management of "C.C." ("Cash and Carry," he was dubbed) Pyle, Grange became the first of the marketable football celebrities. He endorsed Red Grange dolls, a sweater, a cap just like the one he wore, a ginger ale, a candy bar, and even a meat loaf. Sportswriters were frankly asked to submit ideas for a script on which Grange could "ride to fame on the silver screen." He starred in the successful *One Minute to Play* in 1926, and in 1929 played himself in a talkie, *The Galloping Ghost*.[98]

Since the days of Red Grange and "Cash and Carry" Pyle, professionalism has become the standard path for outstanding college athletes. It is time for universities and the NCAA to recognize that while they should retain the line between college and professional sports, they may need to redraw it. They must address the fundamental tension between amateurism and realism as it affects the career choices of the student athlete. Their goal should be to increase the student athlete's ability to make informed decisions. Furthermore, each university and athletic conference has a responsibility to educate its student athletes about the business of professional sports, particularly about agents.

NOTES

1. M. Pachter, Champions of American Sport 266 (1981).
2. "A student-athlete is a student whose matriculation was solicited by

a member of the athletic staff or other representative of athletic interests with a view toward the student's ultimate participation in the inter-collegiate athletic program." Constitution and Interpretations of the National Collegiate Athletic Association, art. three, section 1, Official Interpretation 1, *reprinted in* [1980–81] Manual of the National Collegiate Athletic Association [hereinafter cited as NCAA Manual].

3. *See, e.g.,* Barnes, *Agent's Role Draws Fire,* Washington Post, August 10, 1980, § D at 1 [hereinafter cited as Barnes]; House Select Comm. on Professional Sports, *Inquiry into Professional Sports, Final Report,* H.R. REP. No. 94-1786, 94th Cong., 2d Sess. 70–71 (1977) [hereinafter cited as House Report].

4. Miller, *Bridegroom Tanana Tosses Bouquet at Angels,* The Sporting News, February 4, 1978, at 48.

5. *See generally* WEISTART & LOWELL, THE LAW OF SPORTS 319–333 (1979), especially notes 709–714 and accompanying text [hereinafter cited as Weistart]. *See also* Barnes, *supra* note 3; House Report, *supra* note 3, at 73–76.

6. *See* text *infra* at note 90.

7. *See generally* H. Klein, *The Golden Age of Salaries,* Inside Sports, August 1981, at 58, especially chart at 69.

8. *See, e.g.,* Zinn v. Parrish, 664 F.2d 360, 361 (7th Cir. 1981); Munchak Corporation v. Cunningham, 457 F.2d 721, 722–724 (4th Cir. 1972); Cincinnati Bengals v. Bergey, 453 F.Supp. 129 (S.D. Ohio 1974).

9. Some examples of other benefits are salary guarantees (regardless of whether the athlete makes the team), no-trade or trade limitation clauses, and even a guarantee to start against right-handed pitchers.

10. *See, e.g.,* National and American Leagues of Professional Baseball Clubs v. Major League Baseball Players Ass'n (John A. Messersmith and David A. McNally), Grievance Nos. 75-27 & 75-28, Decision No. 29 (Dec. 23, 1975, Opinion of Impartial Chairman Peter Seitz). The *Seitz* decision, which declared invalid the reserve clause by which major league baseball teams claimed perpetual control over their players, was affirmed on judicial review. Kansas City Royals Baseball Corp. v. Major League Players Ass'n, 409 F.Supp. 233 (W.D. Mo.), *aff'd,* 532 F.2d 615 (8th Cir. 1976).

11. *See, e.g.,* Robertson v. National Basketball Ass'n, 389 F.Supp. 867 (S.D.N.Y. 1975); Kapp v. National Football League, 390 F.Supp. 73 (N.D. Cal. 1974).

12. *See, e.g., Hearings on H.R. 823 and 3287 Before the Subcomm. on Monopolies and Commercial Law of the House Comm. on the Judiciary,* 97th Cong., 1st Sess.,——(July 16, 1981) (Prepared Statement of Lawrence Fleisher). *See generally* Schatz, *In Free Agency Some Players Freer than Others,* Washington Post, April 13, 1980, § N, at 6.

13. *See generally Football prices take short bounce up,* Broadcasting, August 3, 1981, at 40; *Baseball! Rights go out of the Park,* Broadcasting, March 10, 1981, at 33; *Recession, high prices seen hitting ad dollars,* Television/Radio Age, July 14, 1980, at 23.

14. *See generally Sporting Proposition,* Cablevision, May 3, 1982, at 22; Ray, *Cable Can Be a Boon or a Pain to Sports,* The Sporting News, June 13, 1981, at 14; Baker, *Cable Sports: Whose Court Is This Ball In, Anyway?* Cablevision, May 11, 1981, at 38.

15. *See* House Report, *supra* note 3, at 71–72.

16. *See, e.g., id.* at 74–76 (discussion of situation of Spencer Haywood, who signed a professional basketball contract after his sophomore year at the

University of Detroit with the help of an agent who was paid by the league).

17. N.Y. Times, Jan. 18, 1978, § B, at 6.

18. *Id. See also* Montgomery, *The Spectacular Rise and Ignoble Fall of Richard Sorkin, Pros' Agent,* N.Y. Times, Oct. 9, 1977, § 5, col. 1, N.Y. Times, Feb. 2, 1978, at 57, col. 4.

19. *See* Barnes, *supra* note 3. The relevant NCAA rules are set forth at notes 22 to 36 and accompanying text.

20. Chicago Tribune, October 13, 1980, § 4, at 10 (Midwest Edition).

21. The NCAA rules are set forth in the NCAA Manual, *supra* note 2, which includes the NCAA constitution, bylaws, interpretations, executive regulations, recommended policies, enforcement procedures, administation, and case book.

22. *Id.* at 10.

23. *Id.* at 9.

24. *Id.* at 224.

25. *Id.* at 209.

26. *Id.*

27. *Id.*at 210.

28. *Id.*

29. *Id.* at 211.

30. *Id.* at 11, 207.

31. *Id.* at 219.

32. *Id.* at 22.

33. *See id.* at 9–10. *See also* NCAA Guide for the College-Bound Student-Athlete at 2 (February 1981).

34. NCAA Manual, *supra* note 2.

35. *Id.*

36. *See* notes 29–30 *supra.*

37. *See* notes 22, 29 *supra.*

38. NCAA Manual at 209.

39. Telephone interview with Stephen Morgan, NCAA enforcement staff (July 30, 1981). *See also* Barnes, *supra* note 3; NCAA Enforcement Summary (Oct. 1952–Sept. 1977), *reprinted in NCAA Enforcement Program: Hearings Before the Subcomm. on Oversight and Investigation of the House Comm. on Interstate and Foreign Commerce,* 95th Cong., 2d Sess. (Part II, Appendix II, Attachment I) [hereinafter cited as *NCAA Enforcement Program*].

40. See notes 41–42 *infra* and accompanying text.

41. Barnes, *supra* note 3.

42. Sports Talk, WTOP Radio (Washington, D.C.), August 2, 1981.

43. Many agents feel compelled for competitive reasons to make early contact with undergraduates. Hughes Sports Publications solicited members of the Association of the Representatives of Professional Athletes in June 1981 with a flyer that stated, in part: "A list of the top 100 seniors available for the NFL draft of May 1982, with name, position, height, weight, school and hometown; to be available in July so that players can be contacted before the season begins."

44. *See generally* Feinstein, *NBA and Undergraduates: An Anguished Relationship,* Washington Post, May 10, 1981, § D at 1 [hereinafter cited as Feinstein].

45. For example, after Michigan State won the NCAA basketball championship in 1979, its sophomore star, Magic Johnson, signed a professional contract with the Los Angeles Lakers. The next season Michigan State

lost more games than it won. But the coach, Jud Heathcote, was still the coach as of May 1982.

46. Feinstein, *supra* note 44, quoting Lefty Driesell of the University of Maryland.

47. *Id.*

48. *See, e.g.,* Feinstein, *supra* note 44.

49. N.Y. Times, June 3, 1981, § B at 9, col. 4.

50. *See* Indianapolis Star, August 22, 1981, at 28.

51. *NCAA Enforcement Program, supra* note 39, at Part I, 160 (Testimony of Clifton R. Wharton).

52. 1981 Cal. Stats. ch. 929. The recently enacted law requires the California labor commissioner to license and regulate athletes' agencies. The law applies to independent contractors who recruit any person to enter into an agency or professional sports contract or who for a fee procure, offer, promise, or attempt to obtain employment for any person with a professional sports team. It includes a $10,000 bonding requirement, approval of athlete-agent contracts, maintenance of records of clients and fees for inspection by the labor commissioner, and an arbitration procedure. For further discussion, *see* note 86 *infra.* For a legal analysis of the athlete-agent relationship, *see* Weistart, *supra* note 5 at 323–33.

53. Barnes, *supra* note 3.

54. *See, e.g.,* Barnes, *Athletes' Lives and Livelihoods are ProServ's Stock and Trade,* Washington Post, July 19, 1981, § D at 1, col. 2.

55. *Agents Firing Money Pitch at Freeman Williams,* The Sporting News, April 1, 1978, at 40.

56. *See* note 22 *supra.* One tactic some agents employ is to familiarize themselves with the vernacular of a college athlete's home neighborhood. When they meet the athlete they attempt to impress him with their knowledge or their glibness in talking about the in spots, streets, and modes of transportation. The athlete needs to be warned not to be taken in by this glibness, according to George Taliaferro, special assistant to the president of Indiana University, former National Football League Player, and informal adviser to college athletes. Taliaferro recalled his father's standard for anyone who wanted to represent his son: "It had to be somebody who my father trusted with his fourth grade education or else the shot gun comes out." Taliaferro believes the agent problem must be approached from the basis that the college athlete lives in a "fantasy island" and is gullible and unprepared for professional sports, where he will be "chewed up and spit out." Interview in Indianapolis, Aug. 20, 1981.

57. *See* ABA Canons of Professional Ethics No. 2, *Ethical Considerations,* 2-3, 2-4, 2-8; Disciplinary Rule 2-103 [hereinafter cited as ABA Code]. *Reprinted in* Code of Professional Responsibility and Opinions of the D.C. Bar Legal Ethics Committee, 5M–6M, 11M (1976). Some lawyer-agents avoid the bar restraints by not practicing law; others apparently set up corporations and use nonlawyers to solicit business. House Report *supra* note 3, at 73.

58. Indiana State University used this method to help basketball star Larry Bird select an agent in 1979.

59. For a legal analysis of the athlete-agent relationship, *see* Weistart, *supra* note 5, at 323–333.

60. But the athlete will not necessarily prevail. *See* Zinn v. Parrish, 644 F.2d 360 (7th Cir. 1981).

61. *See* Weistart, *supra* note 5, at 332–333.

62. Interview with Richard Moss, agent and former counsel, Major League Baseball Players Association, in New York (December 27, 1977).

63. What was accomplished is a subjective judgment that depends on the context in which the athlete finds himself (e.g., second-round draft choice) and the degree of success (e.g., obtaining the highest salary for a player of similar experience and ability).

64. After studying the various methods of fee calculation, the House of Representatives Select Committee on Professional Sports

> . . . was unable to discern . . . that contingent fee arrangements
> were totally devoid of ethical value or that hourly or flat fees were
> preemptively superior. At best it could be said that contingent fee
> arrangements may be subject to greater abuse than, say, an agreed
> on flat rate, but that an hourly standard favored by many because
> it has the benefit of allowing an agent to focus on the best overall
> bargain rather than the largest dollar package, is also open to abuse
> through the simple device of prolonging negotiations.

House Report, *supra* note 3, at 78.

65. *See generally* Weistart, *supra* note 5, at 328–331; House Report, *supra* note 3, at 76–79.

66. *See generally* House Report, *supra* note 3, at 78; *Inquiry into Professional Sports, Hearings Before the House Select Comm. on Professional Sports,* 94th Cong., 2d Sess. 262 (Ronald Roberts), 308–310 (Jerry Kapstein), 384, 386 (Marvin Miller).

67. Athletes sometimes expect too much from their agents. For instance, hockey player Derek Sanderson once had to make four telephone calls from Honolulu to Boston to reach his agent. Sanderson's hotel room had no hot water, and he wanted his agent to complain to the manager. R. WOOLF, BEHIND CLOSED DOORS 34 (1976).

68. *See* House Report, *supra* note 3, at 78.

69. The *Sporting News* reported on an actual problem involving two Kansas City Royals before the 1981 season. The agent who represented Hal McRae and Frank White refused to settle on White's contract until the Royals agreed to extend McRae's agreement, which had two years left. Royal management asserted that White, who had only one year left on his contract, could have signed a new contract a month earlier if his agent had tried to negotiate.

"I don't think he can use me as leverage to get Hal McRae a contract," White was quoted as saying. "Tony [the agent] said he was going to do Hal's first, but if he has a roadblock there, I don't think he should hold me up." The agent reportedly responded to White's request to go ahead with his contract by saying he'd think about it.

" 'If your agent declines to come in and talk, you're going to have to give him an ultimatum,' White said. 'I'm ready to talk. I really don't want to go to spring training worrying about my contract.' " The Sporting News, January 24, 1981, at 51.

70. *See* ABA Code, *supra* note 57, Canon 5, *Ethical Considerations* 5-14, 5-15, 5-16, 5-19 at 22M–24M.

71. *See id.*

72. Feinstein, *supra* note 45.

73. *See* notes 21–36 *supra* and accompanying text.

74. *See* note 22 *supra.*

75. *See* note 30 *supra.*

76. One area in which this rule apparently has not been strictly enforced

is the obtaining of bank loans by student athletes, based on their athletic ability, to buy athletic disability insurance policies. For a detailed discussion of this issue, *see* Kornheiser, *Insurance for the College Stars,* Washington Post, April 27, 1980, § N at 1. *See also* Benagh, *Sports Insurance Business: A Billion Dollars in Policies,* N.Y. Times, April 7, 1980, § C at 120.

77. NCAA Manual, *supra* note 21, at 7–8.

78. *See, e.g.,* Testimony of C. R. Wharton, chancellor of the State University of New York and former president, Michigan State University; *NCAA Enforcement Program, supra* note 39:

> In summary, what is most disturbing is that neither the NCAA nor the institutions that comprise it have yet to conceive a satisfactory means of controlling intercollegiate sports and of successfully curbing abuses. . . .
>
> A major part of the problem, of course, is that the sports themselves, primarily major football and basketball, have become so overpowering in their presence on some campuses. One shies away from calling them "professional" sports, but referring to them as "amateur" is no less a misnomer. The stakes are too high to treat them simply as an afternoon or evening of high-spirited collegiate fun and competition. The stakes are high for the institutions, for the alumni, the coaches, and of course, the players themselves, who often see a slot on a winning team as the entree into professional ranks.

79. *Id.*

80. A recently formed Center for Athlete Rights and Education (C.A.R.E.) intends to defend the educational and legal rights of high school and college athletes. N.Y. Times, Aug. 31, 1981, § C at 2, col. 1. *See* note 90 *infra;* Indianapolis Star, August 22, 1981, at 28 (report on speech by Ronald J. Waicukauski, director of the Center for Law & Sports of the Indiana University—Bloomington School of Law, criticizing the regulatory efforts of the NCAA in regard to academic standards and the inability of many universities to educate student athletes).

81. This person probably should not be a member of the athletic department, but instead someone affiliated with the university's career center or a law or business school professor.

82. The Big Ten Conference, for example, has taken a step in this direction by holding an "awareness session" on drugs, gambling, and sports agency for the top two football and basketball players from each school. The Collegiate Commissioners Association plans to publish by fall 1982 a pamphlet that will attempt to introduce prospective professional athletes to some of the elements involved in selecting an agent. The NCAA is providing financial support and advice.

83. The NCAA could use part of its television revenues to benefit the athletes responsible for the television contracts.

84. The leagues profess interest in curbing abuses by agents. *See, e.g.,* N.Y. Times, *supra* note 40.

85. The Association of Intercollegiate Athletics for Women (AIAW) had no prohibition on athletes retaining agents. Its president during 1981, Dr. Donna Lopiano of the University of Texas, suggested that agents may help women athletes, whose professional opportunities are much more limited than male athletes. Interview with D. Lopiano in Indianapolis (August 19, 1981). Universities whose women's teams compete in NCAA championship tournaments (which were instituted in 1981) rather than in AIAW competition will have until August 1, 1985, to bring their requirements for

women student athletes into conformity with NCAA rules. NCAA Manual, *supra* note 2 at 86.

86. The California law that regulates sports agents, 1981 Cal. Stats. ch. 929, includes a requirement that the agent, prior to communicating with a student concerning an agency contract or a professional sports service contract, file a copy of its state registration certificate with the university. Also, the statute requires the agent to file a copy of each agency contract and professional sports contract made with a student with the university within five days of when the student signs the contract. If the agent fails to comply with either of these provisions, the contract will be void and unenforceable.

87. Interview with Wayne Duke, Commissioner of the Big Ten, in Indianapolis (August 19, 1981).

88. Feinstein, *supra* note 44, §D at 6.

89. Wayne Duke recalled a meeting of the NCAA Professional Sports Liaison Committee with representatives of the National Football League. When an NFL general manager said he knew of two cases of football players who entered agency agreements before their college eligibility had expired, Duke asked him to reveal their names so that the NCAA could enforce its rules. He declined. Remarks of Wayne Duke at Conference on Amateur Sports and the Law, Indianapolis, August 20, 1981. This committee meets periodically with representatives of professional sports leagues to discuss, among other topics, coordinated efforts to enforce the NCAA eligibility rules. For a general and detailed analysis of NCAA enforcement policies and practices, *see NCAA Enforcement Program, supra* note 39, Parts I & II; *Enforcement Program of the National Collegiate Athletic Association,* Report of Subcomm. on Oversight and Investigations of the House Comm. on Interstate and Foreign Commerce, Comm. Print 95-69, 95th Cong. 2d Sess. (1978).

90. *See* Horn, *Intercollegiate Athletics: Waning Amateurism and Rising Professionalism,* J. COLL. AND U. L. 97, 98 (1978). Dr. Horn criticizes the NCAA for not focusing on "what should be the basic purpose of the organization: the protection of student-athletes from unscrupulous actions by those who would exploit them for their own purposes." *Id.* at 97.

91. For the elements of this tort and a discussion of its application in the context of a professional athlete who is signed to a playing contract by a team in a rival league effective at the expiration of his present contract, *see* Cincinnati Bengals v. Bergey, 453 F.Supp. 129, 145–47 (S.D. Ohio 1974), *see* also Dryden v. Tri-Valley Growers, 135 Cal. Rptr. 720, 723 (1977). For an analysis of the university-NCAA relationship, *see* Weistart, *supra* note 5, at 32–44.

92. Taylor v. Wake Forest University, 16 N.C. App. 117, 191 S.E. 2d 379, 382 (1972).

93. *See* Echols v. California State University and Colleges, No. C 266 777 (Cal. Super. Ct., L.A. County, filed Oct. 22, 1974.) (Seven former student athletes alleged, *inter alia,* that the university breached contracts with each of them by failing to provide the promised educational services. The case was still pending as of August 20, 1981. *See* Indianapolis Star, August 21, 1981, 28.) *See also* N.Y. Times, August 31, 1981, § C at 2, col. 1). *But see* Weistart, *supra* note 5, at 9–12 for a critical view of Taylor v. Wake Forest University, *supra* note 92, and the contractual theory.

94. *See* Weistart, *supra* note 5, at 12–15 (workmen's compensation) and 15–19 (income taxation).

95. *See generally id.* at 37–44.
96. *See* Buckaloo v. Johnson, Ca. Sup., 122 Cal. Rptr. 745, 751 (1975).
97. *Id.* at 752.
98. M. Patcher, Champions of American Sport 266 (1981).

[7]

Rule-Making in Interscholastic Sports: The Bases of Judicial Review

John C. Weistart

INTRODUCTION

Athletic associations and school boards have historically enjoyed a position of virtual legal immunity in their efforts to regulate participation in athletics at the high school level. While the grounds for judicial review of any decision by school authorities were quite limited, athletics seemed to present a particularly compelling case for nonintervention by the courts. Denying a student the opportunity to participate in interscholastic sports did not directly affect the student's standing in the predominant and most important function of the school—its educational venture. Athletics were seen as truly "extracurricular" and thus not entitled to serious legal scrutiny.

The picture changed considerably in the 1970s. Decisions of school boards and athletic associations were challenged on several fronts. Some of these disputes went to the core of the authority of those in charge of athletic programs—the right to demand conforming personal behavior from those who participated in sports activities. The epitome of this shift was in judicial actions invalidating rules requiring athletes to be clean shaven and to wear their hair at a modest length.[1] Many of those on school boards and in athletic associations, who will be referred to here by the general term "athletic administrators," surely saw an ominous sign in these cases. If athletic administrators could not control the physical appearance of those students who were "public representatives" of their schools and whose participation in sports was wholly voluntary, then surely there was some question as to whether any significant restriction on participation could be imposed.

The rules on personal grooming were not the only matters to undergo significant reform in the 1970s. One interested in studying how the law responds to changing social attitudes would be attracted to the cases involving rules that limited the right of married students to participate in interscholastic athletics. Throughout the 1960s, the overwhelming weight of authority upheld the power of athletic administrators to disqualify married students from school-sponsored athletics.[2] The school authorities developed a list of reasons as to why this result was appropriate, and this eventually became the litany that courts recited in their summary affirmance of the administrators' action.[3] Married students, it was said, had new responsibilities and should therefore limit their more frivolous extracurricular involvement. Worse yet, married students had "experiences" supposedly not familiar to those unmarried, and it was feared that the newly wedded might be inclined to talk about these. Such exchanges could be demoralizing to others on the team.[4] And if, heaven forbid, the unmarried students were *not* demoralized, then at least it could be said that they had been corrupted.[5]

Despite, or more likely because of, their quaintness, these marriage rules did not endure the social reforms of the seventies. Case after case came down, first in 1972, then in 1973, 1974, and 1975. In a consistent and rather rapid line of decisions, the learning of the prior seventy years was discarded.[6] And the reform appears to have been complete. Neither commentators nor the courts have indicated doubts about the legal soundness of the results achieved.[7]

The extent to which the cases of the seventies represent an intrusion upon the autonomy of the regulators of school sports should not be underestimated. The administering authorities lost more court cases between 1970 and 1979 than they had in the prior several decades.[8] It is understandable that many administrators emerged from that period quite uncertain about their ability to impose any significant, non–grade-related restraints on the right to participate. There may have been confusion as to why the judicial attitude had changed. Of equal uncertainty were the implications of the judicial reversals for other areas of the administrators' authority. Were the issues of grooming and marriage wholly distinct, or did these cases mean that no action based in personal preference could be infringed upon by official regulation? Relatedly, if something as traditional as good grooming could not be compelled, were there any conventional values that could be required in the administrators' regulatory scheme?

One task that lies ahead for the 1980s seems clear: there is a need to examine the precedent of the past several years and to clarify its meaning for the authority of those who administer school sports. We will undertake this examination in the content of a particular type of regulation. A good deal of recent litigation has been focused on the so-called transfer rules, which, to varying degrees, limit a student's right to participate in athletics after he or she has transferred from one school to another. The frequently stated purpose of these rules is to discourage movements between schools that are athletically motivated, as, for example, when the student or a coach at the transferee school seeks to gain a competitive advantage by virtue of the move.

The present inquiry into these rules is prompted by a number of concerns. It can be noted, for example, that while transfer rules have historically been accorded the great judicial deference shown to other school-sports regulations, a smattering of recent cases has yielded decisions in which particular forms of the rules have been either struck down or seriously disputed.[9] Thus, the transfer rule cases seem to be subject to some of the same forces that prompted reforms in other areas in the 1970s. In addition, however, the transfer rule cases are notable because the regulations in question touch on matters that go to the basic philosophy of regulating school sports. The ostensible basis of rules discouraging transfers is a desire by athletic administrators to discourage an overemphasis on athletics and to maintain the academic side of the school's affairs as the main object of the students' undertaking. These, however, are matters about which students, parents, and coaches may well have different preferences. The question arises then as to how far athletic administrators can go in controlling the philosophical orientation of their athletic programs.

While this discussion focuses on transfer rules, the underlying policy questions are the same as those found in a variety of other regulatory problems. For example, an issue that has a particular affinity to the present inquiry concerns the propriety of a decision to "hold back" a junior high school athlete for a year so that he or she can enter high school competition with increased physical and emotional maturity. As in the case of a transfer decision, such action may be criticized for its singular emphasis on athletics. By the same token, however, students and parents may assert that the matter is one in which their choices should have primacy.[10] Transfer rules were selected as the subject of the present discussion because of the larger body of administrative material and case law that they have generated. The presence of common philosophical themes, however, should suggest the more general application of principles developed here.

TRANSFER RULES: BACKGROUND

It is not difficult to see why the rules governing student transfers have been controversial. For one thing, there appears to be no general agreement on how stringently the rules ought to be drawn. Ostensibly the rules are designed to discourage ill-advised transfers by students and to control improper recruiting by coaches seeking to build strong athletic teams. A student typically loses a year of eligibility if his or her transfer is deemed to be within the prohibition of the applicable rule. Variations occur, however, in the definition of what is a proper transfer. Some authorities permit transfers, without a loss of eligibility, if there is a bona fide change in the parents' residence.[11] Other regulators have rejected this exception and have tried to require the student to sit out for a year even where the transfer was from another state several thousand miles away and was prompted by a change in the student's parents' employment.[12] In still other situations, the rules have been structured to authorize appropriate officials to make an individualized inquiry in certain types of cases.[13] The purpose of the inquiry is to determine whether the athlete has been subjected to improper recruiting pressures. If no such improper influences are found, the transfer is permitted. If generalized to all cases, this approach theoretically would achieve the most just results, for the regulation could be carefully tailored to fit the perceived abuse. Those students who were influenced by improper recruiting would incur a period of ineligibility, while those who moved for independent reasons would be unaffected. By comparison, rules imposing an across-the-board loss of eligibility, or even one that allowed "bona fide" parental moves, are more crude measures and are likely to disadvantage some students whose moves involve none of the evils that prompted the regulations in the first place.[14] But even the wisdom of an individualized approach is subject to debate. One athletic association provided a system of case-by-case review for several years and then abandoned the arrangement.[15] The association found that the decision-makers (the principles at the transferor and transferee schools) were subjected to considerable pressure from parents and other interested parties. In this situation and in others, the concern for the costs and burdens of permitting exceptions has prompted administrators to adopt rules with little flexibility.

The controversy surrounding the transfer rules is further fueled by a lack of sensitivity in the application of the regulations in some situations. Under the historical practice of nearly complete judicial deference to the decision-making of athletic administrators, the courts have found themselves compelled to endorse these rigid pronouncements. A search for dubious interpretations of otherwise reasonable rules yields several candidates. In one case, the student's parents were divorced and living in different school districts.[16] There was later a formal change of parental custody from the mother to the father and a related transfer of the student's residence. The applicable rule provided for a loss of a year's eligibility unless there was a "change in the residence of the parents."[17] When called upon to apply the rule, the appropriate official refused to approve the transfer because, while the student's family situs was altered and while the move was apparently otherwise legitimate, neither parent's residence had changed. This result was decreed even though the student's situation seemed well within the spirit of the exception approving bona fide moves. In a realistic sense, there had been a change in the residence of the student's legal parent. What the administrator, and eventually the court, failed to appreciate is that every formal regulation will require interpretation. Among the techniques of interpretation that are available, unbending literalism is frequently the least preferred.[18]

Another enduring feature of the present regime of transfer rules is that they have acquired the seemingly contradictory characteristics of being simultaneously overinclusive and incomplete in their coverage. The rules are overbroad in that they frequently sweep within their ineligibility period persons whose transfer decisions clearly were not athletically motivated. In one recent case, *Barnhorst v. Missouri State High School Athletic Association*,[19] a female student transferred from one private school to another nearer her home. The court made a specific finding that the transfer was based on the superiority of the academic program in the recipient school and that athletics did not "play any part" in the student's decision. The court also found that the recipient school was not a strong athletic power in the locale, and indeed "often has difficulty in fielding a complete team in certain sports."[20] However, the relevant rule only approved transfers following a bona fide change of residence or a change in parental control or the closing of the student's former school. Since the student's parents had not moved, and because the other grounds were not applicable, the transfer was not permitted. The fact that the case seemed to be outside the evils underlying the regulation did not change the legal result.

The transfer rule may not, however, insure against an excessive emphasis on athletics by parents and students. Indeed, in some states, what the rule does, in effect, is to raise the cost to the parents of pursuing an athletic advantage for their children. Under some rules, parents can move their child to a school offering better competition or better coaching if they are willing to pay the price, namely, the cost of disposing of one residence and acquiring another.[21] Thus, the truly obsessed may be given a way out.

A sociologist might be interested in how the *de facto* availability of this exception is distributed among different social classes. Those living in apartments and those with financial flexibility would seem to be preferred. These distributions can be affected by a variety of other factors as well. For example, rumors continue to circulate about employers who arrange for intercompany transfers of employees whose children enjoy superior athletic skills. An employer subsidy of the cost of making a transfer between cities operates to remove perhaps the most significant barrier to such a move.

Under one view, then, the transfer rules represent a haltering form of regulation. At the same time that the rules fail to except the compelling cases of some persons whose transfers were not athletically motivated, they also leave unregulated transfers for which improved athletic opportunities were the sole motivation. This unevenness provides a further explanation for why the transfer rules continue to attract attention.

CRITICISMS OF THE PRESENT
REGULATORY REGIME

The prior analysis dealt with some of the structural features of the transfer rules. There are other questions, in particular issues of policy, that should be considered. One of the enduring legacies of the cases involving grooming and marriage rules is that the administrators of amateur athletics do not have complete discretion to define the preferences that will be reflected in their regulations. Indeed, the blunt point of those 1970s decisions is that room must be left for some self-direction by those students who participate in athletics. Not only are there nontraditional, nonmajoritarian views that must be tolerated,[22] but in addition certain aspects of student and parental decisions on athletic participation appear to be protected by a veil of privacy that precludes official examination.

There is only the most preliminary consideration of these concerns in the transfer cases decided to date,[23] and the reader will want to note that the following paragraphs are not a reflection of present case law. For the present, we seek only to identify those concerns which might be taken into account in structuring regulations concerning interschool transfers. The policy issues raised here are of the sort that are likely to be considered by a deliberative body—school board or athletic association—that undertook to rethink its previous policy on transfers and summer camps. Whether these policy concerns represent valid legal objections is a much different matter. A later portion of the paper notes the extent to which the grounds for judicial reveiew are drawn in more narrow terms. For now, we simply explore a variety of nonlegal complaints that might be raised against the rules.

As already suggested, the transfer rules reflect a judgment that it is inappropriate for a high school student, either by choice or through enticement by a coach, to pursue athletics as a primary or even a prominent goal in the student's school activities.[24] Devotion to athletics, it is thought, will limit the student's involvement in other important activities, especially the educational venture of his school. The judgment is made that the benefits of athletic participation are likely to be considerably less enduring than those that flow from academic endeavors.

The probabilities against a high school athlete's making a living from athletics are overwhelming. Moreover, participation in the traditional team sports does not insure long-term physical fitness.[25] By contrast, the student's academic undertaking is thought to carry a significantly greater likelihood of a lifetime return. After all, it will be said, the high school curriculum offers an important preparation not only for the student's later vocational efforts but also for his or her family and personal endeavors.

One who was critical of the restraints on transfers might offer two responses to this analysis. As an initial matter, it is not altogether obvious that a student's substantial involvement in athletics is inappropriate. Perhaps more importantly, a question can be raised as to who should have the ultimate right to determine the relative emphasis given to athletics by a particular student. While athletic administrators have traditionally reserved that decision for themselves, there are others—the student and his or her parents—who might also claim a right to make that determination.

While we will consider these responses as they apply to transfer rules, it seems appropriate to note again that the present inquiry bears on other issues that come before athletic administrators. As mentioned, the controversial practice of holding back junior high athletes to enhance their chances in high school competition is often condemned on the grounds that it allows athletic concerns to overshadow the more durable educational aspects of the student's experience. Because the student's suitability for post–high school competition is far from assured, the selection of an athletically dominated career is seen as speculative beyond the bounds of reason.[26] And, as with transfer decisions, the positive values associated with established schoolmate relationships are subverted. By the same token, the hold-back issue generates some of the same objections raised against the regulation of interschool transfers. There are those who regard the financial rewards of athletic success to be sufficient to establish fully the appropriateness of decisions that maximize a student's athletic development. The sports endeavor can be seen as an initial exploration of a potential vocation or as a mechanism for financing the participant's college education.[27] Moreover, regulation by athletic administrators may be seen as an unjustified intrusion into an area where personal and family preferences should predominate. The decision to hold back is likely to be prompted by a mixture of motives. Parents concerned about the social maturity of their children may desire to allow for an additional year's development. Or the parent may be influenced by a perceived lack of educational preparedness on the part of the student. Or the hold-back decision may be related to a concern for the student's athletic-related physical development. Whether these factors appear in combination or singly, parents will argue, they all involve decisions that have traditionally been re-garded as beyond state control.[28] Again, these are concerns that serve to link the regulation of student transfers with other aspects of the administration of interscholastic sports.

We now turn to a more detailed examination of the controversies underlying transfer regulations. The issue of the appropriateness of an emphasis on athletics is not a matter that lacks for controversy. Some commentators have argued that many young people are misled by a singular devotion to sports.[29] This is especially a concern for inner-city youths, perhaps because the lure of professional athletics stands in such sharp contrast to the limited opportunities available under their more traditional vocation options. It is difficult to conclude that this view-point is wholly erroneous. There is, however, another perspective that is likely to gain its own advocates.

It can be observed, for example, that there are some students for whom a consistent development of their athletic talent holds significant social and economic rewards.[30] The clearest cases are those athletes who do in fact attain position on a professional team. There are pres-ently several million-dollar-a-year professional athletes. [31] And for vir-tually all of these, their earnings from sports are greater, by several hundred percent, than the wages attainable in their most likely alterna-ative form of employment. Indeed, assuming constant dollars, there are many athletes who will earn more in a single year than many of us can expect to earn in a lifetime.

Those sympathetic to the observation made above would also point out that for many professional athletes the traditional route of four years of high school followed immediately by four years of college is difficult to justify. We find examples of this in several different sports. Tennis players, for example, may exhibit professional-quality playing while still in high school. Baseball players may develop professional affiliations either without attending college or before their college ca-reers are completed. And recently we have seen basketball players who have moved from high school to professional ranks without the inter-mediate step of four years of college.[32] For many, it cannot be seriously contended that their careers have been enhanced by four more years of school-related competition. With respect to other athletes who moved directly to professional teams, arguments are sometimes made that they would have benefited from several years in college. It will be noted, though, that the benefits hypothesized are those related to ath-letic training and not those that flow from involvement in the college's educational venture.

The athletes affected by the above analysis are the truly exceptional, and they are very few in number. They are not, however, the only ones for whom the conscientious development of their athletic skills makes good social and economic sense. Many parents appreciate that athletic prowess can provide the means for financing a college education. The availability of athletic scholarships is by no means limited to athletes with near-certain professional potential. Indeed, the number of athletes securing positions with professional teams is only a very small portion of the students leaving college after attending on a scholarship.[33] Those players who do not proceed further have still gained a substantial advantage by receiving a financial subsidy for their education.

The amounts involved can be quite substantial. The precise value of the scholarship will vary from school to school. But for an athlete from a middle-class family attending a good private university, a four-year college financial aid package will frequently represent the equivalent of roughly $67,000 in parental earnings. That is, taking account of the effects of taxation, the parents would have to use $67,000 in personal earnings to buy the equivalent of the four-year financial aid package.[34] Understandably, a parent might be pleased to have the $67,000 available for other purposes, while still insuring that the child receives a college education.

Other parents would not make a $67,000 expenditure. Indeed, some could not afford to support the child's education at all. In these cases, the child's athletic involvement is not an obvious evil. It may in fact provide the opportunity for an education that is not otherwise available.

There will be a debate as to whether transfer rules have any significant impact in deterring an athlete from realizing the benefits outlined above. Many athletes have secured significant returns from athletics even in the present system, in which restraints on transfers are commonplace. But this uncertainty has a double edge to it. If the rules have had a significant impact, it will be argued, then the concerns expressed above warrant attention. On the other hand, if the transfer rules have had no substantial effect, opponents will argue, they should be eliminated. While these two positions can be debated, the expenditures made for litigation contesting the rules weigh in favor of the validity of the former proposition.

There is a further criticism that some might urge. It is possible to agree with the notion that athletics should not be allowed to dominate a student's perspective and at the same time doubt the propriety of rules seeking to prevent an overemphasis on the sports. The alternative view is that it is the athlete and his parents, and not the local school board or state athletic association, who should decide the balance to be struck between the student's athletic and educational ventures. A respectable view can be put forth that ultimate responsibility for the nurturing and development of the child should lie within the family unit. The state has traditionally not been allowed to claim an exclusionary role in those endeavors, and while there may have been periods in which state intrusions went unquestioned, it will be argued, we have recently developed clearer notions of the proper role of personal and family autonomy.[35] These have served to identify zones of privacy into which state intrusion is precluded. While numerous examples could be offered, the courts' refusal to enforce grooming and marriage rules in the school sports context will be seen by some as sufficient illustrations. Proponents of this view may raise a rhetorical point: is it not true that decisions concerning career orientation have the same highly personalized qualities that have led to the protection of individual decisions on hair length and marriage? To the extent that an affinity exists between these decisions, there is support for objections to universalized, state-imposed policies concerning the appropriateness of an emphasis on athletics.

It can be noted that there are other areas in which parents have enjoyed expansive, if not complete, discretion to influence their children's development. Indeed, on most other decisions affecting the child's career development, our legal and social institutions seem to assume that these are matters to be resolved within the family. A parent may, for example, make decisions that have the effect of steering the child toward a particular vocational path. The student's enrollment in courses in auto repair or his acceptance of an after-school job in a service station may eventually culminate in permanent employment in that field. The student's endeavors could be the result of conscious parental approval, or of parental deferral to the student's own inclination. Or the particular career direction could be the product of inattention by the parent. Those who dissent from the present system of athletic regulation can observe, however, that none of the above scenarios suggests facts that would support prohibitions imposed by the state.

In particular cases, including those involving athletics, the choice of a particular career direction may be unwise. Jobs may be scarce, or the student may ultimately lack necessary skills. Opponents of pervasive state control will observe, though, that these have not traditionally been accepted as a reason to abandon the restraint on state intrusions into the realm of family and individual privacy.

To this point, the discussion has assumed that the predominance of athletics in a particular student's life represents a career direction. That is not always the case, and it must be accepted that there are innumerable variations in the motives that might influence a parent's or student's decision to seek a transfer to another school. Even here, proponents of milder controls may find grist for their arguments. For example, some parents see athletic participation as the incentive that maintains the child's interest in his or her academic subjects. Studies have shown that students who are not otherwise "interested in" school would resist continued attendance if it were not for the opportunity to participate in athletics.[36] For other children, success in sports may provide the self-esteem that allows them to endure less satisfying experiences in their academic subjects.[37] In cases such as these, it will be argued, decisions to enhance the athletic experience, or to avoid an unpleasant one, are important. For that reason, it will again be urged that ultimate responsibility for the difficult choices to be made in this area ought to lie within the family unit.

A further criticism of the state's role in these matters is that the pursuit of the articulated lofty goals has not always been consistent. For example, as previously mentioned, the rules imposed frequently include exceptions that can be utilized by parents with an inclination, and sufficient resources, to shift their child to a more competitive school. Critics would observe that, in addition, the impact of state policies varies considerably among sports. While the athletic administrators may seek to deny team-sport players the opportunity to refine their skills in specialized summer camps, athletes in other sports, especially tennis, are frequently allowed to continue to pursue individualized instruction and even organized summer tournaments.[38] The parents of the basketball or football player might be able to secure some type of individualized counseling from a skilled instructor. But this is not the equivalent of what the tennis player receives, even if it is otherwise permitted. Without the opportunity to participate in a team venture, the training received would be of limited value. When the state does not pursue its regulatory policies with an even hand, the basic credibility of the policy is undermined, and, opponents would urge, the state's insistence upon its right of control develops a hollow ring.

A final difficulty with the present transfer rules is that there is frequently uncertainty as to whose conduct they are intended to regulate. The discussion to this point has focused on the impact that the rules have upon decisions made by students and parents. Critics will observe, however, that abuses are not always the product of choice made within the family. Many situations giving rise to concern involve efforts by a coach to induce talented athletes to transfer to the local school. Improprieties perpetrated by such persons would seem to raise policy issues different from those generated by a family decision.

A school system may properly decide that it does not want to operate an intense, highly competitive athletic program. And, of course, the school may seek to convince other members of its athletic association to adopt the same view. However, some will observe that the above principles do not necessarily authorize the school system to regulate the highly personalized choices that students or parents might make in connection with a school move. Coaches and other school personnel do not have the same privacy rights as parents. Coaches, for example, are employees of their schools and are obligated to execute whatever goals have been defined for the school system that employs them.

Proponents of reform might note that it would be possible to have a regime of regulation that sought both to prohibit recruiting by coaches and to respect parental decisions concerning the emphasis that a child should place on athletics. Restraints would be placed on activities of coaches and others, and these persons could be subjected to periodic reporting and observation requirements. Parents, on the other hand, would be left free to choose among available athletic alternatives, subject always, of course, to academically based restraints on school transfers.[39] The array of athletic alternatives available might not offer all that particular parents might want, but no direct effort would be made to regulate directly private decisions that were made.

To the extent that present regulations are really intended to control recruiting, they have taken an approach that critics are likely to find sweeps too broadly. While it is true that recruiting will be deterred, it is also true that the rules will affect cases far removed from the concern for improper inducements. As already noted, the prohibition will be extended to situations in which the absence of recruiting is established by specific inquiry[40] or reasonably inferred because of the nature of an accompanying parental move.[41] Detractors of the present approaches would urge that more precision in the mechanism for regulation could insure that the burdens of the controls were borne by those whose actions are most properly the object of concern.

The preceding analysis is intended to suggest that there is indeed "another" view of the problem of overemphasis on athletics. The regulations imposed in this area have reflected little sympathy for this contrary view. The question arises as to whether the future will see a change in direction, particularly a change more sympathetic to the position outlined above. While a reconsideration of present policies could come at the level of decision-making by school boards and athletic associations, our more immediate concern is with the judicial treatment of the rules in question. A specific issue is whether these opposing viewpoints can be translated into legal doctrine that will prompt intervention by the courts. We now turn our attention to that issue. The analysis begins with a review of the courts' traditional approach to transfer and summer camp rules. The outcome of that review has already been indicated: in the vast majority of cases, the courts have refused to intervene in controversies concerning the rules in question. Such a posture means, of course, that the rules have been upheld. A few more recent cases have been to the contrary. These are likely to offer encouragement to those who endorse the views discussed above. A consideration of these recent decisions follows the review of existing precedents.

TRADITIONAL STANDARDS FOR JUDICIAL REVIEW

An interesting feature of the cases considering transfer rules is that they involve at least three different legal theories. Not all of these are considered in each case, and often there is no ready explanation as to why the case was litigated on less than all of the doctrinal bases that might have been offered. In most cases, however, the choice of a different theory would not have changed the ultimate result of the case. As traditionally applied, none of the three approaches placed significant restraints on the rule-making powers of athletic administrators. The relevant doctrine involved application of the law of private associations, principles of state public law, and elements of federal constitutional law.

1. The law of private associations

Our law has historically been highly deferential to internal decision-making by private associations. The general rule has been variously expressed. Some authorities assert that the courts will not intervene to overturn a private association rule unless it violates a criminal statute or is otherwise contrary to natural justice.[42] Other courts reach essentially the same result by suggesting that they will not overturn private association rules in the absence of fraud, mistake, or basic corruption in the organization.[43] The origins of this standard of review is in early English cases involving social clubs and fraternal organizations. Where a group of individuals had joined together and endorsed specific standards of conduct and eligibility, it was thought inappropriate for an outside agency, such as the courts, to impose its own perception of appropriate behavior.[44] This approach was early accepted by courts in this country,[45] and the instances of judicial intervention in the affairs of private noncommercial associations are few in number.

These principles found application in the area of athletic regulation because of the nature of the governing entity. The rules in question were usually adopted and enforced by a state athletic association. The association typically consisted of a group of schools, often including both public and private schools, that voluntarily joined together to promote a common interest in interscholastic sports. Because a school's participation was not mandatory, many courts were led to the conclusion that the group's regulations should be judged according to the standards applied to other private collective bodies. This premise inevitably led to the conclusion that the association's rules would be upheld.[46] Fraud, corruption, and breaches of natural justice were never serious questions in the litigated cases. Hence, the courts perceived that they had before them purely private affairs that gave no reason for judicial scrutiny.

2. State public law

Some courts treated the cases before them as involving not the decision of a private entity but rather a determination by a state instrumentality. This approach was thought to be particularly appropriate where the action under review was one taken by a school board. Such a board was clearly a public body and thus not within theory applicable to purely private entities.[47] Because of the governmental nature of the action, a somewhat more exacting level of review was thought to be appropriate.

The present standard is not limited to school boards, however. Athletic associations have also been subjected to it.[48] The reason for this similarity in treatment presents an important conceptual point concerning the relationship between such entities and the schools that are members. Generalizations are somewhat difficult because of the various organizational structures that are followed. But in most states, a school's participation in the state association is not mandated by legislative rule. Where this is true, the courts may properly view the association as *de jure* or *de facto* delegates of the local school districts.[49] A public school's participation in an athletic association is thus not a purely private affair. If the matter were handled formally, such participation would be with the approval and subject to the ultimate control of the school board. But even in the absence of action amounting to a formal delegation, the school's participation involves tacit public action. Consequently, whatever authority the association exercises would have its source in the association's status as an agent of the state entity.[50] Thus, actions of the association should be subject to the same level of review as would be applied to decisions by the public entity itself.

In terms of its substance, the present standard of review is not an invitation for courts to undertake a close and exacting scrutiny of the rules that have been adopted by the school board or athletic associations. The view is frequently expressed that these entities have been charged with managing a particular sphere of activity, and decisions made in pursuit of that end are entitled to deference.[51] But it is also agreed that review is not foreclosed. Most courts hold, for example, that a rule should be overturned if it is beyond the range of authority that has been granted to the body in question.[52] Thus a school board probably could not attempt to regulate the type of summer jobs that student athletes obtained.[53] Beyond those relatively easy cases, one finds various statements of the level of scrutiny that will be applied. On the surface, these might suggest that there is disagreement about the precise nature of the state law review. In upholding a series of restrictions on participation in summer camps, the Minnesota Supreme Court stated that it was not authorized to inquire into "the propriety, justice, wisdom, necessity, utility, [or] expediency of rules and policies adopted by a school board. . . ."[54] A standard that precludes inquiry into the propriety and justice of a rule would appear at first blush to impose almost no restraint on the rule-making authority of the school board. By contrast, the Iowa Supreme Court in voiding a high school association good-conduct rule operated under a standard that included a "general requirement that a rule promulgated by a governmental subdivision or unit be reasonable. . . ."[55] An inquiry into reasonableness would seemingly permit the court to examine the propriety and justice, and indeed the necessity and expediency, of the rule, matters that the Minnesota court seemed to exclude. A third court, the Missouri Court of Appeals, applied a standard that would allow it to void rules that were unreasonable in the sense of being arbitrary and capricious.[56] To transgress this standard, "the rule would have to be without a rational ground or justification."[57]

While these cases do not yield an indisputable statement of the appropriate standard of review, it is possible to find some coherency among them. The court's ultimate concern again is whether the entity in question had authority to act. If the administrative entity acted in an area that had no substantial connection to the matters within its authority, then its decision should not be respected. But a critical point to be made is that there are other ways in which the school or association can exceed its authority. If it regulates activities of athletes that have no significant effect on athletics, then its action would, in one sense, be beyond its proper jurisdictional claim. Relatedly, if the entity purported to find that a particular rule affected an athletically related objective when all evidence was to the contrary, the resulting rule would be arbitrary. Finally, there is an impermissible arbitrariness in cases in which the athletic administrator attributes undesirable characteristics to an athlete on the basis of conduct which itself was wholly innocent. This deficiency would exist, for example, where students are disciplined for merely associating with those who had engaged in improper conduct.[58] The inappropriateness of the regulation in this setting is that it makes an irrational attribution of misconduct to persons who may be totally innocent.[59] And again there is the characteristic that the regulation ventures beyond the legitimate scope of the regulators' authority; it sweeps within its reach some conduct that bears no appreciable relationship to the goals of the organization.

The present state public law review is not an authorization to courts to sit in judgment of the normal, discretionary rulings made by a regulatory body. If the entity has conscientiously accumulated pertinent data and made deliberate choices based on the information before it, its conclusion will not be disturbed.[60] However, intervention is appropriate where the regulating entity imposes controls without an adequate basis for concluding that such regulation is necessary for the achievement of legitimate athletic-related goals.

In the transfer rule cases decided to date, the authorization for a limited review of state entity actions has not produced significant judicial intrusions into the regulatory efforts of athletic administrators. Where this theory has been used, the courts have typically found the rules in question to be within the bounds of discretion properly claimable by the administrators.[61] While various methods of analysis have been used, the courts frequently undertake a two-step inquiry. The first step is to identify the evidence establishing that a problem of overemphasis exists. This may take the form of a record of a prior formal deliberation by the regulatory body[62] or the accumulation of evidence in the trial court.[63] The courts then determine whether the rule as applied to the particular complainant is responsive to the problem that has been identified.[64] The relevant inquiry does not include consideration of whether the particular regulation is the most effective way to deal with the problem or even whether the degree of regulation is proper in light of the problem that exists. These matters, again, are typically treated as being within the range of discretion that the public regulatory body can claim for itself.

There are few cases in which a school board or association rule of any sort has been overturned. One of these exceptions, however, is the 1972 decision in *Bunger v. Iowa High School Athletic Association*.[65] While *Bunger* dealt with a rule relating to alcoholic beverages and did not directly involve an interschool transfer, the case nonetheless represents an important precedent. The court takes considerable care to present a clear statement of the limits of the regulatory authority of athletic administrators.

The rule in question addressed the situation in which an athlete would lose his or her eligibility because of involvement with alcohol-related activities. In addition to consumption and possession, an offense occurred if one were merely present in a vehicle in which alcohol or dangerous drugs were transported. Bunger was punished under the rule after he was found to be one of four minors occupying a car that contained a case of beer. Bunger apparently had not consumed the beer and was not otherwise responsible for its presence. Moreover, the incident occurred in the summertime.

The Iowa Supreme Court focused its inquiry on whether the rule in question was within the authority of the athletic association and whether it was a rational exercise of that power.[66] Several factors led the court to conclude that the conduct in question was not so substantially related to the goals of the association to justify regulation. The court noted that the incident in question was "outside of the football season, [and] beyond the school year, [and there was] no illegal or even improper use of beer."[67] In light of these considerations, the nexus between the school and the incident "is simply too tenuous."[68]

The *Bunger* court did not purport to present a new theory of state law review. The precedents cited and the standards articulated were those traditionally invoked. The actual application of these principles, however, was more exacting than those undertaken in earlier cases. *Bunger* might then be seen as representing an incremental shift toward a level of review that requires athletic administrators to establish more clearly the factual basis of their regulations. Such an approach would have interesting implications for rules affecting interschool transfers. Among the objections raised against such rules is the complaint that they frequently draw their prohibition too broadly. The evaluation of this and other implications of *Bunger* is undertaken after the following discussion of the third theory of review.

3. Constitutional analysis

The above two theories for the review of athletic regulations have their genesis in state law. The third theory to be considered has a much different orientation. It suggests that school board and athletic association regulations may require application of principles of federal constitutional law. While the present theory is a bit newer than the others, the results is the litigated cases, especially those of the 1970s, were not substantially different.

Two basic constitutional theories were thought to have potential relevance in the present context. The first involves the plaintiff's claim to a right of substantive due process. A regulation can be struck down if it is proven to be incompatible with the substance, or essence, of the federal constitution. Certain rights are thought to be so fundamental that they may be subjected to regulation only by measures that promote a compelling state interest and that are carefully drawn to limit the extent of infringement. The Supreme Court has identified certain types of interests that will trigger these principles of close judicial scrutiny. Among the protected interests are the right to interstate travel[69] and the right to privacy in matters of marriage, childbearing, and child-rearing.[70] Other interests have been specifically deemed by the Court as insufficient to support claims to substantive due process. These include interests in welfare, housing, and education.[71]

A different theory of constitutional review emanates from the Equal Protection clause. While substantive due process involves a frontal attack on disputed legislation, the equal protection theory focuses on the rationality of classifications that are created by a regulatory scheme.[72] The purpose of the constitutional mandate is to assure that persons similarly situated are not subjected to differentiations that are arbitrary, a determination that is made in light of the type of interests involved and the difficulties confronted by the regulating entity. As the latter qualification implies, the degree of judicial scrutiny varies depending on the nature of the problem that is addressed.

Some legislative classifications will be subjected to strict scrutiny under the Equal Protection Clause. This is true where the legislative classification imposes a burden upon persons who are members of a class that historically has been subjected to hostile discrimination.[73] Thus, classifications based on race or alienage are suspect. However, classifications that reflect sex- or wealth-based differences do not invoke this highest standard of review. Where a suspect class, such as race, is involved, the legislation will be upheld only if it is necessary to protect a compelling state interest. Rarely is such an interest found to be present, and few regulations affecting suspect classes are sustained.[74]

Other types of classifications give rise to a different level of judicial scrutiny. The Supreme Court has identified certain types of interests that are not suspect classifications but that nonetheless warrant a review more exacting than that which is applied under the Constitution's most permissive standard. This intermediate level of review is triggered by a variety of classifications.[75] It applies, for example, where a legislative scheme makes differentiations based on gender or illegitimacy, or where the scheme invades a fundamental interest. For present purposes, the interests deemed fundamental are those protected under substantive due process notions.[76] Under the intermediate level of review, a regulation will be upheld only if it is important to a substantial state interest. Thus, it is normally assumed that the characteristics identified above will not be subjected to regulation. Where they are, the state must be able to establish that the classification arrangement involved something more than mere preference and that a significant countervailing state purpose is being served.

Apart from cases in which there is a suspect class and those involving intermediate level interests, the Court has indicated that other legislative pronouncements are entitled to great deference. The basic test is one requiring only a loose rational relationship: if the measure in question furthers a legitimate purpose of the legislating body and if the rule chosen furthers that purpose, then it will be upheld. The Supreme Court has emphasized that the legislative classifications that are chosen need not be precise and need not be the most reasonable that might be selected. Indeed, in recent decisions, the Court has expressed this standard in the form of a question. Once it is determined that the regulation furthers a legitimate purpose, the pertinent issue becomes:

"Was it reasonable for the law-makers to believe that use of the challenged classification would promote that purpose?"[77] Thus as long as the regulatory decision-makers may have thought that a state objective would be furthered, the regulation will be upheld. The fact that there is a substantial body of opinion suggesting that the regulation will not be effective, or even that it will be countereffective, is not enough.[78] Nor is it important that the legislature was wrong in the judgment that it made. Again, all that is necessary is that the regulators *could have* reasonably believed that their legitimate goal would be achieved.

The potential applicability of these principles to transfer rules was raised with fullest vigor in the 1970s. The resulting decisions yielded several clarifying principles. One issue was whether transfer rules affected any fundamental interest so as to invoke the protection of substantive due process or require something more than a permissive level of equal protection review. Whether a fundamental interest is involved may, of course, turn upon facts peculiar to the particular plaintiff. Such would be the case where the plaintiff transferred for a religiously based reason.[79] There are, however, asserted fundamental interests that are more generalized, and the courts' treatment of these can be summarized. It has been held rather consistently, for example, that participation in extracurricular activities does not involve a fundamental right.[80] This conclusion seems correct since the right to an education is not itself fundamental.[81] The courts in other cases found that no suspect class was affected by the regulation of transferrers.[82]

Among the fundamental rights potentially involved, the right to interstate travel is one that might be asserted. One lower court found an infringement of such a right when a transfer restriction was applied to a student who moved from out of state into the regulators' jurisdiction. This holding was reversed on appeal, however. The reviewing court correctly observed that there was no classification scheme that singled out those persons moving interstate. The applicable rule applied equally to all who changed schools, without regard to whether they were originally residents of the state imposing the regulation.[83]

In sum, the decisions of the seventies yielded no cases in which a fundamental interest or suspect class was found to be presented. Hence, the rules in question were reviewed under the least intrusive permissive standard. The task before the courts was merely to determine whether the rule in question bore a reasonable relation to a legitimate state interest.

In pursuing this inquiry the courts considered several issues that were mentioned in our earlier examination of the policy-based criticism that might be raised against the rules in question. Our prior discussion noted, for example, that transfer rules are often applied to students who had changed schools but who had not been subjected to recruiting pressures or other undue influences.[84] Translated into a constitutional argument, the contention would be that the regulatory classification scheme was overinclusive—it included persons who were not participants in the evils that prompted the regulation. In the general jurisprudence of equal protection, such complaints of overinclusiveness are usually not entertained,[85] and the courts considering the transfer rule cases showed a similar disinclination.[86] The response to such objections is found in language of the Supreme Court decisions that indicates that legislative classifications need not be drawn with precision.[87] The fact that some inequality might result from the choice of general classifications is not grounds for invalidating a regulation.[88]

Relatedly, we earlier noted the objection that transfer rules are often applied without an individualized inquiry into whether the athlete in question had been recruited or not. The courts, again, have been unreceptive to this objection. The basis of their response was the admonition of the Supreme Court that the permissive standard of review permits regulators to take into account the burdens and costs involved in administering a particular rule. It is appropriate for regulators to conclude that "the difficulties of individual determinations outweigh the marginal increments in the precise effectuation of [legislative] concern. . . ."[89] In a similar vein, a rule will not be found deficient because the regulators failed to provide for a general hardship exception or to take account of the peculiar equities of the particular case.[90]

A third objection raised earlier was that present transfer rules often do not control all instances of student preoccupation with sports. For example, while summer training in team sports is often controlled, it is frequently true that participants in individualized sports, such as tennis, are able to improve their skills either by individualized instruction or through prearranged competition with better players. While this specific objection has not been considered in the cases, the general point that underlies it has received attention from the Supreme Court. In an oft-quoted passage, the Court has indicated that a "reform may take one step at a time, addressing itself to the phase of the problem which seems most acute to the legislative mind."[91] Similarly, it has been held that the present permissive standard of review does not force a legislature to choose between maximum, pervasive legislation and none at all.[92] Again, the regulator may properly make judgments about the aspect of a problem that warrants first attention.

The unmistakable implication of the above decisions is that regulators will be given great leeway in devising regulations that do not affect suspect classes or invade important personal liberties. Most courts have found rules dealing with the interschool transfers to be well within these bounds. An exception, however, is the 1974 decision by the Indiana Supreme Court in *Sturrup v. Mahon*.[93] The plaintiff changed his residence to his brother's home in Bloomington, Indiana, to avoid a detrimental and unstable situation in their parents' home in Florida. The brother was appointed legal guardian. When the plaintiff sought to participate in varsity sports at his Bloomington school, he was declared ineligible for a one-year period. The pertinent association rule required such ineligibility except where there was a bona fide parental move or an "unavoidable change of residence," as where the parents had died.

The Indiana Supreme Court invalidated the association's finding of ineligibility. The ostensible reason was that the regulations lacked the basic rationality necessary to pass muster under the equal protection clause. The court noted that the object of the rules was to deter recruiting and athletically related school-jumping. In the court's view, all persons not within the two exceptions noted above were presumed to have been the victims of unscrupulous recruiting. But, the court felt, in this respect, the rules "swept too broadly." Those who changed schools for wholly personal or family reasons were indiscriminately lumped with those who had been improperly recruited. The restraints imposed on the former furthered no legitimate associational purpose.

Despite the courage of the Indiana Supreme Court's effort to correct a perceived inequity, it is not clear that the proffered analysis can be sustained under prevailing federal constitutional principles. The court did not suggest that the rule before it called for anything other than a review under the permissive standard. But, as previously noted, the fact of a regulation's overinclusiveness is ordinarily not a reason to invalidate it. Mathematical precision is not required in the definition of the classes of persons to be controlled. The Indiana court was particularly concerned about the fact that guardians were treated less favorably than parents under the applicable rule. An administrative body may decide, however, that some varieties of a particular problem are more demanding of regulation than are others. Or the administrators may conclude that there are some varieties that are of sufficient factual complexity that they should be regulated in gross. The Equal Protection Clause does not provide the grounds for unsettling these determinations. Courts in later cases have shown a greater sensitivity to these principles, and as a result, *Sturrup* has not had a significant impact.

IMPLICATIONS FOR THE FUTURE

A reading of the cases considered above would not suggest that the 1980s would be a period of tumult as far as transfer rules are concerned. Because of other considerations, however, this prediction is not free from doubt. For one thing, the cases to date have not fully considered arguments to be made in favor of increasing the respect to be accorded family and individual choice in these matters. We have previously noted the affinity between these concerns and those that led to the invalidation of grooming and marriage rules. In addition, an appraisal of the future must take account of recent case developments that seem to subject associational rules to closer scrutiny than has been applied in the past. In that same vein, the potential impact of the earlier *Bunger* decision remains to be explored. Finally, the correctness of the early cases should not be taken for granted. This is especially true with respect to the continued invocation of principles from the law of private associations.

1. Reassessing the role of private association law

One development that should come about is the courts' abandonment of any adherence to the law of private associations in legal challenges brought by students. It is difficult to understand how the associational law theory gained such a firm foothold in the first place. Considering the fact that it has been applied as recently as 1977, its durability is equally perplexing.[94]

The general judicial policy of deferring to the internal decisions of private associations is understandable. A wholly private group should be allowed maximum leeway to define its purposes, the character of its membership, and the nature of its venture. Without this freedom to shape their own affairs, private associations would likely evolve according to some undistinguished, modest norm. While all of that is true, it seems to have little to do with complaints raised by students against high school association rules. The essence of private association law is *consent*. The courts can abide an association's rules because the affected members have consented to them. If the member does not like the rule, he can leave the association. In the absence of such a defection, consent will be implied.[95] In any event, internal governing processes are open to the disgruntled member, and he may seek a modification of the offending rule.

That model hardly fits the role of the student in the typical high school athletic association. The student is not a member;[96] nor has he or she participated in the formulation of policy. Further, the activity in question is not a "private affair," but rather is in the form of a public regulation.[97] In short, the consensual premise of the associational theory is absent.

Apart from this basic misconception, the application of this body of law suffers from another significant defect: it introduces a basic logical fallacy into the jurisprudence of judicial review. It will be recalled that the standards for review under private association law and state public law were qualitatively different. Review under a private association theory is virtually foreclosed altogether. Only in the most extreme cases, where there is fraud, corruption, or some other extralegal influence, is judicial intervention authorized. While state public law principles are also highly deferential to the decision-making of state agencies, the deferral is not complete. Actions that are arbitrary or otherwise contrary to the relevant factual circumstances can be overturned. Even if made with complete innocence, these misdirections are not allowed to stand.

There is little dispute that the more exacting standards of review are applicable to actions taken by school boards. And there should be little disagreement in most states that athletic associations obtain their authority by actual or implicit delegation from local school authorities. The associations devise rules on matters—discipline, eligibility, etc.— that the school board would otherwise have to address. Because of this relationship, it can be ventured that whatever level of judicial review obtains to decisions made directly by school boards should not be lessened when the board chooses to operate through a delegate. In other areas of the law the principle is well established that an entity cannot lessen its legal accountability by a simple appointment of a surrogate.[98]

Future litigation should not be burdened by the continued misapplication of association law principles. The nearly complete legal immunity that these notions produce seems inconsistent with the nonconsensual characteristic of the students' involvement in the rules in question. The standard of review that eventually evolves may not be a wholly expansive one. It should, however, be more sensitive than that which normally applies to private, consensual affairs.

2. Case developments

Compared to the litigation of the 1970s, the first decisions of the 1980s would appear to offer encouragement to those seeking to invalidate transfer rules. In two decisions of note, one involving a transfer rule and the other an analogous regulation, the courts have indicated impatience with the tendency of athletic regulators to draw their regulations in sweeping fashion. In each case, the disputed regulations were set aside. Does this forecast a basic shift in judicial emphasis? Because one case indicated a willingness to elevate the role of parental decision-making, the precedents certainly warrant attention. Whether their new direction is an accurate forecast of what other courts will do is, however, a different question.

a. Sullivan v. University Interscholastic League

We earlier elaborated on the tendency of transfer rules to bring within their prohibition persons who indisputably have not been subject to recruiting pressures and whose transfers bear no athletically related motivation.[99] Those same objections underlie the complaint in *Sullivan v. University Interscholastic League*,[100] a 1981 decision of the Texas Supreme Court. John Sullivan had moved to Austin, Texas, from Vermont when his father's employment was transferred. It was accepted that the young man had not been recruited or subjected to other improper pressures. The student was, however, declared ineligible for a period of one year following the transfer. The pertinent rule of the defendant association did not recognize an exception for cases in which there was a bona fide transfer of the parents' residence. Exceptions were allowed in other situations, however. For example, in the case of a student who had only one year of high school eligibility remaining, the rule provided for a specific individualized review under which the transfer would be approved in the absence of evidence that the student had been recruited.[101]

The plaintiff attacked the relevant rule on equal protection grounds, and the court found that the relevant standard of review was the permissive rational relation test. Despite the liberality of that standard, the court held the rule to be constitutionally defective. The court began its analysis by observing that the rule created two classes of persons—those who transferred and those who did not—and afforded significantly different treatment to each of these.[102] One class was denied eligibility for a year while the other was left unaffected. The court found this classification scheme to be irrational in light of the stated goal of deterring the recruitment of athletes. The rule was thought to be "overbroad and overinclusive" because it imposed burdens on some persons who had clearly not been recruited, such as those who moved in conjunction with a change in the parents' employment.[103] The court also noted that the rule did make an exception for seniors and stated that it saw no rational reason why that exception, which included an individualized review, could not be extended to others. In short, the regulation operated too harshly in light of the goal ascribed to it.

While the court purports to decide the case under the federal constitutional principles, it neither cites nor discusses the major Supreme Court precedents that give texture to the rational relation test. An examination of those principles suggests that the *Sullivan* decision contains many of the same defects found in the *Sturrup* decision discussed earlier. The court assumes that an equal protection objection has been validated if the rule in question affects some persons who do not share in the evil that prompted the regulation. That, however, is not the lesson of the equal protection precedents. Regulations may be drawn broadly. The relationship between the state interest to be served and the persons regulated need not be exact.[104] In short, the inequity of overinclusiveness will be tolerated, assuming again that no suspect class or fundamental interest is involved.

It is true that the rule in question did make an exception for seniors and did provide for an individualized inquiry in that case. But contrary to what the court suggests, the fact that one exception is allowed and another equally defensible exception is ignored does not establish the basic irrationality of the regulation. If there ever were any doubt, the Supreme Court has recently confirmed that the equal protection clause does not compel a state to grant all reasonable exceptions merely because some are made.[105] This outcome is consistent with the basic notion discussed earlier that a state is allowed to approach a regulatory problem on a piecemeal basis. Perfect balance in a regulatory scheme is a political ideal, not a constitutional mandate.

The occasional appearance of equal protection analyses like these in *Sturrup* and *Sullivan* may reflect a need among lower courts for more sensitivity to the Supreme Court's basic directives on the permissive standard of equal protection review. It will be recalled that the Court has said that once a legitimate regulatory purpose has been identified, the ultimate question to be asked is: "Was it reasonable for the [rule-makers] to believe that use of the challenged classification would promote that purpose?"[106] This is not an exacting standard and was not intended to be. It will tolerate some rules that are ineffective, some that are countereffective, and some that are simply unwise. The important issue, again, is only whether the rule-makers could have reasonably believed that the rule would further their regulatory purpose.

In the context of the *Sullivan* case, the relevant inquiry is whether the athletic association could have expected that a broad-based rule would promote its desire to discourage recruiting and maintain a proper balance between athletics and academics. On several grounds, the conclusion can be accepted that the association might well have concluded that these goals would be furthered. The rule-makers could conclude, for example, that even when an employment-related transfer occurs, there is still room for athletically related school selection decisions to be made. The fact of the employment change does not refute the possibility that a student might later be subjected to recruiting pressures as he or she decides among the several schools located in the area of the new employment. Relatedly, even when the factor of recruiting is not present, the athletic regulators might decide that the family's selection among competing schools should be influenced by academic considerations and not athletics. A desire to maintain the predominance of academics is a separately recognizable and wholly legitimate goal.

A further ground that the regulators might have relied upon is a concern for the costs and burdens of administering the transfer rules. They could well have decided that the expenditures required to differentiate between athletically motivated and more neutral transfers were simply not justified in light of the incremental increase in refinement that would occur.[107] Given the impressionistic nature of the issue, and the difficulty of exacting neutral testimony, this judgment cannot be readily dismissed as fanciful.

b. Kite v. Marshall: *Protecting Family Privacy?*

The reluctance of the Supreme Court and subordinant courts to overturn state regulations under the permissive equal protection test can be explained on the ground that there is no fundamental, personal interest at stake. By definition, the permissive standard is applied only after we have concluded that there is no substantial, separately protectible interest involved. Thus, for the constitutional law theories to be useful, litigating students must be able to assert an interest of the sort that prompts the more exacting levels of judicial review.

Our earlier discussion of the policy-based criticisms of existing regulatory trends identified one interest that would seem to be of a higher order than those that have been litigated to date. It was suggested that a decision with respect to the relative emphasis to be given athletics might be viewed as a matter of student and family privacy. While administrators could decide on the character of their own programs, they need not be allowed to restrict parental choices among the programs that are otherwise available. If the student and parental interest in controlling the youth's athletic involvement includes a constitutionally protected dimension, then the courts would be compelled to subject the state's intrusions to more exacting scrutiny.

The concern for student and family privacy was given currency for a brief period of time by the 1980 federal district court decision in *Kite v. Marshall*.[108] That decision firmly embraced the notion that parental choices were entitled to primacy in matters relating to child rearing. If left standing, the initial *Kite* decision would have had far-reaching implications for the regulation of interscholastic sports. On appeal, however, the family privacy analysis was pointedly rejected and the initial decision reversed.[109] Nonetheless, the decisions in *Kite* are of considerable importance. As a preliminary exploration of the limits of parental control in athletic matters, they have served to focus debate on the critical issue of the proper interpretation of existing Supreme Court decisions in the privacy area.

The dispute in *Kite* focused on a rule of the Texas high school athletic association that sought to discourage student attendance at specialized summer sports camps. Any student attending such a camp lost a year's eligibility. The prohibition was absolute and, unlike the comparable rules in other states, did not tolerate even one or two weeks' attendance at such camps. Like the transfer rules that have provided the main focus of this chapter, the summer camp rule in *Kite* repre-

sented an effort to control the relative emphasis given to school-related
sports endeavors. The rule was prompted by a prior incident in which
a coach had taken his entire team to a camp for a summer-long practice.[110] There was also proof that some camps continued to place an
undue emphasis on winning and aggressiveness.

The plaintiffs, who were high school athletes and their parents,
grounded their case squarely on the theory that there is a "right in the
family unit to decide what is best for the family," especially as far as
the interests of minor children are concerned.[111] The plaintiffs thus
avoided the weaknesses of prior cases that argued for "a right to participate," a right that has not been recognized. In its essence, the plaintiffs' claim was a claim to substantive due process. The regulation in
question, it was urged, infringed on important constitutional rights
and thus could be sustained only if it were prompted by an important
state interest and were otherwise narrowly drawn.

The federal district court undertook a very deliberate analysis of the
issue before it and ultimately held the rule to be unconstitutional. The
court was able to find a variety of statements from the Supreme Court
that seemed pertinent to the issue before it. For example, the Supreme
Court had recognized the right of parents "to direct the rearing of their
children."[112] Relatedly, the Supreme Court had said that "[t]he child
is not the mere creature of the state; those who nurture him and direct
his destiny have the right . . . to recognize and prepare him for additional obligations."[113] Finally, the district court quoted language in
which the Supreme Court had found in parents a "duty to prepare the
child for additional obligations."[114] The district court accepted these
statements as supporting the view that the parental choice involved in
a summer camp decision was "deserving of constitutional support."[115]

Accepted doctrine required that the court go further, however. Before regulation affecting a constitutionally protected interest could be
struck down, the extent of the state's interest had to be appraised, as
did the question of whether the regulation was drafted with appropriate narrowness. The district court ultimately found that the state had
a "compelling interest" in the matter at hand.[116] The state was charged
with providing the structure for public education. It was thus empowered to insure that the system it devised, including the athletic component, was operated in an efficient and fair manner. But in the court's
view, the rule was not drawn with the "narrow specificity" required of
important constitutional concerns.[117] In effect, the rule chose to control
the offenders (some coaches who used summer camps for recruiting
purposes) by regulating the victims (the athletes who attended the
camps). The conduct of all athletes was impeded, and the prerogatives
of their parents infringed, for the purpose of securing conforming behavior from overzealous coaches. Further, the association had "failed

to show that it is without any other reasonable way to achieve its goals."[118]

Had it been allowed to stand, the district court decision in *Kite* would have had far-reaching implications for the regulation of amateur athletics. If a parental decision on the child's attendance at summer camp is to be respected, should not the same deference be shown for other parental decisions, such as those involved where the parents move for an athletically motivated reason or where similar goals prompt the parents to allow the student to move alone, perhaps to a relative who assumes the position of guardian? Indeed, it would seem that most aspects of eligibility regulation could be viewed as involving some element of parental choice. As noted, however, the case will not have that effect. The initial decision was reversed when the case was appealed to the Fifth Circuit Court of Appeals.

The appellate court revealed itself to be wholly unpersuaded by the multistep analysis of the district court's opinion. Indeed, the reviewing court's rejection of the earlier decision went to the heart of the issue at hand. Although there is a bit of equivocation, the Fifth Circuit's opinion raises a doubt as to whether there is any separately recognizable "right to family privacy." For example, after noting that the plaintiffs' arguments were supposedly based in the Constitution, the court expressed its view that "uncertainty abounds not only as to the constitutional spring from which this family privacy right flows, but also as to its definition and character."[119] The reviewing court also took a different view of the import of the Supreme Court family law decisions. Reference was made to cases involving corporal punishment, teenage abortion, and private segregated academies in which the Supreme Court declined to give controlling weight to parental preferences. In appraising these, the Fifth Circuit observed that when "[c]onfronted with these situations which, at first blush, appear to rest at the heart of parental decision-making, the Supreme Court refrained from clothing parental judgment with a constitutional mantle."[120] Again, an implication of this analysis is to question the very existence of a right to family privacy.

In light of this apparent premise, the Fifth Circuit's ultimate conclusion is not surprising. Its summary appraisal of *Kite* was that "[T]his case implicates no fundamental constitutional right."[121] Since no fundamental interest was involved, the regulation in question would be saved by a showing of mere rationality. The need to control overzealous coaches, to maintain competitive balance, and to reduce pressure on students was thought to present plausible, and hence sufficient, justifications.

It is not certain that the appellate court's decision in *Kite* will represent the final internment of the family privacy argument. The apparent

denial of the existence of a right to the family privacy is a position not
likely to be accepted without question by future litigation.[122] Language
from earlier Supreme Court decisions suggesting the existence of such
a right will likely provide the fuel for a continuing debate. These pronouncements provided the foundation for the district court's opinion
and were never fully refuted in the appellate court's review.

This is not to suggest, however, that the ultimate resolution of the
family privacy issue was incorrect. There is another view of the Supreme Court's decision that would deny *Kite's* complaint but not require a complete refutation of family privacy notions. Specifically, it
can be noted that while the Supreme Court has emphasized the importance of the family in giving direction to children's lives, the actual
issues resolved in the cases in which these concerns appear are far removed from those raised by the plaintiffs in *Kite*. The Supreme Court's
"family privacy" decisions in general deal with matters relating to issues
of abortion, contraception, and the rights of illegitimates.[123] None of
the cases deal with a family decision as far removed from basic issues
of life and personal identity as the question of whether a student will
be allowed to attend a specialized summer athletic camp. While the
Supreme Court has shown itself ready to intervene where basic issues
of human life and control of reproduction are involved, it has not ventured very far into more routine issues involving the accommodation
of family preferences and admittedly legitimate state interests.[124]

Thus, while the notion of family privacy may have validity, its con-
figuration is much more narrow than the district court in *Kite* assumed.
The case that will raise the family privacy claim most strongly is likely
to be one in which the disputed regulation disadvantages a fundamental feature of the parent-child relationship.[125] General claims of "parental preference" are not to be wholly ignored, as suggested in the next
section. They may not, however, be clothed in constitutional protection.

3. Reassessing the policy of extreme judicial deference

As previously noted, the traditional approach to evaluating athletic
regulations was one of extreme judicial deference. The law of private
associations was hardly an intrusion.[126] Even the potentially more exacting state public law principles were applied without a serious, critical examination of the substance of the plaintiff's complaint.[127] Relatedly, the permissive standard of equal protection review almost
inevitably deferred to the "practical difficulties" of drawing and administering precise regulations.[128]

Several courts, however, have indicated a restiveness with the traditional approaches. If the stated legal theories are set aside for the moment, one can see an affinity in the recent decision in *Sullivan*, the dis-

trict court decision in *Kite,* and the somewhat earlier ruling in *Bunger.*[129] In each instance, the court was presented with a regulation that was drawn with an extremely broad sweep. Especially in *Sullivan* and *Bunger,* the disputed rule was applied to someone who seemed far removed from the evils that likely prompted the regulation in the first instance. In the view of the district court, *Kite* similarly presented an example of indiscriminant regulation, for one could doubt, as the court did, that summer athletic camps represented the pervasive evil that the regulation presumed.

These decisions, and some other cases that had less encouraging results for the athlete-plaintiffs, underscore a basic problem with the jurisprudence of this area: if the courts refuse to intervene, one may question whether sufficient incentives exist to insure that rules are drawn with appropriate sensitivity to the risk of overregulation. To raise this concern is not to insist that the rules must except every class that should be exempted and that varying levels in the seriousness of the offense must be exactly calibrated. Nor is it to suggest that regulations must be devised without regard to their administrative cost. Rather the issue to be posed is one of degree. Athletic administrators should have some obligation to make a reasoned effort at exempting cases that need not be regulated and that can be identified with relatively little cost.

The highly deferential premises of the equal protection doctrine and state public law seem to be based on a key assumption about the nature of the underlying political institutions. It is presumed that defects in the regulatory coverage will be corrected through the normal operation of the underlying legislative process. Thus, if a regulatory measure suffers from overbreadth, those who are unnecessarily brought within its coverage can be expected to raise objections to their legislators. The depth and substance of the protestation will be appraised and, if substantial enough, will presumably prompt an appropriate legislative correction.[130]

It is not obvious, though, that this legislative model is the appropriate one where athletic regulations are involved. A significant difference is that the persons regulated—the athletes and vicariously their parents—have limited input into the decisions that are made. As previously noted, they are not members of the rule-making organizations and typically are not consulted in the deliberations that precede governance decisions.[131] Moreover, within the association there are frequently groups other than the athletes that are the focus of the group's deliberations on student-related rules. As we have seen, for example, athletes often bear the burden of regulations that are intended to control the actions of coaches.[132] Thus on the matter of student eligibility, there appears to be a confusion of constituencies. It is by no means certain that the athlete's best interests are the predominant legislative force.

The concern for limitations in the internal processes of athletic associations may not mean that a radical new judicial doctrine needs to be devised. To the contrary, it is a concern that can be accommodated within the confines of existing theories. What is required is a modest adjustment in the level of judicial scrutiny that is otherwise taken. Rather than treating the athletic association with the same deference that would be shown to an entity in the normal political channels, the courts should allow themselves the freedom to insist that the scope of regulation not exceed the limits of the regulatory problem that exists. As at present, the courts would not review the wisdom of a regulation or appraise its merits relative to competing models. The court would, however, be alert to the rule-makers' insensitivity to the potential for unnecessarily burdening innocent parties.

A model of judicial review that is particularly appealing is that applied in the *Bunger* decision. The formal rule in *Bunger* is premised on two questions: did the rule-making entity have authority to regulate the particular activity? If so, was the particular rule or ruling a rational exercise of that authority?[133] It will be recalled that the rule in *Bunger* failed to satisfy the second test. The athletic association had attempted to deny eligibility to a player who, outside the school year, was innocently present in an automobile in which alcoholic beverages were being transported. While the court stated that regulation on some other combination of facts would have been appropriate, in the present case, the regulation was irrational. It attributed to the student a characteristic (improper alcohol use) that was not present and involved an incident that was far removed from the school year.[134]

One can find in other cases a similar quality of irrationality. For example, the result in *Sullivan* could be explained in these same terms: where the purpose of a rule is to discourage recruiting and school-jumping, it is irrational to apply that rule to one who is forced to move because of a family employment transfer.[135] Even *Kite* can be brought within this analysis. The rule involved in that case was adopted because a coach had practiced with his entire team for a substantial part of the summer. While that presents a problem requiring regulation, an absolute, unbending prohibition on attendance at a summer camp has a strong element of irrationality. If the period of attendance is short and if the student's coach is in no way involved, it is difficult to see the reason for the prohibition. A student's participation under these circumstances has none of the characteristics that prompted the adoption of the regulation. Rather than representing a reasoned response, the regulation is more likely explainable as the product of a defective legislative process.

The cases mentioned above are decisions in which the student prevailed on some theory other than the state review provided in *Bunger*. But proper application of *Bunger* should also cause a rethinking of some of the prior decisions that upheld association regulations. For example, a test of basic rationality would allow a court to intervene in a case like *Kentucky High School Association v. Hopkins County Board of Education*.[136] That case involved a situation, mentioned earlier, in which a student transferred schools after parental custody was legally changed from one divorced parent to another. The athletic association denied eligibility to the student for one year because its rule allowed a change of school only if there was a "change" in the parents' residence. The literalistic interpretation applied in this case can be said to lack basic rationality in the face of a legal change in the identity, and hence, the residence of the parent.

This type of case is somewhat different from *Sullivan* and *Kite*. The issue involved is one of interpreting the association's rules, rather than questioning their legal basis. But here again, the application of a rationality analysis seems sound. Without this type of review, there is little to protect the athlete from arbitrary or, more likely, unthinking interpretations of association rules. Errors of interpretation can be made as readily by public entities as by private contracting parties.[137] Since courts are available to provide corrective guidance in the case of wholly private agreements, it would seem that they should be no less available where a public undertaking is involved.[138]

One attraction of a test focusing on a rule's rationality is that it allows a court to make functional differentiations between cases. Once the court identifies the purpose of a rule, it can then inquire into whether the facts and circumstances of the plaintiff's situation indicate that it is one that presents the evil that the athletic administrator sought to control.[139] If there is a risk that recruiting or some other improper influence was present, then the regulation should be sustained. The result should be the same if the risk of an improper influence is unknown. But the court would also be empowered to allow the plaintiff to show that his or her circumstances disprove the possibility of an impropriety.

If the motivations for the student's move are beyond the normal jurisdiction of the administrators, as where they are related to a transfer of employment, then the intensity of judicial scrutiny should be increased. Whether the regulation will be allowed in such a case should depend upon further facts. The association may properly take account of the cost of making individualized determinations and may decline to adopt a general policy to this effect. But where the absence of the evil prompting regulation can be proved with relative ease, the threshold of irrationality is transversed by a rule that fails to admit of such an exception.

A further attraction of this approach is that it offers a state law theory of review. Since athletic associations and school boards operate as state entities, it is appropriate that state law provide a mechanism through which misdirections in regulatory authority can be corrected. Indeed, basic notions of jurisprudence would suggest that the authority that has created an entity has an obligation to provide a vehicle for hearing complaints that the entity has abused the authority that was granted.[140] Such state-based review will also help insure that the process of judicial oversight takes appropriate account of differences among the regulatory structures for school sports in the various states.

It might be asked whether this same approach could not be accommodated under federal equal protection notions, even where the applicable standard is one of permissive review. After all, the basic test in that area is one that nominally requires a rational relation between the purpose of the regulation and the conduct regulated. However, the thrust of the Supreme Court's decisions has been to give regulators maximum leeway where no fundamental interest is involved. As previously noted, the fact of overbreadth is typically not a reason for judicial concern, and the court will accept even some admitted inequities.[141] This tradition of constitutional deference to legislative decision-making as well as basic concerns for federalism, relegated permissive equal protection review to a more limited sphere. Again, the problem at hand seems to be one better suited for an entity charged with insuring the basic integrity of the local legal system.

CONCLUSION

An earlier portion of this chapter set forth some of the policy objections that might be raised against the present rules for regulating inter-school transfers. Among other things, the question was raised as to whether greater freedom ought to be allowed for the exercise of parental choice. In addition, it was noted that transfer rules frequently are drawn with considerable imprecision. A rule may impose a wholesale prohibition affecting even relatively innocent school changes and at the same time allow exceptions that can be used by those with blatantly athletically related motivations. To what extent will the law provide the mechanism for correcting the defects assumed by these objections? The prior analysis should give some idea of the role of judicial review in this area. A pervasive theme of the cases in this area is that the courts are not available to vindicate all objections that might be raised to athletic association rules. It is accepted that school boards and athletic associations must be given considerable freedom to respond to the conflicting interests of affected parties and to take account of practical financial and time limitations on the entity's capacity for administration.

At one time, these considerations produced virtual legal immunity for athletic administrators. Historically, it has been extremely rare for a court to overturn an administrative rule in this area. It appears, though, that that attitude is changing. Contrary to the desires of some, however, the change does not appear to be of revolutionary proportions. Rather, it appears that cases at the margin will now be examined more closely by the judicial institution. It is suggested above that the courts have begun to endorse a somewhat more exacting standard of rationality than had been traditionally applied. The standard should be particularly useful in prompting athletic administrators to except from regulation those cases which represent little or no risk of abuse.[142] Similarly, a rule that regulates insignificant incidents and ignores obvious abuses will be vulnerable under the newly emerging standard.

By the same token, however, there will be many potential objections that will not prompt judicial intervention. For example, the desire of some for complete parental choice is most unlikely to be given judicial consideration. Relatedly, judicial review will not mandate that the administrators ferret out all instances of transfer abuses. The explanation for why such "defects" are tolerated involves a basic point about the nature of the legal process. It is not the obligation of the courts to insure that other political and governmental institutions function with exacting precision. A good deal of slippage in the regulatory apparatus must be tolerated. This is particularly true in the area of athletics, where the affected subject matter has historically been thought not to involve a fundamental right. Thus, there may be important policy objections that have not been fully considered in the administrative processes affecting athletics. These are appropriate agenda items for the deliberations of the administering agencies. They are not, however, translatable into legal objections. Even with the liberalization seen recently, and that anticipated in the years ahead, the function of the judiciary will be limited. While we should see a move toward greater rationality at the margins, basic shifts in the orientation of athletic regulations will have to be the product of actions at a different institutional level.

NOTES

1. *See* Dostert v. Berthold Public School Dist. #54, 391 F.Supp. 876 (D.N.D. 1975); Dunham v. Pulsifer, 312 F. Supp. 411 (D.Vt. 1970). *See generally* Bishop v. Colaw, 450 F.2d 1069 (8th Cir. 1971); Stevenson v.

Board of Educ., 426 F.2d 1154 (5th Cir.), *cert.denied*, 400 U.S. 957 (1970); Breen v. Kahl, 419 F.2d 1034 (7th Cir. 1969), *cert.denied*, 398 U.S. 937 (1970).

2. *See, e.g.*, Board of Directors of Independent School Dist. of Waterloo v. Green, 147 N.W.2d 854 (Iowa 1967); Cochrane v. Board of Educ., 360 Mich. 390, 103 N.W.2d 569 (1960); State *ex rel.* Baker v. Stevenson, 189 N.E.2d 181 (Ohio C.P. 1962); State *ex rel.* Thompson v. Marion County Bd. of Educ., 202 Tenn. 29, 302 S.W.2d 57 (1957); Kissick v. Garland Independent School Dist., 330 S.W.2d 708 (Tex.Civ.App. 1959); Starkey v. Board of Educ., 14 Utah 2d 227, 381 P.2d 718 (1963).

3. *See, e.g.*, Board of Directors of Independent School Dist. of Waterloo v. Green, 147 N.W.2d 854, 858 (Iowa 1967). *See also* Cochrane v. Board of Educ., 360 Mich. 390, 103 N.W.2d 569 (1960); J.WEISTART & C.LOWELL, THE LAW OF SPORTS 86–87 (1979).

4. *See* Board of Directors of Independent School Dist. of Waterloo v. Green, 147 N.W.2d 854, 858–59 (Iowa 1967).

5. *Id.* at 859: "6. Married students are more likely to have undesirable influences on other students during the informal extracurricular activities."

6. Hollon v. Mathis Independent School Dist., 491 F.2d 92 (5th Cir. 1974); O'Neill v. Dent, 364 F.Supp. 565 (E.D.N.Y. 1973); Romans v. Crenshaw, 354 F.Supp. 868 (S.D.Tex. 1972); Moran v. School Dist. #7, 350 F.Supp. 1180 (D.Mont. 1972); Holt v. Shelton, 341 F.Supp. 823 (M.D.Tenn. 1972); Davis v. Meek, 344 F.Supp. 298 (N.D. Ohio 1972); Indiana High School Athletic Ass'n v. Raike, 329 N.E.2d 66 (Ind.App. 1975).

7. *See* H.APPENZELLER & T.APPENZELLER, SPORTS AND THE COURTS 67–71 (1980); Perle & Browning, *Student Classifications and Equal Protection: Marriage and Sex*, 3 J.L. & EDUC. 93 (1974); *Right of Married High School Students to Engage in Extracurricular Activities*, 22 BUFFALO L.REV. 634 (1972). *See also* Goldstein, *The Scope and Sources of School Board Authority to Regulate Student Conduct and Status: A Nonconstitutional Analysis*, 117 U.PA.L.REV. 373 (1969).

8. This conclusion can be sustained by researching the West Key Numbers *Schools and School Districts* 164 to 172 through several Decennial Digests.

9. *See* Kite v. Marshall, 494 F.Supp. 227 (S.D.Tex. 1980), *rev'd*, 661 F.2d 1027 (5th Cir. 1981); Sturrup v. Mahan, 305 N.E.2d 877 (Ind. 1974); Sullivan v. University Interscholastic League, 599 S.W.2d 860 (Tex.Civ.App. 1980), *aff'd in part, rev'd in part*, 616 S.W.2d 170 (Tex. 1981).

10. *See generally* Phillips, *Fattening Them Up for Football*, Time, March 9, 1981, at 41; Norton, '*Holdbacks*' *Slow Down to Get Ahead*, State (Columbia, S.C.), Oct. 25, 1981, at 1, col. 2.

11. *See* Hebert v. Ventetuolo, 638 F.2d (1st Cir. 1981); Denis J. O'Connell High School v. Virginia High School League, 581 F.2d 81 (4th Cir. 1978), *cert. denied*, 440 U.S. 936 (1979); Barnhorst v. Missouri State High School Activities Ass'n, 504 F.Supp. 449 (W.D.Mo. 1980); Kulovitz v. Illinois High School Ass'n, 462 F.Supp. 975 (N.D.Ill. 1978); Dallam v. Cumberland Valley School Dist., 591 F.Supp. 358 (M.D. Pa. 1975); Scott v. Kilpatrick, 286 Ala. 129, 237 So.2d 652 (1970); Sturrup v. Mahan, 305 N.E.2d 877 (Ind. 1974); Kentucky High School Athletic Ass'n v. Hopkins County Bd. of Educ., 522 S.W.2d 685 (Ky.App. 1977); Marino v. Waters, 220 So.2d 802 (La.App. 1969); Josephine County School Dist. #7 v. Oregon High School Activities Ass'n, 15 Ore.App. 158, 515 P.2d 431 (1973); Bruce v. South Carolina High School League, 189 S.E.2d 817 (S.C. 1972).

12. *See* Sullivan v. University Interscholastic League, 599 S.W.2d 860

(Tex.Civ.App. 1980), *aff'd in part, rev'd in part,* 616 S.W.2d 170 (Tex. 1981).

13. The Tennessee Secondary School Athletic Association has used a rule as follows:

> "Except for the eligibility rules in regard to age and to the number of semesters in school, the Board of Control shall have authority to set aside the effect of any eligibility rule upon an individual student when in its opinion the rule fails to accomplish the purpose for which it is intended, or when the rule works an undue hardship upon the student."
>
> "Requests for the consideration of such exceptions shall be acted upon by the Board of Control only twice during each school year—at the fall meeting held the latter part of August and at the January meeting."
>
> "The conditions causing the student to fail to meet the eligibility requirements must have been beyond the control of the school, the student and or his parents, and such that none of them could have reasonably been expected to comply with the rule the violation of which is involved."

Tennessee Secondary School Athletic Ass'n v. Cox, 221 Tenn. 164, 166–67, 425 S.W.2d 597, 598 (1968). *See also* Sturrup v. Mahan, 305 N.E.2d 877, 878–79 (Ind. 1974).

14. *See, e.g.,* Barnhorst v. Missouri State High School Activities Ass'n, 504 F.Supp. 449 (W.D.Mo. 1980) (court finds that athlete was not motivated by athletics and new school did not have good teams, but no relief); Marino v. Waters, 220 So.2d 802 (La.App. 1969); Bruce v. South Carolina High School League, 189 S.E.2d 817 (S.C. 1972); Sullivan v. University Interscholastic League, 599 S.W.2d 860 (Tex.Civ.App. 1980), *aff'd in part, rev'd in part,* 616 S.W.2d 170 (Tex. 1981).

15. Barnhorst v. Missouri State High School Activities Ass'n, 504 F.Supp. 449, 455 (W.D.Mo. 1980).

16. Kentucky High School Athletic Ass'n v. Hopkins County Bd. of Educ., 522 S.W.2d 685 (Ky.App. 1977).

17. *Id.* at 686.

18. In other areas, ranging from contracts law to the judicial interpretation of legislative acts, it is appreciated that legal documents will require interpretation. Some imprecision occurs because of limitations in the drafting skills of the authors. More frequently, though, the need for interpretation is the predictable product of the fact that the authors at the time of drafting cannot anticipate every factual variation that may occur.

Where the need arises to apply a stated rule to an unusual case, courts will frequently seek to ascertain the purpose or "spirit" of the rule and interpret it in a way that achieves a result consistent with this assumption about the drafters' intent. A search for the authors' intent will frequently provide a more accurate guide for interpretation than will a literal application of the language used. *See, e.g.,* 3 A.Corbin, Corbin on Contracts §§ 532–572 (1960).

19. 504 F.Supp. 449 (W.D.Mo. 1980).

20. *Id.* at 455.

21. *See, e.g.,* Sturrup v. Mahan, 305 N.E.2d 877, 878–79 (Ind. 1974). *See also* note 11 *supra* and accompanying text. Some states that otherwise allow a transfer where there is a change in the parents' residence will apparently impose a period of ineligibility in some cases where a further inquiry

reveals that the move was athletically related. *See* Marino v. Waters, 220 So.2d 802, 803–04 (La.App. 1969).

22. "Our institutions do not rely on submerging individual personality in order to create an idealized citizen." Bishop v. Colaw, 450 F.2d 1069, 1078 (8th Cir. 1971). *See also* Dunham v. Pulsifer, 312 F.Supp. 411 (D.Vt. 1970).

23. *See, e.g.,* Kite v. Marshall, 454 F.Supp. 1347 (S.D.Tex. 1978), *rev'd,* 661 F.2d 1027 (5th Cir. 1981). *Cf.* Laurenzo v. Mississippi High School Activities Ass'n, 662 F.2d 1117 (5th Cir. 1981) (action dismissed as moot); Sullivan v. University Interscholastic League, 616 S.W. 2d 170 (Tex. 1981) (court does not reach privacy argument).

24. *See, e.g.,* Barnhorst v. Missouri State High School Activities Ass'n, 504 F.Supp. 449 (W.D.Mo. 1980); Marino v. Waters, 220 So.2d 802 (La.App. 1969). A related policy concern is raised in cases involving limitations on the student's right to participate in specialized summer sports camps. *See* Kite v. Marshall, 494 F.Supp. 227, 239 (S.D.Tex. 1980), *rev'd,* 661 F.2d 1027 (5th Cir. 1981); Brown v. Wells, 288 Minn. 468, 181 N.W.2d 708 (1970); Art Gaines Baseball Camp, Inc. v. Houston, 500 S.W.2d 735, 738 (Mo.Ct.App. 1973).

25. *See* J.Michener, Sports in America 89–92 (1976).

26. One athletic administrator has observed that "having a kid repeat a year just feeds the pipe dream." Phillips, *Fattening Them Up for Football,* Time, March 9, 1981, at 41.

27. *Id.*

28. The parent of a student involved in a hold-back controversy in South Carolina perceived that "the real issue is the right of the parent to decide what's best for his child . . ." State (Columbia, S.C.), Oct. 25, 1981, at 6, col. 4.

29. Underwood, *The Writing Is on the Wall* [*The Shame of American Education: The Student Athlete Hoax*], Sports Illustrated, May 19, 1980, at 36-44; Thomas, *Guidance Is Imperative to Save Student-Athletes,* Chicago Tribune, June 8, 1980, § 4, at 3, col. 4.

30. *See* Luschen, *Social Stratification and Social Mobility Among Young Sportsmen,* in Sport, Culture and Society 258 (Loy & Kenyon, eds. 1969); Otto & Alwin, *Athletics, Aspirations and Achievements,* 42 Sociol.Educ. 102 (1977); Picou, *Race, Athletic Achievement, and Educational Aspiration,* 19 Sociol.Q. 429 (1978); Rehberg, *Behavioral and Attitudinal Consequences of High School Interscholastic Sports: A Speculative Consideration,* 4 Adolescence 69 (1969); Rehberg & Schafer, *Participation in Interscholastic Athletics and College Expectations,* 63 Am.J.Sociol. 732 (1968); Schafer & Rehberg, *Athletic Participation, College Aspirations and College Encouragement,* 13 Pac.Sociol.Rev. 732 (1968); Spreitzer & Pugh, *Interscholastic Athletics and Educational Expectations,* 46 Sociol.Educ. 171 (1973).

31. In baseball these include Dave Winfield (Yankees), Fred Lynn (Angels), Phil Niekro (Braves), Andre Dawson (Expos), Nolan Ryan (Astros), Eddie Murray (Orioles), Dave Parker (Pirates), and Al Hrabosky (Braves). Pope, *Baseball Pays Better Than Politics,* Chicago Tribune, Mar. 8, 1981, § 4, at 6, col. 1. Among basketball players with $1 million contracts are Kareem Abdul-Jabbar, Earvin (Magic) Johnson, Moses Malone, and Otis Birdsong. Magic Johnson recently signed a contract that will pay him $1,000,000 per year for the next twenty-six years. Eskenazi, *Athletes' Salaries: How High Will the Bidding Go?,* New York Times, Aug. 16, 1981, § 5, at 1, col. 1.

Even for players other than these exceptional stars, professional sports can be very lucrative. The average salary in baseball is now in the neighborhood of $180,000. In basketball, the average salary is $193,000 per year, while the football average is $78,657. *Id.*

32. Moses Malone is perhaps the most successful of the basketball players who began their professional careers immediately after high school. New York Times, May 20, 1979, § 5, at 1, col. 4. He was selected the most valuable player in the NBA in 1979. *Id.,* May 23, 1979, § II, at 6, col. 5. For the 1980–81 season, his salary was reputed to be $1,050,000; for 1981–82, it will be $50,000 more. Eskenazi, *Athletes' Salaries: How High Will the Bidding Go?, id.,* Aug. 16, 1981, § 5, at 1, col. 1.

33. One source has reported that chances of a college basketball player securing a permanent position on an NBA roster are on the order of 1 in 18,000. *See* Klein, *Basketball Stars Get Jump on College Life at a Summer Camp,* Wall Street Journal, Aug. 6, 1981, at 1, col. 4.

34. This calculation is based on the assumption that the financial aid package of tuition, room, meals, and books is worth $10,000 per year. Four years of such aid would total $40,000. If the student's parents were in a 40% tax bracket, they would have to earn roughly $67,000 to yield $40,000 after taxes.

This calculation does not discount future years' cost to present value. By the same token, however, no upward adjustment is made for anticipated increases in the value of the package. It may be that these two adjustments would largely offset one another.

35. The Supreme Court has unmistakably marked out certain zones of family privacy into which state regulation can intrude only if there are compelling reasons. Limitations on the state's right to control abortion and choices with respect to contraception provide the clearest evidence of this trend. For a more general discussion of the scope of this right to individual and family privacy, see L.Tribe, American Constitutional Law 921–54, 985–90 (1978).

36. Coleman, Adolescents and the Schools 45 (1965); Landers & Landers, *Socialization Via Interscholastic Athletics: Its Effects on Delinquency,* 51 Sociol. Educ. 299 (1979); Schafer & Armer, *Athletes Are Not Inferior Students,* 6 Transactions 21 (1968).

37. *See* Hanks, *Race, Sexual Status and Athletics in the Process of Educational Achievement,* 60 Soc.Sci.Q. 482 (1979).

38. *See, e.g.,* Dumez v. Louisiana High School Athletic Ass'n, 334 So.2d 494 (La.App. 1976) (prohibition of transfer rule not applicable to golf, tennis, and swimming). *See also* Kite v. Marshall, 494 F.Supp. 227, 229 (S.D. Tex. 1980), *rev'd,* 661 F.2d 1027 (5th Cir. 1981); Caso v. New York State Public High School Athletic Ass'n, 434 N.Y.S.2d 60, 62-63 (S. Ct. 1980).

39. Considerable freedom of choice by parents is allowed under some present forms of regulation. *See* note 13 *supra* and accompanying text.

40. *See* Barnhorst v. Missouri State High School Activities Ass'n, 504 F.Supp. 449 (W.D.Mo. 1980).

41. *See* Sullivan v. University Interscholastic League, 616 S.W.2d 170 (Tex. 1981).

42. *See* J.Weistart & C.Lowell, The Law of Sports 37 (1979); Chafee, *The Internal Affairs of Associations Not for Profit,* 43 Harv.L.Rev. 993, 1014 (1930); Comment, *State High School Athletic Associations: When Will a Court Interfere?* 30 Mo.L.Rev. 400, 402–06 (1971).

43. Sult v. Gilbert, 148 Fla. 31, 3 So.2d 729 (1941); Robinson v. Illinois High School Ass'n, 45 Ill.App.2d 277, 195 N.E.2d 38 (1963); State *ex rel.*

Indiana High School Athletic Ass'n v. Lawrence Cir. Ct., 240 Ind. 114, 162 N.E.2d 250 (1959); Marino v. Waters, 220 So.2d 802 (La.App. 1969); State *ex rel.* Ohio High School Athletic Ass'n v. Judges of Ct. Common Pleas, 173 Ohio St. 239, 181 N.E.2d 261 (1962); Morrison v. Roberts, 183 Okla. 359, 82 P.2d 1023 (1938); Tennessee Secondary School Athletic Ass'n v. Cox, 221 Tenn. 164, 425 S.W.2d 597 (1968). *See generally* 6 Am.Jur.2d § 27 *Associations and Clubs* (1963).

44. *See* Chafee, *The Internal Affairs of Associations Not for Profit*, note 42 *supra. Developments in the Law—Judicial Control of Actions of Private Associations*, 76 Harv.L.Rev. 983, 990 (1963).

45. *See, e.g.*, Shaup v. Grand Int'l Bhd. of Locomotive Eng'rs, 223 Ala. 202, 135 So. 327 (1931); Higgins v. American Soc'y of Clinical Pathologists, 51 N.J. 191, 238 A.2d 665 (1968); Brotherhood of R. R. Trainmen v. Price, 108 S.W.2d 239 (Tex.Civ.App. 1937); Samuelson v. Railroad Trainmen Lodge 852, 60 Wyo. 316, 151 P.2d (1944).

46. *See, e.g.*, Kentucky High School Athletic Ass'n v. Hopkins County Bd. of Educ., 522 S.W.2d 685 (Ky.App. 1977); Marino v. Waters, 220 So.2d 802 (La.App. 1969); State *ex rel.* National Jr. College Athletic Ass'n v. Luten, 492 S.W.2d 404 (Mo.App. 1973); Mozingo v. Oklahoma Secondary School Activities Ass'n, 575 P.2d 1379 (Okla.App. 1978); Bruce v. South Carolina High School League, 189 S.E.2d 817 (S.C. 1972).

47. *See, e.g.*, Davis v. Ann Arbor Public Schools, 313 F.Supp. 1217 (E.D.Mich. 1970); Kinzer v. Directors of Independent School Dist., 129 Iowa 441, 105 N.W. 686 (1906); Fitzpatrick v. Board of Educ., 284 N.Y.S. 2d 590 (S.Ct. 1967).

48. *See, e.g.*, Bunger v. Iowa High School Athletic Ass'n, 197 N.W.2d 555 (Iowa 1972); Brown v. Wells, 288 Minn. 468, 181 N.W.2d 708 (1970); State *ex rel.* Ohio High School Athletic Ass'n v. Judges of Ct. of Common Pleas, 173 Ohio 239, 181 N.E.2d 261 (1962); Morrison v. Roberts, 183 Okla. 359, 82 P.2d 1023 (1938); Tennessee Secondary School Athletic Ass'n v. Cox, 221 Tenn. 164, 524 N.W.2d 597 (1968).

49. *See, e.g.*, Kriss v. Brown, 390 N.E.2d 193 (Ind.App. 1979); Brown v. Wells, 288 Minn. 468, 181 N.W.2d 708 (1970); Morrison v. Roberts, 183 Okla. 359, 82 P.2d 1023 (1938); Anderson v. South Dakota High School Activities Ass'n, 47 N.W. 2d 481 (S.D. 1976). *See also* Spain v. Louisiana High School Athletic Ass'n, 398 So. 2d 1386 (La. 1981).

50. *See, e.g.*, Bunger v. Iowa High School Athletic Ass'n, 197 N.W.2d 555 (Iowa 1972); Anderson v. South Dakota High School Athletic Ass'n, 247 N.W.2d 481 (S.D. 1976). *See also* Spain v. Louisiana High School Athletic Ass'n, 398 So.2d 1386 (La. 1981).

51. *See, e.g.*, Brown v. Wells, 288 Minn. 468, 181 N.W.2d 708 (1970); State *ex rel.* Ohio High School Athletic Ass'n v. Judges of Ct. of Common Pleas, 173 Ohio 239, 181 N.E.2d 261 (1962); Starkey v. Board of Educ., 14 Utah 2d 227, 381 P.2d 718 (1963).

52. *See, e.g.*, Board of Directors of Independent School Dist. of Waterloo v. Green, 147 N.W.2d 854 (Iowa 1967); Brown v. Wells, 288 Minn. 468, 181 N.W.2d 708 (1970); Art Gaines Baseball Camp, Inc. v. Houston, 500 S.W.2d 735 (Mo.App. 1973).

53. *See, e.g.*, Kite v. Marshall, 494 F.Supp. 227, 233 (S.D.Tex. 1980), *rev'd*, 661 F.2d 1027 (5th Cir. 1981); Board of Directors of Independent School Dist. of Waterloo v. Green, 147 N.W.2d 854, 858 (Iowa 1967). *See also* R.Phay, Law of Suspension and Expulsion: An Examination of the Substantive Issues in Controlling Student Conduct 50–61 (1975).

54. Brown v. Wells, 288 Minn. 468, 473–74, 181 N.W.2d 708, 711 (1970).

55. Bunger v. Iowa High School Athletic Ass'n, 197 N.W.2d 555, 564 (Iowa 1972).

56. Art Gaines Baseball Camp, Inc. v. Houston, 500 S.W.2d 735, 740 (Mo.App. 1973).

57. *Id.* at 741.

58. *See, e.g.,* Bunger v. Iowa High School Athletic Ass'n, 197 N.W.2d 555 (Iowa 1972). State *ex rel.* Ging v. Board of Educ., 7 N.W.2d 544 (Minn. 1942).

59. *Compare* Sullivan v. University Interscholastic League, 616 S.W.2d 170 (Tex. 1981).

60. *See, e.g.,* Herbert v. Ventetuolo, 638 F.2d 5 (1st Cir. 1981); Kulovitz v. Illinois High School Ass'n, 462 F.Supp. 875 (N.D.Ill. 1978); Kriss v. Brown, 390 N.E.2d 193 (Ind.App. 1979).

61. *See, e.g.,* Barnhorst v. Missouri State High School Activities Ass'n, 504 F.Supp. 449 (W.D.Mo. 1980); Scott v. Kilpatrick, 286 Ala. 192, 237 So. 2d 652 (1970); Kentucky High School Athletic Ass'n v. Hopkins County Bd. of Educ., 522 S.W.2d 685 (KyApp. 1977); Marino v. Waters, 220 So.2d 802 (La.App. 1969); Mozingo v. Oklahoma Secondary Schools Activities Ass'n, 575 P.2d 1379 (Okla.App. 1978); Bruce v. South Carolina High School League, 189 S.E.2d 817 (S.C. 1972).

62. *See* Kulovitz v. Illinois High School Ass'n, 462 F.Supp. 875, 877 (N.D.Ill. 1978); Brown v. Wells, 288 Minn. 468, 473–74, 181 N.W.2d 708, 711 (1970).

63. *See* Kriss v. Brown, 390 N.E.2d 193 (Ind.App. 1979); Art Gaines Baseball Camp, Inc. v. Houston, 500 S.W.2d 735, 741 (Mo.App. 1973).

64. *See* Barnhorst v. Missouri State High School Activities Ass'n, 504 F.Supp. 449, 463 (W.D.Mo. 1980); Brown v. Wells, 288 Minn. 468, 473–74, 181 N.W.2d 708, 711 (1970); Art Gaines Baseball Camp, Inc. v. Houston, 500 S.W.2d 735, 741 (Mo.App. 1973); Morrison v. Roberts, 183 Okla. 359, 361, 82 P.2d 1023, 1024 (1938); Bruce v. South Carolina High School League, 189 S.E.2d 817 (S.C. 1972).

65. 197 N.W.2d 555 (Iowa 1972).

66. The court stated that one question before it was whether the particular rule was reasonable. As we have already noted, the court apparently meant this to be an inquiry into the basic rationality of the measure. *See* text at notes 54–58 *supra.*

67. 197 S.W.2d at 564.

68. *Id.*

69. Shapiro v. Thompson, 394 U.S. 618 (1969).

70. *See, e.g.,* Bellotti v. Baird, 443 U.S. 622 (1979); Walen v. Roe, 429 U.S. 589 (1977); Wisconsin v. Yoder, 406 U.S. 205 (1972).

71. *See, e.g.,* San Antonio Independent School Dist. v. Rodriguez, 411 U.S. 1 (1973); Lindsey v. Normet, 405 U.S. 56 (1972). *See generally* J.Nowack, Handbook on Constitutional Law 416–19 (1978); L.Tribe, American Constitutional Law 886–990 (1978).

72. *See generally* J.Nowack, Handbook on Constitutional Law 517–35 (1978); L.Tribe, American Constitutional Law 991–1002 (1978).

73. *See, e.g.,* United States v. Carolina Prods. Co., 304 U.S. 144, 152 n.4 (1938).

74. *But see* Korematsu v. United States, 323 U.S. 214 (1944).

75. Some authorities prefer the view that there are not distinctive levels

of review, but rather a sliding scale of intensity of analysis. The more substantial the interest involved, the more exacting the scrutiny to be applied. *See* Massachusetts Bd. of Retirement v. Murgin, 427 U.S. 307, 318–21 (1976) (Marshall, J., dissenting); J.NOWACK, HANDBOOK ON CONSTITUTIONAL LAW 79–80, *Pocket Part* at 75 (1979); Gunther, *Foreword: In Search of Evolving Doctrine on a Changing Court: A Model for Newer Equal Protection*, 86 HARV.L.REV. 1 (1972).

76. L.TRIBE, AMERICAN CONSTITUTIONAL LAW 1002 (1978).

77. Western & Southern Life Ins. Co. v. State Bd. of Equalization, 451 U.S. 648, 668 (1981); Minnesota v. Clover Leaf Creamery Co., 449 U.S. 456, 464–65 (1981).

Rules measured against this standard are virtually certain to survive. In the last fifty years only one case involving a wholly economic regulation was invalidated by the Supreme Court under this test. *See* Morey v. Doud, 354 U.S. 457 (1957). *Morey* was then later overruled. *See* New Orleans v. Dukes, 427 U.S. 297 (1976).

78. *See* Western & Southern Life Ins. Co. v. State Bd. of Equalization, 451 U.S. 648, 667–69, 671–73 (1981).

79. *But see* Chabert v. Louisiana High School Athletic Ass'n, 323 So.2d 774 (La. 1975).

80. Hebert v. Ventetuolo, 638 F.2d 5 (1st Cir. 1981); Kulovitz v. Illinois High School Ass'n, 462 F.Supp. 875 (N.D.Ill. 1978).

81. *See* San Antonio Independent School Dist. v. Rodriguez, 411 U.S. 1, 35–39 (1973). *See also* Barnhorst v. Missouri State High School Activities Ass'n, 504 F.Supp. 449 (W.D.Mo. 1980).

82. *See* Kentucky High School Athletic Ass'n v. Hopkins County Bd. of Educ., 522 S.W.2d 685 (Ky.App. 1977); Chabert v. Louisiana High School Athletic Ass'n, 323 So.2d 774, 779 (La. 1975).

83. Sturrup v. Mahan, 305 N.E.2d 877, 880 (Ind. 1974).

84. *See* text at notes 19–20 *supra*.

85. *See* L.TRIBE, AMERICAN CONSTITUTIONAL LAW 999 (1978). *See also* J.NOWACK, HANDBOOK ON CONSTITUTIONAL LAW 521–22 (1978).

86. *See, e.g.*, Barnhorst v. Missouri State High School Activities Ass'n, 504 F.Supp. 449 (W.D.Mo. 1980); *cf.* Kentucky High School Athletic Ass'n v. Hopkins County Bd. of Educ., 522 S.W.2d 685 (Ky.App. 1977).

87. *See, e.g.*, Dandridge v. Williams, 397 U.S. 471 (1970); McDonald v. Board of Election Comm'rs, 394 U.S. 802 (1969); Williamson v. Lee Optical Co., 348 U.S. 483 (1955); Railway Express Agency, Inc. v. New York, 336 U.S. 106 (1949).

88. *See* Dandridge v. Williams, 397 U.S. 471, 485 (1970); Lindsley v. Natural Carbonic Gas Co., 220 U.S. 61 (1911). *See also* Parish v. NCAA, 506 F.2d 1028 (5th Cir. 1975).

89. Weinberger v. Salfi, 422 U.S. 749, 784 (1975).

90. *See* Barnhorst v. Missouri State High School Activities Ass'n, 504 F.Supp. 449, 454 (W.D. Mo. 1980); Kentucky High School Athletic Ass'n v. Hopkins County Bd. of Educ., 552 S.W.2d 685, 688 (Ky.App. 1977); Bruce v. South Carolina High School League, 189 S.E.2d 817, 819 (S.C. 1972).

91. Williamson v. Lee Optical Co., 348 U.S. 483, 489 (1955).

92. *See* Railway Express Agency, Inc. v. New York, 336 U.S. 106, 110 (1949).

93. 305 N.E.2d 877 (Ind. 1974).

94. *See* Kentucky High School Athletic Ass'n v. Hopkins County Bd. of Educ., 522 S.W.2d 685 (Ky.App. 1977).

95. This is reflected in the notion that the relationship among members is one of contract. Some authorities endorse the view that each participant has agreed to be bound to the association's governing standards. *See* Chafee, *The Internal Affairs of Associations Not for Profit*, 43 Harv.L.Rev. 993, 1001 (1930).

96. *See* Chabert v. Louisiana High School Athletic Ass'n, 323 So.2d 774, 777 (La. 1975).

97. *Compare* Spain v. Louisiana High School Athletic Ass'n, 398 So.2d 1386 (La. 1981).

98. This notion is basic in the law of contracts, for example. While a contracting party is generally free to delegate his contractual duty of performance to another, the delegating party remains fully liable for any defects in his delegate's performance. *See* 4 A.Corbin, Corbin on Contracts § 866 (1967). Similar principles can be found in the law of agency. *See* Restatement (Second) of Agency § 144 (1958). Finally, the same notions have important applications where a public body chooses to allow an external entity to perform its public obligation. *See, e.g.,* Bunger v. Iowa High School Athletic Ass'n, 197 N.W.2d 555, 560 (Iowa 1972).

99. *See* text at notes 19–20, 84–88 *supra.*

100. 616 S.W.2d 170 (Tex. 1981).

101. *Id.* at 171.

102. *Id.* at 172.

103. *Id.* at 173.

104. *See* authorities cited in notes 91–92 *supra.*

105. *See* New Orleans v. Dukes, 427 U.S. 297, 304–05 (1976).

In *Dukes,* the city of New Orleans banned pushcart vendors from the French Quarter but included an exception that allowed two existing operators to continue in business. Other vendors whose business was curtailed raised an equal protection objection. The Court denied their claim, quoting prior decisions that upheld the right of the state to engage in partial reforms. *See* 427 U.S. at 305. *See also* Williamson v. Lee Optical Co., 348 U.S. 483, 899–91 (1955).

106. *See* Minnesota v. Clover Leaf Creamery Co., 449 U.S. 456, 464–65 (1981).

107. *Compare* Weinberger v. Salfi, 422 U.S. 749 (1975). *See also* text at note 89 *supra.*

108. 494 F.Supp. 227 (S.D.Tex. 1980).

109. 661 F.2d 1027 (5th Cir. 1981).

110. 494 F.Supp. at 229.

111. *Id.* at 230.

112. Ginsberg v. New York, 390 U.S. 629, 639 (1968).

113. Pierce v. Society of Sisters, 268 U.S. 510, 535 (1925).

114. 494 F.Supp. 227, 232 (S.D.Tex. 1980), *quoting* Wisconsin v. Yoder, 406 U.S. 205, 233 (1972).

115. 494 F.Supp. at 232.

116. *Id.* at 233.

117. *Id.,* quoting N.A.A.C.P. v. Button, 371 U.S. 415, 433 (1963).

118. 494 F.Supp. at 233.

119. 661 F.2d at 1029.

120. *Id.*

121. *Id.* The abruptness of the court's conclusion that *Kite* involved no protectible right seems to have been tempered somewhat in a later decision from another Fifth Circuit panel. While the court in Laurenzo v. Mississippi High School Activities Ass'n, 662 F.2d 1117 (5th Cir. 1981), ultimately dismissed the complaint before it as moot, the court did find that the plaintiff's allegations of an invasion of family privacy were sufficient to establish federal jurisdiction.

122. *See* note 121 *supra.*

123. For a general discussion of the Court's pronouncements in the area of family privacy, see L.TRIBE, AMERICAN CONSTITUTIONAL LAW 985–90 (1978).

124. Pierce v. Society of Sisters, 268 U.S. 510 (1925), is one of the few cases applying notions of family autonomy outside the areas of conception, contraception, and illegitimacy. The Supreme Court struck down an Oregon law that allowed children to receive their education only in public schools and thus in effect forbade attendance at private schools. The Court objected that this was an attempt by the state "to standardize its children by forcing them to accept instruction from public teachers only." *Id.* at 535.

Pierce lends some support to the notion of the privacy of parental choice in their children's development, a policy that is similar to that involved in *Kite*. Nonetheless, *Kite* is hardly a mirror of the issue in *Pierce*. The regulation in *Pierce* was a pervasive attempt by the state to eliminate a particular type of parental decision—reliance on private schools as the source of educational instruction. The rule in *Kite*, however, affects only a small part of the child's total development and even then represents a limited intrusion. Parents may continue to encourage their children's athletic endeavors. They are only directed to avoid a form of specialized instruction (the summer sports camp) that was apparently thought to present a particular risk that athletics would be overemphasized.

125. For example, a regulation which placed a burden on a transfer of legal custody between divorced parents might require closer scrutiny than the regulation involved in *Kite*. The former affects the child's basic relationship with his or her parents, while the *Kite* regulation touches only on an issue of parental discretion. While the issue of custody transfers has been involved in a couple of cases, no final resolution of the constitutional issue has been achieved. *See* Laurenzo v. Mississippi High School Activities Ass'n, 662 F.2d 1117 (5th Cir. 1981); Kentucky High School Athletic Ass'n v. Hopkins County Bd. of Educ., 522 S.W.2d 685 (Ky.App. 1977).

126. *See* text at notes 42–46 *supra.*

127. *See* text at notes 47–68 *supra.*

128. *See* text at notes 89–92 *supra.*

129. *Bunger* is discussed at notes 65–68 *supra.*

130. *See* L.TRIBE, AMERICAN CONSTITUTIONAL LAW 999 (1978).

131. *See* text at notes 96–97 *supra.*

132. *See* Kite v. Marshall, 494 F.Supp. 227, 233 (S.D.Tex. 1980). *See also* text at notes 38–39 *supra.*

133. *See* Bunger v. Iowa High School Athletic Ass'n, 197 N.W.2d 555 (Iowa 1972); Board of Directors of Independent School Dist. of Waterloo v. Green, 147 N.W.2d 854 (Iowa 1967).

134. *See generally* J.WEISTART & C.LOWELL, THE LAW OF SPORTS 44–59 (1979).

135. This view of the case would require that one avoid a purely specula-

tive appraisal of the rule-makers' motive. Such conjecture is allowed under the permissive standard of equal protection review. *See* text at notes 78–79. The standard suggested in the text seeks to elevate the standard of judicial review and thus would require a more factually based assessment of the rule-makers' purpose.

136. 552 S.W.2d 685 (Ky.App. 1977).

137. The need for judicial review would seem to be stronger where the problem is an error of interpretation, as opposed to a rule that is substantively offensive. In the latter case, some argue that the normal, internal political processes of the rule-making body can be relied on to provide a corrective. *See* note 130 and accompanying text. This justification is not persuasive where there is a misinterpretation of the rule in a particular case. Whatever political pressure is brought to bear to improve the interpretative process, it is not likely to yield retroactive relief for individual cases.

138. *See* note 18 *supra* and accompanying text.

139. *See generally* J.WEISTART & C.LOWELL, THE LAW OF SPORTS 44–59 (1979).

140. Concern for federalism might provide some hesitancy on the part of the federal judiciary to overturn the enactments of state agencies. It seems appropriate that states undertake a more extensive role to insure that state regulatory authorities are subjected to proper accountability. *See* Minnesota v. Clover Leaf Creamery Co., 449 U.S. 456, 477–89 (1981).

141. "If the classification has some 'reasonable basis' it does not offend the Constitution simply because the classification 'is not made with mathematical nicety or because in practice it results in some inequality.'" Dandridge v. Williams, 397 U.S. 471, 485 (1970), *quoting* Lindsley v. Natural Carbonic Gas Co., 220 U.S. 61, 78 (1911).

142. As suggested above, the decided cases included several situations in which this standard might be used to protect students from inappropriate findings of ineligibility. *See, e.g.,* Kite v. Marshall, 494 F.Supp. 277 (S.D. Tex. 1980); Sullivan v. University Interscholastic League, 599 S.W.2d 860 (Tex.Civ.App. 1980), *aff'd in part, rev'd in part,* 616 S.W.2d 170 (Tex. 1981); Chabert v. Louisiana High School Athletic Ass'n, 323 So.2d 774 (La. 1975).

[8]

A Bibliography on Sports and the Law

Keith A. Buckley

Subjects

I. GENERAL MATERIALS

"Affirmance of a Sports Commissioner's Power," 3 GLENDALE LAW REVIEW 322 (1979).

Appenzeller, Herb. *Athletics and the Law.* Charlottesville, Va.: Michie, 1975.

———. *New Trends in Athletic and Physical Education Law.* Kansas City, Mo.: On-the-Spot Duplicators, 1978.

———. *Physical Education and the Law.* Charlottesville, Va.: Michie, 1978.

———. *Sports and the Courts.* Charlottesville, Va.: Michie, 1980.

"Aside: The Common Law Origins of the Infield Fly Rule." 4 JOURNAL OF CONTEMPORARY LAW 233 (1978).

"Athletics" [A Symposium, John C. Weistart, Special Editor]. Contents: Foreword (John C. Weistart); "Collective Bargaining and the Professional Team Sport Industry" (Cym H. Lowell); "An Economic Analysis of Team Movements in Professional Sports" (James Quirk); "Economic Discrimination in Professional Sports" (Gerald W. Scully); "In the Wake of *Flood*" (John P. Morris); "Medical Practices in Sports" (Allan J. Ryan); "Broadcasting and CATV: The Beauty and the Bane of Major College Football" (Philip Hochberg and Ira Horowitz); "Sport: A Philosophical Perspective" (Howard S. Slusher); "A Troubled Cartel: The NCAA" (James V. Koch); "The College Athlete and the Institution" (Harry M. Cross). 38 Law and Contemporary Problems 1 (1973).

Brody, Barton. "The Impact of Litigation on Professional Sports." 14 Trial, June 1980, at 34.

Chamberlain, John D. "The Legal and Moral Aspects of Prize-fighting." 19 Case & Comment 169 (1912).

"The Common Law Origins of the Infield Fly Rule." 123 University of Pennsylvania Law Review 1474 (1975).

"Contemporary Issues in Sport" [A Symposium]. Contents: "Sport and the Social Sciences" (George H. Sage); "Varsity Syndrome: The Unkindest Cut" (Robert Lipsyte); "The Convergence of Work, Sport and Gambling in America" (H. Roy Kaplan); "The Professionalization of Youth Sports" (Johnathan J. Brower); "The Child Athlete: Psychological Implications of Participation in Sports" (Bruce Ogilvie); "The Campaign for Athletes' Rights" (Kenny Moore); "Controversies in College Sports" (George H. Hanford); "Women in Sport: The Synthesis Begins" (Judith R. Holland & Carole Oglesby); "From Chattel to Employee: The Athlete's Quest for Freedom and Dignity" (Edward R. Garvey); "Congress and Professional Sports: 1951–1978" (Arthur T. Johnson); "Sports Within the Veil: The Triumphs, Tragedies and Challenges of Afro-American Involvement" (Harry Edwards); "What Price Victory?: The World of International Sports and Politics" (Andrew Strenk); "The Rise and Demise of Sport: A Reflection on Uruguayan Society" (March L. Krotee); "South Africa: Sport and Apartheid Politics" (Richard E. Lapchick). 445 Annals of the American Academy of Politics and Social Science 1 (1979).

"Courts and Sports: A Changing Picture." 80 U.S. News, Jan. 19, 1976, at 32.

Debevec, Robert M. *Law and the Sportsman.* New York, N.Y.: Oceana Publications, 1959.

Edwards, Harry. *The Sociology of Sport.* Homewood, Ill.: Dorsey, 1973.

Flynn, John J. "A Further Aside: A Comment on 'The Common Law Origins of the Infield Fly Rule.'" 4 Journal of Contemporary Law 241 (1978).

"Focus on Sports" [A Symposium]. Contents: "'Blackouts' and the Public Interest: An Equitable Proposal" (Robert A. Peterson); "Baseball— From Trial by Law to Trial by Auction" (Thomas M. Boswell and Richard B. McKeown); "Monopsony Means Never Having to Say You're Sorry" (Paul W. Shapiro); "Tort Law and Participant Sports" (Dale J. Lambert); "The Impact of the 1976 Tax Reform Act on the Owners of Professional Sport Teams" (Valerie Nelson Strandell); "Aside: The Common Law Origins of the Infield Fly Rule"; "Further Aside: A Comment on 'The Common Law Origins of the Infield Fly Rule'" (John J. Flynn). 4 Journal of Contemporary Law 143 (1978).

Grieve, Andrew W. *The Legal Aspects of Athletics*. South Brunswick, N.J.:
    A.S. Barnes, 1969.
Hodgson, James. *A Digest of Laws Prohibiting Sports or Baseball on Sunday*.
    New York, N.Y.: H.W. Wilson, 1917.
Houdek, Frank G. "Sports and the Law: A Comprehensive Bibliography of
    Law-Related Materials." 2 COMM/ENT 177 (1979).
Humphreys, John O. *Racing Law*. Lexington, Ky.: National Association of
    State Racing Commissioners, 1969–73.
Johnson, Arthur T. "Congress and Professional Sports: 1951–1978." 445
    ANNALS OF THE AMERICAN ACADEMY OF POLITICS AND SOCIAL SCIENCE
    102 (1979).
"Keeping the Illusion Alive: The Public Interest in Professional Sports." 12
    SUFFOLK UNIVERSITY LAW REVIEW 48 (1978).
Koppett, Leonard. "Sports and the Law: An Overview." 18 NEW YORK LAW
    FORUM 815 (1973).
Kornstein, Daniel. "Legal Aspects of Boxing—A 'Big Business' Enterprise."
    186 NEW YORK LAW JOURNAL, Oct. 9, 1981, at 1.
"Legal Aspects of Sports." 24 RECORD 306 (1969).
Nelson, Stephen. "Bringing Sports Under Legal Control," 10 CONNECTICUT
    LAW REVIEW 251 (1978).
"Organized Baseball and the Law." 19 NOTRE DAME LAWYER 262 (1944).
*Pro Sports—Should the Government Intervene?: A Round Table Held on
    February 22, 1977*. Washington, D.C.: The American Enterprise Insti-
    tute for Public Policy Research, 1977.
"The Professional Athlete and the First Amendment: A Question of Judicial
    Intervention." 4 HOFSTRA LAW REVIEW 417 (1978).
"Professional Sports and the Law" [A Symposium]. Contents: "The First
    Great Leap: Some Reflections on the Spencer Haywood Case" (Richard
    K. Simon); "Some Modest Proposals for Collective Bargaining in Profes-
    sional Sports" (David G. Miller); "Tax Aspects of Buying, Selling, and
    Owning Professional Sports Teams" (Leslie S. Klinger); "Television
    Sports Blackouts: Private Rights vs. Public Policy" (Lionel S. Sobel).
    48 LOS ANGELES BAR BULLETIN 144 (1973).
Scanlan, John A., Jr., and Cleveland, Granville E., Sr. "The Past as Prelude:
    The Early Origins of Modern American Sports Law," 8 OHIO NORTHERN
    UNIVERSITY LAW REVIEW 433 (1981).
Sibley, W. W. "Law and Lawful Sports and the Legality of a Sparring
    Match." 37 LAW MAGAZINE AND REVIEW, Feb. 1912, at 137.
Slusher, Howard S. "Sport: A Philosophical Perspective." 38 LAW & CON-
    TEMPORARY PROBLEMS 129 (1973).
Sobel, Lionel S. *Professional Sports and the Law*. New York, N.Y.: Law-Arts
    Publishers, 1977.
"Special Section—Sports and the Law" [A Symposium]. Contents: "Bringing
    Sports Under Legal Control" (Stephen Nelson); "The Political Uses
    and Abuses of Sports" (James A. R. Nafziger and Andrew Strenk);
    "Due Process and Its Future Within the NCAA (Gordon A. Martin, Jr.);
    "A Student-Athlete's Interest in Eligibility: Its Context and Constitu-
    tional Dimension"; "Professional Football—Are Three One-Year Agree-
    ments Signed at One Sitting Actually One Contract? Are Players 'Public
    Figures'?: *Chuy v. Philadelphia Eagles Football Club*, 431 F. Supp. 254
    (E.D. Pa. 1977)"; "The 'Booby' Trap: Does the Violent Nature of Pro-
    fessional Football Vitiate the Doctrine of Due Care in Participant Tort

Litigation?: *Hackbart v. Cincinnati Bengals, Inc.*, 435 F. Supp. 352 (D. Colo. 1977)." 10 Connecticut Law Review 251 (1978).

"Sports and the Law." 5 Oklahoma City University Law Review 659 (1980).

"Sports and the Law" [A Symposium]. Contents: "Swimming Pool Liability" (James Stern); "Torts on the Courts" (Bruce Bortz and Cheri W. Levin); "The Impact of Litigation on Professional Sports" (Barton Brody). 14 Trial, June 1978, at 24.

"Sports and the Law" [A Symposium]. Contents: "An Overview" (Leonard Koppett); "Second and Goal to Go: The Legislative Attack in the 92nd Congress on Sports Broadcasting Practices" (Philip R. Hochberg); "Legalization of Gambling on Sports Events" (Howard J. Samuels); "The Business of Professional Sports: A Reexamination in Progress" (Robert S. Carlson). 18 New York Law Forum 815 (1973).

Swift, Ray L. "Municipal Promotion of Play." 19 Case & Comment 184 (1912).

"Symposium: Professional Sports and the Law." Contents: Introduction (Bowie K. Kuhn); "Taxation of Professional Sports Teams After 1976: A Whole New Ballgame" (Howard Zaritsky); "Player Discipline in Professional Sports: The Antitrust Issues" (John C. Weistart); "Post-Merger Blues: Intra-League Contract Jumping" (S. Phillip Heiner). 18 William & Mary Law Review 677 (1977).

"Symposium: Sports and the Law." Contents: "The Emancipation of Professional Athletes" (Lionel S. Sobel); "Congress Tackles Sports and Broadcasting" (Philip R. Hochberg); "Title IX and the NCAA" (James V. Koch); "The Aftermath of *Flood v. Kuhn:* Professional Baseball's Exemption for Antitrust Regulation" (Philip L. Martin). 3 Western State University Law Review 185 (1976).

"Take Me Out to the Ball Game." 25 Fordham Law Review 793 (1957).

United States. Congress. House. Committee on Education and Labor. Subcommittee on Labor Standards. *Hearings on the Creation of a Federal Boxing Board.* Hearings on H.R. 2726, 96th Cong., 1st Sess., March 28–April 3, 1979. Washington, D.C.: G.P.O., 1979.

United States. Congress. House. Committee on Rules. *Creating a Select Committee on Professional Sports.* House Report 95-41, 95th Cong., 1st Sess., March 3, 1977. Washington, D.C.: G.P.O., 1977.

United States. Congress. House. Committee on the Judiciary. Subcommittee on Monopolies and Commercial Law. *Rights of Professional Athletes,* Hearings, 94th Cong., 1st Sess., Oct. 14, 1975. Washington, D.C.: G.P.O., 1977.

United States. Congress. House. Select Committee on Professional Sports. *Inquiry into Professional Sports, Part 1,* Hearings, 94th Cong., 2d Sess., June 23–Aug. 10, 1976. Washington, D.C.: G.P.O., 1976.

United States. Congress. House. Select Committee on Professional Sports. *Inquiry into Professional Sports, Part 2,* Hearings, 94th Cong., 2d Sess., Sept. 8–22, 1976. Washington, D.C.: G.P.O., 1976.

United States. Congress. House. Select Committee on Professional Sports. *Inquiry into Professional Sports,* Hearings, 94th Cong., 2d Sess., Dec. 10, 1976, Jan. 3, 1977. Washington, D.C.: G.P.O., 1976.

United States. Congress. House. Select Committee on Professional Sports. *Professional Sports and the Law,* Committee Print, 94th Cong., 2d Sess., Aug., 1976. Washington, D.C.: G.P.O., 1976.

United States. Congress. House. Select Committee on Rules. *Inquiry into Professional Sports,* House Report 94-1786, 94th Cong., 2d Sess., Jan. 3, 1977. Washington, D.C.: G.P.O., 1977.

United States. Congress. Senate. Committee on Congress. *Federal Sports Act of 1972,* Hearings on S. 3445, 92d Cong., 2d Sess., June 16, 19, 23, 28, 1972. Washington, D.C.: G.P.O., 1973.

United States. Congress. Senate. Committee on the Judiciary. *Professional Sports Act of 1965,* Senate Report 89-462, 89th Cong., 1st Sess., July 16, 1965. Washington, D.C.: G.P.O., 1965.

Weistart, John C., and Lowell, Cym H. *The Law of Sports.* Charlottesville, Va.: Michie, 1979.

Wilder, L. A. "Baseball and the Law." 19 CASE & COMMENT 151 (1912).

Woolf, Bob. *Behind Closed Doors.* New York: Atheneum, 1976.

II. AGENTS AND ATTORNEYS

Allen, Richard B. "Law, Lawyers, and Baseball." 64 AMERICAN BAR ASSOCIATION JOURNAL 1530 (1978).

Counseling Professional Athletes and Entertainers, 1974. Martin E. Blackman and Frederic B. Gershon, co-chairmen. New York, N.Y.: Practising Law Institute, 1974.

Counseling Professional Athletes and Entertainers. Frederic Gershon and Martin E. Blackman, co-chairmen. New York, N.Y.: Practising Law Institute, 1972.

Counseling Professional Athletes and Entertainers—3d, Robert Needham, editor. New York, N.Y.: Practising Law Institute, 1971.

Counseling Professional Athletes and Entertainers—2d, New York, N.Y.: Practising Law Institute, 1970.

Counseling Professional Athletes and Entertainers, Martin E. Blackman and Miriam I. R. Eolis, co-chairpersons. New York, N.Y.: Practising Law Institute, 1970.

Current Issues in Professional Sports. Durham, N.H.: Whittemore School of Business & Economics, University of New Hampshire, 1980.

"Do Agents Exploit Athletes?" 7 PROFESSIONAL SPORTS JOURNAL, Nov.–Dec. 1979, at 20.

Golenbock, Peter. "Now Calling the Signals, the Lawyer-Agent." 2 JURIS DOCTOR, Oct. 1971, at 49.

Hochberg, Philip R. *Representing Professional Athletes and Teams, 1981.* New York, N.Y.: Practising Law Institute, 1981.

Representing Professional and College Sports Teams and Leagues. Philip R. Hochberg, chairman. New York, N.Y.: Practising Law Institute, 1977.

Representing Professional Sports Teams. Alan I. Rothenberg, chairman. New York, N.Y.: Practising Law Institute, 1974.

Representing the Professional Athlete. Martin E. Blackman, chairman. New York, N.Y.: Practising Law Institute, 1976.

Representing the Professional Athlete, 1978. Martin E. Blackman, chairman. New York, N.Y.: Practising Law Institute, 1978.

Smith, Frederick J., Jr. "Sports Attorneys: Scoring from the Sidelines." 1 CALIFORNIA LAWYER, Dec. 1981, at 40.

"The Sporting Lawyers of Cincinnati." 4 CINCINNATI BAR ASSOCIATION JOURNAL, Summer–Fall 1978, at 16.

Winter, Bill. "Is the Sports Lawyer Getting Dunked?" 66 AMERICAN BAR ASSOCIATION JOURNAL 701 (1980).

III. AMATEUR ATHLETICS (SEE ALSO COLLEGE ATHLETICS AND PRECOLLEGIATE ATHLETICS)

"Administration of Amateur Athletics: The Time for an Amateur Athlete's Bill of Rights Has Arrived." 48 FORDHAM LAW REVIEW 53 (1979).

Lowell, Cym H. "Federal Administrative Intervention in Amateur Athletics." 43 GEORGE WASHINGTON LAW REVIEW 729 (1975).

United States. Congress. House. Committee on the Judiciary. *Amateur Sports Act of 1978*, House Report 95-1627, 95th Cong., 2d Sess., Sept. 25, 1978. Washington, D.C.: G.P.O., 1978.

United States. Congress. House. Committee on the Judiciary. Subcommittee on Administrative Law and Governmental Relations. *Amateur Sports Act of 1978*, Hearings on H.R. 12626 and H.R. 12920, 95th Cong., 2d Sess., June 21–22, 1978. Washington, D.C.: G.P.O., 1979.

United States. Congress. Senate. Committee on Commerce. *Amateur Athletic Act of 1973*, Hearings, 93d Cong., 1st Sess., Nov. 5, 1973. Washington, D.C.: G.P.O., 1974.

United States. Congress. Senate. Committee on Commerce. *Amateur Athletic Act of 1973*, Senate Report 93-380, 93d Cong., 1st Sess., Washington, D.C.: G.P.O., 1973.

United States. Congress. Senate. Committee on Commerce. *Amateur Sports,* Hearings, 93d Cong., 1st Sess., May 22–24, 1973. Washington, D.C.: G.P.O., 1973.

United States. Congress. Senate. Committee on Commerce. *Providing for Settlement of Disputes Involving Amateur Athletics,* Senate Report No. 89-753, 89th Cong., 1st Sess., Sept. 16, 1965. Washington, D.C.: G.P.O., 1965.

United States. Congress. Senate. Committee on Commerce, Science and Transportation. *Amateur Sports Act,* Hearings on S. 2036, 95th Cong., 1st Sess., Oct. 18, 19, 1977. Washington, D.C.: G.P.O., 1978.

United States. Congress. Senate. Committee on Commerce, Science and Transportation. *Amateur Sports Act of 1978*, Senate Report 95-770, 95th Cong., 2d Sess., April 27, 1978. Washington, D.C.: G.P.O., 1978.

IV. ANTITRUST LAW (SEE ALSO LABOR LAW—LIBERTY OF PLAYER MOVEMENT)

Allison, John R. "Professional Sports and the Antitrust Laws: Status of the Reserve System." 25 BAYLOR LAW REVIEW 1 (1973).

Anderson, Mark F. "The Sherman Act and Professional Sports Associations' Use of Eligibility Rules." 47 NEBRASKA LAW REVIEW 82 (1968).

"Antitrust and Baseball: What Justice Ruled." 73 U.S. NEWS, July 3, 1972, at 45.

"Antitrust and Professional Sport: 'Does Anyone Play by the Rules of the Game?' " 22 CATHOLIC LAW REVIEW 403 (1973).

"Antitrust Law—Baseball Reserve System—Concerted Conspiracy—Stare Decisis—Congressional Inaction—Baseball Remains Exempt From State and Federal Antitrust Law." 48 Notre Dame Lawyer 460 (1972).

"Anti-trust Law—National Collegiate Athletic Association Held Subject to the Rule of Reason Test of Sherman Anti-Trust Act, *Hennessey & Hudson v. NCAA.*" 7 Cumberland Law Review 505 (1977).

"Antitrust Law: Procedural Safeguard Requirements in Concerted Refusals to Deal: An Application to Professional Sports—*Denver Rockets v. All-Pro Management, Inc.*, 325 F. Supp. 1049." 10 San Diego Law Review 413 (1973).

"Antitrust Law—Professional Football Immune From Sherman Act as a Team Sport Not Constituting Interstate Commerce, *Radovich v. National Football League*, 231 F. 2d 620." 2 Villanova Law Review 120 (1956).

"Antitrust Laws and Professional Baseball." 19 New York University Intramural Law Review 235 (1964).

"Antitrust Laws—Interstate Commerce—Professional Football." 11 Southwestern Law Journal 516 (1957).

"Antitrust Laws—Professional Football Immune From Sherman Act as a Team Sport Not Constituting Interstate Commerce, *Radovich v. National Football League*, 231 F. 2d 620." 105 University of Pennsylvania Law Review 110 (1956).

"Antitrust Laws—Sherman Anti-Trust Act—Professional Sports, *Radovich v. National Football League*, 77 S. Ct. 390." 36 North Carolina Law Review 315 (1958).

"Antitrust Laws—The Applicability of Federal and State Antitrust Laws to the Sport of Baseball." 1971 University of Toledo Law Review 594.

"Antitrust Laws: The Application of Federal Antitrust Laws to Professional Sports." 18 ALR Federal 489, (1974).

"Antitrust: Preseason Football Tickets and Tie-ins, *Coniglio v. Highwood Services, Inc.*, 425 F. 2d 1286, (2d Cir. 1974)." 1975 Washington University Law Quarterly 495.

"Antitrust—Professional Football—The Rozelle Rule as an Unreasonable Restraint of Trade." 26 University of Kansas Law Review 121 (1977).

"Antitrust—Restraint of Trade—Group Boycott—NFL College Draft." 15 Duquesne University Law Review 121 (1977).

"Antitrust—Servitude in Professional Sport—*McCourt v. California Sports, Inc.*, 600 F. 2d 1193 (6th Cir. 1979)." 2 Whittier Law Review 559 (1980).

"Applicability of the Antitrust Laws to Baseball." 2 Memphis State University Law Review 299 (1972).

"Application of Antitrust Laws to Professional Sports' Eligibility and Draft Rules." 46 Missouri Law Review 797 (1981).

Austin, Arthur D. "The Legality of Ticket Tie-ins in Intercollegiate Athletics." 15 University of Michigan Law Review 1 (1980).

"Baseball—An Exception to the Antitrust Laws." 18 Pittsburgh Law Review 131 (1956).

"Baseball Players and the Antitrust Laws." 53 Columbia Law Review 242 (1953).

"Baseball's Antitrust Exemption and the Reserve System: Reappraisal of an Anachronism." 12 William & Mary Law Review 859 (1971).

"Baseball's Antitrust Exemption: The Limits of Stare Decisis." 12 Boston College Industrial & Commercial Law Review 737 (1971).

"Constitutional Law—Baseball and the Antitrust Law—A Game or a Conspiracy?" 24 NOTRE DAME LAWYER 372 (1949).

"Constitutional Law—Commerce and Supremacy Clauses Exempt Professional Baseball From State Antitrust Statute." 35 FORDHAM LAW REVIEW 350 (1966).

"Constitutional Law—Preemption—Baseball's Immunity From State Antitrust Law, *State v. Milwaukee Braves, Inc.*, 144 N. W. 2d 1 (1966)." 13 WAYNE LAW REVIEW 417 (1967).

Dewey, Addison E. "Professional Athletes—Affluent Elitists or Victims of the Reserve System? An Emerging Paradox—Courts Protect Such Athletes From Antitrust Law Violations But Collective Bargaining Has Resulted in Antitrust Immunity for Leagues and Club Owners." 8 OHIO NORTHERN UNIVERSITY LAW REVIEW 453 (1981).

Ducker, Bruce. "Pros Offside? The Antitrust Laws and Professional Sports." 76 CASE & COMMENT, Sept.–Oct. 1971, at 32.

Eckler, John. "Baseball—Sport or Commerce?" 17 CHICAGO LAW REVIEW 58 (1949).

"The Eighth Circuit Suggests a Labor Exemption From Antitrust Laws for Collectively Bargained Labor Agreements in Professional Sports." 21 ST. LOUIS UNIVERSITY LAW JOURNAL 565 (1977).

Eppel, John P. "Professional Sports." 33 AMERICAN BAR ASSOCIATION ANTITRUST JOURNAL 69 (1967).

"Federal Antitrust Law—Monopolies—Baseball." 22 UNIVERSITY OF KANSAS CITY LAW REVIEW 173 (1953).

"Federal Antitrust Laws—Monopolies—Professional Football, *Radovich v. National Football League*, 77 S. Ct. 390." 26 DICKINSON LAW REVIEW 96 (1957).

"Flood (*Flood v. Kuhn*, 92 Sup. Ct. 2099) in the Land of Antitrust: Another Look at Professional Athletics, The Antitrust Laws and the Labor Law Exemption." 7 INDIANA LAW REVIEW 541 (1974).

Goldstein, Seth M. "Out of Bounds Under the Sherman Act?: Player Restraints in Professional Team Sports." 4 PEPPERDINE LAW REVIEW 285 (1977).

Gromley, Charles. "Baseball and the Antitrust Laws." 34 NEBRASKA LAW REVIEW 597 (1955).

Heydon, J. D. "Recent Developments in the Restraint of Trade." 21 McGILL LAW JOURNAL 325 (1975).

"Illegal Procedure—The Rozelle Rule Violates the Sherman Antitrust Act." 59 MARQUETTE LAW REVIEW 632 (1976).

Jacobs, Michael, and Winter, Ralph K. "Antitrust Principles and Collective Bargaining by Athletes: Of Super Stars in Peonage." 81 YALE LAW JOURNAL 1 (1971).

Johnson, Frederic A. "Baseball, Professional Sports, and the Antitrust Acts." 2 ANTITRUST BULLETIN 678 (1957).

———. "The Law of Sports: The Unique Performer's Contract and the Antitrust Laws." 2 ANTITRUST BULLETIN 251 (1957).

Jones, J. C., and Davies, D. K. "Not Even Semitough: Professional Sport and Canadian Antitrust." 23 ANTITRUST BULLETIN 713 (1978).

Keating, Kenneth B. "The Antitrust Threat to Professional Team Sports." 1959 ANTITRUST LAW SYMPOSIUM 23.

Keefe, Arthur J. "Positively Mr. Kipling! Absolutely Mr. Kuhn!" 58 AMERICAN BAR ASSOCIATION JOURNAL 651 (1972).

Keith, Maxwell. "Developments in the Application of Antitrust Laws to Professional Team Sports." 10 HASTINGS LAW JOURNAL 119 (1958).

Koppett, Leonard. "Antitrust in the Ballpark: What the Rhubarb is All About." 222 NATION, May 15, 1976, at 587.

"The Labor Controversy in Professional Baseball: The *Flood* Case." 23 LABOR LAW 567 (1972).

Leavell, Jerome F., and Millard, Howard L. "Trade Regulation and Professional Sports." 26 MERCER LAW REVIEW 603 (1975).

Lee, Brian F. "A Survey of Professional Team Sport Players—Control Mechanisms under Antitrust and Labor Law Principles: Peace at Last." 11 VALPARAISO UNIVERSITY LAW REVIEW 373 (1977).

Lockman, John S. "Baseball as Interstate Commerce Within the Meaning of Antitrust Laws." 5 NEW YORK UNIVERSITY INTRAMURAL LAW REVIEW 206 (1950).

Martin, Philip L. "The Aftermath of *Flood v. Kuhn:* Professional Baseball's Exemption From Antitrust Regulation." 3 WESTERN STATE UNIVERSITY LAW REVIEW 262 (1976).

"The Modern Trend in Anti-Trust and Professional Sports." 22 ALBANY LAW REVIEW 272 (1958).

"The Monopoly in Baseball." 18 CINCINNATI LAW REVIEW 203 (1949).

"Monopsony in Manpower: Organized Baseball Meets the Antitrust Laws." 62 YALE LAW JOURNAL 576 (1953).

"The NFL Draft and the Anti-trust Laws—The Player Draft of the National Football League Held to Violate the Federal Antitrust Laws, *Smith v. Pro-Football.*" 41 ALBANY LAW REVIEW 154 (1977).

"National Collegiate Athletic Association Held Subject to the Rule of Reason Test of the Sherman Anti-Trust Act." 7 CUMBERLAND LAW REVIEW 505 (1977).

"National Collegiate Athletic Association's Certification Requirement: A Section 1 Violation of the Sherman Anti-Trust Act." 9 VALPARAISO UNIVERSITY LAW REVIEW 193 (1974).

"National Hockey League's Faceoff with Antitrust." 42 OHIO STATE LAW JOURNAL 603 (1981).

"The Nature and Effect of Major Sports: Restrictions on Radio and Television Broadcasting Rights Under the Sherman Act." 21 GEORGE WASHINGTON LAW REVIEW 466 (1953).

"Nearly a Century in Reserve: Organized Baseball: Collective Bargaining and the Antitrust Exemptions Enter the 80's." 8 PEPPERDINE LAW REVIEW 313 (1981).

Nelson, Paul. "Professional Sports and the Non-Statutory Labor Exemption to Federal Antitrust Law, *McCourt v. California Sports, Inc.,* 600 F. 2d 1193 (6th Cir. 1979)." 11 UNIVERSITY OF TOLEDO LAW REVIEW 633 (1980).

Neville, John W. "Baseball and the Antitrust Laws." 16 FORDHAM LAW REVIEW 209 (1947).

———. "Who's on First?" 36 MICHIGAN STATE BAR JOURNAL, April 1957, at 13.

"*North American Soccer League v. National Football League:* Applying 'Rule of Reason' Analysis Under the Sherman Act to Private Bans on Cross-Ownership." 15 NEW ENGLAND LAW REVIEW 697 (1980).

O'Dea, John F. "Professional Sports and the Anti-Trust Laws." 9 HASTINGS LAW JOURNAL 18 (1957).

Pierce, Samuel R. "Organized Professional Team Sports and the Antitrust Laws." 43 CORNELL LAW QUARTERLY 566 (1958).

"Player Control Mechanisms in Professional Team Sports." 34 UNIVERSITY OF PITTSBURGH LAW REVIEW 645 (1973).

"Pre-season Rhubarb: Professional Sports and Federal Antitrust Laws." 69 TIME, March 11, 1957, at 76.

"Professional Sports: Has Antitrust Killed the Goose that Laid the Golden Egg?" 45 AMERICAN BAR ASSOCIATION ANTITRUST LAW JOURNAL 290 (1976).

Robinson, W. Clyde. "Professional Sports and the Antitrust Laws." 38 SOUTH-WESTERN SOCIAL SCIENCE QUARTERLY, Sept. 1957, at 133.

Roger, C. Paul. "Judicial Reinterpretation of Statutes: The Example of Baseball and the Antitrust Laws." 14 HOUSTON LAW REVIEW 611 (1977).

Seiberling, John F., and Mottl, Ronald M. "Should Professional Sports Be Subject to Federal Antitrust Laws?" 102 AMERICAN LEGION MAGAZINE, Feb. 1977, at 22.

Seymour, Harold. "Ball, Bat, and Bar." 6 CLEVELAND-MARSHALL LAW REVIEW 534 (1957).

Shapiro, Paul W. "Monopsony Means Never Having to Say You're Sorry: A Look at Baseball's Minor Leagues." 4 JOURNAL OF CONTEMPORARY LAW 191 (1978).

"The Sherman Act and Professional Team Sports: The NFL Rozelle Rule Invalid Under the Rule of Reason: *Mackey v. National Football League,* 543 F. 2d 606 (8th Cir. 1976)." 9 CONNECTICUT LAW REVIEW 336 (1977).

"The Sherman Act: Football Player Controls—Are They Reasonable?" 6 CALIFORNIA WESTERN LAW REVIEW 133 (1969).

"The Super Bowl and the Sherman Act: Professional Team Sports and Anti-Trust Laws." 81 HARVARD LAW REVIEW 418 (1967).

"Tackling Intercollegiate Athletics: An Antitrust Analysis." 87 YALE LAW JOURNAL 655 (1978).

Topkis, Jay H. "Monopoly in Professional Sports." 58 YALE LAW JOURNAL 691 (1949).

"Trade Regulation—Anti-Trust Acts—Unlawful Conspiracy—Non-Coverage of Professional Football." 25 UNIVERSITY OF CINCINNATI LAW REVIEW 519 (1956).

"The True Story of What Happens When the Big Kids Say, 'It's My Football and You'll Either Play By My Rules or You Won't Play at All.'" 55 NEBRASKA LAW REVIEW 335 (1976).

"Tying Arrangements in the Sale of Season Tickets." 47 TEMPLE LAW QUARTERLY 761 (1974).

United States. Congress. House. Committee on the Judiciary. *Applicability of Antitrust Laws to Organized Professional Team Sports,* House Report 85-1720, 85th Cong., 2d Sess., May 13, 1958. Washington, D.C.: G.P.O., 1958.

United States. Congress. House. Committee on the Judiciary. Antitrust Subcommittee. *Antitrust Laws and Organized Professional Team Sports Including Consideration of the Proposed Merger of the American and National Basketball Associations,* Hearings, 92d Cong., 2d Sess., July 27–Sept. 7, 1972. Washington, D.C.: G.P.O., 1972.

United States. Congress. House. Committee on the Judiciary. Antitrust Subcommittee. *Organized Team Sports,* Hearings, 85th Cong., 1st Sess., June 17–Aug. 8, 1956. Washington, D.C.: G.P.O., 1956.

United States. Congress. House. Committee on the Judiciary. Antitrust Subcommittee. *Organized Team Sports,* Hearings, 86th Cong., 1st Sess., July 29–31, 1959. Washington, D.C.: G.P.O., 1959.

United States. Congress. House. Committee on the Judiciary. Subcommittee on Monopolies and Commercial Law. *Rights of Professional Athletes,* Hearings on H.R. 2355 and H.R. 694, 94th Cong., 1st Sess., Oct. 14, 1975. Washington, D.C.: G.P.O., 1977.

United States. Congress. House. Committee on the Judiciary. Subcommittee on the Study of Monopoly Power. *Organized Baseball,* House Report 82-2002, 82d Cong., 2d Sess. Washington, D.C.: G.P.O., 1952.

United States. Congress. House. Committee on the Judiciary. Subcommittee on the Study of Monopoly Power. *Study of Monopoly Power,* Hearings, 82d Cong., 1st Sess., July 30–Oct. 24, 1951. Washington, D.C.: G.P.O., 1951.

United States. Congress. Senate. Committee on the Judiciary. *Applicability of Antitrust Laws to Certain Aspects of Designated Organized Professional Team Sports,* Senate Report 88-1302, 88th Cong., 2d Sess., Aug. 4, 1964. Washington, D.C.: G.P.O., 1964.

United States. Congress. Senate. Committee on the Judiciary. *Authorizing the Merger of Two or More Professional Basketball Leagues,* Senate Report 92-1151, 92d Cong., 2d Sess., Sept. 18, 1972. Washington, D.C.: G.P.O., 1972.

United States. Congress. Senate. Committee on the Judiciary. *Professional Sports Antitrust Act of 1960,* Senate Report 86-1620, 86th Cong., 2d Sess., June 20, 1960. Washington, D.C.: G.P.O., 1960.

United States. Congress. Senate. Committee on the Judiciary. *Subjecting Professional Baseball Clubs to Antitrust Laws,* Hearings on S.J. Res. 133, 83d Cong., 2d Sess., March 18–May 25, 1954. Washington, D.C.: G.P.O., 1954.

United States. Congress. Senate. Committee on the Judiciary. Subcommittee on Antitrust and Monopoly. *Organized Professional Team Sports,* Hearings, 85th Cong., 2d Sess., July 9–31, 1958. Washington, D.C.: G.P.O., 1958.

United States. Congress. Senate. Committee on the Judiciary. Subcommittee on Antitrust and Monopoly. *Organized Professional Team Sports,* Hearings, 86th Cong., 1st Sess., July 28–31, 1959. Washington, D.C.: G.P.O., 1959.

United States. Congress. Senate. Committee on the Judiciary. Subcommittee on Antitrust and Monopoly. *Organized Professional Team Sports,* Hearings, 86th Cong., 2d Sess., May 19–20, 1960. Washington, D.C.: G.P.O., 1960.

United States. Congress. Senate. Committee on the Judiciary. Subcommittee on Antitrust and Monopoly. *Professional Basketball,* Hearings, 92d Cong., 1st Sess., Sept. 21–23, Nov. 15, 1971, Jan. 25–May 9, 1972. Washington, D.C.: G.P.O., 1972.

United States. Congress. Senate. Committee on the Judiciary. Subcommittee on Antitrust and Monopoly. *Professional Sports Antitrust Bill,* Hearings, 88th Cong., 2d Sess., Jan. 30–Feb. 18, 1964. Washington, D.C.: G.P.O., 1964.

United States. Congress. Senate. Committee on the Judiciary. Subcommittee on Antitrust and Monopoly. *Professional Sports Antitrust Bill,* Hearings,

89th Cong., 1st Sess., Feb. 18–24, 1965. Washington, D.C.: G.P.O., 1965.

Weistart, John C. "Antitrust Issues in the Regulation of College Sports." 5 Journal of College & University Law 77 (1979).

———. "Player Discipline in Professional Sports: The Antitrust Issues." 18 William & Mary Law Review 703 (1977).

Winter, Bill. "Baseball Bill: Again in the Batter's Box." 67 American Bar Association Journal 147 (1981).

V. COLLEGE ATHLETICS (SEE ALSO AMATEUR ATHLETICS)

"The Authority of the College Coach: A Legal Analysis." 49 Oregon Law Review 442 (1970).

Bonaventre, Peter, and Huck, Janet. "Did the Coach Play Too Rough?: The Case of Frank Kush of Arizona State." 94 Newsweek, Oct. 29, 1979, at 91.

Boyle, Robert H. "The Scandal That Just Gets Worse and Worse." 52 Sports Illustrated, June 9, 1980, at 22.

Branchfield, Edward, and Grier, Melinda. "*Aiken v. Lieuallen* and *Peterson v. Oregon State University:* Defining Equity in Athletics." 8 Journal of College & University Law 369 (1981).

"Brief for Appellants in *Handsome v. Rutgers University*." 6 Journal of College & University Law 241 (1980).

Carrafiello, Vincent A. "Jocks Are People Too: The Constitution Comes to the Lockerroom." 13 Creighton Law Review 843 (1980).

Cross, Harry M. "The College Athlete and the Institution." 38 Law & Contemporary Problems 151 (1973).

Deford, Frank. "Fans to Press: Drop Dead." 45 Sports Illustrated, Dec. 13, 1976, at 24.

"The Economics of 'Big Time' Intercollegiate Athletics." 52 Social Science Quarterly 248 (1971).

Evans, J. Robert. *Blowing the Whistle on Intercollegiate Sports.* Chicago, Ill.: Nelson Hall Comp., 1974.

Faccenda, Philip J. "Introduction to the Symposium [Symposium on Athletics in Higher Education]." 8 Journal of College & University Law 291 (1981).

Feinstein, John. "Cheating in Football is a Matter of Degrees: Grade Fixing." 93 Maclean's, Jan. 14, 1980, at 40.

Good, Paul. "Tarkanian vs. the NCAA: Behind the Congressional Probe that May Revamp College Sports." 66 Sport, March 1978, at 37.

"The Government of Amateur Athletics: The NCAA-AAU Dispute." 41 Southern California Law Review 464 (1968).

Hanford, George H. "Controversies in College Sports." 445 Annals of The American Academy of Politics & Social Science 66 (1979).

———. *A Report to the American Council on Education on an Inquiry into the Need for and Feasibility of a National Study of Intercollegiate Athletics.* Washington, D.C.: American Council on Education, 1974.

Hermann, Anne M. C. "Sports and the Handicapped: Section 504 of the Rehabilitation Act of 1973 and Curricular, Intramural, Club and Intercol-

legiate Athletic Programs in Postsecondary Educational Institutions." 5
JOURNAL OF COLLEGE & UNIVERSITY LAW 143 (1979).

"Hit 'em High: The Firing of Frank Kush: Accused of Hitting a Football
Player." 114 TIME, Oct. 29, 1979, at 46.

Horn, Stephen. "Ethics, Due Process, Diversity and Balance." 43 VITAL
SPEECHES, May 15, 1977, at 463.

———. "Intercollegiate Athletics: Waning Amateurism and Rising Professionalism." 5 JOURNAL OF COLLEGE & UNIVERSITY LAW 97 (1979).

"Judicial Review of Disputes Between Athletes and the National Collegiate
Athletic Association." 24 STANFORD LAW REVIEW 903 (1972).

"Judicial Review of the NCAA's Bylaw 12-1." 29 ALABAMA LAW REVIEW 547
(1978).

"Judicial Review of the NCAA's Decisions: Does the College Athlete Have a
Property Interest in Interscholastic Athletics?" 10 STETSON LAW REVIEW
483 (1981).

Kane, John J. "Pre-emptive Purge in the Pac-10." 166 TIME, Aug. 25, 1980,
at 51.

Kirshenbaum, Jerry. "As Bad as Anything That's Ever Come Along." 52
SPORTS ILLUSTRATED, Feb. 25, 1980, at 11.

———. "Restating the Case for Reform." 53 SPORTS ILLUSTRATED, Sept. 1,
1980, at 7.

———. "Victory for Kush, Not for His Methods." 54 SPORTS ILLUSTRATED,
May 4, 1981, at 9.

Koch, James V. "A Troubled Cartel: The NCAA." 38 LAW & CONTEMPORARY
PROBLEMS 171 (1973).

Looney, Douglas S. "Big Ten's Big Mess." 54 SPORTS ILLUSTRATED, May 25,
1981, at 79.

———. "Deep in Hot Water in Stillwater: Accusations of Booster Club Slush
Fund for Oklahoma State University Players." 49 SPORTS ILLUSTRATED,
July 3, 1978, at 18.

McGahey, Robert L. "A Comment on the First Amendment and the Scholar-
Athlete." 6 HUMAN RIGHTS 155 (1977).

McGuire, John F. "The NCAA: Institution Under Constitutional Siege." 2
JOURNAL OF COLLEGE & UNIVERSITY LAW 175 (1975).

Martin, Gordon A. "Due Process and Its Future Within the NCAA." 10 CON-
NECTICUT LAW REVIEW 290 (1978).

———. "The NCAA and the Fourteenth Amendment." 11 NEW ENGLAND
LAW REVIEW 383 (1976).

"The NCAA, Amateurism, and the Student Athlete's Constitutional Rights
Upon Ineligibility." 15 NEW ENGLAND LAW REVIEW 597 (1979).

Papanek, John. "New Mexico: More Tremors." 51 SPORTS ILLUSTRATED, Dec.
17, 1979, at 75.

———. "Now New Mexico Feels the Heat." 51 SPORTS ILLUSTRATED, Dec.
10, 1979, at 32.

Press, Aric, and Foote, Donna. "Do Athletes Have a Right to Play?" 99
NEWSWEEK, Jan. 25, 1982, at 91.

Reid, Ron. "There's the Devil to Pay: Firing of Arizona State Coach Frank
Kush," 51 SPORTS ILLUSTRATED, Oct. 29, 1979, at 26.

Shea, Edward J., and Wieman, Elton E. Administrative Policies for Intercollegiate Athletics. Springfield, Ill.: C. Thomas, 1967.

Steinbach, Sheldon F. "Workmen's Compensation and the Scholarship Athlete." 19 CLEVELAND STATE LAW REVIEW 521 (1970).

"The Student-Athlete and the National Collegiate Athletic Association: The

Need for a Prima Facie Tort Doctrine." 9 SUFFOLK UNIVERSITY LAW REVIEW 1340 (1975).

"A Student-Athlete's Interest in Eligibility: Its Context and Constitutional Dimensions." 10 CONNECTICUT LAW REVIEW 318 (1978).

"Symposium on Athletics in High Education." Contents: "Introduction" (Philip J. Faccenda); "Women in Athletics: Winning the Game But Losing the Support" (Ann V. Thomas and Jan Sheldon-Wildgen); "Taxing the Sale of Broadcast Rights to College Athletics—An Unrelated Trade or Business?" (Larry R. Thompson and J. Timothy Young); "Unsportsmanlike Conduct: The Student-Athlete, the NCAA, and Agents" (Robert H. Ruxin); "*Aiken v. Lieuallen* and *Peterson v. Oregon State University:* Defining Equity in Athletics" (Edward Branchfield and Melinda Grier); "Williams v. Hamilton: Constitutional Protection of the Student-Athlete." 8 JOURNAL OF COLLEGE & UNIVERSITY LAW 291 (1981).

"Symposium on Postsecondary Athletics and the Law." Contents: "Antitrust Issues in the Regulation of College Sports" (John C. Weistart); "Intercollegiate Athletics: Waning Amateurism and Rising Professionalism" (Stephen Horn); "Contract Law, Due Process, and the NCAA" (Jaffed D. Dickerson and Mayer Chapman); "Postsecondary Athletics in an Era of Equality: An Appraisal of the Effect of Title IX" (Mark A. Kadzielski); "Sports and the Handicapped: Section 504 of the Rehabilitation Act of 1973 and Curricular, Intramural, Club and Intercollegiate Athletic Programs in Postsecondary Education" (Anne M. C. Hermann). 5 JOURNAL OF COLLEGE & UNIVERSITY LAW 77 (1979).

Underwood, John, and Sharnik, Morton. "Setting was Ripe for Scandal." 43 SPORTS ILLUSTRATED, Dec. 8, 1975, at 26.

United States. Congress. House. Committee on Education and Labor. Special Subcommittee on Education. *Protection of College Athletes*, Hearings, 93d Cong., 1st Sess., March 5, 19, 26–29, April 2, 1973. Washington, D.C.: G.P.O., 1973.

United States. Congress. House. Committee on Interstate and Foreign Commerce. Subcommittee on Oversight and Investigations. *NCAA Enforcement Program, Hearings, Part 1*, 95th Cong., 2d Sess., Feb. 27, 28, March 13, 14, 1978. Washington, D.C.: G.P.O., 1978.

United States. Congress. House. Committee on Interstate and Foreign Commerce. Subcommittee on Oversight Investigations. *NCAA Enforcement Program, Hearings, Part 2*, 95th Cong., 2d Sess., Sept. 27, 28, Oct. 4, 1978. Washington, D.C.: G.P.O., 1979.

United States. Congress. House. Committee on Interstate and Foreign Commerce. Subcommittee on Oversight and Investigations. *The Enforcement Program of the National Collegiate Athletic Association*, 95th Cong., 2d Sess., Dec. 1978. Washington, D.C.: G.P.O., 1979.

United States. Congress. Senate. Committee on Commerce. *NCAA-AAU Dispute*, Hearings, 89th Cong., 1st Sess., Aug. 16–20, 23–27, 1965. Washington, D.C.: G.P.O., 1965.

United States. Congress. Senate. Committee on Commerce. *Track and Field Disputes*, Hearings, 90th Cong., 1st Sess., Aug. 17–18, 1967. Washington, D.C.: G.P.O., 1967.

"Wearing of Black Armbands by State University Football Players During Game Would Violate Establishment of Religion Clause." 19 UNIVERSITY OF KANSAS LAW REVIEW 316 (1971).

"*Williams v. Hamilton:* Constitutional Protection of the Student-Athlete." 8 JOURNAL OF COLLEGE & UNIVERSITY LAW 399 (1981).

VI. CRIME AND RACKETEERING (*SEE ALSO* LIABILITY AND SPORTS *FOR CRIMINAL LIABILITY ISSUES*)

Axthelm, Peter. "Cocaine and Basketball." 96 NEWSWEEK, Sept. 1, 1980, at 77.

———. "The Good Doctor." 84 NEWSWEEK, Sept. 2, 1974, at 63.

———. "Scandal on the Court: University of New Mexico Scheme." 94 NEWSWEEK, Dec. 24, 1979, at 77.

Baxley, Robert C. "The Mandell Case." 10 JOURNAL OF PSYCHEDELIC DRUGS 385 (1978).

"Bookmaker's Dream." 104 TIME, Sept. 2, 1974, at 86.

"Control of Nongovernmental Corruption by Criminal Legislation." 108 UNIVERSITY OF PENNSYLVANIA LAW REVIEW 848 (1960).

"Crime and Punishment in Sports and Society." 33 JOURNAL OF SOCIAL ISSUES 140 (1977).

De Schaepdrvver, A., and Hebbelinke, M., *International Seminar on Doping.* Ghent and Brussels, Bel. New York, N.Y.: Macmillan, 1965.

"Drug Abuse at the Race Track." 52 CHEMISTRY, March 1979, at 24.

"Drug Factor at the Derby." 1979 BUSINESS WEEK, May 14, at 36.

"Drug Patrol." 115 TIME, Jan. 5, 1980, at 70.

"Fixer." 117 TIME, Feb. 23, 1981, at 102.

Gelbond, Myra. "Banned: Use of the Drugs Butazoldan and Lasix at Maryland Race Tracks." 51 SPORTS ILLUSTRATED, Dec. 3, 1979, at 11.

Hammer, Robert S. "Licensee Discipline and Due Process." 12 CONNECTICUT LAW REVIEW 870 (1980).

Harker, R. Phillip. "Analyzing Sports Betting Records." 48 FBI LAW ENFORCEMENT BULLETIN, Jan. 1979, at 5.

———. "Sports Bookmaking Operation." 47 FBI LAW ENFORCEMENT BULLETIN, Sept. 1978, at 1.

———. "Sports, Wagering, and 'The Line.'" 46 FBI LAW ENFORCEMENT BULLETIN, Nov. 1977, at 3.

Hickman, Dennis P. "Should Gambling Be Legalized for the Major Sporting Events?" 4 JOURNAL OF POLICE SCIENCE ADMINISTRATION 203 (1976).

Hill, Henry, and Looney, Douglas S. "How I Put the Fix In." 54 SPORTS ILLUSTRATED, Feb. 16, 1981, at 14.

Holmes, William L. "Baseball Wagering and Line Information." 48 FBI LAW ENFORCEMENT BULLETIN, June 1979, at 17.

"Horse Racing: Disciplinary Proceedings Against Horse Trainer or Jockey." 52 ALR 3d 206 (1972).

"Interstate Horseracing Act of 1978: An Evaluation." 12 CONNECTICUT LAW REVIEW 883 (1980).

Kaplan, H. Roy. "The Convergence of Work, Sport and Gambling in America." 445 ANNALS OF THE AMERICAN ACADEMY OF POLITICAL AND SOCIAL SCIENCE 24 (1979).

Kennedy, Ray. "427: A Case in Point." 40 SPORTS ILLUSTRATED, June 10, 1974, at 86, and June 17, 1974, at 24.

———. "Non-decision Begs the Question." 43 SPORTS ILLUSTRATED, Dec. 15, 1975, at 74.

Kirsch, Bernard. "Bettors, Beware." 72 SPORT, Sept. 1981, at 79.

Leggett, William. "Judgment at Brooklyn." 52 SPORTS ILLUSTRATED, June 2, 1980, at 54.

Looney, Douglas, S. "New Uproar Over a Controversial Drug." 48 SPORTS ILLUSTRATED, May 22, 1978, at 20.

Quinn, H. "Innocence or Guilt and a Larger Problem." 93 MACLEAN'S, Sept. 22, 1980, at 40.

"Racing on Trial." 115 TIME, May 26, 1980, at 89.

Samuels, Howard J. "Legalization of Gambling on Sporting Events." 18 NEW YORK LAW FORUM 897 (1973).

Shepherd, Almond G. "Horse Racing and the Courts." 19 CASE & COMMENT 176 (1912).

Telias, Bradley S. "Horse Racing and the Law: A Legislative Proposal to Harness Race-fixing." 9 FORDHAM URBAN LAW JOURNAL 253 (1980).

Trivizas, Eugene. "Offenses and Offenders in Football Crowd Disorders." 20 BRITISH JOURNAL OF CRIMINOLOGY 276 (1980).

Underwood, John. "Writing is on the Wall." 52 SPORTS ILLUSTRATED, Sept. 1, 1980, at 81.

United States. Congress. House. Committee on the District of Columbia. *Corrupt Influence in the District of Columbia in the Case of Athletic Contests,* House Report 80-453, 80th Cong., 1st Sess., May 23, 1947. Washington, D.C.: G.P.O., 194.

United States. Congress. House. Committee on the Judiciary. *Bribery in Sporting Contests,* House Report 88-1053, 88th Cong., 1st Sess., Dec. 17, 1963. Washington, D.C.: G.P.O., 1964.

United States. Congress. House. Select Committee on Crime. *Organized Crime in Sports (Racing),* Hearing, 92d Cong., 2d Sess., May 9–July 27, 1972. Washington, D.C.: G.P.O., 1972.

United States. Congress. Senate. Committee on the Judiciary. *Bribery in Sporting Contests,* Senate Report 87-2003, 87th Cong., 2d Sess., Sept. 7, 1962. Washington, D.C.: G.P.O., 1962.

United States. Congress. Senate. Committee on the Judiciary. *Bribery in Sporting Contests,* Senate Report 88-593, 88th Cong., 1st Sess., Oct. 29, 1963. Washington, D.C.: G.P.O., 1963.

VII. INTERNATIONAL SPORTS AND THE OLYMPICS

Espy, Richard. *The Politics of the Olympic Games.* Berkeley, Cal.: University of California Press, 1979.

"Executives' Foreign Relations Power and the New York Courts—A Case of Unwarranted Deferrence." 18 COLUMBIA JOURNAL OF TRANSNATIONAL LAW 557 (1980).

Jacobs, F. G. "Tourism, Sports and Other Forms of Leisure from the Point of View of International Law." 42–43 ANNUAIRE DE L'A.A.A. 52 (1972).

Nafziger, James A. R. "Diplomatic Fun and Games: A Commentary on the United States Boycott of the 1980 Summer Olympics." 17 WILLAMETTE LAW REVIEW 87 (1980).

————. "Legal Aspects of United States Foreign Sports Policy." 8 VANDER-
BILT JOURNAL OF TRANSNATIONAL LAW 837 (1975).

————. "Regulation of Transnational Sports Competition: Down from Mount
Olympus." 5 VANDERBILT JOURNAL OF TRANSNATIONAL LAW 180
(1971).

Nafziger, James A. R., and Strenk, Andrew. "The Political Uses and Abuses
of Sports." 10 CONNECTICUT LAW REVIEW 259 (1978).

"Political Abuse of Olympic Sport—*Defrantz v. United States Olympic Committee.*" 14 NEW YORK UNIVERSITY JOURNAL OF INTERNATIONAL LAW
AND POLITICS 155 (1981).

United States. Congress. House. Committee on Foreign Affairs. *U.S. Participation in the 1980 Summer Olympic Games,* Hearings on H. Con. Res.
249 and H. Res. 547, 96th Cong., 2d Sess., Jan. 23, Feb. 4, 1980. Washington, D.C.: G.P.O., 1980.

United States. Congress. House. Committee on Foreign Affairs. Subcommittee on Europe and the Middle East. *Assessment of the Afghanistan Sanctions: Implications for Trade and Diplomacy in the 1980's,* Committee
Print, 97th Cong., 1st Sess., April, 1981. Washington, D.C.: G.P.O.,
1981.

United States. Congress. House. Committee on Interstate and Foreign Commerce. Subcommittee on Transportation and Commerce. *Alternatives to
the Moscow Olympics,* Hearings, 96th Cong., 2d Sess., Jan. 30, 1980.
Washington, D.C.: G.P.O., 1980.

United States. Congress. Senate. Committee on Foreign Relations. *1980 Summer Olympics Boycott,* Hearings, 96th Cong., 2d Sess., Jan. 28, 1980.
Washington, D.C.: G.P.O., 1980.

United States. President's Commission On Olympic Sports. *Final Report of
the President's Commission on Olympic Sports.* Washington, D.C.:
G.P.O., 1977.

VIII. INVESTMENT AND FINANCING

"Can We Save Our Ball Club?: The Availability of Injunctive Relief for a
Municipality to Prevent the Threatened Breach of a Stadium Lease
Agreement by a Professional Sports Franchise." 2 COMM/ENT 97
(1979).

Demmert, Henry G. *The Economics of Pro Team Sports.* Lexington, Mass.:
Lexington Books, 1973.

Durso, Joseph. *The All-American Dollar: The Big Business of Sports.* Boston,
Mass.: Houghton-Mifflin, 1971.

Hoch, Paul. *Rip Off the Big Game: The Exploitation of Sports By the Power
Elite.* Garden City, N.Y.: Anchor Books, 1972.

Noll, Roger G. *Government and the Sports Business.* Washington, D.C.:
Brookings Institute, 1974.

Quirk, James. "An Economic Analysis of Team Movements in Professional
Sports." 38 LAW & CONTEMPORARY PROBLEMS 42 (1973).

Saiman, Martin S. "Coliseum Use Arrangements: Rome to the Superdome."
81 CASE & COMMENT, Nov.–Dec. 1976, at 3.

"San Diego Requires Solar Heating for Swimming Pools." 1 SOLAR LAW RE-
PORTER 1065 (1980).

"Stadium: Validity of Government Borrowing or Expenditure for Purposes of

Acquiring, Maintaining, or Improving Stadium for Use of Professional Athletic Teams." 67 ALR 3d 1186 (1975).

IX. LABOR LAW

1. General materials

"The Balance of Power in Professional Sports." 22 MAINE LAW REVIEW 459 (1970).

"Baseball and the Law—Yesterday and Today." 22 VIRGINIA LAW REVIEW 1164 (1946).

"Discipline in Professional Sports: The Need for Player Protection." 60 GEORGETOWN LAW JOURNAL 771 (1972).

Garvey, Edward R. "From Chattel to Employee: The Athlete's Quest for Freedom and Dignity." 445 ANNALS OF THE AMERICAN ACADEMY OF POLITICS AND SOCIAL SCIENCE 91 (1979).

Gilroy, Thomas P., and Madden, Patrick J. "Labor Relations in Professional Sports." 28 LABOR LAW JOURNAL 768 (1977).

Hoffman, Robert B. "Is the N.L.R.B. Going to Play the Ballgame?" 20 LABOR LAW JOURNAL 239 (1969).

"Labor Law—Professional Baseball Not Exempt from Federal Labor Laws— *Kansas City Royals Baseball Corp. v. Major League Baseball Players' Association*, 532 F. 2d 615 (8th Cir. 1976)." 5 FLORIDA STATE UNIVERSITY LAW REVIEW 137 (1977).

"Labor Laws and Baseball." 93 MONTHLY LABOR REVIEW, March 1970, at 61.

United States. Congress. House. Committee on Education and Labor. *Labor Reform Act of 1977, Part 2*, Hearings on H.R. 8410, 95th Cong., 1st Sess., Aug. 9, Sept. 7–9, 15, 1977. Washington, D.C.: G.P.O., 1978.

United States. Congress. House. Select Committee on Education and Labor. Special Subcommittee on Labor. *Labor Relations in Professional Sports,* Hearings, 92d Cong., 2d Sess., May 16–29, 1972. Washington, D.C.: G.P.O., 1972.

United States. Congress. House. Select Committee on Education and Labor. Subcommittee on Labor-Management Relations. *Oversight Hearings on National Football League Labor-Management Dispute,* 94th Cong., 1st Sess., Sept. 29, Oct. 2, 1975. Washington, D.C.: G.P.O., 1975.

United States. Congress. Senate. Committee on Human Resources. *Labor Reform Act of 1977, Part 2*, Hearings, 95th Cong., 1st Sess., Oct. 31, Nov. 3–4, 1977. Washington, D.C.: G.P.O., 1978.

2. Arbitration and negotiations (*See also* Collective bargaining)

"Arbitration of Grievance and Salary Disputes in Professional Baseball: Evolution of a System of Private Law." 60 CORNELL LAW REVIEW 1049 (1975).

"Arbitration of Professional Athletes' Contracts: An Effective System of Dispute Resolution in Professional Sports." 55 NEBRASKA LAW REVIEW 362 (1976).

Dworkin, James B. "How Final-offer Arbitration Affects Baseball Bargaining." 100 MONTHLY LABOR REVIEW, Nov. 1977, at 52.

Kiersh, Edward. "Spikes High in Ball Talks." 2 NATIONAL LAW JOURNAL,
    April 7, 1980, at 1.
Seitz, Peter. "Footnotes to Baseball Salary Arbitration." 29 ARBITRATION
    JOURNAL 98 (1974).
Staudohar, Paul D. "Player Salary Issues in Major League Baseball." 33 AR-
    BITRATION JOURNAL, Dec. 1978, at 17.
United States. Congress. Senate. Committee on Commerce. *Sports Arbitra-
    tion Board,* Hearings, 90th Cong., 1st Sess., Feb. 1, 1968. Washington,
    D.C.: G.P.O., 1968.

3. Collective bargaining (*See also* Arbitration and negotiations)

Berry, Robert C., and Gould, William B. "A Long Deep Drive to Collective
    Bargaining: Of Players, Owners, Brawls, and Strikes." 31 CASE WESTERN
    RESERVE LAW REVIEW 685 (1981).
Dworkin, James B., and Bergmann, Thomas J. "Collective Bargaining and
    the Player Reservation/Compensation System in Professional Sports." 4
    EMPLOYEE RELATIONS LAW JOURNAL 241 (1978).
Lowell, Cym H. "Collective Bargaining and the Professional Team Sport In-
    dustry." 38 LAW & CONTEMPORARY PROBLEMS 3 (1973).
Miller, David G. "Some Modest Proposals for Collective Bargaining in Profes-
    sional Sports." 48 LOS ANGELES BAR BULLETIN 155 (1972).
Schulman, Daniel S., and Baum, Bernard M. "Collective Bargaining in Pro-
    fessional Athletics: The NFL Money Bowl." 50 CHICAGO BAR RECORD,
    Jan. 1969, at 173.
Scoville, James G. "Has Collective Bargaining Altered the Salary Structure
    of Baseball?" 100 MONTHLY LABOR REVIEW, March 1977, at 51.
Sloane, Arthur. "Collective Bargaining in Major League Baseball: A New
    Ballgame and Its Genesis." 28 LABOR LAW JOURNAL 200 (1977).

4. Contracts

Alyluia, Kenneth. "Professional Sports Contracts and the Players' Associa-
    tion." 5 MANITOBA LAW JOURNAL 359 (1973).
Brennan, James T. "Injunction Against Professional Athletes Breaching Their
    Contracts." 34 BROOKLYN LAW REVIEW 61 (1967).
"Compensation Planning for the Professional Athlete," 7 SOUTHERN UNIVER-
    SITY LAW REVIEW 235 (1981).
"Contract Matters and Disciplinary Procedures in Professional Sport." 39
    SASKATCHEWAN LAW REVIEW 213 (1975).
"Contractual Rights and Duties of the Professional Athlete—Playing the
    Game in a Bidding War." 77 DICKINSON LAW REVIEW 352 (1973).
Dickerson, Jaffe D., and Chapman, Mayer. "Contract Law, Due Process, and
    the NCAA." 5 JOURNAL OF COLLEGE & UNIVERSITY LAW 107 (1979).
"Employment Contract: Employer's Termination of Professional Athlete's
    Services as Constituting Breach of Employment Contract." 57 ALR 3d
    257 (1974).
"Enforceability of Professional Sports Contracts—What's the Harm in It?" 35
    SOUTHWESTERN LAW JOURNAL 803 (1981).
"Enforcement Problems of Personal Service Contracts in Professional Ath-
    letics." 6 TULSA LAW JOURNAL 40 (1969).

"Equity—Injunctions—Negative Covenant in Personal Employment Contracts —Boxing." 5 NEW YORK LAW FORUM 456 (1959).

Gallner, Sheldon. *Pro Sports: The Contract Game.* New York, N.Y.: Charles Scribner's Sons, 1975.

Heiner, S. Phillip. "Post Merger Blues: Intra-League Contract Jumping." 18 WILLIAM & MARY LAW REVIEW 741 (1977).

"Injunction—Contract for Personal Services—Mutuality, *Philadelphia Ball Club v. Lajore* (S. Ct. Penn. 1902), *American Baseball & Athletic Exhibition Co. v. Harper* (Cir. Ct. St. Louis 1902)." 54 CENTRAL LAW JOURNAL 449 (1902).

"Injunctions in Professional Athletes' Contracts—An Overused Remedy." 43 CONNECTICUT BAR JOURNAL 538 (1969).

Johnson, William O., and Reid, Ron. "Some Offers They Can't Refuse." 50 SPORTS ILLUSTRATED, May 21, 1979, at 30.

"Offer Sheet: An Attempt to Circumvent NCAA Prohibition of Representational Contracts." 14 LOYOLA UNIVERSITY LAW REVIEW 187 (1980).

"Professional Athletic Contracts and the Injunctive Dilemma," 8 JOHN MARSHAL JOURNAL OF PRACTICE & PROCEDURE 437 (1975).

"Professional Football—Are Three One Year Agreements Signed at One Sitting Actually One Contract? Are Players 'Public Figures'? *Chuy v. Philadelphia Eagles Football Club,* 431 F. Supp. 254 (E.D. Pa. 1977)." 10 CONNECTICUT LAW REVIEW 350 (1978).

United States. Congress. House. Committee on Ways and Means. *Effective Date of Basis Limitation for Player Contracts Acquired with the Purchase of a Sports Franchise,* House Report 96-911 on H.R. 4103, 96th Cong., 2d. Sess., April 29, 1980, Washington, D.C.: G.P.O., 1980.

Weil, Jay R. "Depreciation of Player Contracts—The Government is Ahead at the Half." 53 TAXES 581 (1975).

Wietmarschen, Donald A. "Planning for the Professional Athlete: Deferred Compensation Arrangements & Loans in Lieu of Compensation." 8 OHIO NORTHERN UNIVERSITY LAW REVIEW 499 (1981).

Zollers, Frances E. "From Gridiron to Courtroom to Bargaining Table: The New Football League Agreement." 17 AMERICAN BUSINESS LAW JOURNAL 133 (1979).

5. Liberty of player movement (*See also* Antitrust law)

"Baseball and the Reserve Clause." 1 NEW YORK LAW SCHOOL STUDENT LAW REVIEW 159 (1952).

"Baseball Law." 17 LAW NOTES 207 (1914).

"Battle of the Superstars: Player Restraints in Professional Team Sports." 32 UNIVERSITY OF FLORIDA LAW REVIEW 669 (1980).

Boswell, Thomas M., and McKeown, Richard B. "Baseball—From Trial by Law to Trial by Auction." 4 JOURNAL OF CONTEMPORARY LAW 171 (1978).

Carlson, Robert S. "The Business of Professional Sports: A Reexamination in Progress." 18 NEW YORK LAW FORUM 915 (1973).

"Curt Flood at Bat Against Baseball's 'Reserve Clause.'" 8 SAN DIEGO LAW REVIEW 92 (1971).

"Farewell to Feudalism: Court Rulings on the Reserve System." 107 TIME, Jan. 12, 1976, at 45.

"Hockey's Reserve System and the Labor Exemption, *McCourt v. California Sports, Inc.*" 15 NEW ENGLAND LAW REVIEW 765 (1980).

Hofeld, Arthur K. "Athletes—Their Rights and Correlative Duties." 19 TRIAL LAW GUIDE 383 (1976).

Holahan, William L. "The Long-Run Effects of Abolishing the Baseball Players Reserve System." 7 JOURNAL OF LEGAL STUDIES 129 (1978).

Hunt, Joseph, Jr., and Lewis, Kennth A. "Dominance, Recontracting, and the Reserve Clause: Major League Baseball." 66 AMERICAN ECONOMIC REVIEW 936 (1976).

Johnson, William O. "A Legal License to Steal the Stars." 34 SPORTS ILLUSTRATED, April 12, 1971, at 34.

"Legal Implications of the Reserve Clause in Professional Sports." 3 GLENDALE LAW REVIEW 63 (1978).

"The Legality of the Rozelle Rule and Related Practices in the National Football League." 4 FORDHAM URBAN LAW JOURNAL 581 (1976).

"Loss for Curt Flood." 80 NEWSWEEK, July 3, 1972, at 67.

Martin, Philip L. "Labor Controversy in Professional Baseball: The Flood Case." 23 LABOR LAW JOURNAL 567 (1972).

"The Messersmith Decision and the 1976 Basic Agreement: Baseball's Emancipation Proclamation." 46 UNIVERSITY OF MISSOURI AT KANSAS CITY LAW REVIEW 239 (1977).

Morris, John P. "In the Wake of *Flood.*" 38 LAW & CONTEMPORARY PROBLEMS 85 (1973).

"The NBA's Four Year Rule: A Technical Foul?" 1972 LAW & THE SOCIAL ORDER 489.

"The NFL's Final Victory Over *Smith v. Pro Football, Inc.*: Single Entity-Interleague Economic Analysis." 27 CLEVELAND STATE LAW REVIEW 541 (1978).

"National Football League Restrictions on Competitive Bidding for Player's Services." 24 BUFFALO LAW REVIEW 613 (1975).

"National Hockey League Reserve System: A Restraint of Trade?" 56 UNIVERSITY OF DETROIT JOURNAL OF URBAN LAW 467 (1979).

"Organized Baseball and the Law." 46 YALE LAW JOURNAL 1386 (1937).

"Professional Sports: Restraining the League Commissioner's Prerogatives in an Era of Player Mobility." 19 WILLIAM & MARY LAW REVIEW 281 (1977).

"Reserve Clause Anomaly: Decision of the Supreme Court." 24 NATIONAL REVIEW, July 7, 1972, at 731.

"Reserve Clauses in Athletic Contracts." 2 RUTGERS-CAMDEN LAW JOURNAL 302 (1970).

"Safe, Kind of: Reserve Clause Decision by the Supreme Court." 100 TIME, July 3, 1972, at 30.

"The Sale of Minor League Baseball Players During Liquidation—The Application of *Corn Products* to Depreciable Property." 45 TEMPLE LAW QUARTERLY 291 (1972).

Schneiderman, Michael. "Professional Sports: Involuntary Servitude and the Popular Will." 7 GONZAGA LAW REVIEW 63 (1967).

Shapiro, Daniel J. "The Professional Athlete: Liberty or Peonage?" 13 ALBERTA LAW REVIEW 212 (1975).

Simon, Richard K. "The First Great Leap: Some Reflections on the Spencer Haywood Case." 48 LOS ANGELES BAR BULLETIN 149 (1973).

Sobel, Lionel S. "The Emancipation of Professional Athletes." 3 WESTERN STATE UNIVERSITY LAW REVIEW 185 (1976).

"Sport in Court: The Legality of Professional Football's System of Reserve and Compensation." 28 UNIVERSITY OF CALIFORNIA AT LOS ANGELES LAW REVIEW 252 (1980).

Stayton, John W. "Baseball Jurisprudence." 44 AMERICAN LAW REVIEW 374 (1910).

"Whatever Happened to Curt Flood?" 36 EBONY, March 1981, at 55.

6. Unions

Dabscheck, Braham. "Player Associations and Professional Team Sports." 4 LABOUR AND SOCIETY 225 (1979).

Fritz, Sara. "When Pro Athletes Carry Union Cards: Players in the Big Leagues Are in Ferment Over Rules that Bind Them to Their Clubs: The Demand: Freedom to Change Teams for More Pay." 88 U.S. NEWS, March 31, 1980, at 79.

Guback, Steve. "Pro Football Gets a Union Card." 2 WORKLIFE, Oct. 1977, at 28.

Krasnow, Erwin G., and Levy, Herman M. "Unionization and Professional Sports." 51 GEORGETOWN LAW JOURNAL 749 (1963).

X. LIABILITY AND SPORTS

1. Liability and solutions for sports-related injuries

"Aftermath of a Tragedy—Liability of the New York State Athletic Commission for Injuries Suffered in a Prizefight." 14 SYRACUSE LAW REVIEW 79 (1962).

Appenzeller, Herb. *An Analysis of Court Cases Pertaining to Tort Liability for Injuries Sustained in a Public School Program of Physical Education.* Ann Arbor. Mich.: University Microfilms, 1969.

———. *From Gym to the Jury: Who Really Pays the Price for Negligence?* Charlottesville, Va.: Education Division, Michie, 1970.

"Assault and Battery—Liability for Injuries Received in Athletic Contests." 26 MICHIGAN LAW REVIEW 322 (1927).

"Assumption of Risk After *Sunday v. Stratton Corp.*: The Vermont Sports Injury Liability Statute and Injured Skiers." 3 VERMONT LAW REVIEW 129 (1978).

"Assumption of Risk and Vicarious Liability in Personal Injury Actions Brought by Professional Athletes." 1980 DUKE LAW JOURNAL 742.

"Assumption of Risk—Landowner's Liability in Oregon." 1 WILLAMETTE LAW JOURNAL 405 (1960).

Barrett, John C. "Good Sports and Bad Law: The Application of Washington's Recreational Use Statute Limiting Landowner Liability." 53 WASHINGTON LAW REVIEW 1 (1977).

Beumler, Candyce. "Liability in Professional Sports: An Alternative to Violence?" 22 ARIZONA LAW REVIEW 919 (1980).

Blalock, Joyce. "The Sporting Suit." 53 AMERICAN BAR ASSOCIATION JOURNAL 58 (1967).

"The 'Booby' Trap: Does the Violent Nature of Professional Football Vitiate the Doctrine of Due Care in Participant Tort Litigation? *Hackbart v. Cincinnati Bengals, Inc.*, 435 F. Supp. 253 (D. Colo. 1977)." 10 CONNECTICUT LAW REVIEW 365 (1978).

Bortz, Bruce L., and Levin, Cheri W. "Torts on the Courts." 14 TRIAL, June 1978, at 28.

"Bowling Alley Tort Liability." 16 CLEVELAND-MARSHALL LAW REVIEW 294 (1967).

Buxton, John T., Jr. "Baseball and the Law Courts." 39 LAW NOTES, Sept. 1935, at 28.

Chalat, James W. "Colorado Ski Safety Act Updated." 10 COLORADO LAWYER 1610 (1981).

———. "Ski Tips—A Review of Colorado's Ski Safety Act." 9 COLORADO LAWYER 452 (1980).

Cohen, Bernard S. "Gymnastics Litigation: Meeting the Defense." 16 TRIAL, Aug. 1980, at 35.

"Compensating Injured Professional Athletes: The Mystique of Sport Versus Traditional Tort Principles." 55 NEW YORK UNIVERSITY LAW REVIEW 971 (1980).

"The Consent Defense: Sports, Violence and the Criminal Law." 13 AMERICAN CRIMINAL LAW REVIEW 235 (1975).

"Consent in Criminal Law: Violence in Sports." 75 MICHIGAN LAW REVIEW 148 (1976).

"Constitutional Law—Due Process—Horse Trainer Held Strictly Liable for the Condition of Horses." 8 FLORIDA STATE UNIVERSITY LAW REVIEW 365 (1980).

"Controlling Violence in Professional Sports." 2 GLENDALE LAW REVIEW 323 (1978).

"Criminal Law: Consent as a Defense to Criminal Battery—The Problem of Athletic Contests." 28 OKLAHOMA LAW REVIEW 840 (1975).

Epstein, Robert K. "The Case Against Artificial Turf." 13 TRIAL, Jan. 1977, at 42.

"Federal Jurisdiction—Torts—Federal District Court in Diversity Suit May Not Refuse Jurisdiction Over Professional Football Player's Claim for Damages Resulting from Blow Intentionally Inflicted, *Hackbart v. Cincinnati Bengals, Inc.*, 601 F. 2d 516 (10 Cir. 1979, *cert. denied* 100 S. Ct. 275 1979)." 11 RUTGERS-CAMDEN LAW JOURNAL 497 (1980).

Flakne, Gary W., and Caplan, Allan H. "Sports Violence and the Prosecution." 13 TRIAL, Jan. 1977, at 33.

Gabrielsen, M. Alexander, and Olenn, J. Renn. "Swimming Pool Litigation: Educating for Safety." 18 TRIAL, Feb. 1982, at 38.

Goria, Gino. "Decision of the Rota Fiorentina of 1780 on Liability for Damages Caused by the 'Ball Game.'" 49 TULANE LAW REVIEW 346 (1975).

Greenwald, Andrew E. "Gymnastics Litigation: The Standard of Care." 16 TRIAL, Aug. 1980, at 25.

Gregory, I. Francis, II, and Goldsmith, Arthur H. "Sports Spectator as Plaintiff: The Prudent Patron, The Duty to Duck, and the Flying Puck." 16 TRIAL, March 1980, at 26.

Hallowell, Lyle, and Meshberger, Ronald J. "Sports Violence and the Criminal Law." 13 TRIAL, Jan. 1977, at 27.

Hames, Eugene S. "Liability for Ski Injuries Caused by Defective Bindings." 27 FEDERATION OF INSURANCE COUNSEL QUARTERLY 311 (1976).

Hassenhauer, Leo J. and Rollinson, W. D. "Theatres and Shows—Amusements—Negligence." 11 NOTRE DAME LAWYER 93 (1935).

Hechter, William. "The Criminal Law and Violence in Sports." 19 CRIMINAL LAW QUARTERLY 425 (1977).

"Injury from Fall of Seats or Grandstands." 23 LAW STUDENTS' HELPER, March 1915, at 28.

"Judicial Criticism of Baseball Playing." 50 NATIONAL CORPORATION REPORTER 554 (1915).

"Judicial Scrutiny of Tortious Conduct in Professional Sports: Do Professional Athletes Assume the Risk of Injuries Resulting from Rule Violation? *Hackbart v. Cincinnati Bengals, Inc.*" 17 CALIFORNIA WESTERN LAW REVIEW 149 (1980).

Lambert, Dale J. "Tort Law and Participant Sports: The Line Between Vigor and Violence." 4 JOURNAL OF CONTEMPORARY LAW 211 (1978).

Langerman, Samuel, and Fidel, Noel. "Responsibility is Also Part of the Game." 13 TRIAL, Jan. 1977, at 22.

Letourneau, Gilles, and Manganas, Antoine. "Violence in Sports: Evidentiary Problems in Criminal Prosecutions." 16 OSGOODE HALL LAW JOURNAL 577 (1978).

"Liability for Injury to or Death of a Participant in Game or Contest." 7 ALR 2d 704 (1949).

"Liability for Injuries to Spectators." 6 OSGOODE HALL LAW JOURNAL 305 (1968).

"Liability of Polo Player to Spectator Injured While Watching Game." 19 LAW NOTES, July 1915, at 73.

"Liability to Spectator at Baseball Game Who is Hit by Ball or Injured as a Result of Other Hazards of Game." 91 ALR 3d 24 (1979).

Lisman, Carl H. "Ski Injury Liability." 43 UNIVERSITY OF COLORADO LAW REVIEW 307 (1972).

McCarthy, James J. "Aerobatics: Sports Aviation and Student Flying." 14 TRIAL, Aug. 1978, at 24.

Mandel, Bernard. "Negligent Design of Sports Facilities." 16 CLEVELAND-MARSHALL LAW REVIEW 275 (1967).

Markus, Richard M. "Sports Safety: On the Offensive." 8 TRIAL, July 1972, at 12.

Moore, Charles C. "Civil or Criminal Liability for Injuries in Field Sports." 19 CASE & COMMENT 163 (1912).

Narol, Melvin S., and Dedopoulos, Stuart. "Guide to Referees' Rights: Potential Liability." 16 TRIAL, March 1980, at 18.

"Negligence—Landowners—Duty of Baseball Club to Protect Invitees from Injurious Acts of Third Parties." 12 VANDERBILT LAW REVIEW 299 (1958).

"Negligence—Ski Lifts—Common Carriers—Highest Degree of Care." 1 WASHBURN LAW JOURNAL 316 (1961).

"The Negligent Golfer." 18 NEW YORK UNIVERSITY INTRAMURAL LAW REVIEW 167 (1963).

"On Finding Civil Liability Between Professional Football Players: *Hackbart v. Cincinnati Bengals, Inc.*" 15 NEW ENGLAND LAW REVIEW 741 (1980).

Page, Alan. "Violence Act Comes Up Short." 72 SPORT, Feb. 1981, at 10.

"Participant's Liability for Injury to a Fellow Participant in an Organized Athletic Event." 53 CHICAGO-KENT LAW REVIEW 97 (1976).

Peters, George A. "Unsafe Swimming Pools and Spas Claim Unsuspecting Victims." 16 TRIAL, March 1980, at 42.

Peterson, Terri L., and Smith, Scott A. "The Role of the Lawyer on the Playing Field: Sports Injury Litigation." 7 BARRISTER, Summer 1980, at 10.

Philo, Harry M., and Stine, Gregory. "The Liability Path to Safer Helmets."
13 TRIAL, Jan. 1977, at 38.
"Professional Sports and Tort Liability: A Victory for the Intentionally In-
jured Player." 1980 DETROIT COLLEGE OF LAW REVIEW 687.
"The Promoter's Liability for Sports Spectator Injuries." 46 CORNELL LAW
QUARTERLY 140 (1960).
"A Proposed Legislative Solution to the Problem of Violent Acts by Participants During Professional Sporting Events: The Sports Violence Act of
1980." 7 UNIVERSITY OF DAYTON LAW REVIEW 91 (1981).
"Recreational Torts" [A Seminar]. Contents: "Toys-R-Dangerous: Protecting
Children from Hazardous Playthings" (Edward M. Swartz); "Ski Liti-
gation: Elements of the Successful Case" (William A. Trine); "Swim-
ming Pool Litigation: Educating for Safety" (M. Alexander Gabrielsen
and J. Renn Olenn). 18 TRIAL, Feb. 1982, at 28.
Rosenblatt, Albert M. "After the Fall." 5 TRIAL, Feb. 1969, at 44.
———. "Ski Area Liability: What Courts Say." 18 HARVARD LAW SCHOOL
BULLETIN, Jan. 1967, at 12.
"Ski Operators and Skiers—Responsibility and Liability." 14 NEW ENGLAND
LAW REVIEW 260 (1978).
Slonim, Scott. "Goal of Crime Bill to Curb Sports Violence." 66 AMERICAN
BAR ASSOCIATION JOURNAL 1188 (1980).
"The Sports Court: A Private System to Deter Violence in Professional
Sports." 55 SOUTHERN CALIFORNIA LAW REVIEW 399 (1982).
"Sports Liability: Blowing the Whistle on the Referees." 12 PACIFIC LAW
JOURNAL 937 (1981).
"Sports, Torts, Courts: Sports Litigation" [A Symposium]. Contents: "Re-
sponsibility is Also Part of the Game" (Samuel Langerman and Noel
Fidel); "Sports Violence and the Criminal Law" (Lyle Hallowell and
Ronald I. Meshberger); "Sports Violence and the Prosecution" (Gary
W. Flakne and Allan H. Caplan); "The Liability Path to Safer Helmets"
(Harry M. Philo and Gregory Stine); "The Case Against Artificial Turf"
(Robert K. Epstein); "In Defense of Artificial Turf" (F. E. Troy). 13
TRIAL, Jan. 1977, at 22.
"Sports Violence: A Matter for Societal Concern." 55 NOTRE DAME LAWYER
796 (1980).
Stern, James F. "Swimming Pool Liability." 14 TRIAL, June 1978, at 24.
"Tort Law—Reckless Misconduct in Sports." 19 DUQUESNE LAW REVIEW 191
(1980).
"Tort Liability for Players in Contact Sports: Nabozny v. Barnhill." 45 UNI-
VERSITY OF MISSOURI AT KANSAS CITY LAW REVIEW 119 (1976).
"Tort Liability in Professional Sports." 44 ALBANY LAW REVIEW 696 (1980).
"Tort Liability in Professional Sports: Battle in the Sports Arena, Hackbart
v. Cincinnati Bengals, Inc., 435 F. Supp. 352 (D. Colo. 1977)." 57
NEBRASKA LAW REVIEW 1128 (1978).
"Torts—Assumption of Risk—A Professional Football Player Assumes the
Risk of Receiving a Blow, Delivered Out of Anger and Frustration, But
Without Specific Intention to Injure, During a Game." 12 GEORGIA LAW
REVIEW 380 (1978).
"Torts—Assumption of Risk, Lee v. National Baseball Club (Wis.), 89 N.W.
2d 811 (1958)." 18 MARYLAND LAW REVIEW 355 (1958).
"Torts—Assumption of Risk—Matters of Common Knowledge." 32 TEMPLE
LAW QUARTERLY 127 (1958).

"Torts: Athlete States Cause of Action For Injury During a Professional Football Game." 19 WASHBURN LAW JOURNAL 646 (1980).

"Torts—Civil Liability of Athletes—Professional Football Player May Have Tort Claim for Injuries Intentionally Inflicted During Football Game, *Hackbart v. Cincinnati Bengals, Inc.*, 601 F. 2d 516 (10th Cir. 1979)." 84 DICKINSON LAW REVIEW 753 (1980).

"Torts in Sports—Deterring Violence in Professional Athletics." 48 FORDHAM LAW REVIEW 764 (1980).

"Torts—Liability of Owners or Proprietors of Places of Amusement or Entertainment." 12 UNIVERSITY OF DETROIT LAW JOURNAL 169 (1949).

"Torts—Master Servant—Respondent Superior—'Free Time' as Within Scope of Employment." 13 DUQUESNE LAW REVIEW 349 (1974).

"Torts—Participant in Athletic Competition States Cause of Action for Injuries Against Other Participants, *Nabozny v. Barnhill*." 42 MISSOURI LAW REVIEW 347 (1977).

"Torts—Voluntary Assumption of Risk—Contributory Negligence—Injuries to Patrons at Places of Amusement." 10 SOUTHERN CALIFORNIA LAW REVIEW 67 (1936).

Trine, William A. "Ski Litigation: Elements of the Successful Case." 18 TRIAL, Feb. 1982, at 32.

Troy, F. E. "In Defense of Artificial Turf." 13 TRIAL, Jan. 1977, at 46.

United States. Congress. House. Committee on the Judiciary. Subcommittee on Crime. *Excessive Violence in Sports*, Hearing on H.R. 7903, 96th Cong., 2d Sess., Sept. 30, Nov. 19, 1980. Washington, D.C.: G.P.O., 1981.

"Utah's Inherent Risks of Skiing Act: Avalanche from Capitol Hill." 1980 UTAH LAW REVIEW 355.

"Violence in Professional Sports." 1975 WISCONSIN LAW REVIEW 771.

Wells, David. "Liability of Ski Area Operators." 41 DENVER LAW CENTER JOURNAL 1 (1964).

"When Equity Will Enjoin Sport as a Private Nuisance." 21 YALE LAW JOURNAL 414 (1912).

Wilkinson, Allen P. "Sports Product Liability: It's All Part of the Game—Or Is It?" 17 TRIAL, Nov. 1981, at 58.

Zollman, Carl, "Injuries from Flying Baseballs to Spectators at Ballgames." 24 MARQUETTE LAW REVIEW 198 (1940).

2. Miscellaneous civil liability

Johnson, William O. "Walk on the Wild Side: George Atkinson's Slander Suit Against Chuck Noll." 47 SPORTS ILLUSTRATED, Aug. 1, 1977, at 10.

Narol, Melvin S., and Dedopoulas, Stuart. "Defamation: A Guide to Referees' Rights." 16 TRIAL, Jan. 1980, at 42.

———. "Kill the Umpire: A Guide to Referees' Rights." 15 TRIAL, March 1979, at 32.

XI. MEDIA AND SPORTS

"Communications Law—Television—Antisiphoning Rule Governing Movie and Sports Content of Pay Cable Televisions Exceeds Jurisdiction of FCC Under Federal Communications Act, *Home Box Office, Inc. v. FCC* (D.C. Cir. 1977)." 23 VILLANOVA LAW REVIEW 597 (1978).

"Copyright Protection for Live Sports Broadcasts: New Statutory Weapons with Constitutional Problems." 31 FEDERAL COMMUNICATION LAW JOURNAL 277 (1979).

"Copyright Protection for Live Sports Telecasts." 29 BAYLOR LAW REVIEW 101 (1977).

"Copyright Protection for Sports Broadcasts and the Public's Right of Access." 15 IDEA 385 (1971).

"Copyrights—In General—Unauthorized Rediffusion of Live and Film Telecasts of Sports Events to Home Viewers Held Non-actionable." 68 HARVARD LAW REVIEW 712 (1955).

Hickey, Terence N. "Television Broadcasts of Boxing Matches." 16 MARQUETTE LAW REVIEW 260 (1932).

Hochberg, Philip R. "Congress Kicks a Field Goal: The Legislative Attack in the 93d Congress on Sports Broadcasting Practices." 27 FEDERAL COMMUNICATIONS BAR JOURNAL 27 (1974).

———. "Congress Tackles Sports and Broadcasting." 3 WESTERN STATE UNIVERSITY LAW REVIEW 223 (1976).

———. "The Four Horsemen Ride Again: Cable Communications and Collegiate Athletics." 5 JOURNAL OF COLLEGE & UNIVERSITY LAW 76 (1977).

———. "Second and Goal to Go: The Legislative Attack in the Ninety-Second Congress on Sports Broadcasting Practices." 26 FEDERAL COMMUNICATIONS BAR JOURNAL 118 (1973) [reprinted at 18 NEW YORK LAW FORUM 841 (1973)].

Hochberg, Philip R., and Horowitz, Ira. "Broadcasting and CATV: The Beauty and Beast of Major College Football." 38 LAW & CONTEMPORARY PROBLEMS 112 (1973).

Horowitz, Ira. "Market Entrenchment and the Sports Broadcast Act." 21 AMERICAN BEHAVIORAL SCIENCE 415 (1978).

"Importation of Prize Fight Films." 19 LAW NOTES, June 1915, at 144.

Peterson, Robert A. " 'Blackouts' and the Public Interest: An Equitable Proposal." 4 JOURNAL OF CONTEMPORARY LAW 143 (1978).

"Professional Football Telecasts and the Blackout Privilege." 57 CORNELL LAW REVIEW 297 (1972).

"The Property Right in a Sports Telecast." 35 VIRGINIA LAW REVIEW 246 (1949).

"Regulation or Strangulation? Restriction of Radio and T.V. Coverage of Athletic Events." 128 COLLIERS', Nov. 17, 1951, at 86.

Shooshan, Harry M. "Confrontation with Congress: Professional Sports and the Television Anti-Blackout Laws." 25 SYRACUSE LAW REVIEW 713 (1974).

Sobel, Lionel S. "Television Sports Blackouts: Private Rights vs. Public Policy." 48 LOS ANGELES BAR BULLETIN 169 (1973).

"Sports Anti-Siphoning Rule for Pay Cable Television: A Public Right to Free T.V.?" 53 INDIANA LAW JOURNAL 821 (1978).

"Symposium on Entertainment and Sports Law." Contents: "The Sale, Rental and Reproduction of Motion Picture Videocassettes: Piracy or Privilege?" (Joseph J. Beard); "Author's Rights: Waiver, Estoppel, and Good Faith in Book Publishing Contracts" (Jeremiah F. Healy III and Beth M. Alonso); "Celebrity Endorsements: A Case for Alarm and Concern for the Future" (Michael E. Jones); "Agents of Professional Athletes"; "Title IX and Intercollegiate Athletics: HEW Gets Serious About Equality in Sports?"; "The NCAA, Amateurism, and the Student-Ath-

lete's Constitutional Rights Upon Ineligibility"; "Children's Television
Programming and the FCC: Background for Affirmative Regulation";
"*Universal City Studios, Inc. v. Sony Corporation of America:* Appli-
cation of the Fair Use Doctrine Under the United States Copyright Act
of 1909 and 1976"; "*Broadcast Music, Inc. v. Columbia Broadcasting
System, Inc.:* The Copyright Misuse Doctrine"; "*North American Soccer
League v. National Football League:* Applying 'Rule of Reason' Analysis
Under the Sherman Act to Private Bans on Cross-Ownership"; "On
Finding Civil Liability Between Professional Football Players: *Hackbart
v. Cincinnati Bengals, Inc.*"; "Hockey's Reserve System and the Labor
Exemption: *McCourt v. California Sports, Inc.*" 15 New England Law
Review 435 (1980).

Thompson, Larry R., and Young, J. Timothy. "Taxing the Sale of Broadcast
Rights to College Athletics—An Unrelated Trade of Business?" 8 Journal of College and University Law 331 (1981).

"Unfair Competition and Exclusive Broadcast of Sporting Events." 48 Yale
Law Journal 288 (1938).

United States. Congress. House. Committee on Interstate and Foreign Commerce. *Professional Sports—TV Blackouts,* House Report 93-483, 93d
Cong., 1st Sess., Sept. 11, 1973, Washington, D.C.: G.P.O., 1973.

United States. Congress. House. Committee on Interstate and Foreign Commerce. *Sports Broadcasting Act of 1975,* House Report 94-722 on H.R.
11070, 94th Cong., 1st Sess., Dec. 12, 1975. Washington, D.C.: G.P.O.,
1975.

United States. Congress. House. Committee on Interstate and Foreign Commerce. Special Subcommittee on Investigations. *Evaluation of the Necessity for Television Blackouts of Professional Sporting Events,* Committee Print, 93d Cong., 1st Sess., July, 1973. Washington, D.C.:
G.P.O., 1973.

United States. Congress. House. Committee on Interstate and Foreign Com-
merce. Subcommittee on Communications. *Cable Television Regulation
Oversight Hearings, Part I,* 94th Cong., 2d Sess., May 17–July 22, 1976.
Washington, D.C.: G.P.O., 1977.

United States. Congress. House. Committee on Interstate and Foreign Commerce. Subcommittee on Communications. *Communications Act of
1979, V.2, Part 1,* Hearings on H.R. 3333, 96th Cong., 1st Sess., May
14–17, 1979. Washington, D.C.: G.P.O., 1980.

United States. Congress. House. Committee on Interstate and Foreign Com-
merce. Subcommittee on Communications. *Network Sports Practices,*
Hearings, 95th Cong., 1st Sess., Oct. 3, Nov. 2–3, 1977. Washington,
D.C.: G.P.O., 1978.

United States. Congress. House. Committee on Interstate and Foreign Commerce. Subcommittee on Communications. *Sports Anti-Blackout Legislation Oversight Hearings,* 95th Cong., 2d Sess., April 28, 1978. Washington, D.C.: G.P.O., 1979.

United States. Congress. House. Committee on Interstate and Foreign Commerce. Subcommittee on Communications. *Sports Broadcasting Act of
1975,* Hearings, 94th Cong., 1st Sess., Sept. 22, Oct. 31, 1975. Washington, D.C.: G.P.O., 1975.

United States. Congress. House. Committee on Interstate and Foreign Commerce. Subcommittee on Communications and Power. *Professional
Sports Blackouts,* Hearings, 93d Cong., 1st Sess., Aug. 1, 2, Sept. 5–7,
1973. Washington, D.C.: G.P.O., 1973.

United States. Congress. House. Committee on Interstate and Foreign Commerce. Subcommittee on Communications and Power. *Subscription Television*, Hearings, 91st Cong., 1st Sess., Nov. 18–21, 24, Dec. 9–12, 1969. Washington, D.C.: G.P.O., 1970.

United States. Congress. House. Committee on the Judiciary. *Telecasting of Professional Sports Contests*, House Report 87-1178, 87th Cong., 1st Sess., Sept. 13, 1961. Washington, D.C.: G.P.O., 1961.

United States. Congress. House. Committee on the Judiciary. Antitrust Subcommittee. *Telecasting of Professional Sports Contests*, Hearings, 87th Cong., 1st Sess., Aug. 28, 1961. Washington, D.C.: G.P.O., 1961.

United States. Congress. House. Committee on the Judiciary. Subcommittee on Courts, Civil Liberties, and the Administration of Justice. *Copyright Issues: Cable Television and Performance Rights*, Hearings, 96th Cong., 1st Sess., Nov. 15, 26, 27, 1979. Washington, D.C.: G.P.O., 1979.

United States. Congress. House. Committee on the Judiciary. Subcommittee on Courts, Civil Liberties, and the Administration of Justice. *Copyright Law Revision, Part 2*, Hearings, 94th Cong., 1st Sess., June 12, July 10, 17, 23, 1975. Washington, D.C.: G.P.O., 1976.

United States. Congress. Senate. Committee on Commerce. *Professional Sports Antiblackout Law Extension*, Senate Report 94-510 on S. 2554, 94th Cong., 1st Sess., Dec. 5, 1975. Washington, D.C.: G.P.O., 1975.

United States. Congress. Senate. Committee on Commerce. *TV Blackout: Professional Sports*, Senate Report 93-347, 93d Cong., 1st Sess., July 26, 1973. Washington, D.C.: G.P.O. 1973.

United States. Congress. Senate. Committee on Commerce. Subcommittee on Communications. *Blackout of Sporting Events on TV*, Hearings, 92d Cong., 2d Sess., Oct. 3–5, 1972. Washington, D.C.: G.P.O., 1972.

United States. Congress. Senate. Comittee on Commerce. Subcommittee on Communications. *TV Blackout of Sporting Events*, Hearings, 94th Cong., 1st Sess., Nov. 21, 1975. Washington, D.C.: G.P.O., 1976.

United States. Congress. Senate. Committee on Commerce, Science and Transportation. *Cable Television Oversight Hearings*, 95th Cong., 1st Sess., June 6–8, 1977. Washington, D.C.: G.P.O., 1978.

United States. Congress. Senate. Committee on Commerce, Science and Transportation. Subcommittee on Communications. *Amendments to the Communication Act of 1973, Part 3*, Hearings on S. 611, 96th Cong., 1st Sess., May 10, 11, 16, June 5–7, 1979. Washington, D.C.: G.P.O., 1980.

United States. Congress. Senate. Committee on Interstate and Foreign Commerce. *Broadcasting and Telecasting Baseball Games*, Senate Report 83-387, 83d Cong., 1st Sess., June 10, 1953. Washington, D.C.: G.P.O., 1953.

United States. Congress. Senate. Committee on Interstate and Foreign Commerce. *Broadcasting and Televising Baseball Games*, Hearings, 83d Cong., 1st Sess., May 6–12, 1953. Washington, D.C.: 1953.

United States. Congress. Senate. Committee on the Judiciary. *Telecasting of Professional Sports Contests*, Senate Report 87-1087, 87th Cong., 1st Sess., Sep. 20, 1961. Washington, D.C.: G.P.O., 1961.

United States. Federal Communications Commission. *Fifth Annual Report of the Federal Communications Commission on the Effect of P.L. 93-107, The Sports Anti-Blackout Law*, Dec. 1978. Washington, D.C.: G.P.O., 1979.

United States. Federal Communications Commission. *Fourth Annual Report* of the Federal Communications Commission on the Effect of P.L. 93-107, *The Sports Anti-Blackout Law.* Washington, D.C.: G.P.O., 1977.

United States. Federal Communications Commission. *Report of the FCC on the Effect of P.L. 93-107, The Sports Anti-Blackout Law.* Washington, D.C.: G.P.O., 1974.

United States. Federal Communications Commission. *Second Annual Report of the FCC on the Effect of P.L. 93-107, The Sports Anti-Blackout Law.* Washington, D.C.: G.P.O., 1975.

United States. Federal Communications Commission. *Third Annual Report of the Federal Communications Commission on the Effect of P.L. 93-107, The Sports Anti-Blackout Law.* Washington, D.C.: G.P.O., 1976.

XII. MEDICINE AND SPORTS

King, Joseph H., Jr. "Duty and Standard of Care for Team Physicians." 18 Houston Law Review 657 (1981).

"Malpractice on the Sidelines: Developing a Standard of Care for Team Sports Physicians." 2 Comm/ent 579 (1980).

Ryan, Allen J. "Medical Practices in Sports." 38 Law & Contemporary Problems 99 (1973).

Shafer, Nathaniel. "Sports Medicine." 9 Lawyers Medical Journal 31 (1980).

United States. Congress. House. Committee on the Judiciary. Subcommittee to Investigate Juvenile Delinquency. *Proper and Improper Use of Drugs By Athletes,* Hearings, 93d Cong., 1st Sess., June 18, July 12–13, 1973. Washington, D.C.: G.P.O., 1973.

XIII. PRECOLLEGIATE SPORTS

"High School Athletics and Due Process: Notice of Eligibility Rules." 57 Nebraska Law Review 877 (1978).

Phillips, B. J. "Fattening them up for Football." 117 Time, March 9, 1981, at 41.

"State High School Athletic Associations: When Will a Court Interfere?" 36 Missouri Law Review (1971).

XIV. RACIAL DISCRIMINATION

"Black Americans in Sports: Unequal Opportunity for Equal Ability." 5 Civil Rights Digest, Aug. 1972, at 20.

"The Case for Equality in Athletics." 22 Cleveland State Law Review 576 (1973).

Edwards, Harry. "Sports Within the Veil: The Triumphs, Tragedies and Challenges of Afro-American Involvement." 445 Annals of the American Academy of Politics and Social Science 116 (1979).

Eitzen, D. Stanley, and Sanford, David C. "Segregation of Blacks by Playing Position in Football: Accident or Design?" 55 Social Science Quarterly 948 (1975).

Eitzen, D. Stanley, and Yetman, Norman R. "Immune from Racism?" 9 Civil Rights Digest, Winter 1977, at 3.

Ofari, Earl. "Basketball's Biggest Losers: Suit Against California State University by Black Athletes." 43 Progressive, April 1979, at 48.

Scully, Gerald W. "Economic Discrimination in Professional Sports." 38 LAW
& CONTEMPORARY PROBLEMS 67 (1973).
"Sports Integration is Setting an Example in the South: Professional and Col-
lege Sports' Survey." 13 NEW SOUTH, April 1958, at 3.

XV. SEXUAL DISCRIMINATION

"Athletics: Application of State Law to Sex Discrimination in Sports." 66
ALR 3d 1262 (1975).
Brennan, Mary Lynn. "Civil Rights in the Locker Room, *Ludtke v. Kuhn.*" 2
COMM/ENT 645 (1980).
Caliendo, Nat S. "Title IX Athletics." 6 JOURNAL OF COLLEGE & UNIVERSITY
LAW 78 (1980).
"Constitutional Law—Equal Protection—Sex Discrimination in High School
Athletics Unreasonable." 91 NEW YORK LAW FORUM 166 (1973).
"Constitutional Law—Equal Protection—Sex Discrimination in Secondary
School Athletics." 46 TENNESSEE LAW REVIEW 222 (1978).
"Constitutional Law—Sex Discrimination—The Female High School Athlete,
Bucha v. Illinois High School Association, 351 F. Supp. 69 (N.D. Ill.
1972)." 50 CHICAGO-KENT LAW REVIEW 169 (1973).
"Constitutional Law: *Yellow Springs Exempted Village School District Board
of Education v. Ohio High School Athletic Association:* Sex Discrimina-
tion in High School Athletics." 47 UNIVERSITY OF MISSOURI AT KANSAS
CITY LAW REVIEW 109 (1978).
Cox, Thomas A. "Intercollegiate Athletics and Title IX." 46 GEORGE WASH-
INGTON LAW REVIEW 34 (1977).
Davison, Fred C. "Intercollegiate Athletics and Title IX: Equal Opportunity
of Federal Incursion." 108 USA TODAY, July 1979, at 34.
Dessem, R. Lawrence "Sex Discrimination in Coaching." 3 HARVARD
WOMEN'S LAW JOURNAL 97 (1980).
Dunkle, Margaret C. *Title IX: What it Means and Doesn't Mean to Athletic
Programs.* Washington, D.C.: Association of American Colleges, Project
on the Status and Education of Women, 1976.
English, Jane. "Sex Equality in Sports." 7 PHILOSOPHY & PUBLIC AFFAIRS 269
(1978).
"Equal Pay for Coaches of Female Teams: Finding a Cause of Action Under
Federal Laws." 55 NOTRE DAME LAWYER 751 (1980).
"Equality in Athletics: The Cheerleaders v. the Athlete." 19 SOUTH DAKOTA
LAW REVIEW 428 (1974).
Fabri, Candace J., and Fox, Elaine S. "The Female High School Athlete and
Interscholastic Sports." 4 JOURNAL OF LAW & EDUCATION 285 (1975).
Flygare, Thomas J. "Federal Court in Michigan Holds that Title IX Does
Not Cover Athletics." 62 PHI DELTA KAPPAN 529 (1981).
———. "HEW's New Guidelines on Sex Discrimination in Collegiate Ath-
letics." 60 PHI DELTA KAPPAN 529 (1979).
Gaal, John, and Di Lorenzo, Louis P., "The Legality and Requirements of
HEW's Proposed 'Policy Interpretation' of Title IX and Intercollegiate
Athletics." 6 JOURNAL OF COLLEGE & UNIVERSITY LAW 161 (1979).
Gaal, John; Di Lorenzo, Louis P.; and Evans, Thomas S. "HEW's Final 'Policy
Interpretation' of Title IX and Intercollegiate Athletics." 6 JOURNAL OF
COLLEGE & UNIVERSITY LAW 345 (1980).
"Gender Classification and High School Athletics, *Petrie v. Illinois High
School Association.*" 14 JOHN MARSHALL LAW REVIEW 227 (1980).

"HEW's Sex Rules." 105 TIME, June 16, 1975, at 73.

"Half-Court Girls' Basketball Rules: An Application of the Equal Protection Clause and Title IX." 65 IOWA LAW REVIEW 766 (1980).

Hitchens, Donna J. "A Litigation Strategy on Behalf of the Outstanding High School Female Athlete." 8 GOLDEN GATE UNIVERSITY LAW REVIEW 423 (1979).

Holland, Judith R., and Oglesby, Carole. "Women in Sport: The Synthesis Begins." 445 ANNALS OF THE AMERICAN ACADEMY OF POLITICS AND SOCIAL SCIENCE 80 (1979).

Huckley, Patricia. "Back to the Starting Line: Title IX and Women's Intercollegiate Athletics." 21 AMERICAN BEHAVIORAL SCIENCE 379 (1978).

"Implementing Title IX: The HEW Regulations." 124 UNIVERSITY OF PENNSYLVANIA LAW REVIEW 806 (1976).

Ingram, John D. "Sex Discrimination in Park District Athletic Programs." 64 WOMEN'S LAW JOURNAL 33 (1978).

"Irrebuttable Presumption Doctrine: Applied to State and Federal Regulations Excluding Females from Contact Sports, *Yellow Springs Exempted Village High School District Board of Education v. Ohio High School Athletic Association,* 443 F. Supp. 753 (S.D. Ohio 1978)." 4 UNIVERSITY OF DAYTON LAW REVIEW 197 (1979).

Jewett, Susan. "The Equal Rights Amendment and Athletics." 1 HARVARD WOMEN'S LAW JOURNAL 53 (1978).

Kadzielski, Mark A. "Postsecondary Athletics in an Era of Equality: An Appraisal of the Effect of Title IX." 5 JOURNAL OF COLLEGE & UNIVERSITY LAW 123 (1979).

————. "Title IX of the Education Amendments of 1972: Change or Continuity?" 6 JOURNAL OF LAW & EDUCATION 183 (1977).

Koch, James V. "Title IX and the NCAA." 3 WESTERN STATE UNIVERSITY LAW REVIEW 250 (1976).

Kuhn, Janet L. "Title IX: Employment and Athletics Outside HEW's Jurisdiction." 5 GEORGETOWN LAW JOURNAL 49 (1976).

"A Legal Conundrum—Transsexuals in Athletics." 1 COMM/ENT 369 (1978).

McDonald, Eugene J. "Title IX Athletics." 6 JOURNAL OF COLLEGE & UNIVERSITY LAW 73 (1980).

Martin, James P. "Title IX and Intercollegiate Athletics: Scoring Points for Women." 8 OHIO NORTHERN UNIVERSITY LAW REVIEW 481 (1981).

"Pennsylvania Constitution—Equal Rights Amendment—Sex Discrimination—Interscholastic Sports." 14 DUQUESNE LAW REVIEW 101 (1975).

"*Petrie v. Illinois High School Association:* Gender Classification and High School Athletics." 14 JOHN MARSHALL LAW REVIEW 227 (1980).

Podgers, James. "New Title IX Game Plan: Lawyers to Get the Ball." 66 AMERICAN BAR ASSOCIATION JOURNAL 28 (1980).

Seligman, Daniel. "New Rules About Sex: Equal Opportunity in Intercollegiate Sports." 101 FORTUNE, Jan. 14, 1980, at 33.

"Sex Discrimination and Intercollegiate Athletics." 61 IOWA LAW REVIEW 420 (1975).

"Sex Discrimination and Intercollegiate Athletics—Putting Some Muscle on Title IX." 88 YALE LAW JOURNAL 1254 (1974).

"Sex Discrimination—Girls' High School Basketball Rules Held Unconstitutional." 16 JOURNAL OF FAMILY LAW 345 (1978).

"Sex Discrimination in Athletics." 21 VILLANOVA LAW REVIEW 876 (1976).

"Sex Discrimination in Athletics: Conflicting Legislative and Judicial Approaches." 29 ALABAMA LAW REVIEW 390 (1978).

"Sex Discrimination in High School Athletics." 57 MINNESOTA LAW REVIEW 339 (1972).

"Sex Discrimination in Interscholastic High School Athletics." 25 SYRACUSE LAW REVIEW 535 (1974).

"Sex Discrimination—Title IX of the Education Amendments of 1972 Prohibits All-Female Teams in Sports Not Previously Dominated by Males, *Gomes v. Rhode Island Interscholastic League,* 469 F. Supp. 659 (D.R.I. 1979)." 14 SUFFOLK LAW REVIEW 1471 (1980).

"Sexual Equality in High School Athletics: The Approach of *Darrin v. Gould.*" 12 GONZAGA LAW REVIEW 691 (1977).

Smith, Walt. "Enforcing Title IX = Cutting College Sports?" 12 PERSPECTIVES, Summer 1980, at 22.

Stein, Barry. "Title IX and School Sports." 69 TODAY'S EDUCATION, April–May 1980, at 14G.

Stroud, Kenneth M. "Sex Discrimination in High School Athletics." 6 INDIANA LAW REVIEW 661 (1973).

"Termination of Federal Funding to School Athletic Programs Under Title IX of the Education Amendments of 1972." 5 UNIVERSITY OF SAN FERNANDO VALLEY LAW REVIEW 417 (1977).

Thomas, Ann V., and Sheldon-Wildgen, Jan. "Women in Athletics: Winning the Game But Losing the Support." 8 JOURNAL OF COLLEGE AND UNIVERSITY LAW 295 (1981).

"Title IX and Intercollegiate Athletics: HEW Gets Serious About Equality in Sports?" 15 NEW ENGLAND LAW REVIEW 573 (1980).

"Title IX's Promise of Equality of Opportunity in Athletics: Does It Cover the Bases?" 64 KENTUCKY LAW REVIEW 432 (1975).

"Validity Under Federal Law of Sex Discrimination in Athletics." 23 ALR FEDERAL 664 (1975).

Wheeler, Elizabeth. "Is There a Future for Title IX?" 9 MS., March 1981, at 17.

XVI. TAXATION OF SPORTS

Ambrose, James F. "Recent Tax Developments Regarding Purchases of Sports Franchises—The Game Isn't Over Yet." 59 TAXES 739 (1981).

"Amortization and Valuation of Intangibles: The Tax Effect Upon Sports Franchises." 12 LOYOLA UNIVERSITY LAW REVIEW 159 (1978).

Blum, Marc P. "Valuing Intangibles: What are the Choices for Valuing Professional Sports Teams?" 45 JOURNAL OF TAXATION 286 (1976).

Braun, Steven, and Pusey, Michael. "Taxation of Professional Sports Teams." 7 TAX ADVISOR 196 (1976).

"Deferred Compensation for Athletes." 10 TAX ADVISOR 68 (1979).

Dickenson, Charles, and Zook, Sutton. "The Effect of the 1976 Tax Reform Act on the Ownership of Professional Sports Franchises." 1 COMM/ENT 227 (1977).

"Federal Income Tax—Amortization and the Expansion Sports Franchise." 54 WASHINGTON LAW REVIEW 827 (1979).

"Foundation Tax and Player Contract Bills Get Committee Nod." 10 TAX NOTES 634 (1980).

Harmelink, Philip J. "Tax Aspects of Baseball Player Contracts and Planning Opportunities." 59 TAXES 535 (1981).

Horvitz, Jerome S., and Hoffman, Thomas E. "New Tax Developments in the Syndication of Sports Franchises." 54 TAXES 175 (1976).

Jones, John B. "Amortization and Nonamortization of Intangibles in the Sports World." 53 TAXES 777 (1975).

Kaplan, Richard L. "Intercollegiate Athletics and the Unrelated Business Income Tax." 80 COLUMBIA LAW REVIEW 1430 (1980).

Klinger, Leslie S. "Professional Sports Teams: Tax Factors in Buying, Owning and Selling Them." 39 JOURNAL OF TAXATION 276 (1973).

———. "Tax Aspects of Buying, Selling and Owning Professional Sports Teams." 48 LOS ANGELES BAR BULLETIN 162, 176 (1972).

Lowell, Cym H. "Planning Contractual Deferred Compensation Arrangements for Professional Athletes." 10 TAX ADVISOR 68 (1979).

"Professional Sports Franchising and the IRS." 14 WASHBURN LAW JOURNAL 321 (1975).

"The Professional Sports Teams as a Tax Shelter—A Case Study: The Utah Stars." 1974 UTAH LAW REVIEW 556.

Raabe, William, Jr. "Professional Sports Franchises and the Treatment of League Expansion Proceeds." 57 TAXES 427 (1979).

Strandell, Valerie N. "The Impact of the 1976 Tax Reform Act on Owners of Professional Sports Teams." 4 JOURNAL OF CONTEMPORARY LAW 219 (1978).

United States. Congress. House. Committee on Ways and Means. *The President's 1978 Tax Reduction and Reform Proposals, Part 8*, Hearings, 95th Cong., 2d Sess., April 3–4, 1978. Washington, D.C.: G.P.O., 1978.

United States. Congress. Joint Committee on Internal Revenue Taxation. *Tax Revision Issues—1976 (H.R. 10612), I: Tax Shelter Investments*, Committee Print, 94th Cong., 2d Sess., April 14, 1976. Washington, D.C.: G.P.O., 1976.

United States. Congress. Joint Committee on Internal Revenue Taxation. *Tax Shelters: Professional Sports Franchises*, Committee Print, 94th Cong., 1st Sess., Sept. 11, 1975. Washington, D.C.: G.P.O., 1975.

United States. Congress. Senate. Committee on Finance. *Tax Reform Act of 1975*, Hearings, 94th Cong., 2d Sess., March 17–26, 1976. Washington, D.C.: G.P.O., 1976.

United States. Congress. Senate. Committee on Finance. Subcommittee on Taxation and Debt Management Generally. *Miscellaneous Tax Bills, Part 2*, Hearings, 95th Cong., 2d Sess., July 24, 1978. Washington, D.C.: G.P.O., 1979.

Van de Ven, Martha A., and Kauffman, Steven A. "Merits of Incorporating the Athlete." 9 TAX ADVISOR 478 (1978).

Wiesner, Philip J. "Tax Shelters—A Survey of the Impact of the Tax Reform Act of 1976." 33 TAX LAW REVIEW 5 (1977).

Zaritsky, Howard M. "Amortizing a Sport Team's Player Contract: An Analysis of *First North Industries*." 52 JOURNAL OF TAXATION 88 (1980).

———. "Taxation of Professional Sports Teams After 1976: A Whole New Ballgame." 18 WILLIAM & MARY LAW REVIEW 679 (1977).

Contributors

Keith A. Buckley, Reference Librarian, Indiana University School of Law

William G. Buss, Theodore C. Michels Professor of Law, University of Iowa

Mark A. Kadzielski, Member of the California Bar and the firm of Weissburg & Aronson, Los Angeles

Cym H. Lowell, Member of the Indianapolis Bar and the firm of Barnes, Hickam, Pantzer & Boyd

James A. R. Nafziger, Professor, Willamette University College of Law

Robert H. Ruxin, Member of the District of Columbia bar and the firm of Preston, Thorgrimson, Ellis & Holman; Chairman, American Bar Association Forum Committee on Entertainment and Sports Law, Sports Division Legislation Committee

Ronald J. Waicukauski, Assistant Professor, Indiana University School of Law; Director, Center for Law & Sports

John C. Weistart, Professor, Duke University School of Law

Index